THE POLITICS OF IMMIGRATION IN SCOTLAND

THE POLITICS OF IMMIGRATION IN SCOTLAND

Aubrey L. Westfall

EDINBURGH
University Press

Edinburgh University Press is one of the leading university presses in the UK. We publish academic books and journals in our selected subject areas across the humanities and social sciences, combining cutting-edge scholarship with high editorial and production values to produce academic works of lasting importance. For more information visit our website: edinburghuniversitypress.com

© Aubrey L. Westfall, 2022, 2024

Edinburgh University Press Ltd
The Tun – Holyrood Road, 12(2f) Jackson's Entry, Edinburgh EH8 8PJ

First published in hardback by Edinburgh University Press 2022

Typeset in 10/12.5 Sabon by
Cheshire Typesetting Ltd, Cuddington, Cheshire and
printed and bound by CPI Group (UK) Ltd
Croydon, CR0 4YY

A CIP record for this book is available from the British Library

ISBN 978 1 4744 9158 7 (hardback)
ISBN 978 1 4744 9159 4 (paperback)
ISBN 978 1 4744 9160 0 (webready PDF)
ISBN 978 1 4744 9161 7 (epub)

The right of Aubrey L. Westfall to be identified as the author of this work has been asserted in accordance with the Copyright, Designs and Patents Act 1988, and the Copyright and Related Rights Regulations 2003 (SI No. 2498).

CONTENTS

List of Figures, Tables and Appendices vi
Acknowledgements ix

   Introduction: The Political Context of a Unique Scottish Approach to Immigration 1
1 The Past: A Brief History of Migration in Scotland 19
2 The Project: Building a Scottish Nation with 'New Scots' 46
3 The People: Migration and Scottish National Identity 66
4 The Promise: The Benefits of Immigration for Scotland 90
5 The Problem: Promoting Social Cohesion and Anti-racism in Scotland 115
6 The Politics: Party Competition over Immigration in Westminster and Holyrood 139
7 The Press: Newspaper Reporting on Immigration in the UK versus Scotland 175
8 The Public: Attitudes Towards Immigration in Scotland 206
9 The Projections: Alternative Futures for the Politics of Immigration in Scotland 230
   Conclusion: The Prospects for Attracting and Retaining Migrants in Scotland 251

Appendices 260
Bibliography 282
Index 331

FIGURES, TABLES AND APPENDICES

Figures

1.1	Long-term international and EU migration to the UK, in thousands	21
1.2	Net migration to Scotland, in thousands	24
3.1	'How Scottish is someone if they are . . .'	71
3.2	'Who would you consider Scottish?'	72
3.3	'Who should be allowed to vote in Scottish Parliament elections?'	75
3.4	'Some people say that being Scottish is mainly about culture, others say how the country is governed. Where on the scale are you?'	77
3.5	Those born in Scotland: 'How Scottish do you feel?' 'How British do you feel?'	79
3.6	'Scotland would lose its identity if . . .'	81
4.1	Population size of England and Scotland, 1971–2019	93
7.1	Number of articles with 'immigration' in the title or keyword published by newspaper	179
7.2	Percentage of articles with applied frames by newspaper	182
7.3	Tone of coverage by percentage of 'immigration' articles by newspaper	184
7.4	Number of articles published by newspaper, type of article, and tone	185

7.5	Breakdown of utilitarian arguments by newspaper	187
7.6	Tone of articles employing utilitarian arguments by newspaper	188
7.7	Tone of articles employing a political frame by newspaper	190
7.8	Tone of articles employing a moral frame by newspaper	193
7.9	Breakdown of identity arguments by newspaper	195
7.10	Tone of articles employing identity frames by argument and newspaper	197
7.11	'Scotland would begin to lose its identity if more [Muslims/people from East Europe/Black and Asian people] came to live in Scotland'	200
7.12	'Ethnic minority/East European migrants take jobs from Scottish people'	201
8.1	'Do people from outside GB make Scotland a better place?'	208
8.2	'Scotland would begin to lose its identity if more [Muslims/people from East Europe/Black and Asian people] came to live in Scotland'	210
8.3	'Ethnic minority/East European migrants take jobs from Scottish people'	211
8.4	Percentage of SSAS respondents agreeing or strongly agreeing with negative attitudes about immigrants by cosmopolitan indicators	215
8.5	Percentage of SSAS respondents agreeing or strongly agreeing with negative attitudes about immigrants by political party	216
8.6	Percentage of SSAS respondents agreeing or strongly agreeing with negative attitudes about immigrants by national identity and nationalism	217
8.7	Percentage of SSAS respondents agreeing with the notion that migrants/minorities take jobs from Scottish people by socio-economic classification	219
8.8	Frequency of responses about migrant impact	223

Tables

3.1	Markers of nationalism	69
5.1	Conceptual framework for integration	123
7.1	Frames, arguments, and related issues	181

Appendices

A	Parties represented in Westminster's House of Commons in 2019	260
B	Parties represented in Holyrood in 2021	261
C	Monthly brand reach of newspapers in Great Britain, October–September 2018	262

D	Articles with 'immigration' in the title or keyword by newspaper, July 2013–June 2016	263
E	Correlation table of attitudes towards minoritized groups and diversity	264
F	Principle component factor analysis of attitudes towards minoritized groups and diversity in Scotland (varimax rotation)	265
G	Ordered probit model of Scottish attitudes towards immigrants and minoritized groups	266
H	Survey variable descriptions	268
I	Truncated ordered probit model of Scottish attitudes towards immigrants and minorities	275
J	Percentage of pro-immigrant responses by urban/rural classification	276
K	Percentage of pro-immigrant responses by Scottish administrative area	277
L	Ordered probit model of attitudes towards immigrants and minoritized groups in the UK	278
M	Ordered probit model of attitudes towards immigrants and minoritized groups in England and Scotland	279
N	The Anholt Ipsos Nation Brands Index	280

ACKNOWLEDGEMENTS

As I reflect on the years spent working on this project, I am overwhelmed by the number of people who have supported and helped me along the way. The seed of this project was planted during a casual conversation with my friend James Bream, who told me about the campaign to reinstate the post-study work visa. I thought I might write a paper on the visa campaign, and James helpfully provided some introductions and contacts. As the project grew in scope and required many trips to Scotland, James was always available to talk about ideas. I like to think about this project as being the product of friendship.

I owe a great debt to the many people who consented to be interviewed and were so generous with their time. Each interview helped me gain a deeper understanding of the situation in Scotland. The interviews greatly enriched this text and my experience writing it. I also had many valuable conversations with my Scottish colleagues, including Ross Bond, Christina Boswell, Katherine Botterill, Eve Hepburn, Peter Hopkins, David McCollum, David McCrone, and Nasar Meer. Nasar also generously sponsored me as an academic visitor at the University of Edinburgh, making the time I spent in Scotland much more productive. I am grateful to Wheaton College and the Marion and Jasper Whiting Foundation, who funded travel to Scotland and made the interviews and conversations possible. Thanks to Steven Clark for permission to reproduce 'Coming Home'.

I am very fortunate to be surrounded by helpful and supportive friends and colleagues who contribute to my writing process in different ways. Writing group members Jonathan Brumberg-Kraus, Katherine Eskine, Kathleen Morgan, and Srijana Shrestha read many parts of this book over the last few years and read the full manuscript during their holidays. They are an endless source of encouragement to me. Karen McCormack also offered to read the manuscript and she provided very helpful feedback, even to the point of talking me through research problems while we were hitting the trails on our mountain bikes. Gerry Huiskamp and Nick Dorzweiler gave formative advice at the very beginning of the project and helped shape the prospectus. Dana Polanichka and John Partridge are my loyal co-writing companions in Write Now, Right Now. Their company makes writing fun. I can always count on Bozena Welborne to provide valuable feedback and help me 'sexify' my writing. Few people are as lucky in their friends as I am.

The process of research can be a teaching tool, but I often learn as much from my student research assistants as they do from me. I thank the students who have helped with this project, including Jeanne Bedard, Tyler Butler, Zuzka Czerw, Will Entwisle, Joshua Kelly, and Kaitlyn Megathlin. I am especially indebted to Jeanne, Zuzka, and Kaitlyn who worked with me in the final stages of the project. The worst part about working with students is that they graduate. I miss working with them all.

I was privileged to work with Ersev Ersoy and Gillian Leslie at Edinburgh University Press. Their support gave me confidence in this project and I appreciate the way they valued my ideas and opinions. I owe a great debt to the anonymous readers who read the book prospectus, sample chapters, and full draft manuscript. They all provided thoughtful and useful feedback that greatly improved the manuscript.

Everyone says that their projects couldn't have happened without the support of their families, but that is especially true in this case. My spouse, Simon, is Scottish, and his interest and investment in the future of his country means that he is always sending me links to interesting stories, podcasts, and videos about Scotland. James, who set the ball rolling on this project, is Simon's best friend. My in-laws, Alan and Marian McPherson, hosted me or visited with me every time I was in Scotland, as did Alison and Alistair Clark, Simon's aunt and uncle. Marian, my mother-in-law, read the draft manuscript to make sure I didn't come off sounding like too much of a Yank. I am grateful for the love and support of my Scottish family. It was fun to work on something that bridges private and professional life so conveniently. The love of my own parents and siblings has made me who I am and I owe them everything.

INTRODUCTION: THE POLITICAL CONTEXT OF A UNIQUE SCOTTISH APPROACH TO IMMIGRATION

O! we're a' Jock Tamson's bairns,
  We're a' Jock Tamson's bairns;
There ne'er will be peace till the warld again
  Has learn'd to sing wi' micht and main,
We're a' Jock Tamson's bairns
                      Scottish folk song

From Iraq and Somalia,
Your family's coming home
And from Syria and Gaza
Your family's coming home
Seeking rest and refuge
They have never known
They're coming home, Your family's coming home

Coming home to a place they've never been
Coming home to a land they've never seen
Coming home to a family they have never known
A' Jock Tamson's bairns
Are coming home
     'Coming Home' by Steven Clark, songmaker

The Scottish folk song 'Jock Tamson's Bairns' tells a story about universal human equality. In the Scots language, Jock Tamson stands in for 'every man', as Jock is the generic name for a man and Tamson is a derivative of a common Scottish surname. 'Jock Tamson's bairns' metaphorically represents common humanity, and the idea that all humans share a common ancestry. The song by Steven Clark extends a Scottish homeland to everyone, and connects an abstract and uniquely Scottish symbol with concrete, international, and politically charged populations. The invitation would be provocative in many nations, but the extension of a Scottish vision of egalitarian hospitality reflects political consensus about the desirability of immigration and a vision of Scotland as a welcoming place. In reflecting on why he wrote the song, Clark explained:

> The song was originally written in 2004, and came out of witnessing some petty acts of begrudgery and prejudice against refugees/asylum seekers in Glasgow. I travel to work in town on public transport, and the bus services I used went past both the Red Road flats and Sighthill, where many refugees were being housed at the time. I just felt like saying, in whatever way I could, 'You *are* welcome, despite what it sometimes may feel like.' (Personal communication 16 May 2021)[1]

Clark's message of welcome is echoed by the leaders of Scottish political parties, the dominant scholarly voices, and business owners, all of whom discuss migration favourably as a critical part of Scotland's economic and cultural future. What encourages Scottish actors to perceive immigration as an asset and opportunity at a time when much of Europe and the UK government view it as a liability? What drives the Scottish position on immigration? To what extent is it purely an elite-led movement? What are the political elite leveraging the policy for? Is the commitment to immigration genuine, or is it merely political rhetoric intended to augment the differentiation between Scotland and England for purposes of enhanced political power or national independence?

This book attempts to answer these questions and ultimately argues that immigration has become a critical tool of nation-building in Scotland.[2] A central requirement of nation-building is a claim of uniqueness that justifies the creation of distinct governing institutions that represent the unique community. The national endorsement of immigration and diversity is a symbol of Scotland's uniqueness, and it serves genuine moral and strategic interests. The Scottish political leadership views openness to immigrants as a reflection of Scottish values and a solution to demographic and economic problems. This approach contrasts with negative rhetoric about migration in the rest of the UK. The UK's governing Conservative Party, which attracts low levels of support in Scotland, has pledged to reduce immigration, and while the anti-immigrant United Kingdom Independence Party (UKIP) was gaining support in England, it became an object of general derision in Scotland.[3] English–Scottish political divergence around immigration allows Scottish nationalists to demonstrate that Scotland has different practical and ideological interests, differences that should justify further devolved powers or independence.

Political Transformations Enabling National Differentiation

Arguments for devolved Scottish immigration policy have shifted alongside changes in the political climate since 2010. The formation of a UK government led by the Conservative Party emphasised political differences in England and Scotland, because before 2010, no party had governed with such a low share of the Scottish vote (16.7%) (Mitchell and van der Zwet 2010). Conservative Party rule provided an opportunity for Scottish nationalists to argue the UK leadership did not represent Scottish voters, and that decisions made in Westminster were detrimental to Scottish interests. The Conservative victory in Westminster coincided with the growth of right-wing populism in the UK and set the scene for the Scottish independence referendum and the EU referendum (also known as Brexit). These events heightened the sense of Scottish–English difference and primed immigration to become one of the most important symbolic and practical policy issues representing that difference.

The Rise of Populism

The rise of populism in the UK provoked a new politics of immigration in Scotland. Populism is centred on a division between 'the pure people' and 'the corrupt elite', with the latter presented as a unitary mass of the political, economic, cultural, academic, and media establishment who put their own interests – or the interests of others (immigrants, corporations, or foreign countries) – above the interest of the people (Mudde 2004).[4] Populist parties and movements are often led by charismatic individuals who claim to represent 'the voice of the people'. They activate concepts such as common sense, popular sovereignty, nativism, culture, and national identity. They also tend to lie flagrantly, because the lie in itself is a signal that the speaker is not bound by establishment norms. When those lies relate to immigrants, such as with assertions that immigrants are freeloaders draining public funds, the populist claims to say 'what everyone is thinking' (Fieschi 2019).

In the UK, populism primarily manifests on the right side of the ideological spectrum and has capitalised on the UK's relationship with the European Union (EU) and immigration.[5] The UK hosts two populist political parties: the British National Party (BNP) and UKIP (van Kessel 2015). The BNP is a historically neo-fascist political party that has recently attempted to promote a more acceptable image, though the party is still characterised by xenophobic discourse. It usually wins less than 1% of the vote in general elections and is not a viable threat to the mainstream parties.[6] UKIP has been more successful. UKIP was founded in 1993 to advocate for the UK's withdrawal from the EU.[7] Under the leadership of Nigel Farage in 2006, the party broadened its activities to attract people who were alienated by the mainstream political parties. Farage developed a 'fusion strategy' to merge Europe and immigration in the minds of voters by blaming free movement in the EU for rising immigration to the UK (Ford and Goodwin 2014). By campaigning on immigration, the party 'secured ownership of one of the most salient issues in British politics' (Dennison and Goodwin 2015).

In 2010, UKIP won 3.2% of the UK vote, its best result in a national election.[8] It won a substantial share of the votes in a number of districts in several by-elections between 2011 and 2015, and national polls showed growing support. With the experience of the 2010 election and the resulting hung parliament in mind, the Conservative Party leadership viewed UKIP as a competitor on the right. They adapted their strategies to attract or keep the support of potential UKIP voters, which included a tough party line on immigration.[9] In 2013, when public support for UKIP was polling at around 10%, Conservative Prime Minister David Cameron announced a Conservative government would renegotiate the UK's relationship with the EU and give the citizens of the UK the choice about whether to stay in the EU with an in/out referendum. By conceding on UKIP's core issue, Cameron was hoping to attract enough UKIP supporters to ensure a Conservative majority in 2015 (Bale 2018). The Conservative Party won the 2015 election, and secured 330 seats, 30 more than in the 2010 election, and enough of an overall majority to form a government. The party maintained its tough stance on immigration in subsequent elections.

During the general election of 2019, Conservative party leader, Boris Johnson brought populism into the central leadership of the party.[10] He argued that Parliament had been blocking Brexit, which was the will of the people, and he committed to 'get Brexit done'.[11] Though Johnson's campaign was focused on Brexit, he recognised that Brexit was driven by anti-immigrant sentiment. Johnson vowed to stop EU immigrants from seeing Britain 'as their own country', thereby framing immigrants as outsiders. Johnson invoked populist language of popular sovereignty: 'the problem with [immigration] is that there's basically been no control at all. And I don't think that is democratically accountable' (Bulman 2019). The immigration policy introduced by his administration focused on attracting only highly skilled workers while substantially curbing low-skilled migration. He also proposed a change in asylum law to deter asylum seekers from independently crossing into the UK (BBC News 2020).

For the Scottish nationalists, populism exacerbates the contrast between the prevailing political cultures in England and Scotland. The nativist discourse of right-wing UK populism contradicts the image of inclusive Scottish nationalism, and the symbiotic relationship between UKIP and the Conservative Party allows the Scottish leadership to paint both parties with the same xenophobic brush to make strong claims of Scottish difference (Bale 2018).[12]

The Scottish Independence Referendum

In 2011, the Scottish National Party (SNP) formed the first majority government since the Scottish Parliament was formed in 1999. The UK government agreed to an independence referendum in 2014. The referendum primed the Scottish public to consider whether Scotland should take a different trajectory from the rest of the UK.[13] The independence campaign used Westminster's aversion to immigration as a foil for Scotland's progressiveness. First Minister Alex Salmond claimed an independent Scotland would pursue a more liberal policy of migration to offset a predicted pensions deficit caused by an ageing population and demographic decline. The UK government opposed assertions of Scottish distinctiveness in its approach to immigration. Labour Shadow Home Secretary Yvette Cooper said that a Scotland with markedly different immigration policies would not be welcome in the Common Travel Area (CTA) shared by the UK and Ireland, because the agreement relies on closely aligned immigration rules. She also asserted that an independent Scotland would result in 'border controls at Berwick-upon-Tweed' (Carrell 2014c).[14] The UK government also emphasised similar demographic and economic conditions in Scotland and northern England to refute claims that Scotland's needs are distinct from England's.

The independence debate centred on Scotland's relationship with the UK, but EU membership was also at issue. Blair McDougall, the head of the pro-Union Better Together campaign, used EU membership as a carrot to keep Scotland within the UK, asserting (with support from the European Commission) that an independent Scotland would have to apply to the EU as a new member and demonstrate compliance with all of the EU's laws. Independence would therefore work against the efforts of immigration campaigners as it would hypothetically close Scotland to free movement within the EU during the application period.

The referendum result of 55.3% against independence was a blow to independence campaigners. The margin of victory was about 3% larger than expected for the Better Together campaign due to the highest recorded turnout since the introduction of universal suffrage (BBC News 2014). Subsequent analysis suggested the Better Together campaign successfully highlighted the risks and uncertainties associated with independence, like having to reapply to the EU or the economic consequences of separating economies, and convinced people the risks were unnecessary (Curtice 2014; Keating and McEwen 2017). Brexit, however, changed the Scottish electoral landscape, and support for independence was higher post-Brexit, especially amongst the youth and those with a strong Scottish identity. In mid-2020, polls indicated majority support for independence for the first time, with support attributed to diverging views on leadership in Scotland and the UK: while 72% of those polled thought that SNP First Minister Nicola Sturgeon was doing well or very well, only 20% said the same thing about Johnson (Smout 2020). Opinions solidified during the COVID-19 pandemic, when Sturgeon used her devolved powers over health policy to implement strong preventative measures. The pandemic accelerated forces pulling Scotland and England in different directions. Prime Minister Boris Johnson continued to insist that the 2014 referendum was definitive, but polls throughout 2020 continued to demonstrate increasing majority support for a second referendum.

The international political atmosphere around the prospect of a second independence referendum also felt different after Brexit. In 2014, it was assumed that a divorce between the UK and Scotland would be viewed internationally as an 'unwelcome disturbance' (Walker 2014: 745). International analysis of the independence referendum openly questioned why Scotland would unnecessarily rock the boat, and attributed the desire for independence to national identity, parochial attachments to culture, and a self-defeating political obsession on the part of the SNP (Irwin 2014). With Brexit, the UK government was the one guilty of rocking the boat by leaving the EU in an expression of populist nationalism. The divergent results of the EU referendum in Scotland and England therefore allowed Scottish independence to be framed as a *rejection* of parochial identities and isolationism. Though practical concerns about Scottish independence persisted post-Brexit, Scotland became a target of international sympathy, and some of the EU's former leadership signalled that Brexit altered European sentiments towards Scotland (BBC News 2020; Campbell 2019). As Kirsty Hughes (2020), director of the Scottish Centre on European Relations, put it, 'with the UK no longer a member state, and with the ill-will generated by the whole Brexit process, Scotland as a pro-European, remain-voting country is now seen by EU member states (and indeed by EU officials) in a much more positive light'.

The European Union and Brexit

David Cameron called the European Union membership referendum in 2013 to draw support from UKIP and to satisfy Eurosceptics in the Conservative Party, making the referendum a product of right-wing populism in the UK.[15] The Leave campaign's rhetoric of 'taking back control' from the European elite gave the campaign a populist character, which is also reflected in the objective to 'take back control' over the border and immigration. During the Brexit debates, immigration and especially the EU's free movement were disparaged as being uncontrollable and against the UK's national interest. EU citizens living in the UK were characterised as 'lucky' immigrants allowed to come to the UK without regard for domestic economic and physical constraints, and as having easier access to some benefits (like family reunification) than did UK citizens.[16] In 2016, Prime Minister Theresa May said ending free movement was a red line in negotiations about how the UK would leave the EU and the future relationship between the EU and the UK.

The anti-immigrant rhetoric of the Leave campaigners provided an opportunity for highlighting the difference in approach between Scotland and England when it comes to immigration. While there was an outbreak of racist hate crimes across the UK during and after the Brexit referendum, *The Scotsman* reported that hate crimes in Scotland fell (The Newsroom 2016).[17] EU diplomats working in Scotland responded by describing Scotland as a 'haven' for EU nationals and an attractive destination for those fleeing xenophobia in the wider UK or elsewhere (Horne 2016). Furthermore, Scotland benefited from the seamless migration of EU citizens. When the EU referendum was announced, Scotland's economic and political elite immediately recognised the threat Brexit would pose to the Scottish government's plans to increase immigration.[18] Over half of Scotland's immigrants are from the EU and they are more than twice as likely to be employed than non-EU migrants.[19] Because of free movement, EU migrants respond to market forces, and they are more likely to occupy the low-skilled and seasonal jobs that are critical for the Scottish economy.

Ironically, Leave campaigners attempted to use Scotland's pro-immigrant position to attract Scottish support for Brexit. Conservative MP and Secretary of State for Justice Michael Gove visited Scotland in June of 2016 and suggested that the UK government would give Scotland power to set its own immigration quotas through a points-based system after the UK left the EU. SNP Leader and First Minister of Scotland Nicola Sturgeon dismissed Gove's remarks as 'a fib and a half' and tweeted 'politicians who oppose [independence] now pretending that Brexit is a great idea because it will give us powers of [independence] probably shouldn't be trusted!' (Carrell 2016).[20] Sturgeon's suspicions were justified: no devolved immigration plan emerged post-Brexit.

Political transformations since 2010 have made immigration a policy priority and have given it symbolic importance. Absent these changes the low flow of immigrants into Scotland might have kept the issue off the political radar for a number of years. Instead, immigration became the symbol of Scotland's progressive ideology and practical interests. The strain over Brexit underscored Scotland's different understandings and goals for the future. Independence and Brexit amplified political rhetoric about Scotland's distinctive political culture and created a rarefied climate for analysing the politics of migration in Scotland.

Is Scotland Unique?

Are the Scottish politics of immigration worthy of focused attention? Regulating immigration is the state's concern, since border control is a primary principle of sovereignty. However, in federal and devolved states, many sub-state units are stateless nations with distinct cultures and traditions that evolved separately from the state, and with policy preferences that diverge from those of the state. Some sub-state nations may advance a more open immigration policy, as Scotland does, while others will criticise a state's progressive stance towards migration and will push for greater closure (Hepburn 2010a). The rise of the far right in Europe has drawn attention to sub-state nationalist actors who reject immigration and diversity. Many of these actors are members of virulently anti-immigrant parties, such as the Vlaams Belang in Belgium or the Lega Nord in Italy, which attract attention and censure as they push back against democratic norms of inclusion and the principles of integration.

The Scottish case represents a marriage of nationalist sentiment and cosmopolitan identities through the promotion of civic nationalism, which allows people to identify with the nation through attachment to the place and civic participation, rather than through 'primordial ties' of heritage, religion, or cultural customs. Scotland is not the only stateless nation with a civic nationalist tradition and a strong pro-immigrant nationalist political party that is requesting greater regional control over immigration. Nor is it the only country with a nationalist government endorsing the desirability of immigration as a way to bolster economic and political growth – Catalonia and Quebec had civically nationalist sub-state governments that encouraged migration. However, Scotland is unique in its credible and legitimate threat of an independence referendum, in its low barriers to national citizenship, and in the lack of political polarisation around immigration in Scotland.[21]

The Threat of Independence

Semi-autonomous regions with ambitions for independence within mature, democratic states are unusual. Only Scotland, Quebec, and Catalonia have held independence referenda, and of the three, Scotland's referendum is the only one held under agreed-upon conditions between the state and the sub-state nation. Scotland held an independence referendum in 2014, after the UK agreed to make an exception to Scottish devolution, which reserved constitutional issues to Westminster. Both the UK and Scottish governments signed an agreement that stipulated the rules of the referendum, including the single Yes/No question on Scotland leaving the UK and allowing those aged 16 and 17 to vote. The constitutional legitimacy of the referendum signalled that the UK government would accept the result.

Quebec staged referenda in 1980 and 1995 and both were defeated, but the Canadian government never accepted either referendum as binding. Catalonia is constitutionally prohibited from holding referenda, but a referendum was held with the approval of the Catalan Parliament in 2017. In the run-up to the referendum, Spanish police attempted to prevent voting, sometimes with violence, and detained independence proponents. Turnout was low (43%) due to police interference, and because the constitutional political parties urged their supporters not to validate an unconstitutional referendum by voting. Among those who voted, 92% favoured independence. The Catalan President Carles Puigdemont considered the result to be valid and the Catalan Parliament declared independence from Spain, but King Felipe IV and the Spanish government refused to accept the result, calling the referendum 'illegal'.

'Scotland stands out as a unique case of an agreed referendum on an agreed question and a long period of intensive debate' (Keating and McEwen 2017: 1). Some might argue the requirement that the UK give consent to a referendum weakens Scotland's position, but the political legitimacy of the referendum is important. Following the referendum in Catalonia, the Spanish government dissolved the Catalan Parliament and assumed full control over many of Catalonia's powers, and pro-independence politicians were jailed and exiled. While the nationalist movement in Catalonia was disempowered after the independence referendum, Scotland's nationalist movement was strengthened through the legitimacy of the process. Furthermore, votes against independence in Scotland did not signal public commitment to the status quo, since in the run-up to the referendum, the UK government promised to further empower the devolved Scottish Parliament. Ultimately, the energy and excitement of the referendum passed to the SNP (Mitchell 2015). The party retained control of the Scottish government in 2016 and 2019, and it dominated Scottish representation in Westminster in the elections of 2015, 2017, and 2019. SNP Leader Nicola Sturgeon gained an international profile following the referendum, and polls suggested she was the most popular public figure in the UK in 2020.

The SNP may have pitched the referendum in 2014, when polls were not indicating a tremendous surge in support, because they anticipated that returns short of independence would still be advantageous to the party and to Scotland (Keating and McEwen 2017). The referendum secured a sufficient level of support to pressure the UK government to make additional concessions to the Scottish government, and the possibility of a second referendum sustained the nationalist movement. The constitutional validity of an independence referendum incentivises the UK government to take Scottish demands seriously, especially where preferences sharply diverge, as they do with immigration.

Low Barriers to National Membership

The second way Scotland distinguishes itself from comparable regions is in its unusually low threshold for inclusion in Scottish society (Meer 2015). Nationalist parties in Scotland, Catalonia, and Quebec have encouraged migration to their nations. Nationalist governments in Scotland and Quebec have been interested in attracting more immigration to the region to compensate for demographic decline, and both the SNP and the Parti Québécois (PQ), historically the main nationalist party in Quebec, are social democratic parties advancing an ideology of civic nationalism that incorporates newcomers. Catalonia has welcomed immigration ever since its economic expansion in the 1960s, which attracted immigrants from elsewhere in Spain, North Africa, and Latin America. The Convergència i Unió (CiU), the electoral alliance of the two nationalistic parties, consistently promoted immigration as being advantageous for the regional economy, and used their pro-immigrant approach to differentiate Catalonia from the rest of Spain. In the lead-up to the 2017 referendum, pro-independence campaigners wooed immigrants with promises of immediate Catalan nationality upon independence (Reuters 2017). Nationalist politicians in all three countries have therefore used similar arguments and rhetoric to promote immigration for pragmatic and nationalistic purposes.

The parties differ in what they require of immigrants in order to join the nation. In Quebec, the PQ advocated for regional control over immigration in the late 1980s, and those powers were enhanced in 1991. However, the party insisted that any regional policy should focus on recruiting more French-speakers to the province. After coming to power in 1994, the party advanced a package of policies intended to help immigrant integration, including French classes. The party had to grapple with fellow nationalists who believed immigration was a threat to Quebecois culture, which led to a number of conflicts between pro-immigration political elites and anti-immigration advocates. A new anti-immigrant nationalist party, the Action démocratique du Québec (ADQ), was formed in 1994. In response to electoral competition, the PQ tightened its position on immigration and proposed laws limiting political rights and citizenship to French-speaking immigrants.[22] Though the law was eventually tabled, it cast the PQ as a party endorsing an assimilationist approach that treats immigrants as a threat to the national culture until they are fully integrated. In 2018, the conservative and anti-immigrant Coalition Avenir Québec (CAQ) became the main nationalist voice, and its success relegated the PQ to the margins. The CAQ formed a government in the National Assembly of Quebec and worked to reduce the number of immigrants admitted to Quebec by 20%, to strengthen the linguistic and cultural integration requirements, to implement a values test for prospective migrants, and to prohibit religious signs in public places (CAQ 2020).

In Catalonia, the CiU advocated for immigrant rights, and in 2006, Catalonia was granted specific powers over immigration. In subsequent negotiations over Catalan policy, the CiU pushed for strong linguistic rights to ensure that immigrants learned the Catalan language: 'For the CiU, the goal was not to achieve a multicultural society, but to assimilate immigrants into the Catalan community so that the nation remained culturally distinct from the rest of Spain' (Hepburn 2010a: 518). Immersion in Catalan language became a core integration requirement and a condition of residence (Moreno 2006; Arrighi de Casanova 2014). The party also proposed that public services be made available only to those with demonstrable knowledge of Catalan language and culture.

While the nationalist parties in Catalonia and Quebec endorse linguistic and cultural requirements in order for immigrants to achieve full societal acceptance, there are no cultural requirements for immigrants to enter or access benefits in Scotland.[23] While the SNP, PQ, and CiU promoted a national vision whereby anyone living in the territories can be considered part of the political community, and though governments of all three nations have used their progressive approaches to immigration as a tool of differentiation between the regional and central governments, the parties in Catalonia and Quebec have erected barriers that conditionally restrict immigrant rights. The SNP has placed virtually no barriers on civic inclusion and has actively encouraged the political participation of immigrants. This makes Scotland the most civically nationalist sub-state nation.

Lack of Political Polarisation

The most remarkable feature of the Scottish politics of immigration is the lack of political polarisation on the issue. All Scottish political parties endorse immigration, and there is no viable anti-immigrant party in Scotland. The SNP does not face a viable rival nationalist party, which makes its vision of the nation dominant. In Quebec, the CAQ's brand of ethnic and populist nationalism makes contemporary Quebec less comparable to Scotland. In Catalonia, the CiU faces competition on the left and right. The left-leaning party Esquerra Republicana de Catalunya (ERC) provides a nationalist challenge in the same ideological space as the CiU, which provoked the CiU to distinguish itself by imposing more restrictions on immigrants and advocating for reduced flows. Compared with Scotland, the political terrain in Catalonia and Quebec is much more challenging for those with a pro-immigration platform. The national-level political polarisation directs the political energy associated with immigration at other national actors, rather than at the central state. Meanwhile, in Scotland, consensus allows all energy to be devoted to advocating for Scotland's interests relative to those of the UK.

Hepburn (2010a) suggests that one of the main reasons for the Scottish consensus on immigration relates to Scotland's inability to control immigration. While

Quebec selects and integrates its immigrants, and Catalonia has control over immigrant reception and the issuance of work permits, Scotland has no control over immigrant selection, which motivates all of the Scottish political parties to unite in calls for more regional control over immigration. Should Scotland achieve control, it is possible and even likely that polarisation on the issue will develop. Nevertheless, for the time being, the lack of polarisation on immigration and the limited regional control over immigration set Scotland apart.

On the surface, Scotland's pro-immigration nationalist politics do not appear to be unique. Scotland is not the only sub-state nation with a strong civic nationalist party with ambitions for independence and pragmatic and ideological interests in advocating for regional control over more open immigration policy. However, there are several things that distinguish Scotland from the other comparable nations. The first is credible legal access to an independence referendum, which allows regional demands to be attended to in a different way. Second, the nationalist ideology of the SNP-led government imposes no barrier to inclusion in the Scottish polity, while the other states make proficiency in the national language a condition for inclusion.[24] Third, the universal party consensus on the desirability of immigration provides much more accommodating political terrain for the expression of pro-immigration policy preferences in Scotland, while political polarisation has complicated the issue elsewhere. Political consensus around immigration can be traced to Scotland's lack of control over immigration and immigrant reception. While a number of other regional nationalist parties advocate for devolved control over immigration, other nations with a civic tradition have achieved more power over migration than Scotland. This gives the issue unmatched urgency and symbolic nationalistic power in Scotland. Scotland's individuality in its politics of migration justifies focused attention on the politics of immigration in Scotland.

Methodology

This book argues that the Scottish politics of immigration are enmeshed with the politics of Scottish nation-building, which involves many different actors, strategies, and policy audiences, but the Scottish approach to immigration is led by the political elite. Political elites are 'individuals who provide the intellectual element of the governing group within a given society' (Leith and Soule 2011: 121). Research on the elite class often focuses on the people within the halls of power, such as those who occupy executive and legislative offices (e.g. Meer 2015). For the purposes of this work, the definition of elite includes those with a strong stake in and influence over immigration policy, such as members of the business community, trade unions, employees of NGOs, and members of the civil service.

The political dynamics surrounding the independence and Brexit referenda have made 'everyday politics a situation of contending elites who seek to construct a specific sense of national identity' in Scotland (Leith and Soule 2011: 121–2). Scottish political elites have an unprecedented opportunity to proactively define who should be part of the nation, and most are open to a more expansive definition of the nation that includes diverse cultural and ethnic groups. Meer notes that 'political elites of all hues are reaching for some ownership of nationalism in Scotland . . . there is evidence of a consensus across unionists and nationalists that a project of diverse nation-building is under way' (2015: 1482, 1484). Meer suggests the inclusive vision is a 'self-conscious goal among political elites, because it distinguishes Scotland from comparable autonomy-seeking nations' (2015: 1486). This uniqueness provides the Scottish political establishment with greater political legitimacy.

National pluralism, open immigration, and nation-building are therefore intertwined for the Scottish elite class. However, the media and the Scottish public also play a critical role in shaping the politics of immigration in Scotland, and popular understandings of Scottishness place stronger boundaries around the nation than what the elites would prefer (Leith and Soule 2011). The possibility of elite–mass divergence is critically important for immigrants living in Scotland, since they are far more likely to interact with other Scots than with political elites. Nation-building is therefore a complex process involving multiple actors that may work at cross-purposes when it comes to shaping the politics of immigration in Scotland. The book reflects that complexity. Each chapter examines different elements of Scottish culture, politics, and society that converge to make the Scottish situation unique, and they engage with distinct sources of data and varied methodological approaches to develop their contributions to the central argument. The chapters discussing Scottish national identity and public opinion about migration analyse survey data from multiple years of the Scottish and British Social Attitudes Surveys. The chapter on the role of the media in directing the conversation about migration involves content analysis of broadsheet newspaper articles with 'immigration' in the title or keyword. The chapter on political party positions on immigration engages in content analysis of party manifestos and maiden speeches.

Information from a number of interviews with Scottish migration policy stakeholders in 2016 and 2019 is applied throughout the book. The first round of interviews took place during June of 2016, and focused on the post-study work visa, which allowed international students to stay in the UK for two years after graduation. In 2015 and early 2016, several working group and committee meetings were dedicated to debating and exploring the evidence in favour of a post-study work visa in the Scottish and UK governments. Interviews were requested with every participant in the official discussions. The EU referendum was held in the middle of the 2016 interviews, and invigorated the debate about immigration, inflamed the rhetoric, and renewed the conversation about Scottish independence. Several interviewees mentioned how the political situation made it impossible for the Conservative UK government to appear lenient on any forms of migration. Though the uncompromising stance of the UK government was frustrating for the interviewees, it amplified political rhetoric associated with Scotland's distinctive political culture around migration. The second round of interviews occurred in March and April of 2019, timed with the original 29 March deadline for the UK to leave the EU. These interviews involved general immigration policy stakeholders, and revealed how immigration is associated with questions about the future of the Scottish nation inside or outside the EU and/or the UK.

Roadmap of the Book

Nine substantive chapters discuss the ideas, interests, and institutions that create a productive environment for the articulation of a more open sub-state immigration policy in Scotland. Each chapter takes on a central feature of Scotland's social or political environment that provides a political opportunity for the expression of pro-immigration policy preferences. These chapters present a comprehensive picture of the immigration policy landscape in Scotland and explain why immigration is framed as an opportunity, and even a necessity, for Scotland's future success.

The first chapter, 'The Past', reviews Scotland's historical experience of immigration in comparison with the UK and describes the Scottish government's efforts to build a multicultural and immigrant-receiving nation in the new millennium. The second chapter, 'The Project', outlines the development of the Scottish brand of liberal civic nationalism and connects it to the politics of immigration within Scotland, illuminating the mechanisms by which Scottish elites mobilise domestic audiences in support of both nationalism and immigration. A successful nation-building project requires buy-in from a group of people who identify with the vision of the nation and are willing to build the national political community. Chapter 3, 'The People', explores how people living in Scotland understand their national identity. It finds the civic understandings of nationalism are supported by the Scottish public, but many Scots also endorse ethnic nationalist sentiment. The amalgamation of ethnic and civic characteristics of Scottish identity means that immigrant and minoritised groups in Scotland have mixed experiences of belonging, which may undermine the objectives of the political elite to attract more migrants to Scotland. Those objectives are described in Chapter 4, entitled 'The Promise', which reviews the way elites promise that immigration will be a solution to demographic decline, poor economic growth, labour shortages, and underfunded social services. Though migration comes with many economic and demographic benefits, many people are more concerned about the impact of immigration on local culture and community life. Chapter 5, 'The Problem', explores whether increased immigration threatens social cohesion. Evidence from the UK and Scotland contradicts the view that diversity resulting from immigration has a corrosive influence on social cohesion, but only where discrimination is suppressed and social connections link members of diverse groups, two conditions requiring increased attention from Scotland's elite class. Chapter 6, 'The Politics', reviews the immigration policy preferences of Scottish political parties and politicians in Westminster and Holyrood. The chapter examines how Scottish politicians discuss immigration in party manifestos, debates, and maiden speeches. Partisan stances on immigration are much clearer and more oppositional in Westminster, where the issue is politicised. In Holyrood, Scottish parties depart from the positions of their parent parties and there is partisan consensus about the desirability of immigration. Chapter 7, 'The Press', examines the way immigration is represented in the print media. The chapter compares the coverage of immigration in major UK-wide and Scottish broadsheet newspapers, and evaluates the tone and framing in each article with 'immigration' in the title. The analysis reveals that the ideological perspective, rather than national audience, accounts for most of the variance in how frames and tone are applied in articles about immigration. Chapter 8, 'The Public', reveals that the political machinations of the elites are built on a shaky foundation of ambivalent public sentiment. It demonstrates that attitudes towards immigration are very similar in England and Scotland. The main difference is that the issue is very politicised in England and opinions break along party lines, whereas immigration has avoided politicisation in Scotland. Public ambivalence about immigration provides a narrow window of opportunity for Scottish elites advancing a more inclusive agenda. Chapter 9, 'The Projections', demonstrates how immigration has become a symbol for Scotland's ambitions on the international scene, and a central piece of Scotland's future relationships with the UK, the EU, and the international community. The Conclusion brings the many strands of the argument together to reinforce the central claim that immigration has become a critical tool for Scottish nation-building, regardless of whether or not Scotland succeeds at gaining more control over migration post-Brexit. It offers suggestions for how Scotland can attract more immigrants, and discusses strategies that could preserve Scottish openness. The recommendations should be applicable in multiple contexts and at different levels of government.

Notes

1. Clark also mentioned that he deliberately chose to write and perform the song in English, rather than Scots, because 'I wanted the people who it was intended to support to be able to understand it as much as possible – people who might have English as a second language, but would not have Scots.'
2. 'Nation-building' refers to the practice of building a coherent social community that serves as the foundation for a nation-state. It is a process of collective identity formation that allows a group to assert power over a certain territory. It involves

institutions, customs, and traditions, and is the process by which a community defines its national characteristics.
3. In 2013, UKIP leader Nigel Farage was mobbed by Scottish protesters chanting 'UKIP scum, off our streets' and had to retreat into a riot van in Edinburgh after taxis refused him service. After attempting to argue with the protestors, Farage tried to turn accusations of bigotry back on the protestors: 'We've never, ever, ever had this kind of response. Is this a kind of anti-English thing? It could be' (Carrell 2013).
4. Populism can manifest as an ideology, a political style, or a political strategy that can be incorporated into a variety of institutions or agendas, including conservative or progressive, secular or religious, and on the left or right of the political spectrum (Mudde and Kaltwasser 2017).
5. Some question whether the SNP represents a form of left-wing populism, since nationalism, regionalism and populism are easily intertwined (Barrio et al. 2018; Kitschelt and McGann 1995; Stanley 2008). Though the SNP's nationalism is not populist, the party adopted left-wing populist discourse between 2010 and 2017 in its position against the UK-mandated austerity policies (Massetti 2018). Issue-based populism is adopted by the party 'only incidentally and temporarily' (Heinisch et al. 2018: 923).
6. Individual candidates can win a much higher percentage in districts. For example, BNP party leader Nick Griffen won 14.6% of the vote in Barking in 2010. The party's most successful year was 2010, when it fielded 338 candidates and won 1.9% of the vote in the 2010 general election.
7. UKIP's populist character can be seen in how the party leadership criticised elites in the UK and Europe for being corrupt and disconnected from the people, they pushed for the general will by advocating for referenda and direct elections, and they activated a nativist sense of Britishness through assertions of Britain's strength and a natural British desire for independence, especially independence from the EU and freedom from the presence of foreigners.
8. The party won 16% of the vote for the European Parliament in 2004, 16.5% in 2009, and 27.5% in 2014, making it the largest UK party represented in the European Parliament. Farage's post-Brexit party, the Brexit Party, won 31.6% of the vote in 2019.
9. Due to the UK's plurality electoral system, the Conservative Party is unlikely to lose seats to UKIP, but by attracting voters who might otherwise have voted Tory, UKIP risks splitting the conservative vote and increasing the chances of a win by Labour or the Liberal Democrats.
10. The Conservative Party has used populist discourse before. Between 1997 and 2005, the Conservative Party fused Euroscepticism and populism. David Cameron abandoned the fusion in 2006, and created the political space for the rise of a populist UKIP (Bale 2018). Johnson is re-merging the two within the Conservative Party. Though Johnson himself is almost a prototype of the establishment as an Eton-educated, former member of Oxford's high-society Bullingdon Club who studied classics at Balliol College, he has cultivated his image as a leader of the people: he lies shamelessly (Stubley 2019), he deliberately maintains his dishevelled appearance, and he is rumoured to muss his hair before public appearances (Read 2019), and he is regularly photographed running (often in an eye-popping outfit) or riding his bike to work. He loves publicity stunts, even (perhaps especially) when they make him look foolish. His public image is strategic, with each act becoming 'badges of credibility that bridg[e] the class gap' and allow him to style himself as a regular Englishman (Friedman 2019).
11. The assertion that Parliament blocked Brexit is a mischaracterisation. Parliament voted in favour of Johnson's proposed Brexit bill, though it rejected the tight time-

line for scrutinising it. Rather than work toward a compromise solution, Johnson called an election.
12. There is a Scottish branch of UKIP, and Scottish politicians were shocked in 2014 when UKIP won a Scottish seat in the European Parliament elections and again when the Brexit Party won a Scottish seat in the 2019 European Elections. Alex Salmond, who was the leader of the SNP in 2014, had attempted to frame the election as a battle between the SNP and UKIP. Some analysts suggest that this could have backfired, and that people then voted for UKIP as a protest vote against the SNP (Carrell 2014a).
13. The binary option on the independence referendum meant that the result would not be an expression of the preference of the majority. Opinion polls conducted around the time of the referendum suggested that the majority of Scottish voters would have preferred another option of enhanced devolution (known as 'devo plus' or 'devo max'). Prime Minister David Cameron insisted that there be a single question on the ballot paper with a binary option (Sharp et al. 2014).
14. Berwick-upon-Tweed is England's northernmost town. It is strategically located on the Scottish–English border, and possession of the town changed several times during the border wars.
15. Analysts suspect Cameron never anticipated that the referendum results would lead to the UK's withdrawal from the EU. An opinion piece from former Conservative cabinet minister Michael Portillo said the referendum will be remembered as the 'greatest blunder ever made by a British Prime Minister' (Portillo 2016).
16. EU law governs family reunification of EU nationals and is more permissive than the regulations the UK government imposes on UK nationals seeking to reunite with their foreign-born family.
17. In England, 3,000 allegations of hate crimes were made to police in the week before and after the vote, representing a 42% increase in hate crime reporting from the same weeks a year before (Dodd 2016). The Scottish–English contrast in hate crime statistics is striking, but one should not extrapolate much from the difference. Hate crimes are underreported, and England and Scotland have different mechanisms for reporting hate crime.
18. The Scottish public is not as enthusiastic about EU migration as the political elite. One report revealed that while a majority of Scots would like to maintain free trade with the European Union, they would prefer to end freedom of movement, though 63% would accept freedom of movement as the price for free trade (Curtice 2018).
19. In 2018, there were 141,000 foreign workers from EU countries in Scotland, and 57,000 from outside the EU (Scottish Government 2018d).
20. Gove's actions were political strategy, motivated by polls suggesting the national vote was going to be very close, and Scottish members of the SNP could have comprised enough votes to sway the issue.
21. See Hepburn and Zapata-Barrero (2014) for analysis of how a number of European sub-state entities have approached immigration. The volume includes analysis of sub-state politics in Belgium, Canada, the UK, Spain, Italy, and Germany.
22. No immigrant could run for office, campaign, or petition a grievance without a French proficiency test.
23. The vast majority of Scots (around 98%) speak English, and linguistic integration presents the same issues in both England and Scotland, so language is not a salient source of national identity. There is the national language of Scottish Gaelic, which has been promoted through the Bòrd na Gàidhlig, a body charged with advocating for greater respect for Gaelic. Despite efforts to preserve the language, there is virtually no linguistic barrier to Scottishness.

24. Pehrson et al. (2009) find positive relationships between national identification and anti-immigrant prejudice in countries where the people endorse a more ethnic definition of national belonging based on language, and a weaker relationship in countries where the nation is defined in terms of citizenship. Their data comes from the 2003 International Social Survey Programme, which included samples from 31 countries.

I

THE PAST:
A BRIEF HISTORY OF MIGRATION IN SCOTLAND

Britain has been multicultural from the earliest days of human inhabitation, when people arrived on the island from Europe and the Mediterranean. In the Middle Ages, culturally distinct Celtic and Pictish groups inhabited Britain, and subsequent years brought greater diversity through trade and invasion. Roma communities have lived in Britain since the fifteenth century, and in the early modern period, religious conflicts in Europe led many to seek refuge across the Channel. During the eighteenth and nineteenth centuries, imperial ties led colonial subjects from all over the world to seek their fortunes in the United Kingdom, but it was not until the post-war period that the UK experienced consistent positive net migration to England, which resulted in immigration restrictions. Their long history of international immigration makes England secure in its status as a desirable destination. Meanwhile, centuries of emigration have led to Scotland's reputation as a site of departure.

The different experiences of England and Scotland shape the way both countries approach immigration. The English establishment sees immigration as something that must be controlled, while the Scottish political elites believe it should be encouraged. Because Scotland has not encountered challenges of rapid diversification in the modern era, the Scottish elite can learn from the experiences of other nations to prepare their country to welcome newcomers. However, while certain powers have been devolved to the Scottish, Welsh, and Northern Irish Parliaments, control over immigration remains a power reserved to Westminster. Reserving immigration policy to the UK government reflects a central principle of state sovereignty, which requires that state governments have exclusive control over access to their territory. In recent years, concerns about transnational terrorism heightened awareness of immigration as a physical security issue, and reinforced the association between sovereignty and immigration. At the same time, international agreements, legal norms, and economic globalisation erode state control of immigration, and the policies governing the daily life of immigrants, such as housing, education, law enforcement, taxation, and access to social welfare, are governed by local or national authorities. Immigration therefore bridges the gap between domestic and foreign policy and between state and sub-state national policy, though most discussion of immigration control still occurs at the state level. This structure of power has not prevented the political leaders of Scotland from constructing a Scottish approach to immigration, however, complete with independent and devolved immigration policy proposals.

This chapter reviews historical immigration flows that lead Westminster and Holyrood to take different positions on migration. It describes the demographic profiles of immigrant populations in England and Scotland, which explains why immigration is less visible in Scotland. It then outlines how the Scottish government pursues its interest in increased migration through policies that incrementally push devolution further by enhancing Scotland's competencies within the UK-wide system of immigration.

Migration in the UK and Scotland

The UK has grappled with being a major immigrant destination for about a century. Before World War II, the UK was a country of net emigration, meaning that more people left the country than entered it. There were no controls placed on immigration in the UK until the Aliens Act of 1905, which created a bureaucracy of immigration inspectors with discretionary power over 'aliens' (non-Empire or Commonwealth citizens). This created two tracks of immigration control: one for the Empire/Commonwealth, and one for foreign aliens. The clear differentiation in these immigration streams led the UK's immigration trajectory to be intimately connected with its history of Empire. In the post-war context, contracts of citizenship granted citizens of the Old Commonwealth (including Canada, the Americas, Australia, and New Zealand) and the New Commonwealth (including India, Pakistan, Nigeria, and Bangladesh) the right to reside in Britain (Pellew 1989). As the UK experienced growing rates of migration from recently decolonised New Commonwealth countries in the mid-1900s, coordinated efforts to restrict migration resulted in the Commonwealth Immigrants Act of 1962, which introduced many of the first measures to limit immigration (Layton-Henry 1992; Schain 2008). By that point there were already nearly half a million immigrants from the West Indies, India, and Pakistan in the UK, which visibly diversified the domestic population.

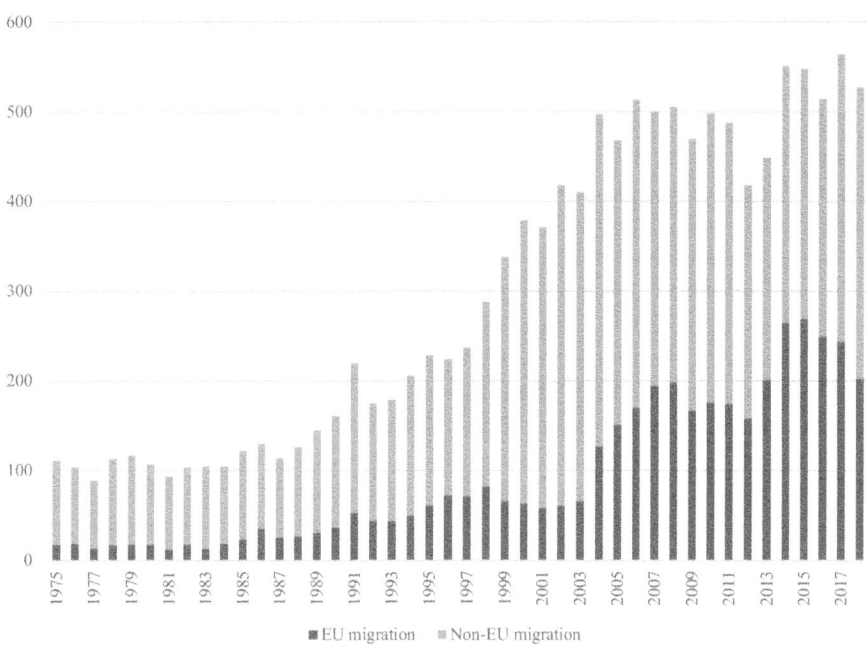

Figure 1.1 Long-term international and EU migration to the UK, in thousands. Source: Office for National Statistics 2018

For the next half-century, those who promoted policies of multiculturalism clashed with those who defined British citizenship with reference to ethnicity and heritage, and political parties started to take sides on the issue (Hampshire 2005; Joppke 1999). Since 1962, government strategies on immigration aligned with the ideology of the party in power. The dominance of the Conservative Party in Westminster between 1979 and 1997 coincided with restrictive policies. The New Labour strategy introduced policies encouraging skilled migration in 1997, which immediately increased immigration from outside Europe, as seen in Figure 1.1. Though the UK joined the EU in 1973, levels of EU migration to the UK remained low until 2004, when ten new states from East Europe joined the EU.[1] While most EU member states initially restricted immigration from these accession states, the UK, Ireland, and Sweden opened their labour markets to the new EU migrants immediately, and EU migration to the UK quickly doubled.

Between 1993 and 2017, the foreign-born population in the UK rose from 3.8 million to 9.4 million, and by 2017, 14% of the UK's population was foreign born. In response to this growth, in 2008, the Labour government introduced a points-based immigration system intended to encourage skilled migration while better controlling low-skilled and family migration. Within the points-based system, a prospective immigrant's eligibility was contingent upon their ability to score points above a certain threshold in a scoring system evaluating education level, skills, private wealth, language ability, age, and the domestic conditions of the UK.[2]

Since the introduction of the points-based system, the public conversation about immigration in the UK has framed it as a problem. People assume that there are too many immigrants in the UK, and that the influx of migrants (often described with the language of uncontrollable natural disaster as coming in 'waves' or 'floods') is not being appropriately controlled. In response to public pressure, in 2010, Conservative Prime Minister David Cameron initiated a change to the immigration system with a promise to reduce immigration 'from the hundreds of thousands to the tens of thousands'.[3] In 2016, Prime Minister Theresa May maintained the goal to reduce net migration and reinforced the 'hostile environment policy', which she implemented as Home Secretary in 2012. The policy sought to make staying in the UK as difficult as possible, so that people without leave to remain would 'voluntarily' leave. Upon taking office in 2019, Prime Minister Boris Johnson promised to scrap the immigration target and to design a system encouraging the 'brightest and best' to migrate to the UK through a new points-based system severely restricting the migration of lower-skilled workers.

Different parts of the UK do not experience immigration in the same way. While London has experienced regular inflows of immigrants, the North-East of England, Scotland, and Cornwall have experienced more emigration than immigration. Excepting Ireland, Scotland's net emigration has been the highest in Western Europe in most decades since the 1850s (Anderson 2018). Emigration was a central feature of Scottish life in every county from the 1400s through the 1990s, motivated by Scotland's harsh climate and its distance from capitals of commerce (Anderson 2018; Devine 2012a).[4] By the seventeenth century, universal parish-school systems created a literate Scottish population and a large, educated middle class, but the Scottish economy remained underdeveloped with a shortage of jobs suitable for an educated population. Many educated Scots (primarily young adults and skilled men) travelled to England, North America, or the Baltic states, and later to the Far East and Africa. For those who remained uneducated or impoverished, Australia and New Zealand were attractive destinations. The majority of Scottish migrants in the nineteenth and twentieth centuries took advantage of the growing British Empire, and many enthusiastically participated in the project of Empire as administrators, soldiers, physicians, and missionaries.[5]

Not all Scots left of their own accord. In the middle of the eighteenth century many Highlanders from the north-west of Scotland were forced to leave their homes in 'Clearances' as landowners recognised that raising sheep was more profitable than crofting (small-scale food production, often involving raising black cattle, kelp, and crops). Facing crippling poverty worsened by potato famine, landowners funded emigration schemes tied to eviction, and many of these efforts received government support.[6] Some victims of the Clearances settled elsewhere in Scotland, but many chose to leave the British Isles altogether to avoid tenement living and harsh working conditions in lowland Scottish cities, preferring to settle in North America where they could continue their pastoral way of life. Mass outward movements from the Highlands after 1820 were significant, especially during the famine of the 1840s and 1850s, but not all emigrants were Highland refugees. Scottish emigrants were a diverse group of people from all regions, social classes, occupations, and backgrounds, many of whom were regarded as the most productive members of their communities (Harper [1998] 2017).

The drama of emigration from Scotland during the 1800s is reflected in migration statistics. In the first half of the nineteenth century, 59% of those who emigrated from the UK were Scottish, half of whom settled in the United States. Scots also made up a quarter of the population of New Zealand at the time. During the full period of mass emigration from Scotland (1841–1931), over 2 million Scots moved abroad, while an additional 750,000 settled in other parts of the UK, leaving only 4.8 million Scots behind (Anderson 2018).

Emigration continued into the twentieth century. Marjorie Harper notes that from 1901 to 1914, 64% more people left the British Isles than in the previous 14 years, but that in Scotland, the increase was 139% (2012: 9). The main destination for these Scots was Canada. After 1914, experiences of world-wide conflict and the economic depression during the interwar years motivated a shift towards migration to England, though skilled Scots continued to move abroad at rates far exceeding skilled migration from other parts of the UK. In the 1920s, nearly half a million Scots moved to destinations outside Europe (many returned during the depression in the 1930s), and the number of Scots-born people in England and Wales climbed by 10% (Harper [1998] 2017). At the same time, policies and opportunities of Empire incentivised 'government-sponsored colonization as a vital tool in securing the increasingly fragile economic, political, and racial cohesion of the British empire' (Harper [1998] 2017: 13). By 1931, between a quarter and a fifth of Scots were not living in their homeland (Finlay 2004). The outbreak of World War II disrupted migration patterns, but emigration gained momentum again in the 1950s and 1960s, encouraged by 'pull' factors, such as active recruitment strategies from the Old Commonwealth, though there were also 'push' factors of high unemployment and troubled industry in Scotland (Jones 1970). An average of 300 people moved away from Scotland every day in the 1960s. Emigration began to fall off from 1966 due to economic downturn and the imposition of immigration controls in many countries overseas, especially Canada (Harper 2012).

Today, the size of the Scottish 'ancestral diaspora' is estimated to be between

Figure 1.2 Net migration to Scotland, in thousands.
Source: National Records of Scotland 2018c

30 and 100 million people, depending on whether those with distant Scottish heritage are included (McNeil 2014). The diaspora is 'the most enduring and pervasive characteristic of Scotland's population history – and has been so for more than 200 years' (Anderson 2018: 124). Rates of net migration (the difference between the number of immigrants and the number of emigrants) in postwar Scotland are depicted in Figure 1.2, which demonstrates low net migration until the 1990s, both from the rest of the UK and internationally. While emigration has slowed, thousands of young Scots still settle in England or abroad.

Despite dominant trends of emigration, people have always immigrated to Scotland. In the early medieval period, people came primarily from Scandinavia, Ireland, and England. The Kingdom of Scotland was built as these people intermingled with indigenous populations. Immigration slowed in subsequent centuries, but industrialisation and urbanisation in the mid-eighteenth century attracted people from all over Europe. By the 1911 census, roughly 400,000 residents in Scotland were born outside the country, amounting to 9% of Scotland's population. The size of subsequent immigrant flows to Scotland in the twentieth century naturally vacillated with cycles of the economy and international conflict.

Irish immigrants were some of the earliest migrants in Scotland, especially in the West of Scotland, but their numbers swelled during the famine years of the 1840s, when migration doubled the Irish-born population, resulting in an Irish population in Scotland that was proportionately twice the size of the Irish population in England and Wales, though absolute numbers were substantially smaller in Scotland (around 207,000 people) (Anderson 2018).[7] Before the famine years, Irish immigrants were stereotyped as being poor and beggarly, though many employers welcomed them as workers. Opinions hardened during the famine, when the influx of immigrants coincided with economic depression in Scotland. Irish immigrants were scapegoated as the source of disease, fuelled by a typhus epidemic in Glasgow in 1847 and cholera outbreaks in 1848, and they were stereotyped as being violent and criminal. Some Scottish workers saw the Irish as strike breakers or competitors for jobs. They believed the Irish depressed wages and damaged working conditions, though Irish workers played a pivotal role in the formation of trade unions and social movements to advance workers' rights, which benefited Scottish workers (Mitchell 1998, 2017).[8]

Among those who held negative perceptions of the Irish, opinions were augmented by religious intolerance. Steps to emancipate Catholics in the United Kingdom were taken in the late 1700s, and the re-establishment of the Catholic hierarchy in England reignited religious conflict in Scotland in the 1850s. On occasion, the conflicts were violent, as when in 1851, Catholic and Protestant groups clashed in Greenock and Gourock (Braber 2012). Things calmed down by the mid-1850s, and after the Catholic hierarchy was restored in Scotland in 1878, backlash against Catholicism and the Irish Catholic community dissipated. Irish Catholics were participants in Scottish society and politics by the end of the nineteenth century, even as they disproportionately occupied the lower rungs on the socio-economic ladder. As Irish influence grew, the establishment of an Irish Free State and the introduction of state-funded Catholic education in 1918 made Scottish people newly aware of the Irish community in Scotland. This awareness fuelled new sectarian conflict during the interwar period, led by the Church of Scotland's anti-Irish campaign. The church sought to lead a nativist anti-Catholic movement to make the church the defender of the faith and the Scottish race, based on the assumption that the Christian Commonwealth and a national church required both racial and religious homogeneity (Brown 1991). These broader motivations allowed the campaign to be presented as having scientific respectability with objectives in defence of the national interest, and gave it broader appeal than a campaign based solely on religion (Rosie 2017). The platform was most notoriously articulated in the Church and Nation Committee of the General Assembly's report in 1923, entitled 'The Menace of the Irish Race to our Scottish Nationality'. The report presented Irish Catholics as a morally corrupting force, and as a population with character flaws resulting from their evolutionary or racial inferiority. The church's efforts were followed by municipal 'No Popery' politics, led by Protestant associations in Glasgow and

Edinburgh (Rosie 2017). As the largest wave of immigrants up to that point, Irish Catholics who migrated during the interwar years experienced a rather unwelcoming Scotland, in which the national church attempted to define Scottish identity in such a way as to exclude Catholics on the basis of religion and the Irish on the basis of race.

Irish Protestants also migrated, and by 1914, about a third of the Irish immigrants in Scotland were Protestant (Braber 2012). In fact, the Irish constituted the greatest number of Episcopalians in the West of Scotland for most of the nineteenth century (Meredith 2017). Irish Protestants were more likely to take skilled employment, and they experienced less hostility, than Irish Catholics. Scottish Protestant churches provided a venue for incorporation, as Irish Protestants joined pre-existing congregations, unlike the Irish Catholics, who had to build their own churches (Vaughn 2005). Many Irish Protestants joined Orange Orders in Scotland, which were set up to oppose Irish home rule, though they also helped Irish Protestants integrate into their local communities (Walker 1992). Despite their integrative potential, Orange Orders did not have a very good reputation among middle-class Scots, who associated them with violence and a foreign struggle that imported tensions into Scotland. While Irish Protestants were a less visible immigrant group than Irish Catholics, the Orange Orders highlighted their presence in Scottish society. Even though Irish Protestants shared a religious tradition with their Scottish hosts, 'whether Protestants or Catholics, the Irish remained Irish above all in the eyes of the Scottish natives' (Vaughn 2005: 190).

Catholic and Protestant Irish immigration to Scotland fell away during World War I, as Irish immigrants flowed in greater numbers to England, the US, and the Old Commonwealth countries. Still, Irish immigrants and their descendants changed Scottish society, and the Irish experience within Scotland was transformed in the twentieth century. Anti-Catholic discrimination entrenched conditions of socio-economic inequality and disadvantage through the 1950s, but post-war political and economic changes provided economic and educational opportunities to the Scots Irish. The Church of Scotland repented of its previous anti-Catholic campaign, and better inter-communal relations between Catholics and Protestants were established. Sectarianism was publicly demonised, most famously by James MacMillan in his speech entitled 'Scotland's Shame', and anti-sectarianism became part of the Scottish public consciousness in the 1990s. Sectarianism became a major interest of concern for the Scottish Parliament when it was established in 1999, resulting in the criminalisation of religious hate crimes. In the twenty-first century, there are positive signs that occupational and social parity between those with Irish and Scottish heritage are within reach, even as the legacy of Catholic victimisation persists (Devine 2017). The experiences of Catholic immigrants, and the Scottish reckoning with how those immigrants were treated, laid the foundation for Scotland's future campaigns for immigration, inclusivity, and anti-racism.

The Irish were not the only historical group of immigrants that came to Scotland seeking a new life. English people were attracted by industrialisation in Edinburgh and by the late 1800s, English-born residents outnumbered Irish-born residents.[9] German immigrants were a feature of Scottish life since the Middle Ages, and they were well-regarded entrepreneurs in most communities until World War I, when they were targeted for internment and deportation. Other international migration remained low before the world wars, during which time about 40,000 people came primarily from Europe, especially Italy, Russia, and modern-day Lithuania and Poland. Many migrants were Jews fleeing persecution in Russia, Latvia, Lithuania, and Estonia. Native attitudes towards Jews were largely ambivalent, and though Jews did experience some prejudicial stereotyping, individual Jews achieved economic and political success in Scotland (Braber 2012).[10] Most international migrants came fleeing the pressures of a fast-growing population, depression, or oppression, such as Belgian refugees that were settled in Glasgow during World War I or Jewish immigrants, many of them children, fleeing Hitler's persecution during World War II. Many groups of refugees established cultural communities in the Central Belt that persist to this day. Even with a diverse array of new arrivals, international migrants made up less than 1% of the population in 1945, and the national origins of Scotland's immigrants resembled those in the rest of the UK. The international immigration experiences of Scotland and England began to diverge after the world wars.

In the early post-war period, England attracted migrant workers from the New Commonwealth, but Scottish employers did not need new sources of labour because unemployment was high and the textile industry was collapsing. Instead, half of those who immigrated to Scotland had origins in the United States, Australia, Canada, New Zealand, and South Africa (Jones 1970).[11] The rest came from all over the world, and included refugees from Vietnam fleeing the war, Chileans fleeing the 1973 coup d'état, and many Poles, Tamils, Ghanaians, Afghans, Somalis, Kurds, Ugandans, Balkans, and Kosovars who settled in Scotland in the 1980s and 1990s (Braber 2012).[12] Migrants from India, China, and Pakistan arrived in Scotland in the 1950s, many moving from their original settlements in England, and they diversified Scotland economically, socially, and culturally. Many Asian migrants were entrepreneurs, starting businesses that transformed Scottish cityscapes and broadened culinary horizons (Devine and McCarthy 2018). Though Scotland received new groups of immigrants in the post-war period, immigration from North America, the Old Commonwealth, and Europe continued to dominate flows until 2000. Immigration only outpaced emigration in the new millennium.

Scotland continues to receive a very small share of the UK's international immigrants, as only 4.7% of the UK's foreign-born population lives in Scotland.[13] By the 2011 census, 93% of Scotland's population was born in the UK, and 83% were born in Scotland, leaving 7% of Scotland's population with birthplaces outside the UK. Most international immigrants settle in the Central Belt, around the cities of Glasgow and Edinburgh. Though the population of immigrants in Scotland is small, it has changed substantially in a short time. Every region in the UK is experiencing growing numbers of immigrant residents (Vargas-Silva and Rienzo 2017), but Scotland has seen the most growth, and its foreign-born population nearly doubled between 2001 and 2011 (Vargas-Silva 2013). Fifty-two per cent of Scotland's immigrants come from outside the EU, while most of the EU immigration comes from the accession states, especially Poland. Poland is the third most common country of birth in Scotland, after Scotland and England. The large Polish population in Scotland is partly explained by the history of Polish immigration to the UK (Piętka-Nykaza 2018). After World War II, the British government arranged for Polish servicemen and their families to settle in the UK, while also allowing for displaced people to migrate with the European Voluntary Workers Scheme. A second wave of Polish migration began with the admission of Poland into the EU in 2004, and Polish immigrants have settled throughout Scotland in a mix of urban and rural areas. The 2011 census established that Polish immigrants make up almost half (47%) of the resident EU nationals in Scotland (Hudson and Aiton 2016), though movement from all ten accession states increased after they were admitted to the European Union. Meanwhile, extra-EU migration has visibly diversified the Scottish population. Migration from the New Commonwealth in the immediate post-war period grew Scotland's ethnically minoritised population to 1.3% of the total population. By 2001, that proportion was 2%, and by 2011, minoritised groups made up 4% of the population.[14] The Asian population is the largest ethnically minoritised group (3% of the population or about 141,000 individuals), and a third of the Asian population is Pakistani. Migration from India before the 1947 partition of the subcontinent was facilitated by the disproportionate involvement of Scots in Empire and the East India Company. After partition, many Indians in Scotland became Pakistanis overnight, and Pakistanis comprised the biggest group of post-war migrants to Scotland from the subcontinent. From the 1950s through the 1980s, migrants from India and Pakistan were drawn to Scotland by work opportunities, especially as Irish labour migration slowed. By the 1970s, many migrants had prospered and opened their own businesses, mostly settling in the main cities of the Central Belt. Today those of Indian and Pakistani heritage are dispersed across Scotland. Both groups retain their cultural and religious practices and exhibit high rates of entrepreneurship, bringing a South Asian flavour to every main Scottish town.[15]

African, Caribbean, or Black individuals make up an additional 1% of the Scottish population. People of African origin and descent have had a long history of contact with Scottish people. The eighteenth-century association is inexorably mired in slavery, though African and Caribbean people also came to Scotland for employment and study. The population has grown substantially, increasing six-fold between 2001 and 2011, largely because the UK named Glasgow as a site of refugee dispersal with the Immigration and Asylum Act of 1999. Groups of Congolese, Ivoirians, and Cameroonians living in Glasgow built vibrant co-ethnic associational lives, and their celebrations became 'visible and proud assertions of cultural origins and African-ness in Scotland', though the lived experiences of African migrants vary substantially by context (Piacentini 2008: 187). After 2015, an especially visible population in Scotland were Syrians. During the Syrian refugee crisis, a fifth of the UK's Syrian refugees were settled in Scotland, and they were settled in every local authority in the country.

Terrorist attacks by al-Qaeda and ISIS and the reception of large Muslim populations during the Syrian refugee crisis led to anxieties across Europe about the growing Muslim presence in immigrant communities (McLaren and Johnson 2007). In the UK, concerns are amplified because the Muslim population is the fastest-growing population, projected to double by 2021. The Muslim population is much smaller in Scotland than in England. In 2011, for every 1,000 Scots, 16 were Muslim, well below the average of 39 Muslims for every 1,000 English people (Office for National Statistics 2011). The Muslim population in Scotland exhibits higher levels of affluence and social class compared with the Muslim population in England, and as a result may have different experiences with segregation or social unrest within their communities (Hopkins 2008). Nevertheless, for Scotland's predominantly Muslim Pakistani community, Muslimness 'became a core public identity following the changes in public attitudes towards Muslims after the Rushdie Affair in 1988–9 and the terrorist attacks on the United States in 2001' (Bonino 2018: 85).

The profile of minoritised communities in Scotland is not a microcosm of wider UK trends. According to the 2001 and 2011 censuses, many of the top ten sending countries are the same (Poland, India, Pakistan, Ireland, Germany), but England attracts many more immigrants from Bangladesh, Nigeria, and Jamaica than Scotland. In some ways, the ethnic profiles of the main immigrant groups make Scotland look more like other European countries than the rest of the UK. For example, the age profile and countries of origin of unaccompanied asylum seeker children who sought refuge in Scotland from 2001–4 looked more like minors who sought asylum in Scandinavia than those who arrived in England (Hopkins and Hill 2006). Scotland is changing, but the nation's recent experience as a country of immigration and the cultural profile of its immigrants mean Scotland does not yet confront the same challenges of immigrant incorporation facing England.

A consequence of the divergent English and Scottish histories of migration is different national perspectives on the relationship between race and immigration. Scotland is experiencing its first generation of phenotypically different immigrants. Issues of modern racism and immigration are therefore bound together in Scotland, meaning that the conversation about one inevitably becomes a conversation about the other. To some extent, this has always been the case in Scotland, as during the nineteenth and twentieth centuries, the Scots, Irish, English, and Welsh were understood to be distinct races, and Scottish people racialised Irish immigrants by justifying anti-immigrant sentiment with notions of racial inferiority (Brown 1991). The Scottish history of immigration and racism illustrates how 'race' is defined by society and has no objective meaning. Modern discourse differentiates between race, used to describe phenotypic characteristics (white, Black, Asian), and ethnicity, which refers more to heritage or culture (Irish, Jewish, Kurdish), though the UK government prefers to forgo use of the word 'race' completely in favour of 'ethnicity'. In England, where generations of minoritised groups have been born in the country, immigration and racism are handled as independent but related phenomena. In Scotland, the politics of immigration can obfuscate problems of racism, and it is difficult to disentangle the meaning of any resistance to immigration and whether it is rooted in racism or xenophobia.

To summarise, while both England and Scotland are historically countries of emigration, the UK experienced net inflows of migrants in the 1980s, 20 years earlier than Scotland, and at a much higher rate. Immigration to England has been more visible due to the ethnic heritage of the migrants, while Scotland's migration has primarily been from Europe and North America. Nevertheless, the English experience has been the reference point for designing UK immigration policy that does not reflect Scotland's experiences nor serve Scottish interests. The UK and Scotland have divergent narratives about the role of immigration in society. It is taken for granted that people want to migrate to England, and the policy priority is to shield society from 'floods' of migrants from less privileged and culturally different places. In Scotland, projections of population decline have sustained concerns about Scottish emigration. This has resulted in national humility that manifests in arguments about the importance of making a deliberate national-level effort to attract migrants.

These differences justify an examination of the politics of migration in Scotland, as distinct from the politics of migration in the UK. While ample scholarly work discusses the politics of immigration, citizenship, and ethnicity in the UK, most work does not engage with Scotland, thereby missing an opportunity to explore alternative social and political possibilities under a common legal system.[16] Furthermore, many of these works generalise research based in London or Manchester to all areas of the UK. This book exploits these oversights to provide a more comprehensive vision of the politics of immigration in Scotland.

THE SCOTTISH APPROACH TO IMMIGRATION IN THE TWENTY-FIRST CENTURY

Immigration policy is decided by the UK government and managed by the Home Office in London. There is no requirement for the UK government to consult with devolved governments on reserved issues. This is a problem for the Scottish government, as the UK and the Scottish governments have vastly different views on immigration and its role in their countries' future. The Conservative UK government committed itself to reducing net migration, while the Scottish government wants to maintain high levels of migration to combat demographic decline and support the economy.

The Scottish government recognises its constraints under the current system and has found alternative ways to pursue Scottish interests. The Scottish Executive is taking an incremental approach to what it hopes will be a comprehensive national immigration regime. The One Scotland campaign (previously called One Scotland, Many Cultures) seeks to celebrate diversity and address structural racism and discrimination at all levels of Scottish government and society. The Scottish Executive expanded its powers over immigration with the Fresh Talent Initiative in 2005, which included the implementation of a post-study work visa, a two-year visa intended to allow graduates from Scottish universities to stay in Scotland to find employment. The New Scots Refugee Integration Strategies of 2014 and 2018 planned to better integrate new arrivals, provide a welcoming image of Scotland, and demonstrate Scotland's commitment to global citizenship. Immigrant integration has always been the purview of the Scottish national government and the New Scots Strategy is an expression of the desire to make Scotland an attractive destination. Though it has not been implemented, Scotland's most comprehensive immigration strategy short of independence is a devolved immigration policy, which the Scottish government has presented as a feasible option within the UK-wide post-Brexit immigration policy.

These policies include both immigration and integration strategies and target particular groups of migrants. With the exception of the proposal for a devolved immigration policy, the initiatives are limited in scope and specific in their implementation. They are more realistic than a grand immigration strategy in the current political climate, in which interests and issues around immigration, national interest, and nationalism are conflated and politicised. Together, these initiatives provide a multidimensional image of the goals of the Scottish Executive, and an indication of the government's power to achieve them.

One Scotland

The One Scotland campaign emphasises Scotland's diversity and its challenges with racism. The Scottish Executive introduced the campaign in 2002 against a backdrop of increased attention to racial violence, political devolution, and new legal responsibilities to address racism.[17] The campaign had two elements. First, it helped the Scottish Executive take responsibility for ensuring no person or group is disadvantaged in the development, design, and delivery of government policies or services. Second, it included an outward-facing publicity campaign to raise public awareness and celebration of Scotland's cultural diversity, intended to change the attitudes and behaviours of Scottish citizens. The campaign assumed that appreciation for equality can be learned. It taught Scots what discrimination looks like and spread the message that anti-racism and multiculturalism are fundamental features of the Scottish national ethos. Advertisements focused on racist language, behaviour, and attitudes were launched on television, cinema, radio, and posters (Penrose and Howard 2008).

The One Scotland campaign reflects the attention given to inter-ethnic relations following devolution in 1999. While the Scottish government does not have the power to develop race relations legislation, it can promote equal opportunities and inclusion in distinctively Scottish ways.[18] The campaign connects Scottish history and symbolism to national pride in multiculturalism (Meer 2018). For example, the campaign published a timeline of the social and cultural changes that have shaped Scotland, demonstrating that Scotland has never been exclusively white, that it is a nation of immigrants, and how transition and change describes the Scottish experience much more than cultural and racial homogeneity. This effort attempted to dissolve fear of immigration and social change, making the One Scotland campaign a foundation for the Scottish Executive's approach to more open immigration.

By shedding light on instances of racism, the campaign upset the idea that Scotland is a place without racism and helped to displace unwarranted complacency among Scottish decision makers and the public (Hopkins 2008: 118). Racism is an everyday occurrence for Scots who are members of minoritised groups, most of whom are immigrants or have an immigrant background.[19] All elements of the One Scotland campaign shape the politics of immigration by constructing an image of a multicultural and tolerant Scotland, but the initiative takes up immigration explicitly with its 'We Are Scotland' webpage, which illustrates why Scotland needs immigrants to fill skills shortages and to supply a working population to compensate for demographic decline and ageing. It also features stories about Scots with migrant backgrounds, highlighting their contributions and commitments to Scotland. Even though the main audience for the One Scotland campaign is the majority white, native-born Scots, the campaign focuses on creating a national environment prepared for greater diversification, and lays the foundation for subsequent efforts to attract and retain migrants.[20]

The Post-Study Work Visa

The creation and implementation of a Scottish post-study work visa built on One Scotland to attract and retain international university graduates. The UK government consented to grant Scotland unique control over student migrants through the 2005 Fresh Talent: Working in Scotland Scheme, which allowed foreign nationals who graduated from Scottish universities to remain in the UK for two years post-graduation without having to apply for a work permit. The policy is the only example of a devolved immigration policy in the UK's history. It was devised by Jack McConnell, first minister of Scotland from 2001 to 2007. Faced with declining birth rates, McConnell was interested in increasing highly skilled migration to bolster the Scottish economy. The human capital provided by immigrants, and especially those already studying within Scotland, seemed like a natural, if partial, solution. The scheme was designed to link the issues of economic growth, population decline, entrepreneurship, and migration in one policy package administered by the Scottish government.

Fresh Talent employed three major strategies to attract and retain migrants. First, it expanded international networking activities and marketing efforts to present Scotland as a desirable place in which to live and work. Second, it marketed Scotland as a region of promising employment prospects with promotional materials and seminars educating prospective employers about the new worker's permit. Third, the government focused on retaining students already in Scotland by allowing a two-year visa extension to enable a job search. Scholarships were also offered to students interested in postgraduate degrees. To qualify, participants must have graduated from a Scottish college or university with at least a Higher National Diploma (a semi-vocational/semi-professional qualification earned in two to three academic years), or have earned a degree in a postgraduate programme.[21]

A 2008 evidence review of the policy declared early success. Between 2005 and 2007, non-European international enrolments in Scottish universities increased by 3,000 students, growing the international student body by about 8%. Between 2005 and 2008, over 8,000 students enrolled in the scheme (Cavanagh et al. 2008). The report found that the 'attraction' element of the Fresh Talent Initiative worked most effectively, as it led to enhanced cooperation between the universities and governments to send a strong message about the benefits of studying, living, and working in Scotland. In terms of employment, the enrolments did not yield universally optimal results, as the experience of many students suggested that the right kind of skilled work was not always available to them. The Scottish government suggested improving the support given to international graduates in order to manage expectations and to more effectively orient employers and prospective employees towards each other.

Almost immediately after the implementation of Fresh Talent, institutions of higher learning in England objected, insisting that the scheme unfairly advantaged Scottish institutions by allowing them to pull international students away from English institutions. In response, Chancellor of the Exchequer Gordon Brown proposed a similar UK-wide post-study visa programme based on the Fresh Talent model to go into effect in May 2006, and in May 2007 the Scottish programme was absorbed into a new UK-wide International Graduates Scheme (IGS). The main difference between Fresh Talent and IGS is that while the Scottish scheme allowed a two-year extension of the visa, the UK programme allowed one year, and the Scottish scheme qualified students with Higher National Diplomas while the UK policy did not. Scottish universities objected to the UK-wide scheme, claiming that the new but similar programme damaged the Fresh Talent Initiative by removing the incentive for students to choose Scottish institutions. In other words, with introduction of the IGS, Scotland lost its competitive advantage.[22]

In June of 2008, Westminster announced the UK's new comprehensive points-based immigration system. It did not include any flexibility that would allow the Scottish Executive to encourage migrants to settle in Scotland rather than England. Both the IGS and the Fresh Talent Initiative were absorbed into the Tier 1 point system for 'high value migrants'. The post-study work visa within this tier of the UK-wide system operated from 2008 until 2012 when the post-study work scheme along with the whole of Tier 1 was eliminated by the Conservative UK government as part of its effort to reduce net migration to below 100,000.[23] The government claimed that the volume of student migration created by the tier was a burden on the UK Border Agency, and it accused colleges and universities of fraud and neglecting their responsibilities as migrant sponsors. The government also suggested that economic migrants were using the student visa to illegally access the labour market and mandated that only graduates with a 'skilled graduate level job' paying at least £30,000 annually would be able to stay in the UK after graduation under a Tier 2 visa.[24] It also imposed English language skill requirements and removed the right of family reunification for students enrolled in anything other than postgraduate work. At the same time, the government increased the accreditation requirements for colleges and universities hoping to recruit international students. As the then Secretary of State Theresa May explained:

> The package of measures that I have outlined today is expected to reduce the number of student visas by between 70,000 and 80,000 – a reduction of more than 25% – and it will increase the outflow of foreign students after they have concluded their studies. There will be a proper system

of accreditation to root out bogus colleges; tough new rules on English language skills, financial guarantees, working rights and dependents, to root out bogus students; and new restrictions on post-study work to make sure that all but the very best return home after study. This package will stop bogus students studying meaningless courses at fake colleges, protect our world-class institutions, stop the abuse that became all too common under Labour, and restore some sanity to our student visa system. (May 2011)

May's claims about fraudulent student visas are exaggerated, though university watchdog groups have compiled a list of fake institutions guilty of degree fraud, which should prompt concerns about fraudulent credentials rather than visa fraud (Weale 2019). Though the BBC uncovered instances of fraud in English tests used to qualify for a visa, a vast number of those whose visas were cancelled for cheating were falsely accused and given no opportunity for appeal (Wright 2018). The treatment of these students illustrates the consequences of May's 'hostile environment' for legal immigrants.

The consequences of this policy change were quickly felt in Scotland. In its 2016 report on the issue, the Scottish Affairs Committee estimates that since 2012, retention of non-EU students fell by 80%. The report also concludes that the closure of the Tier 1 visa 'has harmed Scotland by making Scotland less competitive in the global education market, with other nations able to offer prospective students greater employment opportunities after graduation' (UK Parliament 2016). In February 2015, the UK Parliament's All-Party Parliamentary Group (APPG) on Migration considered the post-study work visa for the UK.[25] The group concluded that the elimination of Tier 1 reduced the number of skilled international students remaining in the UK more than anticipated, and that the requirements of the Tier 2 visa simultaneously presented a substantial barrier to employment for non-EEA graduates. The APPG recommended that the post-study work visa be reconsidered.

In 2014, Scotland began a new effort to introduce a Scottish post-study work visa, fashioned on the previous Fresh Talent Initiative. Discussions about the policy occurred within the context of the independence referendum under the presumption that an independent Scotland would need a comprehensive immigration policy platform. In August, Humza Yousaf, the Scottish Minister for Europe and International Development, set up a working group on the post-study work visa. The group brought together stakeholders from the business and higher education communities to consider the impact of post-study work opportunities within Scotland. After Scottish voters decided against independence in September 2014, the ambitions of the working group shifted away from post-independence policy and towards a new post-study work visa within the UK government's promise to devolve more powers to Scotland after the independence referendum.

Prime Minister David Cameron asked Lord Robert Smith of Kelvin to lead a Devolution Commission (colloquially called the Smith Commission) to reach an agreement about what new devolved powers would be granted to Scotland. The findings of the Commission were eventually implemented with the Scotland Act of 2016. The Smith Commission provided an opportunity for the stakeholders supporting the reinstatement of the visa to present their arguments. The Scottish government and Colleges Scotland submitted statements emphasising the need to consider a scheme similar to Fresh Talent. The Scottish government identified the Fresh Talent Initiative as an 'early example of UK policy in a reserved area responding positively within the devolution settlement', and suggested that such a policy could therefore be successful again (Scottish Government 2018g: 6). The Smith Commission responded by including the post-study work visa in its report under 'additional issues for consideration' where formal devolved powers may not be required. The charge was for the Scottish and UK governments to 'work together to ... explore the possibility of introducing formal schemes to allow international higher education students graduating from Scottish further and higher education institutions to remain in Scotland and contribute to economic activity for a defined period of time' (The Smith Commission 2014: 28). The relegation of the visa to 'additional issues' outside of devolved powers and the unambitious mandate to 'work together' caused hopes of devolved power over any form of immigration to fade.

The result was deeply frustrating for proponents of the post-study work visa. Initially, campaigners had many reasons to believe that the reinstatement of the visa was a viable proposal: it set up a 'best case scenario' for devolved immigration decision making (involving high-skilled, Scottish-educated migrants); it enjoyed essentially unanimous support across the political parties in Scotland; UK government committees endorsed reconsidering the scheme; it was part of a solution to demonstrable demographic and economic need and was backed by important and powerful lobbying groups from universities and economic sectors; and there was the legal precedent set by the Fresh Talent Initiative, which demonstrated how the policy could be legally justified. As a representative of the Scottish Trades Union Congress put it:

> We think that students who study in Scotland are really a valuable resource to the cultural life of the university. It's good for our economy, and ultimately our economy benefits when employers get access to the skills of people who have trained and studied in Scotland and are socialised into Scottish culture with good language skills. (Personal interview 9 June 2016)

Even for those who resent or fear immigration, the relatively small numbers of highly skilled and well-integrated immigrants attracted by the post-study work visa takes some of the sting out of the prospect of increased immigration, because they are theoretically the most beneficial and least costly group of migrants and the least controversial in terms of any economic or cultural threat. As a Labour Member of the Scottish Parliament (MSP) said:

> It's difficult to make any rational case against a Fresh Talent approach, where it's not so difficult to make a rational case against large-scale unskilled migration which makes people quite genuinely feel threatened if they themselves are in low-paying jobs. They fear that they'll either lose their jobs or wages will be driven down further because of low-skilled migrants. That's not to say they're right in their reactions, and sometimes they're wrong, but [their feelings are] understandable. People are not going to feel the same way about doctors, dentists, engineers, and computer scientists. The people in those professions will have confidence in their own ability to carry on doing what they do and will not feel threatened in the same way. And people in other professions or in other aspects of society are going to see the benefits of more able young people contributing to the economy. (Personal interview 27 June 2016)

Nevertheless, in 2017 the Conservative government stated that there would be no reintroduction of a post-study work visa scheme, declaring that the issue was 'dead' (Macdonell 2017).

In September 2019, Boris Johnson's newly elected government announced the return of the post-study work visa, seven years after the programme had been scrapped by Theresa May. International students who started their studies in the UK in 2020 were once again eligible for the post-study work visa for two to three years under the new post-Brexit immigration policy. The reintroduction of the visa was attributed to Boris Johnson's brother, former Universities Minister Jo Johnson, who (along with Labour MP Paul Blomfield) added the visa in an amendment to the government's post-Brexit immigration bill, which won support from 26 Conservative MPs, including the Prime Minister. Jo Johnson subsequently called for the government to double the visa offering from two to four years in order to help Britain recover from Brexit and the COVID-19 pandemic and to send 'a clear signal that Global Britain is open and welcome, with a best-in-class student visa offer' (McIntyre 2020). Jo Johnson's stance reveals the consistency between the post-study work visa programme and the UK's government's goal to attract highly skilled migration to the UK and demonstrates that the previous resistance to the policy was political and not practical.

The Scottish government's reaction to the reintroduction of the policy noted its constant advocacy for the post-study work visa, and attempted to reclaim the policy: 'It should not have taken seven years for the UK Government to accept the arguments from partners across Scotland and reverse their decision' (Scottish Government 2019b). Though the Scottish government said the reintroduction of the visa is a 'welcome step', it also argued that it is only one of several steps required to fix a problematic immigration system: 'The UK's current and proposed post-study work offer is far less attractive than in its competitor countries. Brexit and the negative atmosphere around immigration also discourages international students from coming to the UK, especially those from EU countries' (Scottish Government 2019a, quoting Paulina Trevena). Maintaining a competitive edge, according to the report, requires greater support for those wishing to stay, including language and employability support, integration programmes, and better advice on employment. Fortunately for Scottish decision makers, the powers to implement many of these programmes are already devolved.

The New Scots Refugee Integration Strategy

Since the Smith Commission made it clear that the UK government would not consider any plans to devolve powers of immigration to Scotland, the Scottish government investigated other ways to make Scotland appear to be a welcoming country to immigrants. One such strategy emerged in the context of the Syrian refugee crisis, the largest international refugee crisis since the end of the Cold War. In September 2015, moved by the image of drowned toddler Aylan Kurdi, Scottish First Minister Nicola Sturgeon said that Scotland would accept 1,000 refugees as a starting point for a meaningful discussion about further help, and urged David Cameron to increase the UK's commitment to accepting at least 10,000 refugees (it had accepted 216 when Sturgeon made her commitment). Sturgeon also committed to set up a task force to coordinate Scotland's response to the growing crisis (BBC News 2015a). Sturgeon admitted that 'we don't control the borders of the UK' and unless the UK government changed its plan to accept more refugees, the conversation about accepting more refugees in Scotland was 'academic' (Ferguson 2015). But only a few days later, Cameron committed to take 20,000 refugees from 2015 to 2020 with the Vulnerable Persons Resettlement Scheme, and almost exactly a year after Sturgeon's commitment, the thousandth refugee was settled in Scotland.

Sturgeon's objective in citing a figure of 1,000 was to state her readiness for Scotland to accept a proportional share of the UK's refugees, but she committed to take at least 2,000 by 2020 as part of the government's resettlement scheme. By 2016, Scotland settled a hugely disproportionate number of the UK's refugees, hosting nearly a third of the refugees settled in the UK. Angela Constance, the Scottish Equalities Secretary, highlighted the milestone in 2016 by pointing out the widespread effort to house refugees: 'It is a great credit that 29 out of 32 local authorities in Scotland have now taken Syrian refugees, in marked contrast to what has happened south of the border' (Brooks 2016). By 2018, a third of the UK's local authorities had yet to take a single refugee (Easton and Butcher 2018).[26] By December of 2017, three years ahead of schedule, Scotland met its goal to host 2,000 Syrian refugees, and by 2018, all 32 local authorities in Scotland were hosting refugees.

Most of the Syrian refugees in Scotland were settled through the Syrian Vulnerable Persons Resettlement Scheme, which is managed and funded by the UK government. All Scotland's leaders could do was express their willingness to host, but the Scottish government was interested in moving forward with its own national plan for welcoming asylum seekers and refugees. It made inroads with national-level legislation relating to asylum seeker children with the Children (Scotland) Act of 1995, which placed a duty on local authorities to ensure the welfare of all children in need, including asylum seeker children.[27] Furthermore, the Scottish Executive controls the integration of immigrants and refugees, since devolved powers include control over essential services like housing and education.

The first efforts to coordinate the organisations supporting refugees and asylum seekers took shape in the New Scots Refugee Integration Strategy from 2014 to 2017. The duration of the Syrian crisis motivated the Scottish government to extend the New Scots Refugee Integration Strategy to 2018–22. The new strategy was the result of collaboration with the Scottish Refugee Council, the local government body Convention of Scottish Local Authorities (COSLA), and nearly 700 refugees and asylum seekers. It was described as an 'approach to support the vision of a welcoming Scotland' (Scottish Government 2018c). A representative of the Scottish Refugee Council described it as

> encompassing all refugee populations in Scotland, not just those who've come from this asylum route. More local authority actors are involved in this, and it's moved away from a sort of 'emergency aid' response to actually really focusing on integration as a two-way process and a longer-term issue. (Personal interview 3 April 2019)

In contrast to UK immigration law, which distinguishes between asylum seekers and refugees and provides full support only to refugees, the Scottish strategy aims to support asylees from the day of their claim.[28] In early 2018, the Scottish government extended the right to vote in local council elections and Scottish Parliament elections to everyone legally residing in Scotland, including asylum seekers and refugees. As Green Party MSP Ross Greer put it, 'what better way could we show refugees and asylum seekers that they truly are welcome and that Scotland is their home than by giving them the right to vote?' (Green 2018).

These efforts reinforce the strategy articulated in the One Scotland and the Fresh Talent Initiatives to attract and improve the retention of migrants by demonstrating that Scotland is a good place to live. The signal of inclusiveness impacts the quality of life of all immigrants who settle in Scotland. Naomi McAuliffe, programme director of Amnesty International in Scotland, pointed to the importance of the general climate for the successful integration of refugees: 'Scotland has demonstrated that it does have a far more positive response to these kind of humanitarian disasters and therefore it is quite positive for refugees to come into that context' (BBC News 2015a). There is an added benefit to the progressiveness of the Scottish approach because it supports Scotland's international reputation. The strategy has been endorsed by the United Nations Refugee Agency and was acknowledged to be 'leading the way' by the European Council on Refugees and Exiles (2018). Refugees are therefore not the only ones advantaged by Scotland's inclusive policies – other immigrants and the Scottish government also benefit.

Devolved Immigration Policy

The Scottish government has advocated for more control over immigration since the Scottish Parliament was re-established in 1999. Their strategies shifted in 2008, with the introduction of the UK-wide points-based system and the question of whether the system could increase immigration to Scotland while reducing levels of migration to the rest of the UK. There is no reason to assume a points-based system will result in lower numbers of immigrants, and the allocation of points based on individual characteristics raises the possibility that points can be applied for where the migrant intends to settle. Such a policy has been implemented before – Canada, Australia, and New Zealand provide models of points-based systems that allow for regional differentiation.[29]

Regional differences are most strongly reflected in the Canadian immigration system, which makes the Canadian case most comparable to a potential devolved immigration system in Scotland. In Canada, all of the provinces have immigration agreements with the federal government in Ottawa, which take their specific territorial considerations into account. 'Provincial Nominee Programs' in each territory split responsibility for immigration between the federal and provincial governments. Through the programmes, an applicant immigrant could theoretically face a lower points threshold if they agree to live, work, and stay in a province for a set period of time, usually three years, at which point the applicant is eligible for citizenship.[30] The Canada–Quebec accord grants more authority to the territory of Quebec, where immigrants apply directly to the provincial, and not the federal, government. Quebec also uses a points-based system, but the weighting reflects Quebec's priorities alone.[31] Canada's example provides a clear route for the UK, should the government pursue immigration policy that meets regional needs.

After Brexit, the UK government created a single immigration system for European and non-European citizens. The Scottish government anticipated the policy change, and based on past policies of Conservative governments, Scottish decision makers inferred that the new policy would be damaging to Scottish interests. They were concerned by proposals to end free movement, and the idea of a single points-based immigration system with universal skills and salary requirements that did not reflect the needs of Scottish employers or the cost of living in most of Scotland. Even before the UK published a white paper outlining the proposed policy, the Scottish government called for devolved policies over immigration, often called the Scottish Green Card or Scottish visa, with the publication of a discussion paper entitled 'Scotland's Population Needs and Migration Policy' (Scottish Government 2018g). The paper reinforced claims that 'different parts of the UK had different needs and expectations of migration' and argued UK immigration policies were detrimental to Scotland (6). The Scottish government believed it would be better served by a differentiated system that allowed Scotland more say over who can come to Scotland. The Scottish Executive wanted continued participation in the free movement policies of the EU. Barring that, the Scottish government planned to pursue new devolved powers on migration to ensure 'for future EU citizens coming to Scotland, their experience is the same as free movement within Europe and they are able to continue to live and work in Scotland as they do currently' (31). Devolved powers would also apply to non-EU migrants, and would include provisions for a Scotland-specific visa within the existing points immigration system. The visa would restrict migrants to living in Scotland, and Scottish ministers would determine the criteria and thresholds for the points. Scottish ministers would also control policy regulating family migration, since the migration of families indicates better prospects for settlement and integration. They did not want to be constrained by a net migration target or quota. When the discussion paper was published, prospects for devolved policy were poor, and Prime Minister Theresa May was not interested in discussing devolution or Scottish independence while uncertainty surrounding Brexit persisted. Scottish claims were further undercut by the Migration Advisory Committee in Westminster on 18 September 2018, when it announced that it did not believe Scotland's needs differ substantially from other areas in the UK.

The Scottish government was not deterred, and in 2020 it published a paper entitled 'Migration: Helping Scotland Prosper' detailing how a tailored migration policy within the UK framework could meet Scotland's needs. The paper built upon the Scottish government's previous work, to propose broad changes to the UK's migration policy (including reintroducing the post-study work visa) alongside two tailored policy options. The first was the Scottish visa from the 2018 discussion paper, but the 2020 paper provided details: compliance could be monitored with the existing Scottish tax code, which determines Scottish taxpayer status by residency. The visa introduces an 'added option' in the UK system, with partial devolution of immigration, where the Scottish and UK governments share responsibility. The paper presented five models for how power could be shared across dimensions of policy formation, immigrant selection, legislation, and admission. The second tailored policy was a plan to attract and retain migrants in rural areas, a policy already supported by members of the UK government. In the paper, Scotland committed itself to pilot the policy though its Ministerial Task Force on Population, with the assumption that the policy could complement the Scottish visa proposal.[32]

Comparative examples of devolved immigration policy and the viability of the Scottish proposals within a UK-wide system reveal that the main barrier to the Scottish visa is political will in Westminster. Think tanks and committees at Westminster and Holyrood have endorsed the principles underlying the Scottish visa, but the policy proposal is unlikely to succeed in the current political environment.[33] A few days after the publication of the paper proposing the Scottish visa in January 2020, Boris Johnson asserted that a Scottish visa would result in the construction of a 'wall and border posts' between Scotland and England, and called the idea of a Scottish visa 'fanciful and deranged' (Gourtsoyannis 2020). Until something changes in Westminster, Scotland will have to rely on its existing devolved powers to pursue its goals.

Conclusion

Scotland's past experiences with emigration incentivised the construction of a policy regime that attracts and incorporates immigrants, even as the UK retains control over immigration policy. The One Scotland campaign, the post-study work visa, the New Scots Refugee Integration Strategy, and the proposal for a Scottish visa demonstrate the Scottish government's consistent interest in steadily pushing for an immigration and integration system that advances its national interests, distinct from those of the rest of the UK. While the One Scotland campaign and the New Scots Strategy focus on devolved powers, the post-study work visa and the devolved immigration policy push devolution further to give Scotland more control over immigrant entry. All of the policies confirm Scotland's willingness to work within the dominant UK-wide system, and all political parties in the Scottish Parliament support them because the policies do not require independence. The consensus demonstrates that the political will required to make Scotland a destination for immigrants is present at the national level, but the barriers are in Westminster. Though the policy objectives of the Scottish government are thwarted by the UK government, the oppositional stance between Holyrood and Westminster supports the nationalist argument that the UK government is insensitive to Scotland's needs, which makes the continued push for devolved policy a central pillar of Scottish nation-building. The intransigence of the UK government further supports nationalism by providing an adversary perceived to be working against Scotland.

Scotland's package of immigration and integration policies communicates the breadth of the Scottish Executive's unreserved acceptance of all immigrants. Many governments, even anti-immigrant ones, welcome highly skilled immigrants like those targeted with the post-study work visa. The Scottish government is eager to attract and retain educated immigrants, but it also welcomes asylum seekers and refugees. The contrast between the Scottish and UK-wide approach allows the SNP-led Scottish government to frame Scotland's response to immigration as a central example of Scotland's different interests, and the inclusion of asylum seekers and refugees adds moral superiority undergirded by the international human rights regime. The breadth of Scotland's openness activates the interests of many groups in Scottish society, from economic and educational stakeholders to humanitarian and religious groups. The range of immigration, integration, and anti-discrimination policies gives full expression of the interests and strategies of the Scottish government as it engages with immigration as a tool of nation-building and strategic national differentiation.

Notes

1. Ten accession states were admitted to the EU in 2004 (Cyprus, Czech Republic, Estonia, Hungary, Latvia, Lithuania, Malta, Poland, Slovak Republic, and Slovenia), and two more in 2007 (Romania and Bulgaria).
2. The points-based system consisted of five tiers, each of which contained multiple categories of visa. Tier 1 was for high-value and exceptional talent, and Tier 2 was for skilled workers sponsored by an employer. Tier 3 was for low-skilled workers, though it was never implemented. Tier 4 was for students, and Tier 5 for temporary workers.
3. David Cameron included asylum seekers, family, students, and EU and non-EU migration in his measure of net migration. When he left office in 2016, net migration was 249,000.
4. Before the late twentieth century Scotland did not record the timing and pattern of individual moves, meaning that most of what is known about early migration is the product of inferences made from imperfect sources.
5. See Fry (2001), MacKenzie and Devine (2011), or Devine (2012b) for overviews of Scottish involvement in Empire and colonialisation.
6. The Emigration Act of 1851 made emigration more possible for the poorest Scots by providing a mechanism for landlords to borrow money to pay for the migration of families.
7. Nearly 3% of the population in England and Wales were Irish in 1851, while Irish people made up 7.2% of the population in Scotland (Devine 2012a).
8. Many scholars argue that discriminatory attitudes towards immigrants were widespread, but Mitchell (2017) argues that if attitudes towards strike breakers is put aside, there is little evidence of open popular hostility toward the Irish presence among the working-class Scots who lived alongside immigrants.
9. The English population grew from 47,000 in 1851 to over 194,000 in 1921, and to 230,000 by 1951.
10. Jews were subjected to large-scale violence in 1947, during riots sparked by events in Palestine.
11. Statistical information on overseas migration was not available on a uniform basis

until recently. The best estimates prior to about 2001 come from the International Passenger Survey, which interviews a stratified random sample of passengers entering the UK on planes, ships, or trains. Migrants are considered to be those who declare their intention of residing in the UK for at least a year. Because these figures are grossed from sample data, they are subject to error and should only be used for broad estimates.
12. The Scottish Refugee Council was established in 1985 in Edinburgh to assist with refugee resettlement. It moved to Glasgow in 1999 when the city became a primary dispersal area for refugees in the UK.
13. Wales receives approximately 2% of the migrant population and Northern Ireland 1%. London houses 37% of the immigrant population, and the remaining 55% is distributed throughout the English regions.
14. This is below the UK average. About 14% of the English and Welsh population identifies as a member of a minoritised group. In London, the figure is 40%.
15. The Indian and Pakistani communities took different educational and socio-economic trajectories after coming to Scotland. In the first decades of the new millennium, Indians were employed at rates equivalent to white residents, while Pakistanis' rates were lower than average, though higher than those of Pakistanis in England (Bonino 2018).
16. For example, Hansen (2000) references Scotland/Scottish on four pages of his 264-page book, about immigration in post-war Britain. Spencer's (1997) review of *British Immigration Policy since 1939* does not include Scotland in the index.
17. The legal responsibilities came out of the Race Relations (Amendment) Act of 2000, which outlawed racial discrimination and placed a duty on public officials to work towards the elimination of unlawful discrimination and to promote equality of opportunity.
18. The Scottish government describes the distinct 'Scottish approach' to policy making as 'a large number and mix of specific reforms, aims, and principles ... distinct from the more general academic notion of "policy style"' that dominates elsewhere (Cairney et al. 2016: 339).
19. Minoritised Scots face disadvantages including higher rates of poverty, lower rates of employment, and health inequities (Equality and Human Rights Commission 2018). In a cross-sectional survey of 501 minoritised Scots, nearly one in three reported experiencing discrimination within the last five years. They reported discrimination in a number of areas, including employment, housing, health, and education. Sixty per cent of those surveyed who claimed to have experienced discrimination did not report it (Meer 2018).
20. Interviews with young Scottish people suggested that they had positive views about the campaign and believed that it accurately portrays Scotland's multicultural nature (Ross et al. 2008).
21. Eligible applicants must also have spent the majority of their studies living in Scotland and prove that they and their dependents would be able to support themselves without having recourse to public funds.
22. Removing the Scottish advantage in competing for immigrants with England was evidently a prime motivation for the creation of the UK-wide programme, as Home Secretary Charles Clark (2004–6) stated in the Home Affairs Committee on 8 February 2005: 'The Scottish Parliament and the Scottish Executive have a Fresh Talent Initiative which is specifically designed to bring people into the country because that enables them to deal with some of the de-population which they otherwise worry is causing problems for their economy and society in Scotland. That would be true of some parts of England as well, so I certainly think that is a consideration which has to come through' (House of Commons

2005).
23. The inclusion of students in the net migration calculations has been widely criticised. Students do not behave like a typical non-European Economic Area (EEA) migrants because their visas are temporary.
24. Average gross annual pay in Scotland in 2016 was £22,918, well below the UK Tier 2 visa income threshold of £30,000.
25. The mission of the APPG is to 'provide a continued opportunity for evidence-based political debate about the challenges and opportunities relating to contemporary migration flows in the UK' (see <https://appgmigration.org.uk/about/>).
26. Councils are under no obligation to accept Syrian refugees. If they do, the first year's resettlement costs are covered by the UK government. After that, funding tapers off to £5,000 peer refugee in the second year and £1,000 in year five.
27. Policy on children falls under the purview of the Scottish government, and in the mid-2000s the Scottish government argued that raids to remove asylum seekers were traumatising asylee children and violating their rights. Labour First Minister Jack McConnell asked for more of a Scottish say in the implementation of deportation decisions, and was rebuffed by Westminster (Shaw 2009: 34–5).
28. Support includes access to appropriate housing and proximity to services, access to the labour market and skills development, immediate access to and equitable treatment within the education system, language training, and access to health care and health literacy resources.
29. Canada introduced a points-based system in 1967, and the system was replicated by Australia in 1973. New Zealand introduced its system in 1987. All systems include regionalist criteria in their policies, but regionality is less central in Australia's and New Zealand's policies. Switzerland offers another policy model of regional differentiation, called a 'two-level quota system', where the federal government and the cantons get an annual quota of immigration permits, but different cantons get a different number of permits.
30. This policy was intended to encourage more diffuse immigrant settlement outside the main cities of Toronto, Montreal, and Vancouver. It was also motivated by the empirical reality that once a person spends more than two years in a place, they are more likely to stay in that location (Wright and Mosca 2009).
31. Quebec awards fewer points for the human capital characteristics like education and qualifications, and more points for knowledge of the French language.
32. For a Scottish visa to work, the UK government must be prepared to enforce it, even to the point of deporting violators in Scotland. Fortunately for Scotland, evidence from Canada suggests non-compliance may not be a big concern, since inter-provincial moves were rare (Wright and Mosca 2009). The five-year rates for inter-provincial moves were between 2.8 and 3.5%, and one-year rates were between 0.8 and 1.0%. Inter-provincial moves were less frequent for immigrants than they were for native-born Canadians.
33. Boris Johnson is hostile towards any proposals that enhance devolution and refused Sturgeon's request for the legal power to hold an independence referendum post-Brexit. SNP MP Ian Blackford accused Boris Johnson of a devolution 'power grab' through legislation that withholds the power of devolved nations to control state aid after the Brexit transition (Marlborough 2020).

2

THE PROJECT: BUILDING A SCOTTISH NATION WITH 'NEW SCOTS'

This chapter outlines the building blocks of Scottish nationalism and connects them to the politics of immigration within Scotland, illuminating how Scottish elites mobilise domestic audiences to support both nationalism and immigration through the nation-building project. It begins by defining the scholarly ideal types of civic and ethnic nationalism and describes how elites attempt to implement civic nationalism in Scotland. Scottish nationalist political elites are the vanguard of a movement for territorial sovereignty that paradoxically embraces multicultural, pro-European (or post-national), and pro-immigrant ideology.

The second half of the chapter focuses on how immigration fits into notions of Scottish nationalism and highlights how openness to immigration is discussed as a reflection of Scottish values and a solution to distinct Scottish problems. From the perspective of the Scottish political leadership, the UK government's restrictions on immigration are failing Scotland, and control over immigration is one of the most important objectives for those seeking territorial sovereignty. Scottish political elites make explicit connections between the forces driving modern immigration and Scottish historical experiences with emigration and forced relocation. The comparisons make an emotionally resonant case for immigration and reinforce openness to migrants as part of the national ethos. This chapter provides the foundation for the central argument of this book, which links the politics of immigration in Scotland to the political ambitions of the nation. The legitimacy of the independence claim rests on a coherent and democratically acceptable civic definition of the nation, which Scottish elites describe with Scotland's openness to outsiders.

Defining the Scottish Nation

Nation-building refers to the practice of building a coherent social community that serves as the foundation of the nation-state. It is a process of collective identity formation that allows a group to assert legitimate power over a territory (Anderson 2006). It involves institutions, customs, and traditions, and an ideology of nationalism, which defines how a social or political community defines itself relative to other communities in the world. Scholars debate the origins of nationalism and nation-building. Traditionalists claim that nations took shape before the advent of modernity in the cultural-political configurations of empires and tribal structures and conflicts (e.g. Hirschi 2012). During conflicts, forces of resource-based expansion motivated a reactionary force among the would-be conquered, and the common enemy provided an incentive to work on a mobilising identity around what could be identified as a nation. Modernists understand nationalism to be a modern political ideology, rooted in the international system of states, industrialisation, and empire (e.g. Gellner 1983). Ethno-symbolists adjust the modernist argument to stress the importance of memories, myths, and symbols from the pre-modern community that support the modern process of nation-building (e.g. Smith 1996). Viewed from different angles, the Scottish case provides evidence for all perspectives. Public figures describe very early traces of a Scottish national character: the image of Scottish people uniting as early as the first century AD, and fighting against external oppression from Romans, Anglo-Saxons, Scandinavians, and the English, features prominently in the Scottish political consciousness. However, the vision of nationalism advanced by Scottish political elites is very modern and is not grounded in a narrative of liberating an oppressed tribe or people, nor do they envision Scottish nationalism as an effort to preserve a threatened culture. The political leadership has noticeably avoided rhetoric of threat and fear of or anger towards an oppressive 'other', in order to brand Scottish nationalism as modern, progressive, and forward-looking. Elite-level Scottish nationalists mobilise around political independence as the surest way to promote a progressive Scottish political agenda and ensure Scottish prosperity within the modern context. This concept of Scottish nationalism emerged within the last 50 years, coming into full force in the 1980s and 90s as a form of 'civic nationalism' that upholds distinctly Scottish values of equality, humanity, and decency, embedded within what is argued to be a less inclusive UK state.

Civic nationalism and ethnic nationalism are analysed as dichotomous types of nationalism in Europe.[1] Under civic nationalism, attachment to a territory or community is achieved through personal attachment to a place, rituals affirming territorial statehood (pledges of allegiance, flag waving, etc.), and civic participation. Ethnic understandings of the nation also appeal to territorial claims and rituals but emphasise connection through 'primordial ties', which can include race, language, religion, and customs (Geertz 1963). The objective of ethnic nationalists is to protect the authenticity or purity of their culture from those who would dilute it by introducing different cultural practices. In the modern democratic climate, these two forms of nationalism are associated with strong normative frames that rhetorically legitimise or discredit particular nationalistic movements: civic nationalism is assumed to be benign, tolerant, and compatible with democracy, while ethnic nationalism is perceived to be backward and exclusionary.

Ethnic and civic nationalism represent ideal types or abstractions and do not accurately represent real-world nationalism. As Hearn explains:

> The difference between a useful distinction and a misleading dichotomy can be difficult to discern ... Minimally, we should bear in mind that what these pairs ultimately define is opposing styles of arguments about what nations are and how social values are created, rather than actual types of nations or societies. (Hearn 2000: 194)

Kuzio (2002) rejects the distinction between ethnic and civic nationalism and argues that all so-called civic nations have evolved systems of nationalism centred on the political and cultural institutions of a dominant ethno-national group. Kymlicka (2000) similarly argues that the process of moving from an ethnic to a civic nation often involves nation-building through cultural homogenisation that requires the repression or eradication of competing ethno-national groups, resulting in the conflation of and constant tension between civic and ethnic considerations in how modern citizenship and nationality are constructed. Kymlicka (2001) also highlights the similar cultural constituents of nominally civic and ethnic states, and argues that both are fundamentally cultural forms of nationalism. Looking at the Scottish case, Leith and Soule (2011) discuss how both civic and ethnic nationalism are present at elite and mass levels and argue that it is impossible to separate the two.

The concept of civic nationalism includes two ideal types: liberal and republican civic nationalism. Liberal civic nationalists define their nations as 'historical communities that possess a societal culture – that is which possess a set of institutions, operating in a common language, covering both private and public life', but with 'nothing in the idea of a societal culture that precludes the incorporation of new ideas and practices from other parts of the world' (Kymlicka 2001: 211). The liberal civic national culture is allegedly open and pluralistic, recognising ethnic pluralism and allowing for diversity, but maintaining a national frame of reference for national belonging in the public sphere, usually through language or political ideology. From this perspective, other cultures do not present a threat to national cultural purity. The liberal civic nationalist is happy to draw on other cultures to create a rich and diverse nation, and will usually tolerate the maintenance of alternative cultural groups in the private sphere. In contrast, civic republicanism 'justifies assimilation to the majority through a rhetoric of freedom and equality set against a communitarian background, as cultural homogeneity is deemed to provide a framework through which all citizens can participate in society on an equal footing' (Dupré 2012: 231). This form of civic nationalism is also open to ethnic pluralism in that it does not restrict membership to any particular ethnic group, but it expects full conformity to the dominant majority culture in public and sometimes private life.

Liberal and republican civic nationalism pair with different state traditions. Keating classifies civic republicanism as civic nationalism paired with a strong state, wherein

> membership of the national community is in principle open to all living on the national territory and all are equal before the law. Individual liberties are respected, but precisely in consequence of the doctrine of popular sovereignty, forms of collective action other than through the national state are not regarded as legitimate. (Keating 2001a: 25)

With liberal civic nationalism, the state is weaker and 'national identity is carried by the state but also in the institutions of civil society. There is room both for individual liberty and for forms of collective action outside the state, within the limits of the national value system' (Keating 2001a: 25).[2]

Strong versus weak state traditions link forms of nationalism with a spectrum of integration strategies (understood as the mechanism by which a national outsider can become an insider) ranging from assimilation to multiculturalism. Assimilation requires the outsiders to reject their previous affiliations and absorb the culture of their new nation. Multiculturalism seeks to improve the representation and accommodation of ethnocultural groups in state institutions and society, with policies providing group members legal protection from discrimination and access to equal opportunity. Sometimes multiculturalism allows for policies or resources supporting cultural retention in the private and public sphere. Strong state republican civic nationalism is likely to be assimilationist, and weak state liberal civic nationalism is more consistent with multiculturalism (Brubaker 1992). Both republican civic nationalism and liberal civic nationalism are theoretically inclusionary, but when cultural assimilation is the integration requirement for belonging to a civically nationalist community, republican civic nationalism can look very much like ethnic nationalism in policy terms, and integration can be a violent, intolerant, and narrowly applied process. Those who do not wish to adopt the values or lifestyles of their host nation risk being branded as traitorous or treasonous, which means the language of civic nationalism can be used to 'crush' minorities, even within the territory of the civic nation (Kymlicka 2001: 273). Liberal civic nationalism leaves more room for multicultural expression and practice, though again, the concept is not without its ambiguity. No matter how inaccurate these concepts of nationalism are, they (and especially the simple dichotomy between civic and ethnic nationalism) continue to guide the thoughts and actions of the political elite in Scotland, and are useful for understanding how the image of the Scottish nation is constructed.

Liberal Civic Nationalism in Scotland

Scottish nationalism is a form of liberal civic nationalism. Elite Scottish nationalists celebrate their cultural heritage while professing openness to the inclusion of cultural others and express no desire to enforce cultural assimilation. Former SNP First Minister Alex Salmond (2014) described the 2014 independence campaign as 'a peaceful, inclusive, civic – and above all democratic and constitutional movement'. One of the best examples of this civic portrayal of Scotland comes from the white paper on independence, entitled 'Scotland's Future'. The opening paragraphs identify the Scottish constituents as 'We, the people who live here', an inclusive definition of national identity based on residency (Scottish Government 2013b). The Scotland Is Now campaign was similarly inclusive. The campaign intended to put Scotland in the international spotlight and showcase the country's assets. Its inaugural video features Scotland's scenery, history, culture, art, and innovation, while conveying the message of warm welcome with images of people of different physical abilities, races, and origins. Each image corresponds with a spoken script describing what Scotland 'now is', and at the climax about halfway through the video, the narrator says, 'Now is the welcome for all those who come.' As Nicola Sturgeon explained when she opened the campaign in China, 'The message at the heart of "Scotland is Now" is of a bold and positive country offering the warmest of welcomes, rich in history and heritage and with a progressive, pioneering and inclusive approach to our future' (Thorburn 2018).[3]

A challenge for the Scottish nationalist movement relates to distinguishing their social culture from that of the rest of the UK, especially England. England could make many of the same claims about landscape, history, art, innovation, and a tradition of inclusively constructed British identity, and the UK is also considered to be a liberal, civically defined state. Unlike with Quebec and Canada, Flanders and Belgium, and Catalonia and Spain, the other oft-cited cases of sub-state civic nationalism, Scotland and England share their primary national language, which means Scotland cannot use language to define its identity, though efforts to preserve 'indigenous' Gaelic, Doric, and Scots correspond with identity claims of linguistic difference. Intermarriage and migration over centuries have blended Scottish and English peoples and cultural practices, though the Scottish Presbyterian Kirk is maintained as the national church of Scotland, as opposed to the Anglican Church of England. The political and military traditions of both nations have informed and influenced each other since the Union in 1707, even as devolution has allowed for different institutional trajectories. Through there are unmistakable differences between England and Scotland, it is difficult to make strong claims about fundamental cultural, ethnic, or linguistic difference, and Scottish nationalists face an uphill climb in justifying Scotland's need for completely independent institutions. Threats of invasion and the logic of defence consolidated the nation in the past, but modern Scottish political elites are eager to avoid defensive nationalism or nationalism defined with reference to someone or something other than Scotland. Other-oriented justifications of the nation hark back to exclusionary ideals that form the basis of ethnic nationalism, ideals that would undermine the modern Scottish multicultural project. Nevertheless, for Scottish nationalists, distinguishing between Scotland and England is required to make a case for independence.

To advance a legitimate pro-democratic nationalist claim that avoids cultural or identity threat, elite-level Scottish nationalism advocates for a return to a natural political order that acknowledges different democratic trajectories and political values. Despite the desire to avoid divisive nationalism, some of these arguments tap in to narratives of oppression. For example, Hechter (1975) presents the UK as a relic of imperialism, which he argues hampered the development of both England and Scotland. By extension, the Scottish independence movement is likened to post-colonial independence movements in Africa or Asia, and allows Scotland to claim an affinity with those international movements. Another oppression-based justification appeals to the under- or mis-representation of Scotland by British historians who have focused almost exclusively on England and the English experience, with the other nations of the UK becoming part of the central historical narrative only after union with England. Pre-Union Scotland is portrayed in these narratives as a backward and impoverished place, brought into the Enlightenment only through its association with England. As explained by Pocock:

> When such a series as the Oxford History of England (1934–65) or the New History of England (1978–) arrives at the years 1707 or 1801, the momentous Acts of Union marked by these dates are of course given thorough and proper treatment; but there is no caesura, no change of key or structure, no sense that the history of England has become part of something else and requires to be written in new terms ... it is not to be expected that any attempt will be made to depict it as continuing an already living Scottish or Irish history. That perspective is left to the authors of histories of Scotland or Ireland, who write as if they were addressing themselves to different reading publics. (Pocock 1982: 312)

Scottish historians resent their erasure, though Scottish counter-histories can be equally controversial and revisionist, aiming to refute claims of the English Crown and to root sovereign authority in the Scottish people (Kearton 2005). These scholars identify the Declaration of Arbroath in 1320 as the source of limited monarchy (Cowan 2003). It is also heralded as the founding document of the Scottish nation, which asserted the right of the Scottish people to reject the English monarch and also gave them the authority to reject Scottish royals if they betray the trust of the people. Scottish historiography also leans towards the European continent, in contrast to the English narrative of England as 'something apart from Europe and in opposition to it' (Keating 2001b: 34).[4] Nationalist historians affirm the political institutions of pre-Union Scotland, highlighting the separation of powers in the Crown, Parliament, courts, and the church, and illustrating the democratic traditions within Scottish social institutions. Scots Law is distinguished by historians as a continuous source of legal authority dating back to the Middle Ages, and a legal system that is more European and rational than its English counterpart (Thomson 1995). The Union of 1707 is perceived as an agreement between sovereign nations, which like treaties of today, cannot be altered except by mutual consent: 'The United Kingdom of Great Britain and Northern Ireland, has always been a state based on a series of unions, rather than one having its basis in a common nationality' (Pittock 2014: 16). Political arguments can be broken when the terms no longer benefit both parties. The 'union' is also presented as incomplete because the British government was not historically active in the Scottish domestic public sphere or civil society, and the agreement allowed for the substantial independence of Scottish society and institutions (Pittock 2012). These claims led to the Claim of Right of the Scottish Constitutional Convention in the 1980s, out of which came the assertion that it is the right of the Scottish people to choose the form of government that best suits them.

Nostalgic historicity focusing on the civic culture and democratic institutions of medieval Scotland speak to how democratic consolidation in a nation may be a prerequisite for the creation and maintenance of civic nationalism (Kuzio 2002). Scottish historians claim the democratic veins in Scotland run deep, much deeper than in most other European contexts. This should make it more possible for Scotland to avoid the pitfalls of ethnic nationalism. At the same time, justifying nationalism with deep ties to history resembles claims of ethnic nationalism (Seymour 2000). Scotland avoids some of the ethnic overtones by disassociating its nationalism from linguistic preservation, but the social and political nostalgia inherent in Scottish nationalism is inevitably associated with symbols of blood lineage that could easily morph into understandings of ethnic nationalism. Furthermore, the nationalist emphasis on freedom from England cannot avoid images of war and oppression, which carry anti-English implications.

Scottish nationalism remains neither wholly ethnic nor wholly civic, but a sometimes uncomfortable mixture of the two. As Leith and Soule point out:

> While politicians (and academics) may explicitly affirm their commitment to civic and inclusive criteria of national identity, they do so within a discourse laden with atavistic tendencies, historical references and irrational collectivism. Even when the stories are about the heritage of the Scottish Enlightenment, proud educational traditions or respected legal institutions, these civic narratives cannot escape an emotive presentation. (Leith and Soule 2011: 143)

Political actors are aware that 'within the masses, a sense of history, culture, ancestry, and birthright combines to create a Scottishness that cuts across the political, ideological, and social spectrum' (Leith and Soule 2011: 149). The cross-cutting appeal of a national narrative rooted in history, culture, ancestry, or birthright makes it a tempting tool for politicians who are seeking to build public support for their platforms. However, the same narratives of shared heritage that unite native-born Scots can alienate foreign-born Scots who do not have Scottish ancestry and 'feel excluded by thoughtless mono-cultural symbolism' (Hussain and Miller 2006: 135).

Scottish modernists reconcile this contradiction by rejecting the assumption that Scottishness has been constructed in the same way throughout time or in a linear fashion. Ideas of the nation and national identity are culturally specific constructs that are made and remade over time (Anderson 2006). This process of creation is referred to in the publicised efforts of the Scottish government to create a 'new Scotland'.[5] Some modernists turn to definitions of Scottish values as a national frame of reference that avoids nostalgia and cultural romanticism. Related to ideas about democracy's deep roots in Scotland, Scottish values are held to be inclusive and democratic. Angus Roxburgh, a Scottish foreign correspondent for *The Guardian*, identifies Scottish values as 'scorn of privilege' and 'pursuit of fairness', principles that endorse notions of democratic equality (Roxburgh 2014). Even these egalitarian ideals savour of anti-Englishness, however, because they are used to distinguish Scotland from the more elitist England. England's neoliberal economic principles are also perceived as a threat to a Scottish political culture of social democratic corporatism. As Jackson explains:

> For many nationalists the core of the case for Scottish independence ultimately reduces to the argument that Scots want to build a social democratic or socialist country while the English do not (the views of the Welsh and Northern Irish are usually put to one side). On this account, Scottish statehood is not so much about the expression of a national identity as an instrumental device for the realization of a more egalitarian society. (Jackson 2014: 52)

When the UK Conservative Party became the home of neoliberal ideas and reforms during Margaret Thatcher's regime, her actions cemented the politicisation and nationalisation of economic and political models. The Scottish social democratic model also forms the foundation of opposition to the modern Labour Party, which Scottish nationalists believe has abandoned the roots of the Labour movement in order to win power in London. A new Scottish state freed from neoliberal shackles offers Scots the chance to achieve the traditional social democratic goals of the Labour Party. While Jackson claims that socio-economic models are something separate from national identity, the entrenchment of the ideals of a communitarian Scottish morality and identity reinforces political and value-laden descriptions of Scottish civic nationalism (Jackson 2014).

Despite efforts on the part of the Scottish political elites to develop consensus around ideals of liberal civic nationalism, Scotland represents a complex configuration of nationalist ideas. Underlying contradictions between civic and ethnic understandings surface regularly. The contradictions become obvious in conversations about Scotland's ideal relationship with the EU.

Scottish Civic Nationalism in the EU

Scottish elites articulate a liberal civic national vision, and they argue that Scottish values are reinforced within the EU. Their pro-EU position contrasts with nationalist movements in Europe that oppose the supranational EU because it erodes the importance and power of state sovereignty. Many of these movements endorse visions of ethnic nationalism in an attempt to preserve the purity of their national culture, and they resent the globalising impact of the EU. Free movement within the EU's Schengen Area is particularly threatening to these nationalists.

Conversely, Scottish elites believe that

> the demise of the traditional model of absolute state sovereignty allows Scotland to participate in an era in which Scottish institutions can take over some important powers previously held at Westminster while in other domains simultaneously remaining subject to institutions at a European and perhaps even British level. (Jackson 2014: 5)

The creation of a European layer of governance substantially changed the Scottish vision for statehood and opened new possibilities for alternative arrangements between Scotland and the UK government. Under the multi-level system, Scotland could share certain services with the UK government (like monetary policy or functionalist bureaucracy) while additional rights and powers could be granted at the European level, independent of the UK.[6] As such, Scotland is 'presenting very complex claims to greater autonomy and enhanced recognition *within* the UK, while at the same time attempting to negotiate some measure of discrete personality in the international institutions to which the UK (and Scotland) belongs' (Tierney 2005: 162).

The SNP leadership were not always proponents of European integration. In the 1960s, many within the SNP opposed integration as an assault on sovereignty, though the party position softened around the time of the 1975 independence referendum, when the party held off on declaring a position on European Community membership until after independence, at which time Scots could decide for themselves. In the 1980s, the vision of an independent Scotland *within* Europe emerged. The shift was primarily attributable to the Thatcher government's strident anti-European position and the pro-Europe position of the Labour Party, which was the SNP's major electoral competition. There is now a general pro-European political consensus in Scotland that has grown stronger after Brexit.

Scottish nationalism within Europe is not conventionally nationalistic, a contradiction noted by Scottish nationalists like Alex Salmond, who identified himself as a 'post-nationalist' (Torrance 2011: 244). From a post-nationalist perspective, Scotland exists in a 'post-sovereignty' international order, which provides opportunities for Scottish decision making to be diffused across multiple layers of government (Keating 2004). Multi-level governance is a deliberate strategy pursued by nations in the age of 'late sovereignty, where the power of the nation state is declining through the influence of international normative sites, but where, through playing a full role within these fora, territorial politics can yet retain considerable influence' (Tierney 2005: 162). The European outlook internationalises the nationalistic claims of Scotland, and provides a venue for Scottish leaders to seek improved recognition, constitutional autonomy, and representation in the UK and in the international community.

The 'Scotland in Europe' vision is ironic, as it proposes changing one form of multinational governance within the UK for another form of multinational governance within the EU. Scottish nationalists claim that in exchanging English rule for European rule, they would be aligning themselves with a political partner that more naturally and enthusiastically endorses the Scottish vision of civic nationalism and multiculturalism. During Brexit, when stopping immigration was a primary motivation for Leave voters, maintaining immigration under free movement became the symbol of Scotland's national interest within the EU. The SNP's 2019 European Election Manifesto discusses free movement as the most critical right conferred by EU citizenship. Reporting on the manifesto quoted Sturgeon:

> in this manifesto you will see strong and unequivocal support for free movement. It is good for Scotland and it is good for Europe. The SNP celebrates and values all those who choose to make Scotland their home,

and SNP MEPs will take that welcoming message to the heart of Europe. (BBC News 2019)

Though small states in the EU have big ambitions, they experience disadvantages because of their limited bargaining power and constrained resources. They must also confront the complex and changing global environment where state power endures but is under growing pressure. As Tierney says:

> It would be disingenuous, and indeed unsustainable, for the nationalist movement not to acknowledge that the pressures which undermine state power will also, albeit in different ways, undermine the scope for action of new, smaller nation-states or increasingly autonomous units within larger states. (Tierney 2005: 174)

Scottish nationalist elites are reticent to publicly grapple with the changing social and geopolitical order that could ultimately undermine the legitimacy and practicality of their territorially based bid for independence, and are more enthusiastic about arguing for advanced opportunities for Scotland within the EU. At the very least, Scotland benefits from supranational European policies over free movement, and the prospect of losing access to European membership with Brexit provided a major motivation for campaigns linking immigration to Scottish nationalistic claims.

Connecting Migration to Nationalism

The 'national interest' describes what a nation needs to support its future. Where there are sub-state nations, national interest can differ across the nations within the state or between a nation and the state. Where there is divergence, advancing a different policy position from the state contributes to the effort of nation-building and justifies devolution or independence. Many powers have been devolved to Scotland under various Scotland Acts, most notably taxation and education. Calls for further devolution of powers are premised on the claim that status quo devolution has not worked, and that Scotland's needs remain unmet by the UK government. Chapter 4 describes how devolved control over immigration has been framed as a viable solution to Scottish problems, with reference to demographic decline, stagnant economic growth, the hiring needs of local industries, and supporting social services. These arguments outline why admitting more people to Scotland would serve the national interest. But open immigration has also been framed as a policy that is consistent with Scottish values and ideologies, projecting an image of a welcoming and diverse Scotland where people of many different races, religions, and cultures belong to the nation. For example, the One Scotland campaign linked nationalism to multiculturalism with nationalistic imagery: in one of the campaign's videos, the words 'racism' and 'discrimination' are painted graffiti-style on a blue wall, then sprayed over with a white X, creating the Saltire, the Scottish national flag.

The marketing of multicultural Scottish identity is supported by a number of Scottish policy initiatives, proving that the link between nationalism and immigration is not just rhetorical. The Fresh Talent Initiative raised awareness of Scotland abroad and promoted Scotland as a welcoming and dynamic nation, and the Fresh Talent: Working in Scotland Scheme introduced a post-study work visa that allowed international graduates from Scottish universities to live and work in Scotland. The policy was introduced with a document entitled 'New Scots: Attracting Fresh Talent to Meet the Challenge of Growth' (Scottish Executive 2004). The title of 'New Scots' transmitted the government's belief that foreign students can become Scottish, affirming a vision of liberal civic nationalism where national identities are earned and performed rather than inherited. All of the government's immigration initiatives, but especially the Fresh Talent Initiative, frame immigration as an opportunity for Scotland to meet its distinctly national interest in a manner that is sensitive to Scottish values, where the nation is the primary unit of social and economic activity, and where the status of outsiders is contingent on their ability to contribute to national goals. As Skilling notes, 'The most important features of this discourse are its emphasis on national interests and national goals, its presentation of immigration as primarily an economic process, and the centrality accorded to talent as an appropriate criteri[on] for admission or exclusion' (2007: 102).

The claim that immigration yields national benefits is strongest in the case of student migrants, because they have been educated within Scottish universities, simultaneously demonstrating their professional potential and their ability to integrate into Scottish professional life. The link to universities likewise allows universities to argue that the post-study work visa is critical for attracting and retaining lucrative international students. Ejecting Scottish-educated students is framed as a waste of Scottish resources. These arguments are materialistic, nationalistic, and inward-focused, dwelling on the benefits migrants bring to Scotland.

Scottish nationalists have made similar claims with reference to refugees, a much costlier group of immigrants. The New Scots Refugee Integration Strategy again uses the expression 'New Scots' to confer national membership on resident refugees. While the policy was being promoted, the government placed heavy emphasis on how to help refugees use their skills to benefit Scotland. As Cabinet Secretary for Communities, Social Security and Equalities Angela Constance said, 'As refugees and asylum seekers rebuild their lives here they have to make Scotland stronger, more compassionate, and a more successful nation' (BBC News 2018b). Sabir Zazai, the chief executive of the Scottish Refugee Council, expressed similar themes:

The new Scots who live and work alongside us bring a wealth of experience and talent to Scotland and the new strategy will help us unlock and develop that potential. At the end of the day these refugees will be our neighbours, our colleagues and our customers. We don't want them to live in poverty, we want them to prosper and be proud of their own identities, proud of being Scottish, proud of being new Scots. (BBC News 2018b)

Zazai transfers national identity to the new population, while emphasising the benefit that refugees bring to Scotland as skilled workers and consumers.

The refugee population also featured in a discussion about the extension of the franchise. The 2016 Scotland Act devolved powers over running elections, and in 2020 the Scottish Parliament granted refugees voting rights.[7] Minister for Parliamentary Business Joe FitzPatrick explained, 'Scotland is a welcoming country and our intention to extend the opportunity to vote to all those who are legally resident in Scotland, whatever their place of birth, should include refugees and asylum seekers' (Shedden 2018). Zazai argued the vote is a 'hugely significant point in their journey towards integration, citizenship and the ability to play an active role in society' (Shedden 2018), reflecting the civic republican notion that national membership is earned through engagement rather than lineage.

The Scottish Executive is consistent in its messaging about the civic character of Scottish nationalism and pairing that image of nationalism with a strong desire to attract and retain immigrants. The elite consensus around the desirability of immigration developed after devolution, when it became clear that the devolved powers granted to Scotland were not enough to allow Scotland to pursue its national interests relating to population growth. Part of the challenge for political elites is to link this relatively new policy ambition with the well-established narrative of Scottish nationalism, hoping to make immigration fit in to the narrative of how the Scottish people understand themselves. They do this through appeals to the Scottish memory of emigration, which build a collective sense of empathy for those seeking to enter Scotland.

Nationalism and the Scottish Memory of Migration

Historical nostalgia and memory are critical for constructing nationalism in Scotland, even though sustaining heritage sits uncomfortably with the values of civic nationalism. The way Scottish elites use the country's memory and experience of migration to justify modern immigration illustrates the tension. There are two primary memories of migration that are of great importance to Scottish nation-building: the place of diaspora in national identity and the memorialisation of the Highland Clearances.

The Diaspora

Scotland is historically a country of emigration. The Scotland Is Now campaign estimates that there are about 50 million people around the world who claim Scottish ancestry. The sheer size of the emigration flows means that most Scottish families have members living abroad, and through these connections, Scots are familiar with the difficulties and advantages of a migration experience. As Frank Angell, a former SNP local council candidate expressed it, 'Scots are very tolerant people. I think the fact that Scotland has a large diaspora has something to do with that. Scots have often seen themselves as a persecuted minority, that makes them very sympathetic' (Elgot 2014). Accepting immigrants might also be seen as part of a *quid pro quo*, where acceptance is required to compensate for the welcome Scots have received abroad. A Liberal Democrat MSP put it this way:

> If you stay here two years, or five years, or their whole lifetimes, I'm not too bothered, our Scots go off and work in Canada, India, Europe, around the world. New Zealand is a particularly good example at the moment, and we shouldn't be any different. (Personal interview 27 June 2017)

Familiarity with migration may be part of what makes Scots slightly more open to immigrants and immigration, though typically emigration is linked to immigration by promoting return migration. As First Minister Jack McConnell said:

> There are many thousands of Scots living and working elsewhere and we will actively encourage these expatriate Scots to return home. The extent of the Scots diaspora means that there are millions of people across the globe who have a strong emotional and cultural link with Scotland. Friends of Scotland and GlobalScot will be reorganized to create a more focused relationship with this group, to encourage some of them to live and work in Scotland. (Scottish Executive 2004: 7)

Because of efforts to encourage people of Scottish descent to return to their ancestral land, people of Scottish descent play a prominent role in the economics of tourism.[8] The most famous example is the Homecoming, an event designed to draw people with Scottish heritage to Scotland every five years. The primary objective of the event and others like it is economic, but diaspora-oriented events also have socio-political impacts. They reflect a deliberately constructed image of Scotland and promote nationalist sentiment by reinforcing the cultural affinity shared by the diaspora and the native Scots. Ancestral tourism provides opportunities to see citizens of different nations and states as Scottish.

Diasporic communities often maintain strong emotional, social, and political connections to their countries of origin, and a sense of Scottish identity is a central element of the personal identity of many descendants of Scottish emigrants.[9] Diasporic identities are typically rooted in an overly romantic and sentimental imagined view of Scotland, though they also include real-world, modern interactions. Devolution changed how the Scottish government engaged with the diaspora and empowered the Scottish Executive to be a resource for those who want to maintain links to Scotland, demonstrated through government sponsorship of Homecomings, the Tartan Weeks in America, and the 2010 Diaspora Engagement Plan (Sim 2012). Due to outreach and the ease of communication and travel, the diaspora is increasingly knowledgeable about Scottish constitutional change, and personal aspirations towards Scottishness amongst the heritage tourists correspond with political aspirations for Scottish independence (Bhandari 2016). Recognising the support for independence among the Scottish diaspora, the Scottish government suggested that a Scottish parent or grandparent would be an eligible criterion for Scottish citizenship upon independence (Scottish Government 2013b).[10]

One should not be overly optimistic about the potential of the diaspora for helping develop a nationalism that is open to diversity and immigration. Nation-building with a diaspora is typically analysed as a version of ethnic nationalism because of its fixation on roots and ancestry. Brubaker calls this form of nation-building

> homeland nationalism . . . directed outward across the boundaries of territory and citizenship, towards members of their own ethnic nationality, that is towards persons who 'belong' (or can be claimed to belong) to the external national homeland by ethnonational affinity, although they reside in and are (ordinarily) citizens of other states. (Brubaker 1996: 111)

The Scottish government's strategies of ancestral tourism appear to promote ethnic qualities of Scottishness through ancestry. However, much of the promotional material discusses emotional bonds and a sense of belonging, a subjective sentiment that could theoretically be felt by anyone. Furthermore, the acceptance of a multi-generational descendant as Scottish allows for substantial degree of blood mixing, which presumably would compromise ethnic purity.

Accepting the descendants of Scottish-born people as Scottish requires the Scottish people and government to grapple with Scotland's role in slavery. Since the death of George Floyd in the United States in 2020 and the rise of the Black Lives Matter movement, activists in Scotland have campaigned for Scotland to come to terms with its own slave-owning history, and the reality that Scottish emigrants owned slave plantations in the Caribbean and elsewhere, including a third of the plantations in Jamaica. This call involves recognising generations of Black Scots, to recognise that 'Black people have been part of this country and shaping the culture and social development of this country for a very, very long time' and committing to reparations (Lane 2020, quoting May Sumbwanyambe). Recognising the entitlement of the descendants of Scottish-owned slaves, many of whom also have Scottish ancestry, significantly complicates ethnic definitions of Scottishness.

While the efforts of the Scottish government to connect with the diaspora are interesting, it would be a mistake to interpret these strategies as an expression of a deep philosophical commitment to anything other than a revenue stream. That said, the diaspora does surface in discussions of national interest as part of a narrative about population decline, as a strategy for increasing revenue through tourism and investment, and as a political boon for nationalist causes. Immigration is also purported to be a solution to all of these challenges, which means there is at least a tangential or spurious relationship between past emigration and modern immigration.

The Highland Clearances

The experience of the Highland Clearances is highly present in Scottish nationalist discourse. The Clearances were one of the drivers of Scottish emigration in the mid to late eighteenth century, during which time thousands of Highlanders were removed from their generational homes to end up in coastal settlements, in central Scotland participating in industrialisation, or emigrating.[11] The Clearances represent a time when Scots were forced migrants or refugees, removed from their homes at the will of landowners who saw more profit in sheep than in people working the land. Though this experience directly affected a small percentage of the Scottish population from one specific geographic area, the remembered injustice of forced or nearly forced migration rankles broadly. The memory represents a critique of the landowning class and the power they had in the region, and contributes to the narrative of how Scotland has identified itself against England, whereby Scotland privileges fairness and rejects elitism, especially the kind of capitalistic elitism that gives a wealthy individual almost absolute power over those in the lower classes. The Clearances are

> one of the significant elements around which the present identity of the crofting (small-scale farming) districts of Scotland is conceptualized and constructed. The period has the ability to elicit intense emotions as it is bound up with the notions of trauma, dislocation and oppression as well as a sense of loss and betrayal. It is read as seminal and is often inserted in historical discourses of origin and used as a point of cohesion, uniting a people. (Gouriévidis 2000: 125–6)

The Clearances involve

> a kind of 'postmemory' [a form of memory that is drawn from narratives that precede people's birth by one or more generations, but which nevertheless provides a powerful thread running through people's lives (354)] revolving around a series of iconic motifs and ... this provides a framework for interpretation and action in the present. (Jones 2013: 346)

The motifs of the Clearances are vivid and violent: burning homes, evil landlords, weeping refugees, and scenes of poverty. The continued use of these images and individual stories in poetry, song, theatre, and art have kept the memory of the Clearances alive and feed into the national narrative about the collective experience of Scottish people (Miyares 2017).

While the memory of the Clearances is used to build a historical narrative that feeds into national identity, it has also been used to activate empathy for modern people in similar situations. For example, in a pamphlet published by the Scottish Faiths Action for Refugees, the section about Scotland's relationship with refugees opens with the statement 'In Scotland's history, the Clearances in the nineteenth century are a useful reminder that we've been here before; but on that occasion it was forced migration from Scotland to many other parts of the world' (2017: 12). The Clearances represent a parallel experience and create a sense of obligation to refugees. At a public meeting discussing the relocation of five Syrian refugee families to Dingwall, a Highland city in the east of Scotland, civic leader Margaret Peterson highlighted the relationship between the Clearances and modern-day refugee politics when she said, 'We are very friendly people and, in the past, when we had to leave Scotland's shores in the Highland Clearances, we were made welcome elsewhere and we will never forget that' (North Star 2017).

On occasion, the Clearances are invoked to argue for the benefits of immigration. From 2015 to 2017, Dr Paul Monaghan was the Member of Parliament for Caithness, Sutherland and Easter Ross, a constituency that experienced the Clearances. In his maiden speech, Monaghan described the importance of learning from history, and used the unintended consequences of the Clearances to make a case for free movement:

> These dispossessed highlanders travelled the world and applied their creativity and resource in ways that have benefited all of humankind. The economic and social contribution of the ancestors of people from my constituency stand today as a shining example of why the free movement of people is something no Government should hesitate to encourage. (Monaghan 2015)

The Scottish memories of emigration are leveraged for political purposes, but in a variety of ways. The general diaspora is framed as a resource for Scotland with little reference to the original migration experience. The memory of the Clearances is used symbolically as a national grievance against England, even though many political leaders endeavour to discourage grievance-based nationalism. As the Syrian refugee crisis has developed, the memory has also been used to encourage public affinity with refugees housed in Scotland. Both resource and symbolic frames present a positive national case of welcoming migrants, and embed an obligation of hospitality within Scottish history.

CONCLUSION

This chapter reviews the way Scottish nationalism is constructed by political elites. The political investment in creating a civic national identity for Scotland reveals how 'identity has moved from that which might be unconscious and taken for granted, because implicit in distinct cultural practices, to conscious and public projections of identity and the explicit creation and assertion of politicized identities' (Modood et al. 1997: 337). The conscious projection of a Scotland that is open and welcoming to outsiders is part of a strategy to legitimise Scotland's government and differentiate between England and Scotland.

The construction of Scottish liberal civic nationalism has not been easy or natural. Public imaginings of Scottishness still involve symbols and practices that project an ethnicised version of identity, and in an effort to capitalise on economic opportunity, the Scottish government has been complicit in emphasising connectedness through Scottish heritage. The fetishisation of Scottish culture among Scottish Americans raises especially uncomfortable questions about the consequences of an explicit celebration of clan, warrior, and war and a perhaps implicit endorsement of white supremacy through the celebration of Scottish culture.[12] These symbols have the potential to work against the construction of a civic national identity that is open to outsiders.

One way the Scottish elites straddle this precarious line of constructing a nationalism that both looks backward at history or lineage and also moves forward towards internationalism and multiculturalism is through connecting their national memories of migration to current trends in human movement. Through making direct comparisons between Scottish past experiences of emigration and forced migration and the modern experiences of immigrants and refugees, they appeal to historical nostalgia while advocating for change. Another way Scottish elites negotiate this delicate position between parochialism and cosmopolitanism is through advocating for liberal civic political institutions as an expression of Scottish values and the inclusion of immigrants as solutions to distinctively Scottish problems, against the backdrop of a UK state that cannot meet Scottish needs. Aggressively differentiating between Scotland and the rest of the UK harks back to oppositional and defensive politics linked to ethnically defined nations threatened by an external 'other', but in this case England is framed as a political foe that does not accept Scotland's liberal civic political culture, nor Scotland's efforts to include ethnic or cultural outsiders. The civic and pro-diversity argument makes the England–Scotland differentiation normatively acceptable by democratic standards, and it legitimises the nation-building project of the Scottish political elites.

Notes

1. Civic and ethnic nationalism are attempts to describe the character of nationalism. There are many other typologies of nationalism that focus on its ambitions (unification, separatist, state, sub-national, anti-colonial, etc.).
2. Stateless national movements like those in Quebec and Scotland dwell in a third 'No state' category. The sub-state nations must negotiate layers and potentially competing systems of belonging that complicate the issue of their preferred expression of nationalism. For example, if Quebec were independent, its government would endorse civic republicanism, but Quebec's presence within multicultural Canada moves its regional government more towards liberal civic nationalism than would be its preference. Dupré argues that the Quebecois case walks a thin line between liberal civic nationalism and civic republicanism, as notions of Quebecois majority culture hinge strongly on the French language and increasingly on secularism: 'While language nationalism can be reconciled with pluralism, increasing calls for an absolutist form of secularism by civic and cultural nationalists constrain the development of an openly pluralistic stance on citizenship in the province' (2012: 230).
3. See <https://www.gov.scot/news/global-campaign-takes-scotland-to-the-world/>.
4. The Scottish narrative transmits stories of the continental travels of the Scottish academic elite and alliances made with European countries in support of Scottish monarchs (Herman 2001).
5. The idea of a new Scotland has been a recurring theme in the discussions of Scottish politics since the Scottish Parliament reconvened in 1999 (see Paterson et al. 2001; Hassan and Warhurst 2002a, 2002b). The implication of those who casually invoke the image of 'new Scotland' is that Scotland is transforming to become a better place, a more confident, diverse, and pluralist country under its new institutional configuration.
6. The politics of Brexit substantially reduced the multi-level outcomes Scotland is willing to consider. Moving forward, an institutional relationship with the EU may require a complete break from the UK or a change in EU policy.
7. At the time, British, Irish, Commonwealth, and EU citizens residing in Scotland were eligible to vote in Scottish elections.
8. Ancestry tourism is said to be worth £400 million for the Scottish economy, and the Scottish government has pursued business people of Scottish heritage to improve opportunities for international trade or skills development (Kuznetsov 2008). The GlobalScot network was designed to identify skilled people with Scottish connections whose expertise could benefit Scottish industry.
9. There are substantially weaker Scottish identities amongst the Scottish diaspora in England, compared with North America (Leith and Sim 2017). In the second generation, the Scottish identities weaken further (Leith and Sim 2012). The difference between the English and overseas experience may be attributable to England's proximity to Scotland, which makes the individual preservation of identity less necessary.
10. Other potential citizens include legal residents, people who lived in Scotland for ten years, and migrants on qualifying visas: 'This Government proposes an inclusive model of citizenship for people whether or not they define themselves as primarily

or exclusively Scottish or wish to become a Scottish passport holder' (Scottish Government 2013b).
11. There were also many outside forces driving emigration at the same time, including changing economics, potato blight, and political oppression following the Jacobite uprising.
12. See Ray (2001) for an anthropological description of the construction of Scottish American Heritage in the American South, especially North Carolina. She highlights the constructed nature of the version of Scottish history celebrated in the US, and is fully aware of the paradoxes and absurdities that come with it. She disclaims the linkages that have been made between the celebration of Scottish American culture and white supremacy, though others have documented the way neo-Confederates of the American South have adopted theories in which they see themselves and Southerners as being 'Celtic', even to the point of introducing a Confederate Memorial Tartan (Sebesta 2000).

3

THE PEOPLE: MIGRATION AND SCOTTISH NATIONAL IDENTITY

The previous chapter outlines how immigration relates to nation-building in Scotland. It discusses elite consensus around a more modernist, civic conceptualisation of the nation, one that is inclusive, and where national identity is based primarily on residency, and not ancestry, ethnicity, or history. While '"it is in the elite that concepts of the nation are shaped and modified"; nevertheless, it is in the masses that the nation is given form and concrete substance' (Leith and Soule 2011: 152, quoting Kearton 2005: 25). Is there divergence between elite and mass ideas about who the Scottish people are?

What does it mean to be Scottish? What characteristics does someone need to be considered Scottish? Who gets to decide? Identity questions are at the centre of political conversations in Scotland, because political actors across the ideological spectrum capitalise on who 'we' are, and what 'we' need. Defining identity is dialectic and intrinsically othering – deciding who 'we' are also determines who 'they' are, and linking a nationalist movement with an identity risks branding the movement as tribal or ethnic and parochial. And yet, as evidenced by the many proud citizens of immigrant-receiving nations, it is possible to have a strong national identity and to be welcoming to others who would like to join your nation. Some argue that 'a strong national identity, albeit of a particular kind, is a prerequisite for a multicultural society', because all nations are *de facto* multicultural in the sense that all nations contain diverse populations (Asari et al. 2008: 2). The construction of an inclusive and voluntaristic national identity that reflects this reality is vital for ensuring peace.

The Scottish political elites are developing a vision of Scottishness that is open and welcoming, but also one that (sometimes uncomfortably) grafts on to beloved distinctive elements of Scottish culture, music, literature, dialects, customs, laws, and institutions. Though the explicit conversation about nationalism and national identity occurs among the elites, the message targets the Scottish public, many of whom do not spend much time following politics and are not introspective about who they are as Scots and why it matters. This chapter examines public understandings of Scottish identity and whether Scottish people extend Scottish identity to minoritised groups. It also considers how members of minoritised groups relate to Scottish identity, and whether their experience with Scottish nationalism mirrors that of native-born Scots.

THE NATIONAL IDENTITY OF SCOTS

Compared with other forms of identity (gender, religious, class, personal, etc.), national identity is outward-focused because the purpose of the identity is to define a political community. It is 'a public project rather than a fixed state of mind', a 'form of social order – a mechanism by which otherwise autonomous individuals agree to accept the rules and authority of the collective' (Zimmer 2003: 174; Asari et al. 2008: 3). National identity determines how social and political activity is organised and defines the boundaries distinguishing community insiders from outsiders.

The power of community gives national identity gravitas, but for most people, national identity is not salient except during events like football matches, patriotic holidays, and elections. However, Scots engage in forms of 'everyday nationhood' when they talk about, select, perform, and consume Scottishness (Fox and Miller-Idriss 2008). Events such as the devolution referendum in 1997, the opening of the Scottish Parliament in 1999, the independence referendum in 2014, and the Brexit referendum in 2016 activated Scottish national identity, and brought questions about Scottishness to the front of people's minds on a fairly regular basis.

Defining one's identity is a complicated process involving two streams of thought: claiming the identity and being accepted as a member of the identity group. Individual identity is partly socially constructed, requiring recognition by others, especially if one hopes to access group benefits. Identity claims are recognised through identity cues or markers:

> Identity markers are those social characteristics of an individual that they might present to others to support their national identity claim. Markers are also those characteristics that people use to attribute national identity to others and to receive claims and attributions made by others ... [Identity markers] are probabilistic rules of thumb whereby,

under certain conditions and in particular contexts, identity markers are interpreted, combined or given precedence over others. (McCrone 2002: 208–9)

There are many different types of national identity markers, including accent, place of birth, appearance or phenotypic traits, name, place of upbringing, place of education, ancestry, values, residency, length of residency, or dress. Some markers are fluid, meaning that an individual can change them over time, while others are fixed and unalterable. Some markers are more detectable or accessible to those evaluating an identity claim. Accent, appearance, name, and dress are all relatively easy to recognise and understand, while someone would have to explicitly communicate political values or family history (Kiely et al. 2001).

Chapter 2 explains the theoretical differences between civic and ethnic nationalism, and describes why the dichotomisation is problematic when it comes to explaining real-world nationalism.[1] Nevertheless, the development of a strong civic national identity is assumed to be a shared goal in Scotland. As one ranking member of the SNP said:

> there is a majority feeling that there's a more cohesive national view, which means that it doesn't matter if you were born here or if you're white or black, that you can still be a Scottish person every bit as much as if your family lived here for 2,000 years. (Personal interview 10 June 2016)

If the Scottish public agrees with this civic characterisation of their national identity, they will emphasise the importance of fluid markers of Scottishness, such as residency or political values. However, if a Scot endorses ethnic nationalism, they would place more weight on fixed markers, such as race or ancestry. Occasionally, fixed markers can be civic in nature (birthplace), and some fluid markers can carry an ethnic association (national clothing and religion). Table 3.1 illustrates marker quality (fixed vs fluid) by the nationalism ideal types (civic vs ethnic).

A few markers straddle categories. Religion straddles the fixed/fluid categories. Because of the personal stakes (such as reincarnation or going to heaven or hell), the socialisation involved with religion, and associations between religion and other fixed markers like race or birthplace, religion can seem like a fixed identity. However, a person can convert and change their religion or stop identifying with a religion, which would make religion a fluid identity marker. Language and accent straddle all of the categories. Anyone can learn a language, which makes it a more fluid identity marker, and the endorsement of linguistic markers can be consistent with ideas of civic nationalism, especially since a common language creates opportunities for social solidarity

Table 3.1 Markers of nationalism

		Nationalism ideal types	
		Civic	Ethnic
Marker quality	*Fluid*	Residency Length of residency Place of education Naturalisation Political/personal values Political participation Attachment to territory Affinity with people or place Shared experiences	National clothing Consumption/food
		——— Language/accent ——— Religion ———	
	Fixed	Birthplace Upbringing/socialisation	Family name Ancestry Skin colour Phenotypical characteristics

and facilitates participation. However, the preservation of language is often a central feature of nationalistic movements, and the principle of preservation carries ideas of cultural purity, which makes the marker function as a tool of ethnic nationalism. The added layer of accent makes language an even more complicated marker, because though some people can learn to mimic accents, they are typically a product of socialisation from a young age, giving accent a fixed character tied to birthplace or upbringing. Even some of the more easily categorised markers can be complicated. Shared experience is civic in character, but in situations where there has been internal conflict, the events or persons that provoke community and pride in one group may be a source of feelings of betrayal in another. One can also change one's name, which would imply a degree of fluidity in the family name marker, but because a family name attached to a person at birth is a signal of ancestry, it is categorised as fixed. Even some of the most fixed identity markers, like skin colour and phenotypical characteristics, are changeable with plastic surgery and cosmetic treatment.

Scottish national identity is rooted in a sense of place, rather than tribe or blood (McCrone and Kiely 2000). As a result, many of the most widely endorsed markers of Scottish identity are place-centred, including accent, birthplace, upbringing, and residency. Some of these markers are fixed and unchangeable, like birthplace, upbringing, and perhaps accent. Others are more fluid, like residency or attachment to Scotland. People who consider themselves Scottish according to fluid markers of identity might find their claims undermined by the absence of a critical fixed marker, like accent. The multiple and potentially conflicting markers reflect the complexity of Scottish nationalism, which is a product of both ethnic and civic characteristics.

Research on Scottish national identity evaluates the relative strength of identity markers for native and non-native Scots. Kiely and colleagues (2001) conducted hundreds of interviews with members of the economic and cultural elite in Scotland, including equal numbers of native and non-native Scots. Their findings revealed some telling rules for national identity claims (how a person claims an identity for themselves), attribution (assigning an identity to someone else), and reception (accepting or rejecting someone else's identity claim) in Scotland. The strongest national identity claims and attributions were based on place of birth, ancestry, upbringing, and residence, but Kiely et al. find place of birth stands on its own as the strongest marker of identity. It was much harder to form rules about the reception of national identity claims: 'The audience who receive claims and attributions are not homogeneous in their conception of national identity. The audience may interpret the markers used in contrasting ways, with the end result that some people uphold a claim or attribution while others reject it' (2001: 51). In later research, Kiely et al. (2005) used narratives of national identity in post-devolution Scotland to examine the extent to which identity claims based on blood, birth, or belonging were used by English migrants and Scottish nationals. The vast majority of their interview participants defined identity with place of birth and upbringing. This does not mean that claims are not made on the basis of other markers, such as ancestry or a sense of belonging, but that birth and upbringing (and other markers that come along with it, like accent) are the most widely accepted and least contested identity markers among those who live in Scotland.[2]

While researchers achieve consensus about the importance of birthplace as a Scottish identity marker, the 2011 Scottish Social Attitudes Survey (SSAS), a probability survey of over 1,197 Scots, included a battery of questions about identity attribution. Figure 3.1 provides the percentage frequencies of approximately 1,175 responses to questions about how Scottish someone might be according to their residential and ancestral identity markers.

The majority of respondents believe a person born in Scotland and living in England is Scottish, affirming research suggesting that one of the strongest markers for national membership is birthplace (Bond 2006; Kiely et al. 2001). However, intent to return to Scotland matters, suggesting an attachment to the Scottish territory and plans for residency are also important. Sixty-three

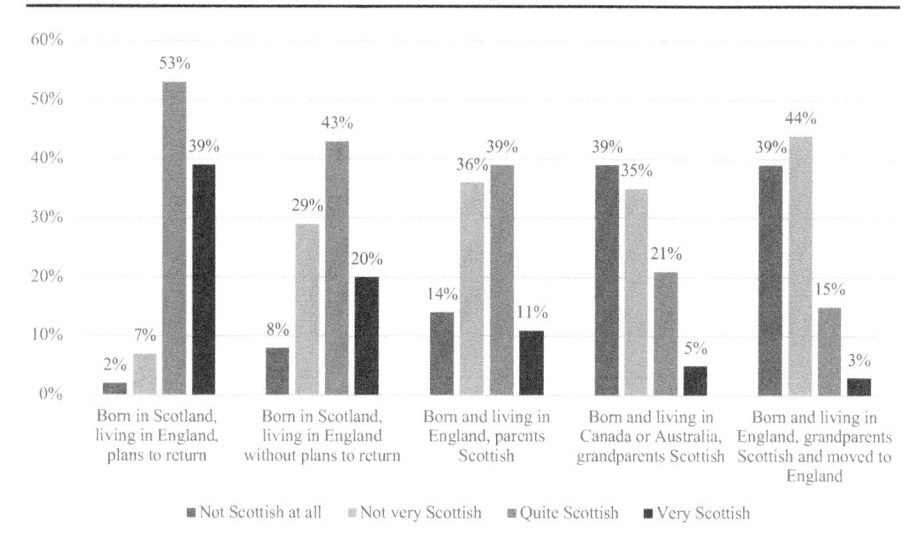

Figure 3.1 'How Scottish is someone if they are ...'
Source: 2011 Scottish Social Attitudes Survey (ScotCen Social Research 2013)

per cent of respondents identify a person born in Scotland living in England without plans to return as quite or very Scottish, but that number jumps to 92% when the person plans to return.

The assessments of the other identity markers in Figure 3.1 relate to Scottish ancestry. The first questions the Scottishness of someone who was born and lives in England but has Scottish parents. The respondents are split on this question, with 50% identifying that person as quite or very Scottish. When the relationship to the Scottish ancestor moves to the grandparents, only 18% of respondents believe that the individual is quite or very Scottish.[3] The difference could reflect the perceived importance of Scottish socialisation, since parents presumably play a much greater role in socialising their children. However, the moderate responses even with Scottish parentage suggest that the survey respondents believe nationality is diluted in foreign contexts, presumably due to other socialising influences in the foreign country, like schools, public institutions, or intermarriage. The survey respondents are a bit more acceptant of those with Scottish grandparents who live in the Commonwealth countries of Canada and Australia than they are of those born and living in England with Scottish grandparents: 26% of respondents identify the people living in Canada or Australia as quite or very Scottish, compared with the 18% who affirmed the Scottish identity of those who live in England. This difference may reflect the perception of stronger Scottish ties with Canada and Australia compared with England, or recognition of the efforts of those with Scottish heritage in those states to keep their Scottish heritage alive.

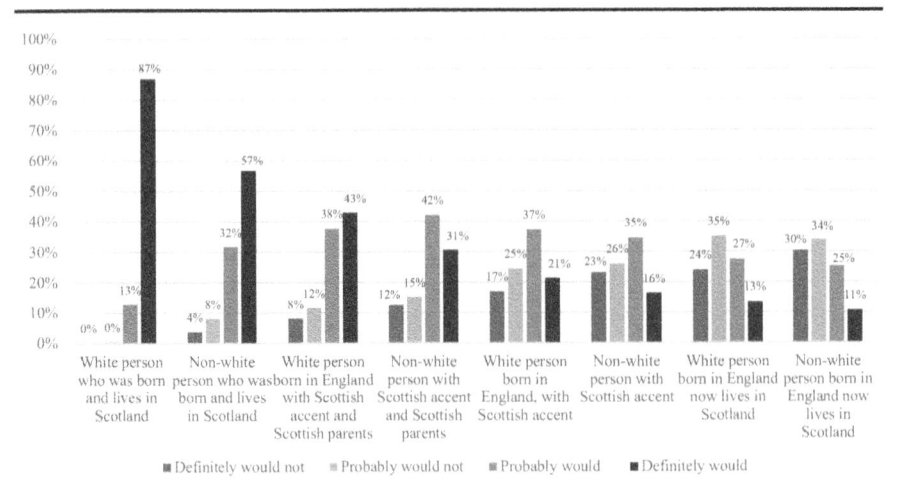

Figure 3.2 'Who would you consider Scottish?'
Source: 2009 Scottish Social Attitudes Survey (ScotCen Social Research 2010)

In 2009, the SSAS included a battery of questions about the identity of hypothetical residents of Scotland, and frequencies of the responses are illustrated in Figure 3.2. The questions ask respondents to assess a variety of identity markers for hypothetical white and minoritised residents of Scotland and reveal two major trends. First, with reference to both white and minoritised residents, birthplace in Scotland is the least controversial marker of Scottish identity, followed by ancestry. This finding is not new, since the dominance of birthplace as the most agreed on marker of Scottishness is well established (Bond 2006; Kiely et al. 2005). Second, while the most important markers are the same for both white and minoritised residents, some respondents differentiate based on race, and about 10% of the sample demonstrates an unwillingness to perceive a member of a minoritised group as Scottish, regardless of adherence to the other Scottish identity markers. Residency in Scotland is the marker that gains the least recognition from the survey respondents, regardless of whether the prospective Scot is white or a member of a minoritised group. The Scottish government regularly asserts that 'if you live here, you're Scottish', but these data suggest that the image of Scottish national identity promoted by the Scottish Executive may not match the ideas of the wider public.

Many of these trends were affirmed in a YouGov poll of Scots in 2016, which found that birthplace and parentage are the least controversial markers of Scottish identity (Smith 2016). That poll asked a few questions about residency, specifically about whether living in Scotland for up to five years, between five and ten years, or more than ten years, makes a person Scottish. Fifty-eight per cent of Scots in the sample do not believe that living in Scotland for more than ten years makes someone Scottish. That grows to 70% for those living in

Scotland between five and ten years, and 75% for those living in Scotland for less than five years. The overwhelming lack of public support for residency as a marker of Scottishness, even when the residency is quite long, strikes another blow against the Scottish Executive's vision of national identity.

The YouGov poll tests the power of the theoretical makers of identity attribution (birthplace, parentage, where someone grew up, affinity, and residency) by asking survey respondents to identify celebrities as Scottish or English. The list of celebrities includes those born in Scotland of two Scottish parents and having lived their whole lives in Scotland (Nicola Sturgeon, Ruth Davidson), those born and raised in Scotland but living elsewhere (Ewan McGregor, Billy Connolly, Alex Ferguson), those born in Scotland but raised elsewhere (Gordon Ramsay, Tony Blair), those born elsewhere but living in Scotland (J. K. Rowling), those with two Scottish parents (Alastair Campbell), and those with one Scottish Parent (Rod Stewart, Tony Blair). If people's theoretical markers were directly applied to the celebrities, those born in Scotland should be identified as Scottish, though Scottish-born Tony Blair scores the lowest with only 10% of respondents attributing a Scottish identity to him. Those born and raised in Scotland (Nicola Sturgeon, Ruth Davidson, Ewan McGregor, Billy Connolly, Alex Ferguson) are most likely to be identified as Scottish, though there is remarkable variance. Both Sturgeon and Davidson embody the same markers of birthplace, parentage, and upbringing, but while 87% identify Sturgeon as Scottish, only 61% identify Davidson as Scottish. This is likely because of Davidson's affiliation with the Conservative Party, which would suggest that political values play into Scottish identity. That McGregor, Connolly, and Ferguson do not live in Scotland did not prevent more than 75% of people from identifying them as Scottish; however, residency does seem to matter for J. K. Rowling, who is considered Scottish by 46% of respondents. She was identified as Scottish more frequently than those with Scottish ancestry (Campbell, Stewart, and Blair), a result that contradicts responses to the theoretical question suggesting residency and ancestry are the most important identity markers. The exercise with celebrities reveals the difficulties of identity attribution and the way theory falls apart when confronted with real people. Theoretically, a person may believe place of birth and ancestry matter for Scottishness, but these markers are invisible. Those who are raised in Scotland and therefore have a Scottish accent, and who embody or perform their Scottishness (politicians in the Scottish Parliament, a folk singer/comedian with shows featuring strong Scottish themes, a player/manager for Scottish football teams), will more easily have Scottish identity attributed to them, though even then, the attribution of identity may be compromised by other things, like Conservative political affiliation. 'One cannot simply add up criteria of Scottishness so that one person is more Scottish than another', at least not with any consistency (Kiely et al. 2005: 152).

English residents in Scotland express similar understandings of what makes someone Scottish. In interviews with English migrants living in Scotland, Kiely et al. (2005) found that the English migrants typically defined their identity with reference to birthplace, which meant they identified as English or British (used interchangeably), and did not envision a possibility of becoming Scottish because they were not born there. Most of them attributed Scottish identity to their Scottish-born children, especially if the children spoke with a Scottish accent. English individuals also placed a much stronger emphasis on ancestry than Scottish natives. English-born Scottish residents seldom made claims to Scottishness because they believed such claims could be challenged or rejected by 'true' or 'real' Scots who were born in Scotland and who have Scottish accents (Kiely et al. 2005). This reflects a gradated system of nationality in the minds of the English-born residents, where markers of affinity to Scotland, birthplace, and ancestry are all at play, but where affinity is a necessary but insufficient marker of Scottishness. As one of their respondents explained, 'I live the Scottish way, but that doesn't make me a Scotsman' (Kiely et al. 2005: 157). Such a perspective recognises the host society as the ultimate authority by which membership is granted.

The English-born participants recognised the importance of accent as an identity marker, because it signals where someone grew up. English accents signalled their birthplace and hindered their ability to be recognised as Scottish. Based on survey data in Figure 3.2, the English residents were correct, and Bond (2006) also found that Scots were more likely to identify a resident member of a minoritised group with a Scottish accent as Scottish than they were to identify a permanently resident English-born person as Scottish. While this might be disappointing to English-born residents of Scotland, it suggests 'accent is a hybridized code of cultural belonging which reverses the negative evaluation of phenotypically categorized non-whites', which can give hope of belonging to minoritised residents of Scotland (Virdee et al. 2006: 4).

Many Scots accept fixed and ethno-symbolic markers of Scottishness. The least controversial marker of birthplace aligns with ideas of civic nationalism, since it is ethnically blind, but it is a fixed marker. The marker of the Scottish accent works similarly, since it is contingent on parents or upbringing in Scotland. The overtly ethnic marker of Scottishness is ancestry, and in the surveys, Scots attributed Scottishness to white and minoritised residents differently. The popular attribution of Scottishness with fixed markers runs counter to elite understandings of Scottishness as a highly flexible identity based on residency. It also means that those who lack these fixed markers but who claim Scottishness based on the messaging of the Scottish government will have their Scottishness called into question by many members of the Scottish public.

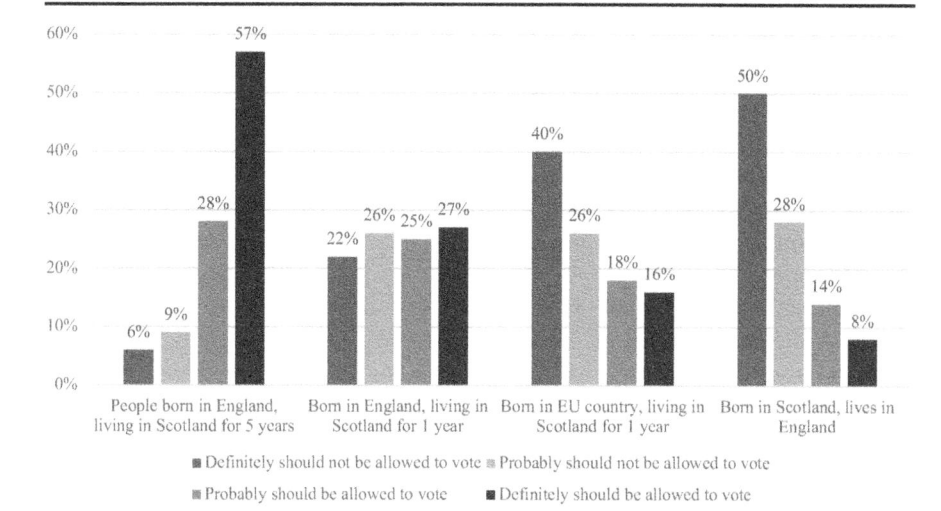

Figure 3.3 'Who should be allowed to vote in Scottish Parliament elections?'
Source: 2011 Scottish Social Attitudes Survey (ScotCen Social Research 2013)

Political Belonging

Questions about national identity attribution help define who Scottish people accept into their national political community. Acceptance drives political inclusion and determines who gets a say about what kind of country Scotland is going to become in the future. The 2011 SSAS includes a battery of questions asking respondents about who should be allowed to vote in Scottish Parliament elections, illustrated in Figure 3.3.

The overwhelming majority (85%) of respondents agreed that those born in England and residing in Scotland for five years should probably or definitely have the right to vote in Scottish Parliament elections. Support dropped when such English-born residents were resident for only one year, though half of the respondents agreed that the English-born residents should definitely or probably be allowed to vote. The difference reflects the greater commitment to Scotland associated with long-term residence, and therefore a greater degree of belonging. Survey respondents were notably less enthusiastic about an EU citizen's participation, with a third of respondents approving of allowing someone who was born in the EU and resident in Scotland for one year to vote. The difference between the EU- and the English-born residents could reflect the closer ties and greater familiarity Scots feel with the English, or the trend of circular migration among EU migrants, which reduces the probability that an EU migrant will settle in Scotland.

The importance of residency is affirmed by the question asking whether Scots living in England should be given the right to vote in Scottish elections.

In this case, the overwhelming majority (78%) suggests that person should probably or definitely not have the right to vote. The 22% of respondents who believe that Scots living in England definitely or probably should have the right to vote suggests there are those who approve of granting political rights through birthplace. However, the much stronger support for residency as a criterion for voting and the stronger support for political inclusion with longer residence emphasises the dominance of location as a critical criterion for political incorporation.

To belong, a person must claim community identity and be recognised as a member by other group members to be given group rights and privileges. Concerns about whether native Scots will recognise a prospective Scot can hinder the prospective Scot's sense of belonging. Answers to questions about Scottish identity and political integration in the SSAS and YouGov polls suggest that Scots differentiate between national identity and civic inclusion. Similarly, the data from 2009 in Figure 3.2, in which 59% of respondents indicated that they would not consider an English person permanently residing in Scotland as Scottish, contrast with the data presented in Figure 3.3, which suggest that such a person should be allowed a vote. Ascribed national identity does not correspond perfectly with a public understanding of the rights of representation in Scotland: Scottish national identity does not automatically translate into Scottish civic incorporation, nor does Scottish civic incorporation automatically confer Scottish identity.

The 2009 SSAS includes another question that confirms that most Scots think about Scottishness as a cultural rather than political identity. Figure 3.4 displays the frequency of the responses to the question 'Some people say that being Scottish is mainly about culture (landscape, music, language, literature), others say how the country is governed. Where on the scale are you?'[4]

The majority of respondents (55%) fall on the cultural end of the spectrum, while 26% are neutral, leaving almost a fifth to understand Scottishness in a civic, which is to say political, way. In a follow-up question in which respondents are asked to evaluate the importance of cultural and civic elements of Scottishness, 90% of respondents affirm the importance of culture, including many of those who understand Scottishness as a civic identity. Sixty-eight per cent agree that governance is an important element of Scottishness. Defining Scottishness primarily as a cultural identity does not reduce the importance of the political culture of Scotland in the minds of many survey participants. Individuals endorse a combination of the cultural and civic constructions of national identity and make a strong case for conceptualising national identity as a combination of ideas communicated by interrelated markers, rather than a dichotomous understanding of civic versus ethnic nationalism.

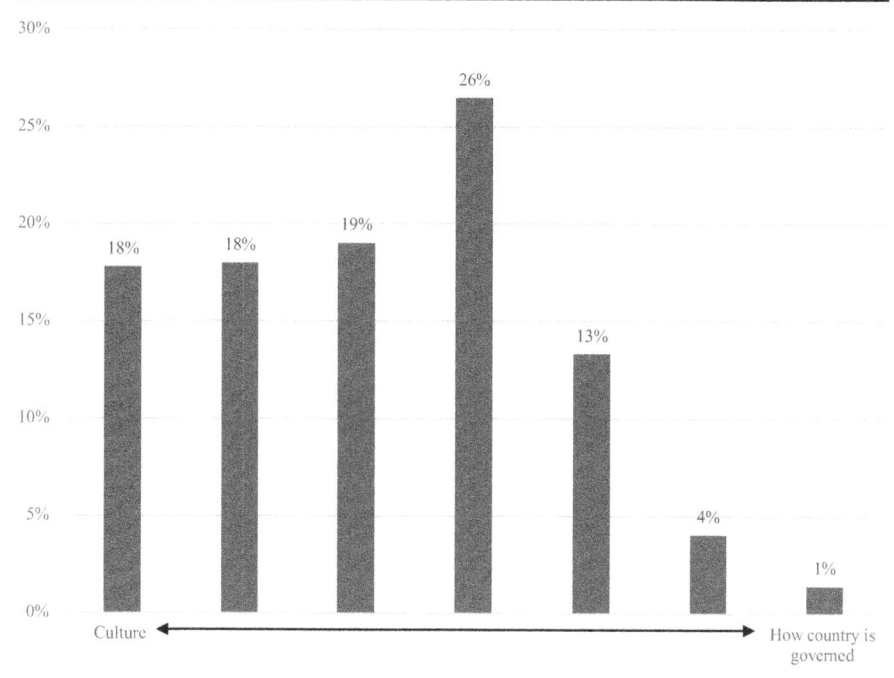

Figure 3.4 'Some people say that being Scottish is mainly about culture, others say how the country is governed. Where on the scale are you?'
Source: 2009 Scottish Social Attitudes Survey (ScotCen Social Research 2010)

SCOTTISHNESS AND BRITISHNESS

The variety of Scottish identity markers tell a complex story of identity construction. The salience of an identity and its associated markers depends on the presence of other competing identities. For example, when there was an influx of Irish Catholic immigrants into Scotland in the nineteenth century, religion became an identity that differentiated national communities. One persistent identity contest is between Scottishness and Britishness, which appeal to different parts of the Scottish experience. Mobilising the disparate parts of the UK towards an imperial project required a construction of British identity that allowed for cultural or ethnic diversity under a unifying political identity created and reinforced by the UK state. Political loyalty became a marker of British identity, and it was open to all of the constituent nations of the UK and the subject colonies. Even though the constituent nations of the UK asserted their own cultural identities, they were assumed to be nested identities, with Britain providing the state or civic identity, overlaid on top of Scottish, Northern Irish, and Welsh cultural national identities. Today, English and British identities are held to be interchangeable to the point that

Englishness is not seen as a meaningfully distinct identity, due to the long-standing domination of the British Isles by English language, English culture, English law, and English political institutions (Kumar 2010).[5] Britishness is imbued with Englishness, which could make it less appealing to those who do not identify as English. The meaning attached to the British identity functions differently in the nations of the UK. Those who claim to be British in Scotland are likely to be right of centre and pro-union in their political views, while in England, the self-identified British are more left-leaning than those identifying as English (Paterson et al. 2001).[6] South of the border, being British carries the civic nationalistic character that Scottishness holds in the north (McCrone 2002).

Even though British identity is Scottish-inclusive, and despite the fact that the elite construction of the civic Scottish identity is tolerant of dual identities (see Leith and Soule 2011), many Scottish public opinion surveys encourage participants to think of Scottish and British identities as competing identity constructs. National surveys routinely include questions asking respondents to rank their affinity to Scottish identity contrasted against their feelings of Britishness. For example, when asked to select their national identities from a range of choices, the vast majority of the 1,288 Scots (79%) surveyed in the 2015 SSAS identified as Scottish. When the survey introduced an element of prioritisation, and asked which identity best described them, 68% reported Scottish identity. Another question asked individuals to measure their level of Scottishness relative to their level of Britishness, and 27% of the survey respondents identified as Scottish and not British, while another 28% identified as more Scottish than British. Thirty-three per cent identified as 'equally Scottish and British'. When those who identified as both Scottish and British were asked to pick which of the identities best describes them, two-thirds of them selected Scottish.

The attractiveness of the Scottish identity may be due to its flexibility, transmissibility, and informality. A representative from the Scottish Refugee Council highlighted the civic character of Scottishness as an 'institutional' rather than ethnic identity and pointed to the advantage of not linking Scottish identity to citizenship:

> Because Scottishness is not official, in terms of the law, then it's an identity you can assume quite easily, and is open and adaptable. You'll hear people talk about being Scots Asian or Scots Ethiopian, or this and that – if you can take that identity quite quickly, whereas Britishness is not – you have to have gone through this process to be rubber stamped. (Personal interview 3 April 2019)

On the one hand, this statement raises questions about whether independence and the formalisation of Scottish citizenship would change the degree to which

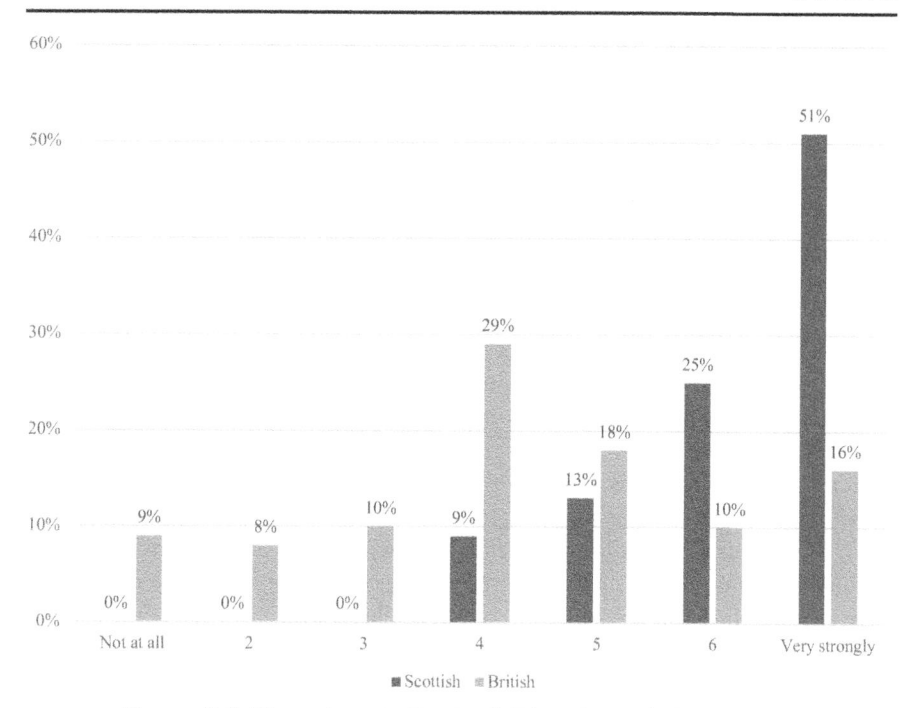

Figure 3.5 Those born in Scotland: 'How Scottish do you feel?'
'How British do you feel?'
Source: 2011 Scottish Social Attitudes Survey (ScotCen Social Research 2013)

Scottish identity is seen as inclusive. On the other hand, legal status could reinforce the civic character of an already 'institutional' identity.

Feelings of Scottishness dominate the pan-national British identity in Scotland. Data from the 2011 SSAS nuance this finding, because participants were not asked to prioritise their identities and instead were asked to indicate the strength of their Scottish and British identities on a seven-point scale. As illustrated in Figure 3.5, a majority of Scots claim a very strong Scottish identity, and nearly everyone else registers a Scottish identity somewhere above the middle category. When asked to rank their Britishness, the same respondents distributed themselves in a roughly normal curve, with nearly a third of the sample identifying as middling British. Of the five people who identify as weakly Scottish (scores of 1 and 2), four of them identify as very strongly British. However, many more respondents demonstrate the compatibility of holding both Scottish and British identities: of the 490 people who identify as strongly Scottish, 24% also identify as strongly British, and 16% identify as weakly British.[7]

National identities are complex and overlapping. Even so, Scottish survey data reveal strong preferences for Scottish national identity and a marked tendency to define Scottishness with reference to birthplace and residency. The next section considers how these identities relate to political attitudes, and particularly support for independence, which would determine whether autonomous control over immigration is granted to Scotland.

Extending National Identity to Minoritised Groups

Are native-born Scots open to the idea that a migrant or a member of a minoritised group can become Scottish? What if they hold different cultural or religious values? Scots endorse some fixed and ethnic definitions of Scottishness, and the emphasis on birth and ancestry sets restrictive boundaries around the nation, and presents a barrier to minoritised groups seeking to integrate into Scotland. While a birth criterion is not included in the most civic understanding of national membership through naturalisation, residence, participation, and affinity, it does allow entry to the nation for anyone whose parents were in Scotland at the time of their birth. If immigration policies do not discriminate, a birth criterion allows for diversity within the national membership, though only the Scottish-born children of migrants will be considered Scottish. However, as the YouGov poll on Scottish celebrities revealed, theoretical criteria for what makes someone Scottish are not always applied in real life (Smith 2016).

Kiely et al. (2005) asked Scottish nationals about whether migrants could become Scottish. The most common response was to deny that it is possible:

> Become Scots? I would say no, myself, but there are certain people I've met, from other countries, that they just seem to fall in love with Scotland and they've been here for quite a few years and they like to sort of think thersel as Scots and I wouldnae knock that . . . I would accept it to their face but I think deep down I would say to masel 'well he wants to be Scots, he loves it up here' and I wouldnae knock it but he'll never be Scots. (Kiely et al. 2005: 167)

Most of the respondents in their study understood their own identity and the identity of others as a matter of birth, and not affinity or residency. At the same time the quote suggests that migrant affinity to Scotland and claims to Scottishness may not be overtly challenged by native Scots, meaning that there might be no rejection, but social acceptance might never occur. There were other interview subjects from the same study who were much more open to conferring nationalism on those who love and contribute to Scotland:

> If they feel Scottish, who am I to tell them that they're not? Who am I to say 'no, no, you're no Scottish, you wernae born here . . . if this is your home and this is where you want to be, then why not? (Kiely et al. 2005: 168)

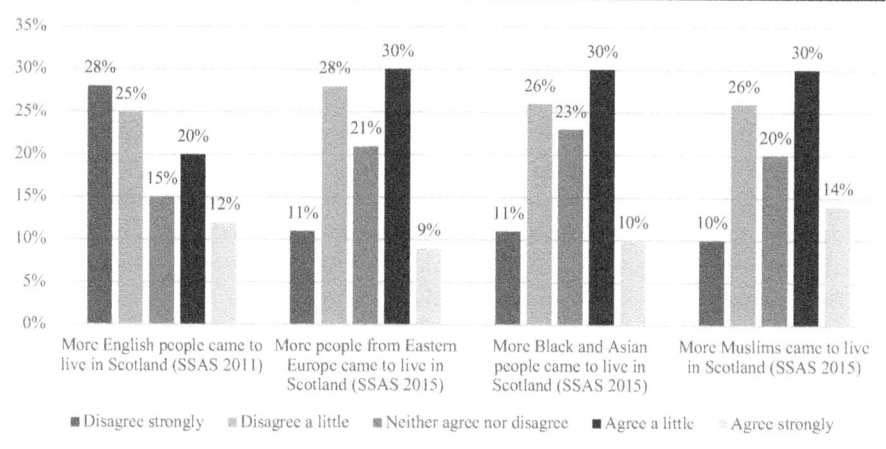

Figure 3.6 'Scotland would lose its identity if . . .'
Source: 2011 and 2015 Scottish Social Attitudes Surveys
(ScotCen Social Research 2013, 2017)

Figure 3.6 illustrates survey data suggesting a majority of people in Scotland believe Scotland's identity is tolerant of migrants, based on whether they perceive a threat to Scottish identity from a variety of migrant groups (English, Muslims, East Europeans, Black and Asian people). Though the data about the English migrants are drawn from an earlier survey and cannot be directly compared with the other frequencies with great confidence, survey respondents saw much less threat to Scottish identity from English migrants. One might expect people to differentiate between Muslims, East Europeans, and Black and Asian people since these groups activate different perceptions of religious, economic, and racial threat, but the distribution of responses looks remarkably similar. Scottish survey respondents believe Muslims represent the greatest threat to Scottish identity by a small margin, followed by East Europeans.

In a more direct question about identity attribution from the 2009 SSAS, 11% of Scottish respondents thought true Scottishness was restricted to white individuals. The question read 'I'd like you to think of a non-white person who you know was born and lives permanently in Scotland. This person says they are Scottish. Would you consider this person to be Scottish?' Of the 1,481 respondents, 3.7% reported that they would definitely not consider them to be Scottish, and another 7.9% said they probably would not consider them to be Scottish. Among those who accept minoritised Scots, individual acceptance could be watered down or challenged by what Scots believe other Scots think. Leith (2012) demonstrates that a large majority of Scottish survey respondents personally accept minoritised individuals as Scottish but believe only half of the Scottish population feels the same way, expressing a lack of confidence in a more expansive concept of Scottishness among the Scottish public.

Aggregate public opinion data conceal the way designations of Scottishness are reconfigured with reference to local experiences. For example, at the neighbourhood level in Glasgow, ethnic understandings of Scottishness are challenged through the everyday interactions between ethnically different residents. Virdee et al. (2006) describe the way residents in a neighbourhood in Glasgow reached an understanding about the racialised other through regular interactions with them in marketplaces and public transportation. They argue that this new understanding causes ethnic understandings of Scottishness to lose their persuasiveness and ability to cohere communities.

Despite the richness of these encounters, members of minoritised groups continue to face social exclusion in Scotland. Virdee and colleagues note that Muslims have been targeted by those who hold both ethnic and civic understandings of Scottishness. Exclusion on the basis of religion is discriminatory and conflicts with norms of multiculturalism, but many Scots may justify it with the belief that Islamic fundamentalism is at odds with Scotland's liberal civic nationalism. This conflict especially emerges with reference to the national identity of women who wear the Islamic headcovering:

> Whilst white respondents did not object to the practice of Islam, or even to Islam being compatible with Scottish national identity, they did object to the enforcement of beliefs, which the burqa and the hijab are deemed to represent. It was contended that values associated with fundamentalism such as the wearing of the burqa in particular, were incompatible with Scottishness. (Virdee et al. 2006: 8)

The distinction between religion and fundamentalism presumes that the average person can discern the degree of fundamentalism endorsed by an individual Muslim. People often confuse culture or religiosity with fundamentalism and will use cues of culture or religiosity, such as wearing the headscarf or beard length, to mark out a 'fundamentalist' Muslim who deserves exclusion. In reality, UK residents who wear headscarves or beards are unlikely to hold fundamentalist beliefs. A person's race or ethnicity may also cue religious identity, which triggers a chain of stereotypes linking phenotype to religion and religion to fundamentalist values, conjuring up a 'foreign Muslim' threat to Scottish society. Forms of exclusion, even when made with reference to civic values, challenge the development of a multicultural Scotland that will attract and welcome immigrants.

Ultimately, the openness of Scottish identity to minoritised groups is contingent on who is asked, what the group represents, and whether the members of the group embody important markers of Scottishness. Most Scots are theoretically open to a diverse conceptualisation of Scottishness, though some fixed markers of Scottishness persist (accent, birth in the territory) which make it difficult for first-generation immigrants to be included in the public vision of a Scottish person, regardless of the level of attachment that immigrant has to Scotland or the effort the migrant makes to integrate. Such a closed definition of identity certainly impacts levels of attachment to Scottishness, which could ultimately undermine the elite-led Scottish multicultural nation-building project.

NEW SCOTS

Up to this point, this chapter has focused on national identity from the perspective of the Scottish majority. This section considers the degree to which Scottish national identity is embraced amongst migrant and minoritised groups and the groups' experiences as they integrate into Scottish society. A migrant's enthusiasm about integrating into a nation hinges on what integration means, and what they must do to join the nation.

Most research on the national identities of minoritised groups in the UK focuses on state identities and the extent to which members of minoritised groups identify as British. Quantitative research has demonstrated a reluctance among minoritised individuals in England to identify as English, because they perceive Englishness to be an ethnic identity that cannot include a racially diverse population. Consequentially, they demonstrate a greater propensity to identify as British, which they understand to be a diversity-acceptant identity constructed out of a legacy of international empire (Bond 2017c). However, research on Britishness neglects variance in the national identities of members of minoritised groups at the sub-state level. Sub-state national comparisons are difficult to make because ethnically minoritised groups are often too weakly represented in survey data to support comparative analysis across nations.[8] Furthermore, Scottish nationalism and national identity has largely been developed with reference to England and Englishness, and has not historically included a discussion about linking Scottish civic nationalism to members of minoritised groups.

Researchers have uncovered a more inclusive character of Scottish nationalism in that Scottish-based members of minoritised groups are more likely to describe themselves as 'Scottish Muslim', 'Scottish Pakistani', or 'Scottish Asian' (Hussain and Miller 2006). Saeed et al. (1999) note a strong preference for dual ethnicity labels among Pakistani teenagers in Scotland as 59% of their survey sample used bi-cultural terms to describe themselves.[9] Meanwhile, England-based ethnically minoritised individuals will typically identify as British or with British hybridised identity, and not English. The 2011 census asked about national identities for the first time, which made it possible to compare sub-state national identity across ethnic groups and revealed that ethno-religious minorities are less likely to identify as English and more likely to identify as Scottish (Bond 2017b). However, just because members of minoritised groups are more likely to identify as Scottish than they are to identity as English does not mean that Scottishness is absolutely inclusive – just that it is more inclusive than Englishness. Henderson and colleagues examined the national identities of those born in Scotland, those born in the rest of the UK, and those born outside the UK, and they found that 'those born outside the UK are almost three times as likely to describe themselves as Scottish rather than British as those born in the rest of the UK. Those born in the UK are the only group to prioritise their sense of Britishness over other identities' (50% compared with 5.6% for those born in Scotland and 19% for those born outside the UK) (Henderson et al. 2018: 242). The comparative willingness of members of minoritised groups to identify with Scotland does not excuse instances of exclusion and racism faced by some minoritised groups within Scottish society. Clayton (2005) relays several anecdotes of exclusionary behaviour by Scots, including a few instances where Scottish-born minoritised individuals are told to go 'back home'. The automatic assumption that ethnic or racial otherness is perceived as being incompatible with being at home in Scotland demonstrates the presence of explicitly racist ethnic understandings of Scottishness.

What is the political meaning of these Scottish, British, and ethnic identities for minoritised groups within Scotland? There are many possible reasons for why immigrants might be less likely to support Scottish independence. They might feel a greater sense of attachment to the state that facilitated their immigration, or they may have less of a sense of regional grievance. If they are economic migrants, they may fear the implications of instability and economic risk that accompanies constitutional change. Many migrant groups come to Scotland with negative personal experiences of nationalistic politics in their home countries, and these experiences may explain why members of a minoritised group are less likely to support independence and are warier of devolution. Botterill and colleagues (2016) interviewed 382 young members of minoritised groups during the period of the independence referendum campaign, and they find that while they are proud of being Scottish, many young minoritised Scots planned to vote No in the independence referendum because they were concerned about increasing divisions within society, an experience that was sometimes informed by their own family's experiences with the division of India and Pakistan or the Soviet Union. For some members of the Scottish Jewish community, Scottish nationalist politics activate trepidation relating to their community's experiences with anti-Semitic nationalism in Europe (Sales 2014).[10] Sadiq Khan, the first British-Pakistani and Muslim mayor of London, tapped into these sentiments in his comments on Scottish nationalism: 'there is no difference between nationalists trying to divide Scottish and English people and those who try to divide us on the basis of our background, race, or religion' (Liinpää 2019). Khan was communicating innate suspicion of political nationalism, even when it is civically defined. These understandable fears of nationalism push members of minoritised groups towards Britishness, but in the devolved political climate where the Scottish identity is increasingly rarefied and salient and defined in part by cultural separation of the UK, members of minoritised groups who embrace Britishness may feel further alienated. However, recent political actions may have changed how these identities work. Jewish support for the SNP and independence appears to be growing in the post-Brexit environment, bolstered by Nicola Sturgeon's outreach to the Scottish Jewish community. Mark Gardner, the director of communications at the Community Security Trust, a watchdog group on anti-Semitism, said 'clearly, the Scottish leadership have realised that the anti-Semitism issue is a litmus test of sorts for Scottish society and we are seeing serious efforts to address the community's concerns' (Liphshiz 2016). A poll by Asian radio station Awaz FM suggested that almost two-thirds of Asians in Scotland would vote in favour of independence (Elgot 2014).[11] Contrasted with the anecdotal evidence suggesting a greater hesitancy to support independence on the part of other groups, Asian preference for independence implies that the degree to which an ethnic or religious group endorses Scottishness and nationalism may vary depending on the group's experiences within Scotland and within their home countries.

It is difficult to make direct associations between the national identities of minoritised groups and political preferences because of the limited data available. Henderson and colleagues (2018) made a substantial contribution with three waves of the Scottish Referendum Study, which included asked questions about levels of engagement, satisfaction with the referendum campaign process, and constitutional preferences, and allowed for comparisons across place of birth. They found that those born outside the UK were much less likely to be involved in the referendum campaign than those of Scottish birth, and comparisons with those born in the rest of the UK differed by the type of engagement. Similar patterns emerged with measures of satisfaction with the referendum process. When it comes to support for independence, those born in Scotland were most likely to support Yes (53%), while those born outside the UK were more likely to support the status quo (57% No), but the biggest gap between Yes and No supporters was among those born in the rest of the UK (72% No). In support for independence and in attitudes towards Yes and No arguments, those born outside the UK occupy the space somewhere between the Scottish-born and those born elsewhere in the UK, leading Henderson et al. to conclude that 'we can distinguish, therefore, not between Scottish-born and migrants, but between a polarized vision of politics held by those in different parts of the UK and the middle ground views of those from outside the UK' (2018: 246).[12]

Immigrant groups from outside the UK are quite small in Scotland, making up just 4% of the population all together, but the small size of the minoritised populations does not stop political actors from seeking to mobilise them. The SNP is very enthusiastic about highlighting the ethnic inclusivity of the independence campaign and Scottishness more generally, 'both to disprove charges of ethnic exclusion and to build internal consensus' (Kymlicka 2011: 294). The party regularly mentions the Scots Asians for Independence as an important symbolic political partner that achieves the dual objectives of demonstrating the diversity of its constituency and building support for its cause.

Compared with racism and ethnic inequality, sectarianism and the extent to which a Catholic–Protestant divide continues to reflect inequalities in Scotland has received substantial attention from Scottish journalists, politicians, and academics (Raab and Holligan 2012; Law 2018). While younger generations of Catholics and Protestants are experiencing socio-economic equality, there are still signs of disadvantage among older Catholics in Scotland, and some spaces in Scotland where the residual culture of Protestant privilege is recognised and experienced by Scottish Catholics (Slaven 2018). Persistent conflicts around religion within Scotland reflect the identities differentiating in-group from out-group within an ethnically homogenous population. The salience of religious identity is a product of historical conflicts over the Reformation and Irish migration, and ongoing nationalist/religious conflicts in Northern Ireland. Though sectarian conflict is often described as a feature of Scotland's history, Catholics, who make up about 16% of the population, are still the victims of over half of faith-related crime in Scotland (Scottish Government 2018e). An example of the continued relevance of these identities is the ongoing conflict over Orange marches (parades organised by Orange Orders, which are Protestant fraternal orders committed to defending Protestantism and Unionism) in Glasgow. In 2018, a priest was verbally attacked and spat on as the parade passed his church. In response, the Archdiocese of Glasgow used its Facebook page to criticise the event and to ask, 'What kind of society is it that allows ministers of religion and churchgoers to be intimidated and attacked by a group which has a long history of fomenting fear and anxiety on city streets?', thereby blaming bigoted actions on society's tolerance of xenophobia, and raising questions about the inclusiveness of Scottish culture (Record Reporter 2018).

Protestantism is incorporated into ideas of Scottish identity, but Catholic versus Protestant sectarian arguments do not graft neatly on to Scottish nationalism because both religious identities are exterior to Scotland with links to British Unionism and anti-Catholic colonial history in Northern Ireland:

> Sectarianism is the product of the relationship between groups whose exteriority with respect to Scotland reflects an ambivalence between their extra-Scottish origins and loyalties (strong determinants of their identity) and their desire to integrate within Scottish society. There is no

doubt that Protestants feel very much a part of Scottish society, not least because their construction of Scottish-ness is usually Unionist, and able to accommodate their sense of belonging to Britain. However, the same cannot be said for Catholics. (Clayton 2005: 110–11)

Protestants feel a sense of cultural privilege that attaches them to Scotland, but Protestant privilege is not unique to Scotland, which weakens it as a Scottish identity marker. Meanwhile, links between Protestantism and Unionism could explain why the SNP was able to attract sizable Catholic support for the 2014 independence referendum, which suggests Catholics may envision a brighter future for themselves in an independent Scotland, compared with the Protestants who might feel more of an affinity for the Union.

Experiences of sectarianism in Scotland do not translate to the experiences of other minoritised groups, but continued sectarian conflict over more than a century exhibits the potential for persistent identity-based conflict in Scotland. As Scottish society diversifies, the religious identity conflict may expand to involve minoritised religious groups, like Muslims.[13] Even though some identity groups are privileged, discussions of Scottish nationalism do not usually involve identity conflicts. The separation of identity politics and Scottish nationalism presents an opportunity for a multicultural understanding of Scottish national identity, even if lived realities of minoritised groups do not always reflect those understandings.

Conclusion

The campaign for Scottish civic nationalism is elite-driven, and only partially supported by the Scottish public. The civic marker of being born in Scotland is the most widely accepted standard for Scottishness. Though birth in Scotland is culturally neutral, it is a fixed marker that excludes first-generation immigrants from joining the nation. Meanwhile, ethnic nationalist sentiment persists, as evidenced by the continued emphasis on Scottish ancestry as an entitlement to Scottishness. Expressions of civic and ethnic nationalism can be promoted by the same individual, demonstrating that the dichotomous constructions of civic and ethnic nationalism are ideal types and are never found in real-world nations or individual national identity.

The amalgamation of ethnic and civic characteristics of Scottish identity means minoritised groups within Scotland have mixed experiences. Elite rhetoric presents Scotland as welcoming, and that effort is acknowledged by many minoritised groups. However, words are not always matched with decisive action. Scottish leaders have been criticised for hiding behind Scotland's civic identity and being very slow to acknowledge instances of systemic racism (Davidson and Virdee 2018). As Labour MSP Anas Sarwar, chair of the Cross-Party Group on Tackling Islamophobia, said, 'Scotland is an open and diverse country, but we should never allow our national pride to blind us to the fact that good and bad people live everywhere' (University of Glasgow 2018). Implying that the 'bad people' are responsible for racism in Scotland is a bit disingenuous, as there are examples of systemic racism and widely held discriminatory beliefs in Scotland. The survey data considered in this chapter indicate racial preferences in terms of those whom Scots would be willing to consider Scottish, and Scots are almost evenly split about whether they believe that immigrants present a threat or benefit to Scottish identity. To live up to its own rhetoric of civic nationalism, the Scottish government and society must tackle issues of formal and informal racism and discrimination, discussed at greater length in Chapter 5.

The most significant national identity conflicts in Scotland have been with Ireland and England. As a result, issues of race as they are understood within the modern context have not entered the Scottish conversation about nationalism. Nowadays, instances of Irish/Catholic discrimination are labelled as sectarian rather than racist, and minority and race politics in Scotland were not widely interrogated until recently.[14] The lack of self-reflection impacts the prospects of a multicultural Scotland, where persistent anti-English and sectarian divisions hint at an ideological framework that could be reactivated by the enhanced presence of foreign 'others'. The activation of xenophobic expressions of nationalism would contradict official rhetoric labelling Scotland as a more tolerant country than its neighbours and could compromise the notion of Scottish exceptionalism that undergirds the prospect of independence.

Notes

1. Civic nationalism defines attachment to a nation through civic participation, while ethnic nationalism defines individual links to the nation with 'primordial ties', including biological characteristics like race and ancestry, but it also can include cultural characteristics like language, religion, and clothing, as these things connote cultural continuity and privilege.
2. Different identity claims are prevalent within specific groups. Bechhofer and colleagues (1999) find ancestry is a stronger marker of national identity among the landed and cultural elite, though other markers of birth, upbringing, accent, residence, and commitment to the nation were also mentioned by their research participants.
3. The low levels of Scottish identity attribution based on a grandparent's nationality contrasts with the Scottish government's suggestion that upon independence, those with a parent or grandparent who is eligible for Scottish citizenship could themselves apply for Scottish citizenship (Scottish Government 2013b).
4. The definition of cultural identity in this question is benign compared with more ethicised versions of cultural identity. Defining culture with reference to cultural artefacts like music, literature, and landscape is open to wide participation and appreciation, and therefore can be much more compatible with civic understandings of Scottishness than an understanding of Scottishness based on cultural purity, for example. The meaning of 'how the country is governed' is vague. As a result, the respondent to the question could activate ideas about territorial politics, devo-

lution, the Scottish Parliament, the current political leadership in Scotland or the UK, or the political culture. The ambiguous nature of 'governance' could explain why a relatively small proportion of respondents selected governance as part of their definition of Scottishness.
5. This conflation has been challenged by survey data and recent political developments. Consistent numbers of people still identify as British, but the number of people who prioritise British identity relative to the other identities has declined (Heath et al. 2007). This coincides with a political effort to assert English identity (Kenny 2016). In the 2010s, there was an emergence of the 'English question' in reaction to parliamentary devolution to Scotland and Wales, with calls for an English Parliament, and English votes for English laws in the House of Commons.
6. There is a link between English nationalism and Euroscepticism, while those who felt more British than English were the most positive in their attitudes about the EU (Henderson et al. 2016).
7. The two indicators of identity are very weakly correlated in a negative direction (r=-0.08, p=0.01). The negative relationship could be interpreted as supporting the idea that these identities are competing and oppositional, but the weakness of the relationship indicates that the identities sometimes compete and sometimes complement each other in the minds of Scots.
8. For example, the 2010 Ethnic Minority British Election Study sampled 2,787 ethnic minorities across Britain, and only 39 lived in Scotland. The 2015 SSAS likewise included only 38 minoritised respondents (Barclay et al. 2019).
9. Hybridised identities are difficult to negotiate for many members of minoritised groups. Second-generation immigrants report particular struggles, because they feel they are denied an authentic experience of both cultures making up their identities (Clayton 2005). Saeed et al. noted their interview subjects' preference for their Muslim identity, and they suggest that the white British majority 'will have to work harder at accepting an Islamic element as a legitimate component of Scottish or English identity' (1999: 841).
10. Scottish Jews also tend to be strongly unionist due to their ties with the Labour Party and concerns about the SNP's position on Israel.
11. Scottish Asian is a term defined within the 2011 Scottish Census as including people of Bangladeshi, Indian, Pakistani, or other Asian ancestry resident in Scotland.
12. Henderson et al. constructed a demographic model of independence vote choice, and found 'once we control for the fact that people who are born in different places hold different views, then place of birth ceases to exert an independent influence on vote choice' (2018: 246).
13. Muslims make up roughly 1.5% of the Scottish population, yet were victims of 18% of the instances of reported religiously aggravated offending (Scottish Government 2018e).
14. The publication of the edited volume *No Problem Here: Understanding Racism in Scotland* in 2018 (Davidson et al. 2018) attracted widespread attention as a response to public rhetoric of civic nationalism that neglects the lived realities of racism and Islamophobia in Scotland.

4

THE PROMISE: THE BENEFITS OF IMMIGRATION FOR SCOTLAND

The central UK state has the constitutional power to protect borders and regulate the economy, both of which involve controlling migration. Scotland has not possessed these powers at any point in the modern industrialised era and has always been dependent on the broader British or European economic and political environment. Representatives of the UK government have used mutual dependency as an argument against independent Scottish policy on immigration, claiming such a policy would create social and economic boundaries between the populations of England and Scotland. With Brexit distancing Scotland from Europe alongside Westminster's commitment to reducing international immigration, growing numbers of Scots believe more power should be delegated to the Scottish government, especially where the interests of Scotland diverge from those of England. This chapter describes why immigration is promised to be a solution to economic difficulties that compromise Scotland's status as a nation. Three key areas in which Scottish and UK interests differ and where immigration is presented as a benefit to Scottish interests are population growth, economic growth and employment, and support for social services.

Population Growth

Steady population growth is understood to be a prerequisite for future prosperity. A growing population corresponds with a growing economy, and in the modern welfare state, citizens look to population growth for assurances that there will be a working population of sufficient size to support future dependents. Most European countries are experiencing natural population decline – birth rates are at an all-time low while average lifespan is longer than ever before.[1] Because of immigration, the UK has experienced population growth above the European average, but growth has not been evenly distributed. Rural areas in the UK, like 95% of Scotland's landmass, are experiencing dramatic population decline.

Extensive emigration in the post-war period shrank the Scottish population. Even as emigration slowed in the 1970s, the population continued to decline from a peak of 5.25 million in 1974 to 5.06 million in 2002 (National Records of Scotland 2019). Concerns about the demographic situation in Scotland climaxed with the publication of the 2001 census, which reported Scotland's population at its lowest level since World War II. The accompanying report attributed the decline to emigration, weak immigration, and falling fertility rates. The Scottish population was also ageing while life expectancy was increasing – the number of Scots aged over 65 outnumbered those under 15 for the first time in 2011.[2] Forecasters predicted the population of the UK would continue to grow (though at a lower rate than all the other the EU-15 countries except Germany), but the population in Scotland was expected to fall to 4.5 million by 2050. The Scottish government had set 5 million as the symbolic population size required for Scotland's sustainability, and the predictions provoked a 'population crisis'.

Jack McConnell, the Labour politician who became first minister of Scotland in 2001, identified population growth as the single biggest challenge facing Scottish policy makers. He confronted the change by encouraging the immigration of 'new Scots' while discouraging emigration. He explicitly described immigration as being in the Scottish national interest and, in doing so, struck a balance between nationalistic and multicultural claims. In his legislative speech at the opening of the Scottish Parliament in 2004, McConnell outlined his agenda and introduced the Fresh Talent Initiative:

> Five years ago, the decline of Scotland's population was considered inevitable. Government was planning for it, not reversing it. But now – in a world where some think that movements of people are a threat, Scotland is bold enough to say that it is in our national interest – in every way – to welcome fresh talent alongside the development of our home-grown talent. Fresh Talent is more than just growing our population. It is about our ambitions. That Scotland will be the best place in Europe to live and work. And we will be the most welcoming place too. We will welcome all those who want to make their lives in Scotland. We value their contribution and we welcome students from overseas, seasonal workers, professionals – and we welcome those fleeing persecution from unstable states too. (BBC News 2004)

McConnell linked an expansive immigration policy including many different forms of migration (students, temporary workers, high-skilled migrants, and refugees) to population growth, which he associated with economic growth. The explicit connections between economic growth, population growth, and immigration are striking when compared with rhetoric in England that attributes economic benefits only to highly skilled migrants. While describing the Johnson government's plan to restrict low-skilled migrants from entering the UK, Secretary of State Priti Patel said the new system would 'attract the brightest and the best from around the globe [those with a job offer with a minimum salary threshold of £25,600], boosting the economy and our communities, and unleash this country's full potential' (Castle 2020). In contrast, McConnell explicitly included low-skilled migrants and refugees in his vision of Scotland's future population. His inclusive stance emphasised his view that when population growth is the objective, the quantity of people entering matters more than the quality of the individual immigrant's skill set or net economic contribution. While the macroeconomic impact of high-skilled immigrants might be more immediately felt, economic benefits associated with sheer numbers of immigrants will manifest in the future.

As illustrated by the index of Scotland's and England's population size in Figure 4.1, the Scottish population started to recover right after the 2001 census. The biggest jump occurred after 2004, as citizens from the ten new EU member states took advantage of the UK's decision not to restrict labour market access.[3] The public tone about demographic decline shifted after the 2011 census, which registered 5.30 million people living in Scotland, representing a 5% increase since the 2001 census, the fastest population growth rate in a century. The growth was almost entirely (86%) attributed to immigration, and especially EU migration (50%) (Hudson and Aiton 2016). After the publication of the 2011 census, Scottish Cabinet Secretary for Culture, Tourism and External Affairs Fiona Hyslop said that the potential for more growth represented a 'historic moment' for Scotland:

> A decade and more of devolution has delivered a growing and record high population. That is not simply a sign of the dynamic, attractive nation we are building. It is also a key factor in delivering economic growth in future years. (Carrell 2012)

The positive trend prompted the Scottish government to enact an official Population Growth Target to match Scotland's population growth to that of the EU-15 member states from 2007 to 2017. The strategy focused on developing comparative advantage and attracting and retaining migrants (Scottish Government 2016b). Though it is risky to make future projections of population growth based on immigration because return migration is always possible and even likely, especially for EU migrants, the growth

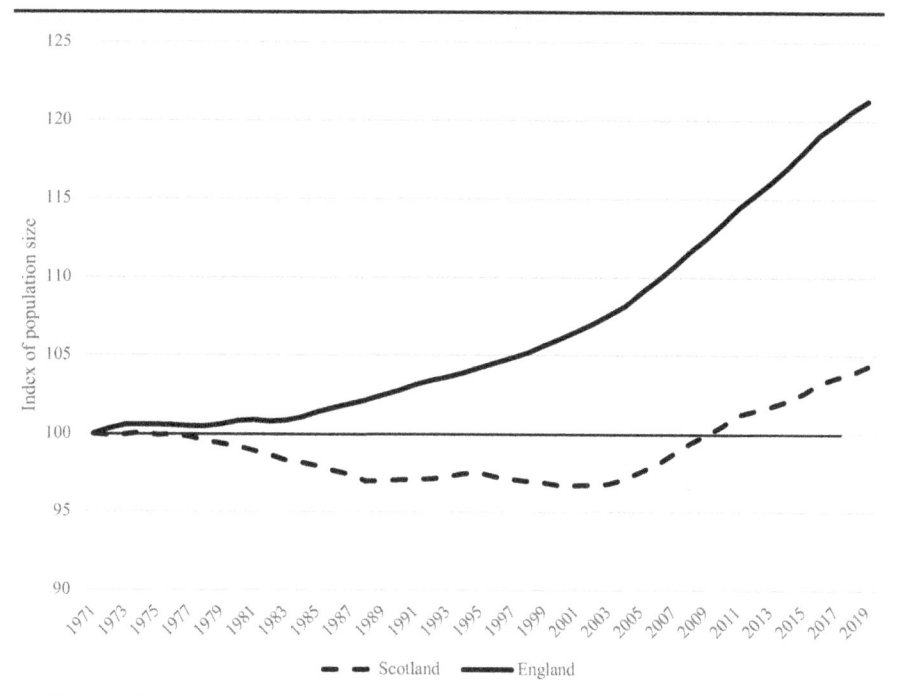

Figure 4.1 Population size of England and Scotland, 1971–2019 (1971=100). *Source:* Office for National Statistics 2018; National Records of Scotland 2018a

has continued.[4] Meanwhile, natural change (births minus deaths) has not contributed to population growth, as the number of deaths exceeds births in Scotland. Scotland is wholly reliant on continued migration for population growth.

Population growth is not experienced evenly across Scotland. The urban centres of the Central Belt and the sparsely populated Highlands and Islands have very different experiences with demographic change.[5] In 2018, two-thirds of Scotland's 21 councils reported population increase over the previous ten years, but a third reported further decline, including many islands off the west coast of Scotland.[6] For example, the population of the Outer Hebrides, a chain of interconnected islands off the west coast of mainland Scotland, is predicted to experience population decline of nearly 14% by 2039, the steepest decline of any Scottish region. The working-age population in Scotland's rural areas is projected to fall by a third by 2046 (Copus 2018). The Scottish Executive promotes migration as a critical part of the effort to sustain and repopulate rural areas of Scotland, especially since some of these areas are home to industrial sectors that are heavily reliant on migrant labour, such as tourism, hospitality, agriculture, and food processing. Immigrant preference for cities conflicts with the wishes of the government, as immigrants are even more likely than native

Scots to live in urban centres, which house 94% of the EU nationals living in Scotland (Hudson and Aiton 2016).

That population growth since 2001 is entirely attributable to immigration leads Scottish decision makers to conflate the issues of demography and immigration. The Scottish population is vulnerable to the growing political push in Westminster to restrict migration, and Brexit complicated the issue. The Scottish government knows that if European migration to the UK is reduced with the suspension of free movement, Scotland's population size will shrink. There will be knock-on effects of fewer working-age adults to contribute to the pensions and services required by the ageing native Scottish population. Such effects were foreshadowed immediately after the Brexit vote, with a reduction in net migration from 31,700 people in 2016 down to 23,900 in 2018. Scottish leaders are worried that their experience with population growth over the last 20 years will be reversed by the politics of Westminster, and are incentivised to advocate for national control of migration to maintain positive demographic trends and their hope for future prosperity.

The Economy

The UK economy provides a useful benchmark for evaluating sub-state economic performance, and discussions about the health of the Scottish economy almost always occur with reference to England. Where divergence exists, the comparisons can be politically useful for nationalists seeking justifications for independence. Grievance-based arguments, describing Scotland's past exploitation by the UK, became very popular in the 1970s when Scotland's economic past was analysed using systemic frameworks like Wallerstein's world systems theory, which divides the international system into an industrialised economic core and a dependent periphery. Debates about whether Scotland (or at least the Highlands) could be theorised as the periphery in its underdevelopment interested political economists, and the political culture was receptive to the idea that Scotland was externally controlled by, and perhaps even a colony of, England. The latter argument was made by Michael Hechter in 1975. He claimed that the situation of the Celtic fringe in the British Isles was analogous to that of less developed countries, and that Ireland, Scotland, and Wales were economically suppressed by and made dependent on England. Such accounts ignore the reality that Scotland, along with Britain, made the earliest transition to industrial capitalism in the world. 'What cannot be denied, however, is the powerful imagery which "dependency" and "colonialism" brought to academic study as well as political practice' (McCrone 1992: 62). Language of colonialism is still symbolically and politically useful for scapegoating Scotland's difficulties and sets up a Scotland–England contrast.

Scotland was an industrial powerhouse and leader in manufacturing at the beginning of the industrial revolution. It has a strong legacy of producing diversified goods and services, ranging from textiles and jet engines to whisky and shortbread. Manufacturing has declined, and today the service sector is the largest sector in the Scottish economy. In terms of absolute and per capita GDP and controlling for size, Scotland falls in the top third of European countries, in the neighbourhood of Finland, Denmark, and Ireland. However, aggregate statistics mask difficult economic conditions tied to market fluctuations. The 2008 recession had negative effects on Scotland's economy, and its post-recession growth rate lagged behind that of the UK and most EU countries. Economic challenges returned in 2016 with the downturn of the oil and gas sector. Today the Scottish economy is, in the words of the Scottish Fiscal Commission (2018), 'subdued', with growth under 1% and real wages below what they were a decade ago. About 20% of Scots live in regions where GDP per capita is below €20,000. Derek McKay, Scotland's finance secretary, credited the UK government with Scotland's economic woes, blaming spending cuts, curbed immigration, and Brexit for undermining the Scottish economy. McKay told the Scottish Parliament that if Scotland experienced population growth commensurate to England's, Scottish economic growth would mirror the UK's. He advocated for Scottish control over its immigration to grow the population and make Scotland more economically competitive (Dickie 2018). This section describes how immigration provides needed skills and has a neutral effect on native worker employment and wages, and how immigrants contribute to the economy through taxation.

Immigrant Labour

Scotland's population is growing, but it is experiencing a relative decline in the size of the working-age population. Migration continues to be the best immediate solution to a dwindling workforce, as the vast majority of migrants are of working age.[7] As explained by demographer Robert Wright (2017), 'whether we like it or not, our future prosperity is dependent on our ability to attract foreign-born workers to substitute for the native-born workers who were never born'. An effective migration management strategy must ensure that the nation can attract and retain migrants by matching up skills and jobs. The UK-wide points-based system was designed to allocate points to migrants based on their skills in relation to the needs of the UK labour market. However, points are distributed with reference to the UK labour market as a whole and are not sensitive to the particularity of regional skills gaps or labour conditions (de Lima and Wright 2009). Scottish visa proposals call for the distribution of extra points to migrants who commit to settle in Scotland, since Scotland can absorb more workers: Scotland's unemployment rates are lower than in the rest of the UK, and migrant groups in Scotland have an employment rate of nearly 78%, 5% higher than the Scottish average.[8] Among migrants from the EU ascension countries the rate is nearly 85%.

Migrants are more successful than native-born Scots at finding work because migrants move in response to skills shortages or job opportunities that are not appealing to native-born Scots. Six per cent of employers in Scotland reported skills shortage vacancies in 2015, up from 3% in 2011, and the proportion of vacancies that were hard to fill grew from 15% to 24% (Skills Development Scotland 2017).[9] The Scottish government observed the ways migrants meet sectoral demand:

> Migrants, particularly recent EEA migrants, tend to be concentrated in hospitality and catering; in agriculture; and in food processing sectors. In general, migrants meet demand for low-skilled labour, and address sector-specific skills shortages at the higher end of the labour market. In addition, migrants act as a flexible supply of labour when demand exceeds local labour supply. However, in sectors such as agriculture, where employers find it difficult to source labour regardless of prevailing economic conditions, demand for seasonal migrant labour remains more constant. (Scottish Government 2016b)

This statement signals a critical distinction between high-skilled and low-skilled migration and their respective benefits to the Scottish economy.

Highly skilled migrants

High-skilled migration, or migration of the 'creative class', is an important route to economic growth and productivity in the modern knowledge economy. Scotland experiences some skills shortages in critical industries, like manufacturing, and 'STEM skills are particularly difficult to obtain for employers' (Scottish Government 2019b: 31). A representative for Scotland IS, a trade body for the digital technologies industry, explained:

> We have had, for very many years, a falling workforce because so many of our young people go elsewhere to work. So, back filling our own workforce with people from overseas has been a trend for quite a long time and is hugely valuable to the economy. (Personal interview 14 June 2016)

The Fresh Talent post-study work visa gave international graduates from Scottish universities permission to stay in Scotland based on the assumption that university graduates are the most productive and talented workers. As a Labour MSP explained:

> The most valuable inward migration is of the most skilled and best qualified people, so as a focus that allows you to enable more of the best qualified and most skilled people to settle here, or at least come and work here for a period and decide whether they want to settle here, focusing on

people who have already made the choice to come here to study has an obvious advantage. (Personal interview 27 June 2016)

Recruiting students will not fill all of the shortages in the economy, however. As the Scotland IS representative explained:

> we have a skill shortage where we need around eleven thousand new people coming into our industry every year. We think we get about, somewhere between four and five thousand from college, universities, and career changes. So, we've got a shortage of about five thousand people. And we currently have a hugely growing start-up community in technology, particularly in Edinburgh. So, we've got an industry that's in growth mode, and we have a skill shortage. (Personal interview 14 June 2016)

Proactive immigrant recruitment strategies are more likely to fill shortages in growth industries like digital technology.

Long-term self-employment and entrepreneurial activity were predicted to be the main economic benefits of the post-study work visa (Houston et al. 2008). Entrepreneurship and creativity are critical for economic growth, and immigration is associated with higher levels of both. Having more immigrants in a locality enhances entrepreneurship, and an increase in ethnic diversity within a community at first decreases but then ultimately increases the likelihood of start-up activity (Mickiewicz et al. 2017). The effect is attributable to the propensity of immigrants to be 'self-selected risk takers by virtue of their willingness to leave their homeland to make their way in a foreign country' (Parker 2009: 176). Immigrants are more risk-acceptant and are more confident in their skills, compared with UK life-long residents (Levie 2007). Immigrants also recognise a wider range of economic opportunities in their new country because their diverse experiences and thought patterns lead to innovation, risk-taking, experimentation, and creativity (Cruz et al. 2014). Immigrants combine pre-existing knowledge from their home countries with the knowledge they gain in the host country to come up with innovative business ideas.

Everyone in the community benefits from immigrant entrepreneurship. Those who meet immigrants access new knowledge and experiences, which they can combine with their existing knowledge to identify and act on opportunities. The Scottish government highlights this impact in Scottish institutions of higher learning, claiming that diverse perspectives brought by migrants enrich the learning experience for everyone and help native-born Scots to become more productive. Community diversity does not automatically lead to entrepreneurship, however. A community must lower communication barriers, so that knowledge or information can travel, and social capital can be developed (Efendic et al. 2015).[10]

Migrants in low-skilled jobs

A large proportion of migrants in Scotland (30% of European migrants) are working in low-skilled jobs, doing the work that native-born workers avoid (Hudson and Aiton 2016). The work is vital for the Scottish economy, though it is often overlooked in policy discussions. The Fresh Talent Initiative was criticised because the post-study work visa applied to a select group of high-status student migrants and left other groups untouched, including migrants already in the country and EU migrants in low-skilled jobs, many of whom live in the rural areas of Scotland that are most in need of a population injection (Williams and de Lima 2006). Workers from the EU accession states make up 7% of the UK's agricultural workforce, significantly more than in most other industrial sectors (Gilpin et al. 2006: 20). EU nationals and especially those from the EU accession states make up 12% of those employed in the UK's accommodation and food services. Unfortunately for the migrants, many of these jobs are associated with low pay, limited possibilities for advancement, and risk of exploitation (de Lima and Wright 2009). Migrants working these jobs are often underemployed. EU migrants are more likely than native Scots to hold degree-level qualifications, but nearly a quarter of those with degrees are working in unskilled occupations, far outpacing the 3% of Scots who are in a similar situation.

Employer attitudes about migrant workers

Employers express positive attitudes about migration, and often favour migrants for their positive work ethic, reliability, and flexibility (de Lima and Wright 2009). In the summer of 2013, over 700 employers across Scotland were asked, 'How important are visa and immigration issues to your business?' Those sectors that scored above the sample average include health and social care, hospitality and tourism, construction, retail, property, agriculture, wholesale, and transport and storage (Tindal et al. 2014). High-value sectors in the Scottish economy with employers that did not identify immigration as vitally important, but which are nonetheless important for how attractive the economy is to migrants, include finance and insurance, oil and gas, and higher education.

The consensus of the Scottish government, employers, and academics is that migrants, and especially EU migrants, already contribute to the Scottish economy in important ways. A wide range of business sectors and public services in Scotland rely on migrant workers to meet their skill and labour needs. Brexit animated discussions about those areas of the Scottish economy that rely on EU migration for low-skilled labour, like social care, agriculture, food processing, construction, and hospitality (Hudson and Aiton 2016). Employers fear that without the free market, they will lose access to a critical source of labour and skills, especially since the Johnson government aims to end Britain's reliance on low-skilled workers with its points-based immigration policy. A Migration Advisory Committee report in January 2020 estimated that around 70% of EU workers would not qualify under the new rules (Migration Advisory Committee 2020). Following the Brexit referendum, there were signs of labour shortages as early as 2017. Agricultural sectors, like in the soft fruits sector, could not employ enough pickers, and fruit rotted in the fields.[11] Scotland's fruit farms have traditionally depended on seasonal workers from Central and East Europe, and the current labour shortage of about 10–20% is predicted to grow substantially worse. A survey of workers in 2018 suggested that only 40% of workers were sure they would return (BBC News 2018a).[12] Across the UK, the health industry is predicting serious shortages, as high numbers of nurses and care workers have left the UK since 2016 (Scottish Government 2018a).

Given the heavy reliance on migration in sectors that are of particular importance to the Scottish economy and tied to Scotland's geography and natural resources, many Scottish elites frame Scotland's economic reliance on migration as critical. Chris Murray of the Institute for Public Policy Research demonstrated that business sectors employing high numbers of migrant workers represented a bigger proportion of the Scottish economy than they do in the English economy, and argued that changes to migration flows would have a greater impact on Scotland than on the rest of the UK (Scottish Affairs Committee 2018). Scottish nationalists in the SNP argue the most appropriate solution would be autonomous Scottish control over immigration policy, where Scottish decision makers could determine their own policies. Others suggest that some version of the Scottish green card within the UK system would also meet employer concerns and could also be applied to struggling regions in England as well. In either case, the political consensus in Scotland is that a sensible immigration policy should be sensitive and responsive to Scotland's economic and demographic situation.

The impact of immigration on Scottish workers

If it is managed properly, migration is conducive to the aggregate economic welfare of a country (Giordani and Ruta 2011). It contributes to growth by raising the supply potential of the economy, filling skills shortages, and increasing domestic productivity (Longhi et al. 2005). That said, macroeconomic figures do not address the economic experiences of individuals. A failure to consider how immigration affects the average Scottish worker could undermine a national or state-level effort to promote open immigration policies, especially if workers experience losses they blame on the presence of migrants.

The average person who makes negative assumptions about the economic impact of migration is not thinking about long-term macroeconomic conditions. They are worried about the immediate effects of immigration on native employment and wages.[13] They also form opinions about people entering the country, and forget to account for emigration. Immigration is assumed to continually increase the local population, pushing host communities close to their carrying capacity. The supply of labour is assumed to perpetually grow, and immigrants are seen as competitors for jobs and resources. Because immigrants come to a new country in search of opportunities they would not have at home, they might settle for lower wages than the native worker would. Then, the story goes, access to cheaper labour suppresses wages for everyone, even as GDP grows.

These assumptions are contradicted by data, which provide very little evidence that immigrants have a negative impact on native labour market outcomes like wages or unemployment. The absence of an effect is related to the size of migrant flows. In a study of migration from the newly admitted EU-10 to the older EU-15 member states, the European Commission concluded that the migration was not large enough to affect the general EU labour market (European Commission 2006).[14] Minimal or insignificant negative wage effects of migration are found in research on European states, including the UK (Friedberg and Hunt 1995; Heinz and Ward-Warmedinger 2006; International Organization for Migration 2005; Longhi et al. 2005; Zorlu and Hartog 2005). Research focusing on the UK also provides little evidence of adverse outcomes on overall native wages, employment, or unemployment (Blanchflower et al. 2007; Dustmann et al. 2005, 2013; Lemos and Portes 2008; Lucchino et al. 2012).[15] The UK government's Migration Advisory Committee conducted an extensive analysis of the association between immigration and native employment between 1975 and 2010 and found no systemic correlation between overall immigration and native employment (Migration Advisory Committee 2012). It found a negative relationship between immigration and employment during economic downturns, but when the analysis was limited to EU migration there was no relationship during any time period. Migration does not suppress overall wages because migrants and UK workers are imperfect substitutes, meaning that they are more likely to have complementary, rather than competing, skill sets (Manacorda et al. 2012).

The economic effects of immigration at the individual level may vary by wage group or region, particularly since migrants have a propensity to settle in urban centres and because the economies of certain regions (like the Highlands) are increasingly reliant on migrant labour (Green et al. 2008). International migration might also impact movement within the UK, thereby displacing the economic impact of international migration to other regions within the country.[16] Pouliakas and his co-authors (2014) investigated regional responses to migration with a simulated model of the effects of immigration on remote European regions, including Scotland. They found that free movement of labour could have significant positive short-term consequences for the GDP levels of the regions – a 10% increase in total labour supply in Scotland should correspond with a 5.62% increase in GDP. Because GDP does not automatically translate to quality of life, they looked at the impact of labour supply on living standards and found modest positive effects, though they predict skilled and unskilled labour migration might suppress wages in the remote areas (9–12%), because their economies are smaller and less diversified. In sum, there is little evidence that migration has reduced wages or employment opportunities for resident workers overall, but effects will vary based on the diversification of the local economy.

Public Finances

British citizens are very concerned about whether immigrants contribute enough to the tax and welfare systems, and policy makers respond by restricting immigrant access to social benefits, such as when the Labour government under Tony Blair coupled openness to labour migration from the new EU member states with restricted immigrant access to the welfare system until the migrant had been employed in the UK for a year. David Cameron placed similar restrictions on migrants from Romania and Bulgaria. Public service providers must adapt to a changing population, but the question for the system's sustainability is whether those who need services pay for them through taxation. Immigrants residing in the UK have been less likely than UK-born individuals to receive state benefits or tax credits and are also less likely to live in social housing (Dustmann and Frattini 2014). Meanwhile, immigrants from the European Economic Area (EEA) made positive fiscal contributions even during economic downturns. Under free movement, European migrants move to work, and if the conditions for work are not favourable, many choose to return to their home countries rather than draw on UK benefits (Blanchflower et al. 2007). Most EU migrants do not bring their families with them, which minimises their impact on education and health services.[17] Immigrants from outside the EEA have historically had a fiscal effect similar to the native born, which is a negative net contribution.[18] However, all immigrants who arrived in the UK in 2016 were predicted to reduce the fiscal burden for native workers, with immigrants paying £27 billion more than they took out in the form of services or transfers over the entirety of their stay (Oxford Economics 2018). This effect is partly because of the younger age profile of the migrants (only 4% of EU nationals living in Scotland are over 65, compared with 18% of the native population), though the positive fiscal effect persists across comparable age, education, and labour market cohorts (Scottish Government 2017). Immigrants also share the costs of fixed expenditures with the native population (those expenses that cost the same regardless of use, like infrastructure, transportation, and schools).

Immigrants are also net contributors to the Scottish economy. Scottish government analysts found that the average EU citizen in Scotland adds £10,400 to revenue and £35,400 to GDP each year (Scottish Government 2018f). If the Conservative UK government's pledge to reduce migration is fulfilled, the Scottish economy is expected to suffer disproportionately. Government estimates predict a 4.5% reduction in Scottish GDP, compared with 3.7% across the rest of the UK, amounting to a cost of approximately £5 billion by 2040 (Scottish Government 2018g).

SOCIAL SERVICES

Welfare concerns play a more important role than labour market concerns in driving resistance to immigration (Dustmann and Preston 2007). Will an influx of migrants place additional strain on critical public services like health care, housing, and education? Theresa May connected immigration and strain on public services in an address to the Conservative Party Conference in May 2015 when she said, 'when immigration is too high, when the pace of change is too fast, it's impossible to build a cohesive society. It's difficult for schools and hospitals and core infrastructure like housing and transport to cope' (BBC News 2015b). While it is intuitive to expect that a growing population will require more services and worsen conditions of strain, immigrant engagement with these systems comes with positive externalities, and the benefits of immigrant inclusion outweigh the drawbacks. To promise immigration as a viable solution for Scotland's demographic and economic challenges, the political elite must correct mistaken assumptions about immigration's negative impact on critical services while acknowledging and addressing concerns. They must foreground the positive outcomes immigration has on Scotland's health, housing, and education systems.

Health

The UK's National Health Service (NHS) is underfunded and UK citizens worry that immigrants will overwhelm the already stressed system. During the Brexit debate, Nigel Farage of UKIP activated these fears when he claimed that EU membership was detracting from public finances that could go to the NHS, and the pro-Brexit justice secretary Michael Gove said that projections of future immigration to the UK from hypothetical new EU member states would make the NHS unsustainable (Mason 2016). Those who accept these claims make two erroneous assumptions. The first is that immigrants provide no opportunities to expand the NHS and are merely a draw on fixed resources. The second is that immigrants coming from less developed countries exhibit poorer health and require greater expenditure than UK citizens. Longitudinal data on use of health services in the UK demonstrate that immigrants do not self-report poorer health than native-born people and they use health services at equivalent rates (Wadsworth 2013).

The COVID-19 pandemic illuminated how immigrants contribute to the NHS with their labour. Foreign-born doctors who died of the virus were held up as exemplars of immigrants who paid the ultimate price for the health of the UK citizenry.[19] Of NHS staff whose ethnicity is known, about 21% identify as a member of a minoritised group, and 13.8% say their nationality is not British (UK Parliament 2020). Thirty per cent of doctors are non-British, as are 21% of nurses (excluding health visitors) (NHS 2018). In Scotland, 7% of the health care workforce is foreign born. Thirty-six per cent of doctors receive their training and qualifications outside the UK (Trewby 2017). These figures make the UK more reliant on foreign-born health care workers than any other European country, except Luxembourg: over half of the increase in the health and social care workforce in the UK is attributable to immigration (Crew 2019). Immigrants are also critical workers in the social care sector, which includes nursing home services. In the UK, at least 18% of care workers are foreign born, and 60% of care workers in London are born outside the UK (Shutes 2011). In Scotland, 5.6% of social care nurses come from Europe, equating to about 10,000 workers (Scottish Government 2018a).

The Scottish and UK governments recognise the NHS's reliance on foreign labour. A Liberal Democrat MSP began an interview by emphasising the importance of immigration for the NHS:

> The big picture is that Scotland needs people. I would argue this is for the whole UK. We are dependent across lots of sectors, particularly our National Health Service, for doctors, nurses, and medical staff who come from other countries. That's not just from Europe, but from a wider field. At home, we have some consultants at our only hospital who have come in the past from as far as South Africa and India. So, I think immigration debate, particularly in the context of the [Brexit] referendum, has been nasty, negative and incredibly narrow in its definitions. Because the NHS, both in Scotland and across the UK, would fall apart were it not for the staff, the trained staff who come in from all parts of the world. (Personal interview 22 June 2016)

The shortage of health care workers became even more critical during the COVID-19 pandemic, when the UK government offered a one-year automatic visa extension for all health care workers. The Home Office proposed a fast-track system for health care workers under Johnson's points-based system, but most social care workers will not be included in the scheme. Recent polls indicate that the NHS is a top priority for the British public, overtaking immigration as a top concern in 2019. Restricting immigration could therefore have serious political implications, in addition to the consequences for public health (Blinder and Richards 2020).

Housing

The UK is in a housing crisis, and millions of people are living in unaffordable or unsuitable homes. Research is inconclusive about whether and to what degree immigration impacts housing prices.[20] Basic analysis by the Ministry of Housing, Communities and Local Government in 2018 found house prices in England grew by 320% over the previous 25 years, and suggested that immigration may be accountable for about 21% of that growth, but the estimate is based solely on immigration's contribution to population growth.[21] Using simple supply-and-demand logic, the report assumed that positive net migration increases the demand for housing, which impacts housing prices. Using a comparison between England and Scotland, Levin et al. (2009) also found that demography determines house prices, especially when population growth is in age groups associated with first-time home ownership (age groups 20–29 and 30–44). It is also possible that an influx of immigrants could drive down housing prices in some areas. Sá (2015) finds that a 1% increase in the population of immigrants is associated with a 1.7% decrease in house prices due to the mobility of the native population, which responds to immigration by moving. The relationship between immigration and housing prices is complicated and difficult to predict.

In Scotland, the impact of immigration on housing markets has not been a major focus of research, because the country has been more concerned about population decline. Levin et al. (2009) predicted that the gap between house prices in Scotland and England/Wales will widen in the future because of population decline in the critical age groups in Scotland: the young adult population continues to decline in Scotland despite increases in immigration, falling from 37% of the population in 1990 to 32% in 2019. Nevertheless, Scotland is facing a housing crisis related to a chronic undersupply of homes and rising house prices that outpace income growth.[22] Government analysis does not mention immigration as a cause of Scotland's housing woes, but the housing shortage certainly affects immigrants and refugees, who have difficulty gaining access to appropriate accommodation. Considering the role of immigration in driving population growth in Scotland, it is reasonable to assume that immigration contributes to competition for housing, though the impact is limited to the urban centres where most immigrants are living.[23] For example, estate agents in Aberdeen reported a lower supply of rental housing and increased competition as consequences of migration (Whitehead et al. 2011).

Due to affordable housing shortages across the UK, there are widespread concerns that immigrants may receive preferential treatment in the allocation of social housing.[24] The UK-wide tabloid media often encourages these perceptions, such as in one 2012 story in the *Daily Mail* claiming over half of social housing in parts of England goes to immigrants (Peev 2012). In reality, immigrants in England are less likely than the UK-born population to be accommodated in social housing because many migrants are not eligible for social housing (Vargas-Silva and Fernández-Reino 2019). In Scotland, 87% of households in social rented housing were born in Scotland, 5% were born in England, about 4% were born in Europe, and 3% were from the rest of the world. Three per cent of social housing units are rented to minoritised residents (Scottish Government 2019b). Since Scotland's population is 9% foreign born and 4% of the population are members of minoritised groups, the number of social units going to immigrant and minoritised populations is proportional to their presence in the general population. One SNP MSP emphasised how social housing shortages are attributable to reduced supply, rather than increased demand resulting from immigration: 'The lack of council housing is about selling off council housing, it's not about anything else. They've sold off huge amounts of council housing because of the right to buy. [In Scotland] we've cancelled the right to buy' (personal interview 24 June 2016). This MSP suggests that political decisions to reduce supply have caused the affordable housing crisis in London.

Instead of being advantaged in the housing market, there is substantial evidence that migrants and ethnic minorities experience disadvantage and discrimination in both private and public housing systems. In 2013, the Runnymede Trust found that over a quarter of minoritised survey respondents felt discriminated against when seeking housing, and in 2016, the Human City Institute reported that housing stress in minoritised communities is much higher than average (Gulliver 2016). Members of minoritised communities wait longer for housing, are offered poorer-quality homes, and are more frequently offered flats, rather than houses (Scottish Government 2016a). Migrants are also more likely to live in overcrowded and unsuitable housing (Vargas-Silva and Fernández-Reino 2019).

Institutional racism in housing is a product of both formal and informal practices. Though discrimination is outlawed, and the Race Relations Act of 1965 prohibited common practices such as demanding to see a passport before providing housing services, there is substantial evidence of persistent subtle discrimination at work in private and public rented housing (Lukes et al. 2018). Discrimination is more visible in the public housing sector, where housing policy is made at the national level. Because the policy is enforced at the local level, varied policy implementation results in differential outcomes (Guentner et al. 2016). According to Lukes et al., 'The local variations in social housing and the private rented sector reflect the historical "slippery" discrimination experienced by migrants and minorities as a result of the devolution of housing policies and weak regulations governing the private rented sector' (2018: 3193). For example, some local authorities avoided housing asylee populations and publicly advocated for comprehensive policy change, arguing that the allocation system favoured migrants. This resulted in a long-term trend where

> successive measures to cut access to housing for migrants over the past two decades have been underpinned by rhetoric about fairness, showing how public perceptions may be used to justify potentially discriminatory policy – even if they are known to be inaccurate. (Guentner et al. 2016: 401)[25]

Excluding migrants from social housing was a product of general discrimination before the 1990s, but since then, public policies have excluded migrants by restricting access based on immigration status. The 2014 Immigration Act required private landlords to check the immigration status of all new occupants and evict those who do not have appropriate documentation.[26] The 2016 Immigration Act amplified the measure and made it a criminal offence for landlords to rent to those with no 'right to rent'. Landlords who did not comply with the Right to Rent scheme could suffer a five-year prison sentence and/or a substantial fine. Opponents of the bills predicted the checks would lead to discrimination in the rental markets, and since December 2014, assessments by the Home Office and the Joint Council for the Welfare of Immigrants highlight the potential for discrimination against minoritised tenants, where visible minorities are more likely to be seen as an 'other' and to have their documents checked. The embodiment of immigration control in landlords creates an outsized power differential between landlords and tenants and a relationship in which non-UK citizens are immediately identified as problematic (Anderson 2015; Guentner et al. 2016; Leahy et al. 2017). Disentangling citizens from non-citizens

> creates an atmosphere of mistrust, is a further catalyst to maintain division within society, and serves to draw attention away from state practices and place blame and an air of suspicion on all those who 'appear' to be outsiders. It serves to further instil a hierarchy between citizens and non-UK citizens. (Leahy et al. 2017: 614)

Rather than creating problems, placing immigrants in public housing may yield positive externalities. Refugees and asylum seekers are dispersed across the UK based on the availability of necessary support and cultural characteristics of the host community. In Scotland, they have primarily been placed in areas of Glasgow with available accommodation, which usually means less popular areas with high vacancy rates, higher proportions of low-income households, and limited community facilities. Placement in underserved communities presents challenges for immigrant communities, but there is a long-term benefit. Once migrants settle into a previously neglected community, the local area is economically and socially regenerated (Scottish Parliament 2010). These benefits could justify allocating *more* social housing to immigrants, as their settlement will bring advantages to all residents of a community.

Scotland is a complex environment for disentangling the link between immigration and housing because while housing is a devolved power, immigration is not. Laws that blend housing policy and immigration control like the Right to Rent scheme oblige Scottish housing organisations to enforce conditions set by Westminster, which infringes upon Scotland's self-determination. Leahy et al. (2017) reported that the general sentiment towards the Immigration Act among housing stakeholders in Scotland was overwhelmingly negative for both practical and ideological reasons. One housing lawyer expected the tension between state and national powers to cause resistance in Scotland, rooted in the ideology and objectives embedded within Scottish social democracy. Nevertheless, when faced with vague legislation carrying severe consequences for landlords, most self-interested landlords might take the easy option and avoid renting to members of a minoritised group. The imperative of control enforced at the individual level undermines the objectives of the Scottish government around anti-racism and increasing immigration to Scotland and forces elements of Scottish society to work at cross purposes. Scottish stakeholders feel that the Immigration Acts create incentives for behaviours that threaten to undo much of Scotland's social progress in the housing sector.[27]

Claims that immigrants are causing the UK's housing crisis are unfounded. There is mixed evidence about the impact of demographic change on housing prices, no evidence that immigrants receive preferential treatment in social housing, and ample evidence of systemic housing disadvantages for minoritised community members. While a growing population will naturally place strain on housing systems, the most direct response should be found in housing policy, not immigration policy.

Education

As immigration to the UK accelerated after 2004, anti-immigration activists argued that it was causing a rapid injection of students into the school system, resulting in overcrowding and competition for resources. The proportion of students with an immigrant background in the UK increased between 2009 and 2018, from 11% to 20% (OECD 2019). The growth of the migrant student population is directly related to fertility trends in the UK. According to the ONS, a third of the babies born in the England and Wales in 2017 had at least one parent born outside the UK. The estimated total fertility rate for foreign-born women is 1.95 children per woman, higher than the UK-born rate of 1.79, but fertility rates for both foreign-born and UK-born women are declining, and rates converge in subsequent generations.[28] The impact of incorporating immigrant families in schools should even out in the second generation. In terms of straight enrolments, there is a surplus of primary school places across the UK, though the balance between pupils and places varies between and within the UK's nations. Scotland has many undersubscribed schools, and about a quarter of schools in south-west Scotland are operating at less than 50% capacity (McLaughlin 2020).[29] Undersubscribed schools would benefit from increased student numbers. In Scotland, asylum seekers have been placed in deprived estates experiencing population decline, and asylum seeker children helped to keep local schools open by increasing enrolments (Sim and Bowes 2007).

Another concern is that immigrants are disproportionately consuming educational resources with the requirement that schools provide English as an additional language (EAL) or bilingual support for students. The Scottish government estimates that between 4% and 6% of students in Scottish primary and secondary schools have English as an additional language (Scottish Government 2015). Teachers from Glasgow and the surrounding areas said they needed more training in how to help bilingual learners, and in how to best promote cultural and linguistic exchange within the classroom (Anderson 2013). While training and bilingual resources are an added expense, the costs must be weighed against the advantages immigrants bring to an education system. Educators in Glasgow reported positive impacts of migrant children in the classroom, where the children increased the native-born students' awareness of other cultures and languages (Dillon 2013). Immigrant children are also perceived by educators as being high achievers, who help improve school statistics in Glasgow (Dillon 2013). Importantly, there is no relationship between the proportion of immigrant students and native-born student achievement (Ohinata and van Ours 2013). The advantages associated with diversifying the classroom more than compensate for the costs.

A final concern relates to immigrant demand for faith schools, which activates long-standing debates about state-funded religious education in Scotland. Arguments against faith schools take many forms, and reflect wider disagreements about belonging and national identity in Scotland. The one that relates most closely to the immigrant communities is the concern that faith schools promote the deliberate self-exclusion of religio-ethnic groups, and that they contribute to sectarianism. Proponents of faith schools believe the schools promote tolerance of religious pluralism, support community cohesion, and develop social capital (McKinney and Conroy 2015).

Publicly funded Catholic schools date back to the 1918 Education (Scotland) Act, but modern waves of immigrants have reignited the debate about the role of faith schools in Scottish society. Scottish leaders have refused to meet demands for the state funding of Islamic schools, despite the fact that Muslims are the largest non-Christian religious community in Scotland. Sarrouh (2018) argues that the refusal is attributable to historical church–state relations, and particularly the political focus on anti-sectarianism.

Among those who support and want to enrol their children in a faith school, immigration could increase competition for limited spots.[30] The rapid increase in Polish-born immigrants after 2004 increased the demand for spots in Catholic schools, resulting in a lower probability of native-born students attending Catholic schools (Pasini 2018). Though their reasoning is different, both those who oppose and those who support faith schools might see immigration as a threat.

Educated immigrants who migrate in adulthood bring educational savings to the UK government because they arrive with educational qualifications paid for by their country of origin. Compared with other West European states, the UK has a much larger share of immigrants with a tertiary education.[31] Between 1995 and 2011, European immigrants endowed the UK labour market with human capital that would have cost £14 billion if it had been produced through the British education system, and non-European migrant educational savings were equivalent to £35 billion (Dustmann and Frattini 2014). Since a student with a migrant background often accompanies one or more qualified working parents, the cost of educating the child is offset.

Concerns about the impact of immigration on social policy provision are understandable. It is intuitive to expect injection of immigrants into society to correspond with heavier demands on social services, and when those services are already experiencing strain, they should be less equipped to absorb newcomers. However, this perspective ignores the contributions that immigrants make to services. As one SNP MSP put it:

> if [public services] haven't kept up, that's not the fault of people coming here, it's the fault of the population growth for whatever reason, and the fact that the public services should have built a new school or should have built an extra ward in that hospital. The thing about people coming to this country is that they're being taxed. So why is their tax money not being used to fund those public services? ... Why is it not keeping up? It's a bit of a political decision not to do this, and to spend money on other areas. It's the fault of the politicians rather than the fault of the population. (Personal interview 24 June 2016)

Immigrants consume services proportionally, while they make a greater contribution than native-born residents through taxation. With the potential exception of housing, even social systems experiencing strain would be worse off without the contributions of migrants. The discrimination some migrants face while accessing services is deeply unjust.

Conclusion

The UK's immigrant population is well educated and achieves good employment and participation rates, which results in net gains for the UK economy. There is little evidence that their presence detracts from native-born citizens' wages, employment opportunities, or social services. Instead, migrants rejuvenate local communities and attract services. Much of the Scottish campaign to justify and endorse immigration focuses on dispelling myths about the effect of migration on the labour market and demonstrating that immigration is beneficial to the Scottish economy and Scottish workers. Migration is presented to the Scottish people as a win–win solution.

Not all Scottish elites accept the argument that immigration will be a panacea for Scotland's demographic and economic challenges. Demographer Robert Wright warned that even if rates of immigration to Scotland doubled, it would not be enough to resolve the economic and demographic challenges. The critical strategy is to focus on growing the workforce, and developing strategies for improving productivity: 'Having a managed migration system that we have control of, that meets labour market needs is critical to that, but it's not the answer' (MacNab 2014, quoting Wright). Though Scottish decision makers do not deny the need to consider alternative policy options – such as educational programming to match students with employers or raising the retirement age – they continue to push migration as the main solution to Scotland's most pressing problems and to lobby the UK government to adopt a differentiated strategy for migration.

Pursuing immigration as a policy objective introduces a political problem because the UK government has been forceful in its desire to restrict immigration. This allows Scotland to contrast English and Scottish interests and argue that the UK government is thwarting Scotland's goals. As the Scottish government's Europe Minister Alasdair Allan said: 'The evidence is clear that the UK government's position on migration does not work for Scotland's needs' (McCall 2018). In response, the UK's Home Secretary Amber Rudd asked the UK government's Migration Advisory Committee to research the immigration system and consider whether Scotland's population and economic situation was serious enough to warrant a unique Scottish-tailored immigration policy. In 2018 the committee concluded that Scotland does not have a greater need for immigrants than other demographically challenged areas, like northern England or Wales, and that 'demography does not respect administrative and political borders' (Migration Advisory Committee 2018b: 13). It did not find Scotland to be economically distinct either, and argued that Scotland is less dependent on migrant labour than the rest of the UK. Part of the evidence considered by the committee was submitted by Benedict Greening of Migration

Watch, an immigration and asylum research organisation and think tank, who pointed out that the Labour Force Survey indicated that only 10% of the Scottish workforce was born outside the UK, compared with 17% of the UK workforce, and argued that this indicated that Scotland was therefore less dependent on migrant labour than the UK (Scottish Affairs Committee 2018). The Migration Advisory Committee concluded that the problems facing Scotland are not national: 'overall, we were not of the view that Scotland's economic situation is sufficiently different from that of the rest of the UK to justify a very different migration policy' (2018a: 123). While acknowledging that a solution should be found, it asserted that the solution should be drawn up at the state level and applied to all areas of the UK that are suffering the same ills. The committee did not completely close the door on the possibility of a differentiated system, but emphasised that 'this decision would be a political one' and not one driven by empirics (2018a: 131).

The findings from the committee were previewed by David McCrone's (1992) analysis of the industrial, occupational, and sectoral change in Scotland compared with changes in England and Wales from 1851 to 1981. McCrone finds the similarities north and south of the border are much greater than the differences:

> Far from being a specialised 'region' of Britain, however, Scotland throughout its industrial history has had a very similar profile to Britain as a whole, while containing considerable internal specialisation, reflecting its position as a distinct country within the United Kingdom. (McCrone 1992: 74)

On the one hand, the similar economic profiles of Scotland and England undercut claims that Scotland deserves independence or autonomous control over migration in order to react to particular Scottish economic conditions. On the other hand, advocates for independence could take heart from Scotland's diversified economy, which as McCrone argues, speaks to Scotland's capacity as and potential to be a 'distinct country'. The Scottish elites who responded to the 2018 report did not share McCrone's optimism. Ben Macpherson, Minister for Europe, Migration and International Development, emphasised that the report would be 'deeply disappointing to businesses and employers across Scotland' and rejected the report's findings (Scottish Parliament 2018). Macpherson noted that the report 'did not fully consider the social and cultural benefits that come from being an open and connected European nation' and suggested these omissions would direct future Scottish work on migration (Scottish Parliament 2018).

Scottish elites can move ahead with their commitment to increase immigration because most migrants are looking for economic opportunities as the prerequisite of the decision to move (Houston et al. 2008). Scotland's devolved powers make it possible for Scotland to create and broadcast economic opportunities in Scotland. However, under the post-Brexit immigration policy, only the most highly skilled and lucrative positions will translate into enough points for a work visa. The Scottish government must therefore continue to advocate for a different policy that will allow for the entry of lesser-skilled workers. It must retain the current immigrant population, which requires work with the Scottish population to overcome parochialism and discrimination and efforts to create community cohesion. The next chapter explains why this could present a challenge to Scottish elites in their pursuit of a migrant-acceptant society.

Notes

1. Exceptions are Ireland, France, and the Netherlands, where birth rates are above the replacement rate of above 2.1 children per woman.
2. Pensions rely on a workforce paying in to the system. A growing elderly population increases health and social care costs. These costs are high in Scotland, where free personal care is provided to the elderly in their homes. The costs of that policy increased 150% between 2003 and 2010 to £342 million. The number of elderly people is expected to rise by 62% by 2030 (Carrell 2012).
3. The UK, Sweden, and Ireland were the only EU countries to immediately open their labour markets to these new EU citizens.
4. Rendall and Ball (2004) find that between half and two-thirds of the UK's immigrants that were born in the continental EU, North America and Oceania emigrate within five years, while 15% of those born in the Indian subcontinent do so.
5. Rural areas account for 95% of Scotland's landmass but 18% of the population.
6. Those councils reporting a decline over the last ten years include South Ayrshire (-0.8%), East Dunbartonshire (-1.1%), North Ayrshire (-1.4%), Dundee City (-1.7%), Na h-Eileanan Siar (-3.4%), Argyll and Bute (-5.4%), West Dunbartonshire (-5.9%), and Inverclyde (-8.9%) (National Records of Scotland 2018b).
7. Eighty per cent of EU nationals in Scotland are of working age, compared with 65% of the Scottish population as a whole.
8. In December 2019, Scotland's employment rate was 74.5%, which was lower than the UK's 76.2%. Unemployment in Scotland was 3.7%, which was lower than the UK's 3.8%. The low employment and unemployment levels in Scotland are partially due to higher levels of economic inactivity in Scotland, at 22% (i.e. those out of work but who do not meet the criteria for unemployment). The COVID-19 pandemic reversed many of these trends, and Scotland suffered higher unemployment and lower employment in 2020.
9. These trends are in line with UK-wide levels, though the proportion of vacancies was 1% higher in Scotland.
10. It is possible for inter-ethnic communities to exist with very little cross-cultural communication, which may lead to fractionalisation or polarisation. Fragmented societies will have a narrow knowledge base, which will negatively affect social capital formation and economic growth aspirations.
11. Scotland's soft fruit industry is largely centred in Tayside and Fife in the east of Scotland, and is worth about £115 million a year. The worth of these crops has doubled over the past decade as Scotland has built a strong reputation around the quality of its strawberries and raspberries.
12. Employers are urging policy makers to adopt a UK-wide Seasonal Agricultural

Workers Scheme, similar to that which allowed East European migrants to work on British farms before their countries were eligible for free movement in 2014.
13. Perceived competition for resources was a strong determinant of negative attitudes towards a fictional group of immigrants in Canada (Esses et al. 1998). Survey research reveals more nuance, demonstrating that an equal proportion of Europeans agree and disagree with the idea that average wages are brought down by immigrants, but the beliefs interact with economic self-interest to influence perception of immigrants (Malchow-Møller et al. 2008).
14. The public has a very poor understanding of the scale and nature of immigration, which could account for some of the disconnect between perceptions and empirics. In a survey in the UK, the average guess was that foreign-born people make up 31% of the UK's population, far more than the official estimate of 13% (Duffy and Frere-Smith 2014).
15. Dustmann et al. (2013) find that over the period from 1997 to 2005, immigration held back wage growth for those below the 20th percentile of income, but only by a very small amount. Meanwhile, immigration has increased wages above the 20th percentile quite substantially. Overall, immigration to the UK has had a positive impact on average native wages. Manacorda et al. (2012) argue that the group whose wages have been depressed by immigration are immigrants who were already living in the UK.
16. Hatton and Tani (2005) investigate this possibility and find that for the most part, effects are only felt in Southern England where immigration is most concentrated.
17. This will change if EU immigration is restricted. Before the 1970s, many European governments recruited foreign workers, most of whom were young and male. Both migrants and policy makers assumed that the migration was temporary. Once the economic crisis resulted in a freeze in the recruitment of foreign workers, an unintended consequence was the permanent settlement of migrant labourers, and those labourers brought their families into the host countries. The migration of migrant families substantially changed the composition of immigrant communities. After Brexit, European workers in the UK faced the same choice to leave or permanently settle.
18. In 2016, the average European migrant contributed £2,300 more to public finances than the average UK adult. Each non-European migrant contributed over £800 less than the average (Oxford Economics 2018).
19. Reporting in May 2020 revealed that 60% of health workers killed by COVID-19 infections were members of minoritised groups (Marsh and McIntyre 2020). The population of the UK is 92% white.
20. The Migration Observatory listed 'little systematic evidence of direct and indirect impacts of immigration on house prices, rents, and social housing at national and local levels' as one of the top ten deficiencies in the UK's evidence base about immigration (Blinder et al. 2011). In a brief in 2019, it reported that there is some evidence that migration may be contributing to increased housing costs.
21. That same year, the Migration Advisory Committee (2018) found that a 1% increase in the UK's population due to migration increased house prices by 1%, but cautioned that the results depend substantially on the statistical approach taken.
22. In response to the growing need for housing, the SNP-led government promised in 2015 to deliver 50,000 affordable homes between 2016 and 2021, though Housing Minister Kevin Stewart announced on 3 April 2020 that the COVID-19 pandemic made achieving that goal unlikely. Meanwhile, the need for housing is much greater than even the government's target could satisfy – the Scottish Federation of Housing Associations said that at the beginning of 2020, there were around

160,000 households on waiting lists for social housing. The problem involves many barriers to the delivery of new homes in the post-2008 environment, including mortgage availability, reduced lending to small-scale builders, no long-term commitments to funding affordable housing, a reduction of the housing sector workforce, insufficient funding for infrastructure, low levels of support for home building in the local authorities and neighbourhoods, and the lack of a centralised planning system (Barklay and Swift-Adams 2018).
23. Though migrants are attracted to cities, the most dramatic housing shortages are in the rural areas, islands, and Highlands, where rising rent prices are forcing people out of their homes. These price hikes are attributed to holiday rentals, not immigration (Carrell and McEnaney 2019).
24. One might expect these concerns to be especially serious in Scotland, where wages are below the UK average and expenditure on public services is approximately 20% higher than in England (HM Treasury 2019). Average public expenditure per head in Scotland is £11,247, while in England it is £9,296. This measure includes money spent on a wide range of services, including housing, and includes money spent by the UK and devolved governments as well as local councils and public corporations.
25. Guentner et al. (2016) highlight the role of senior councillors of the London Borough of Tower Hamlets, who were avoiding requests to house Bengali families throughout the 1980s. The borough used laws on homelessness to expel housing applicants from temporary accommodation and actively lobbied for changes in immigration law that would allow them to uproot long-standing Bengali residents.
26. The 2014 and 2016 Immigration Acts were introduced as part of the Conservative government's agenda to create a 'hostile environment' for irregular migrants in the UK.
27. For example, Leahy et al. interviewed an advocate in a homelessness and housing charity, who described Scottish legislation, saying, 'The whole point about that was to get a clear message to landlords that every eviction has to be subject to a process . . . I think [the Immigration Act] reinforces all of that bad practice about illegal evictions, which we have been trying to eliminate' (2017: 612).
28. The lower fertility rates of daughters of immigrants from high-fertility countries is partly explained by their higher educational enrolment, compared with their mothers (Dubuc 2012).
29. There is also a teacher shortage in Scotland, and the government has hoped to recruit teachers from abroad to fill the shortage (BBC News 2017).
30. Catholic schools in Scotland are on average better-performing schools, and are also over-subscribed. In 2020, there were 369 state-funded Catholic schools in Scotland educating around 120,000 pupils.
31. In 2015, 47% of immigrants of working age in the UK had achieved tertiary education, much more than in Germany (19%), France (29%), Sweden (36%), and Switzerland (38%). Only Poland and Ireland have a larger share of tertiary-educated migrants. Across the EU, the average rate is 30% (Alfano et al. 2016).

5

THE PROBLEM: PROMOTING SOCIAL COHESION AND ANTI-RACISM IN SCOTLAND

Immigration is a partial solution to Scotland's demographic and economic challenges. When confronted with empirical evidence demonstrating that immigrants help the economy without harming native workers, anti-immigration activists fall back on arguments that immigrants damage social cohesion. For example, at the 2015 Conservative Party Conference Theresa May said, 'when immigration is too high, when the pace of change is too fast, it's impossible to build a cohesive society' (BBC News 2015b). Comments like May's speak to an assumption that solidarity depends on conformity with an underlying shared culture that is threatened by newcomers. Former Conservative MP Enoch Powell vividly made this point in his 1968 'Rivers of Blood' speech, in which he claimed that immigration made Englishmen 'strangers in their own country'. Powell argued that feelings of strangeness make the native population feel deprived and resentful, which would have disastrous social and political consequences, resulting in rivers 'foaming with much blood'. Powell's message was clear: when immigrants damage social cohesion, the end result will be the literal or symbolic death of English/British culture. Meanwhile, Scottish political elites present migration as a way to make Scottish society better or stronger: 'Migration is not just about economic prosperity . . . People from overseas who come to Scotland to live, to study or work, or to raise their families are our friends and neighbours. They strengthen our society and we welcome them' (Scottish Government 2018g: 3). This statement from Fiona Hyslop, the Cabinet Secretary for Culture, Tourism and External Affairs, illustrates the Scotland-centric nature of the narrative about the benefits of migration, which does not mention the migrant experience in Scotland or their quality of life in Scottish society. An exclusive focus on increasing future immigration risks neglecting deeply rooted social problems of discrimination and racism that could undermine the Scottish government's agenda.

This chapter elaborates on one of the biggest challenges or problems facing Scotland in its attempt to attract and retain migrants: the disconnect between the national strategies to welcome and integrate immigrants and the responses to immigrant populations at the street level. Scottish political elites encourage local authorities to improve migrant quality of life, but there are persistent problems that require constant attention in order to ensure that Scotland is a welcoming place for all groups of immigrants. The chapter opens by considering the impact of diversity on community cohesion, which describes the ability of a community to foster a sense of belonging. It then describes models of immigrant integration and Scotland's multicultural policy of acculturation, before discussing racism and the threat it presents to Scotland's community cohesion and immigrant integration. It concludes with a discussion of the Scottish Government's anti-racism efforts

COMMUNITY COHESION

One of the main criticisms of migration is that it negatively impacts 'community cohesion', which is the ability of a community to foster a sense of solidarity and to grow in harmony. Social disorder or conflict within a community reflects a lack of solidarity. The concept gained a lot of traction in the UK in the early 2000s, when civil disturbances involving Pakistani-Muslim communities, white communities, far-right groups, and the police were held up as examples of a failed British policy of multiculturalism (Hepburn 2020). The UK government subsequently adopted a 'community cohesion' approach to immigrant integration, which required immigrants to take part in shared experiences, aspirations, and values, and did not highlight or support difference. The UK's approach to community cohesion is inherently conservative, because it assumes that the status quo represents the best possible situation and that any change would be detrimental. From a more progressive perspective, immigration expands and diversifies the idea of what the community is, which will make the community more resilient to change. It is difficult to assess whether the conservative or progressive perspective is more accurate, because community cohesion is complex, multifaceted, and difficult to define and measure. The Migration Advisory Committee admitted this difficulty in a 2012 report on the impacts of immigration in the UK:

> [we are] least able to provide a firm conclusion on the overall impact [of immigration] on social cohesion and integration . . . because we felt that there was insufficient evidence in the existing literature to enable us to

define and accurately measure the impacts of migration on social cohesion and integration. (Migration Advisory Committee 2012: 91)

Assessments of community cohesion are most typically done with public opinion data, looking at attitudes about political trust, assessments of neighbourhoods, or self-reported social capital, which is made up out of the quality of an individual's social networks.

Some evidence suggests immigration and increased diversity can lead to better outcomes in community cohesion than would be possible without the injection of diversity into a community. The mechanism of the positive relationship between diversity and cohesion is rooted in quality contacts between people of diverse backgrounds. First theorised by Allport (1954) as the 'intergroup contact hypothesis', as different types of people get to know each other and work together, the social contact should erode the social importance of differences between them. Contact enhances solidarity and social cohesion by reducing prejudice towards the people engaged in the contact *and* the groups to which they belong (Pettigrew 1998; Putnam 2000). Even better, the reduction in prejudice against a specific cultural group can be generalised to other groups, which leads to greater acceptance of minoritised groups of many different types (Pettigrew 1997). Pettigrew (1998) theorised that the effect would be strongest under conditions of structured contact, such as with contact between diverse groups of parents and between diverse groups of students in a common educational system. In Scotland, clubs and sporting activities enabled migrant and non-migrant children to interact with each other in a way that builds solidarity by increasing positive social contacts (Sime and Fox 2015). Even unstructured contact, like simple social interactions, can reduce prejudice across many different types of groups (Pettigrew and Tropp 2006).

Over time and with widespread engagement, shifts in personal values resulting from regular contact should change the local culture, making a community more open and welcoming to diversity, and more cohesive across groups. Diverse communities with strong cohesion exhibit tolerance, open-mindedness, cosmopolitanism, and respect for diversity (Figueira et al. 2016). The shift in values cycles back into other benefits for the community: 'Tolerance and inclusiveness becomes embedded, which makes a neighbourhood or region more attractive; as a result, it draws and retains a large number of talented individuals with diverse cultural backgrounds' (Mickiewicz et al. 2019: 82). The creation of socially supportive culture (endorsing a humane application of sensitivity, friendliness, tolerance, and cooperation) is associated with higher levels of quality entrepreneurial activity and economic improvement, which benefits everyone (Stephan and Uhlaner 2010).

Not all social contacts are equally effective for developing social cohesion. Social capital is a concept capturing the quality of social networks and the benefits derived from them. 'Bonding' social capital is built within groups (like within an ethic community), while 'bridging' social capital is built across groups (between immigrants and native groups or across different immigrant groups, for example) (Putnam 2000). While the two types of social capital are not mutually exclusive, the distinction is important when thinking about the impact of immigration on social cohesion, because bridging social capital is expected to yield positive benefits for both immigrants and the host society. Bonding social capital supports a migrant or minoritised group member by connecting them with others in a similar situation, but it can also result in a greater degree of withdrawal from the mainstream Scottish public. For example, Hopkins and Smith (2008) interviewed Muslim men in the Pollokshields area of Glasgow, the most residentially segregated area of Scotland, where 50% of the local population identifies with a South Asian heritage and 40% identifies as Muslim. The men describe a protective element of their neighbourhoods, where the ethnic majority community provides a safe haven from racism.[1] However, bonding social capital may also lock people into social niches. In empirical analysis, cross-cultural bridging social capital is associated with positive labour market outcomes (Lancee 2010) and creativity (Leung et al. 2008), while bonding social capital is not. A Conservative MSP suggested that Scotland's minoritised populations are more likely to live in ethnic enclaves, compared with their counterparts in England:

> My sense of it is the way immigration works in Glasgow is very different from how it works from say, cities in England. Immigrant communities in Glasgow are still very heavily ghettoised. So, the Jews live where the Jews live, and the Pakistani community lives where the Pakistani community lives, and the Bangladeshi community lives where the Bangladeshi community lives. There's not much dispersal. You can walk and walk and walk and walk in Glasgow, and not see anybody who doesn't look like us. There's no city in England where you could do that. So, I don't know why this is, but if you look at the primary school figures of ethnic breakdowns of primary schools in the southside of Glasgow, you'll see it's really stark. There are schools that are 98% this and then 98% that. And again, I just don't think you'd see the same Liverpool or Birmingham or Winchester. It's quite different. (Personal interview 26 March 2019)

While the small size of the Scottish minoritised communities could account for their lower visibility, their concentration in urban neighbourhoods could present challenges for building bridging social capital in Scotland.

Theresa May's assumption that diversity will negatively impact social cohesion and trust within a community is supported by 'conflict theory', which suggests that for various reasons, but especially conflict over limited resources, diversity fosters distrust of those who are different and solidarity between those who are similar. Goodhart (2004) argues that the UK is built on a system of risk-pooling and sharing limited resources, which manifests in public services and the democratic political system. One could argue that Scotland's system is even more reliant on concepts of social solidarity, given the public provision of university education and home elder care for Scottish residents. Such sharing, Goodhart argues, is best facilitated by taking for granted a shared set of values and assumptions and a common culture. Risk-pooling is hypothetically more likely if people recognise the beneficiaries and believe them to be like themselves, facing the same difficulties they themselves might face. Goodhart alleges that the diversification of Britain through immigration has eroded that common culture. International research, and especially research from the United States, provides some support for this theory.[2] Alesina et al. (2001) asked why the US does not have a European-style welfare state, and concluded that Americans see ethnic and racialised groups as part of a different social group, and unworthy of shared sacrifice. Likewise, Putnam's (2007) 'hunkering down' thesis, also based on data from the US, suggested that in ethnically diverse neighbourhoods, people of all races tend to hunker down, or pull into their ethnic community. Using data from the white population of the US and Canada, Stolle et al. (2008) found a negative relationship between neighbourhood diversity and generalised trust.[3] Cross-national research likewise found positive relationships between the ethnic homogeneity of a country and higher levels of social trust (Delhey and Newton 2005). However, 'different kinds of [ethnic and linguistic] heterogeneity matter differently for different behaviours and attitudes associated with civil society', meaning that increased diversity leads to higher levels of some citizenship behaviours, while diminishing others (Anderson and Paskeviciute 2006: 797). In Anderson and Paskeviciute's (2006) cross-national and individual-level study, they found that heterogeneity did not determine many citizenship behaviours in developed democracies, but linguistic heterogeneity reduced political interest and ethnic heterogeneity reduced interpersonal trust. In less democratic countries, linguistic diversity increased organisational membership and political interest, while ethnic heterogeneity stimulated political discussion. The effect of diversity on social cohesion depends on context, what type of diversity is present, and how social cohesion is measured.

The mechanisms of conflict and contact are presented as competing explanations for the effect of diversity on social cohesion, but both of these processes operate in tandem (Stolle et al. 2008). Within each community there might be some people who are motivated to avoid social engagement and to distrust strangers. Others might engage in direct interactions with the new groups, thereby reducing their distrust of newcomers. The best way to interrogate the relationship between diversity and community cohesion is through examining the interaction between diversity and levels of interpersonal contact on community cohesion, rather than assuming a direct link between diversity and cohesion (Sturgis et al. 2011).

Researchers have grappled with confounding factors in the relationship between diversity and social cohesion in Europe. Using data from 25,000 people in the UK, Sturgis and colleagues (2011) found no relationship between neighbourhood ethnic diversity and general trust in people. They found a trivial negative relationship between neighbourhood diversity and strategic trust (trust in people with whom we are acquainted), but the effect is contingent on low levels of interpersonal contact. Laurence (2013) used 2001 General Household Survey data from the UK and found a difference between local social connectivity and general social connectivity, and that diversity shares a negative relationship with local connectivity but not with general connectivity.[4] Laurence concludes that native people in diverse neighbourhoods are 'hunkering away' into their extended social networks rather than hunkering down into local ethnic communities. However, minoritised residents in these communities may not respond to diversity in the same way. Fieldhouse and Cutts (2010) compared the UK and the US and found that neighbourhood diversity resulted in fewer shared values for white residents, but more diverse neighbourhoods usually coincided with higher rates of co-ethnic residency, which helped build more cohesive communities. They found that Britain's minoritised residents were more comfortable living in diverse areas, even when the diversity reflected the presence of groups other than their own.

Most research considers alternative structural explanations that could make the relationship between neighbourhood diversity and trust either indirect or spurious. In a study of social capital in 28 European countries, Gesthuizen et al. (2008) found national-level economic inequality and a national history of continuous democracy in European societies were more important than diversity for explaining cross-national differences in social capital in Europe. At the neighbourhood level, Gijsberts et al. (2011) suggest that reduced social cohesion in more diverse neighbourhoods in the Netherlands is attributable to relative socio-economic disadvantage within those communities. In the UK, Laurence and Heath (2008) argue that deprivation undermines cohesion and that diversity does not interact statistically with deprivation to create greater divisions in areas with larger minoritised populations. Sturgis and colleagues (2013) focus on London and perceptions of the local area as an indicator of community cohesion. They found opinions were driven more by social and economic deprivation rather than new migration, and that once economic deprivation is accounted for, ethnic diversity is positively associated with perceived community cohesion, as long as the diversity is not accompanied by segregation. The Migration Advisory Committee conceded that evidence from the British case indicates that 'it is economic deprivation rather than ethnic diversity which is negatively related to social cohesion' (2012: 92). These results suggest that empirical associations between neighbourhood diversity and community cohesion at the level of the community are spurious.

A growing body of research investigates links between diversity and social cohesion in multiple contexts, though research focusing on the relationship in Scotland is rare. Much research on conflict theory focuses on the effects of ethnic and linguistic pluralism, and while Scotland has experienced linguistic diversity with its historical immigration flows, it has not experienced much ethnic pluralism until recently, so the effects of immigration on social cohesion may be muted. Furthermore, most immigrants in Scotland are concentrated in the urban centres, which makes the relationship between diversity and social cohesion relevant for a geographically concentrated community. This may change as Scotland receives more ethnically different immigrants who move into rural areas. Even so, there is evidence from Scotland that corroborates the findings of the European and UK-wide research. Kay and Morrison (2012) found that tensions between migrant and native-born Scots arise when the native-born groups suffer poverty and social exclusion prior to the arrival of the newcomers. Migrants who suffer disproportionate rates of poverty and social exclusion are believed to strain already strapped social services. Where services are targeted at the migrant community instead of the whole population, deprived native-born communities feel resentment.

Testimony from immigration experts in Glasgow suggests that the growing diversity of Scotland could have a healing effect on the historical problem of sectarianism (Kay and Morrison 2012). One educator explained how the addition of many minoritised communities diluted an old us versus them dynamic between Irish Catholics and Scottish Protestants: 'it's not like the sort of two-tribe-syndrome any more, you know, it's mini tribes' (Kay and Morrison 2012: 8). Other Glaswegian interview subjects also noted the way cultural diversity

> changed the 'feel' of the area, softening a tendency for outsiders of any kind to feel vulnerable to attack or harassment and increasing the range of retail and leisure outlets, thus turning rather grim and forbidding streets into much more welcoming places. (Kay and Morrison 2012: 8)

Immigrant entrepreneurship led to regeneration of the area, and these subjects suggested that the changing culture was felt in immigrant and native-born communities alike. Many interview subjects noted how a community that once felt unsafe felt much safer after the injection of new populations. Similarly, a representative of the Scottish Trades Union Congress (STUC) was describing the community outreach of the organisation and recalled:

> When we were in these communities the refugees were actually replacing flats that were empty, that were potentially being used as drug dens, that were very, very poor areas in Glasgow. There were a couple [refugee]

> families coming in who were actually had a lot of get-up-and-go about them. They actually really wanted to be there, and were so pleased to be in Drumchapel, whereas everybody else felt gutted to be in Drumchapel. They were sending their kids to school and were supporting their children's education, and were very good members of the community. It didn't take very long for people to go 'wait, hang on a minute, this refugee is miles better than that junky' . . . They were rehabilitating the community . . . That meant that local people just adopted them and started doing things like locking arms to stop the dawn raids and all of this kind of stuff. They started to say 'you can't take these people they are our people'. It was just a complete adoption of families because they were valued in the community. (Personal interview 9 June 2016)

The STUC representative suggested that a community with competition for resources, or where the political discourse did not support the refugee communities, might see a different outcome.

There are mixed answers to the question of whether diversity negatively impacts social cohesion. Research from the US suggests a negative relationship, but evidence from Europe finds economic inequality and deprivation are the real culprits behind societal discord. It is hard to reach consensus on this issue because it is difficult to define and measure community cohesion. It is also difficult to make strong claims about the impact of immigration on community cohesion, since most research on the subject looks at the effect of ethnic or linguistic diversity, which is not solely a product of immigration. Nevertheless, there is evidence that diversification does not necessarily lead to community conflict. If diversification is managed so that native populations do not see themselves as competing with new populations for resources, communities can prevent resentment. This requires investment in deprived areas so that the injection of a migrant population does not exacerbate an already difficult situation. Communities can build resilience to deprivation when they promote behaviours that have a positive effect on cohesion. If immigrant communities positively interact with the native population in a structured environment, diversity can make communities richer and stronger. These kinds of connections are less frequent in poorer neighbourhoods: 'while there is no deficiency of social networks in diverse communities, there is a shortage of them in economically disadvantaged ones' (Laurence and Heath 2008: 42). Efforts should target these communities. Scotland is just beginning to experience diversification, which means Scottish elites have an opportunity to pre-emptively develop structures and institutions to ensure the best possible outcome.

Immigrant Integration

The government can help encourage the links that lead to improved social cohesion with their immigrant integration strategy. There is disagreement over the correct definition of integration, but nearly all scholarly definitions of integration communicate an idea of how migrants become part of the public and private dimensions of society. Integration in the public sphere involves providing rights to migrants, and the exercise of those rights. Integration in the private sphere speaks to the experiences and social networks of immigrants, and the degree to which those experiences align with those of the native population. Integration policies provide resources for and direct the process of integration and address the different needs of migrants based on how long they have been in the country. Newly arrived migrants focus on language acquisition and getting to know their host society with the help of orientation policies. Once migrants are established within a community, they benefit from policies intended to further their long-term social, political, and economic inclusion.

The policies and public–private dimensions of integration are mutually reinforcing and involve a complex interplay of a number of domains and factors. Using data from the UK, Ager and Strang (2008) developed a conceptual framework for integration by breaking concepts of 'successful' integration into four normative themes: 1) the legal foundation of rights and citizenship; 2) the facilitators of integration, like learning the language and culture and feeling safe within the community; 3) processes of social connection within the group and wider community; and 4) achievement of and access to employment, housing, education, and health. A successfully integrated immigrant will display healthy markers of integration (full employment, educational attainment, good health, secure housing) by virtue of the foundations, facilitators, and social connections that made their success possible. The framework is illustrated in Table 5.1.

While most researchers and policy makers agree with the markers of integration depicted at the top of Table 5.1, they disagree about the ideal strategy to achieve them. Assimilationist approaches involve a method of one-way

Table 5.1 Conceptual framework for integration.

Markers and means	Employment	Housing	Education	Health
Social connection	Social bridges	Social bonds		Social links
Facilitators	Language and cultural knowledge		Safety and stability	
Foundation	Rights and citizenship			

Source: Adapted from Ager and Strang 2008

integration where a migrant is absorbed into the host culture, which theoretically remains homogenous and unchanged after the inclusion of migrants. Acculturation models of integration expect migrants and native-born people to participate in a learning process of second-culture acquisition and to contribute to a common changed culture (Berry 1997; Strang and Ager 2010). Policies endorsing assimilation and acculturation will differ based on the degree to which they require cultural conformity or allow for cultural differences. Policies that protect cultural differences are called 'multicultural policies'.

The foundation of integration is access to citizenship and legal rights, and the policies and laws governing them fall under the reserved powers of the UK government. All other elements of integration are regulated by the devolved governments. The policy areas that influence a migrant's incorporation into their host society – health, education, housing, legal services – are the purview of the Scottish government.[5] Immigrant integration is therefore primarily a national rather than state responsibility, which provides the Scottish government with an opportunity to develop an integration strategy that would best meet Scotland's needs. The Scottish integration strategy endorses acculturation and the dynamic two-way relational process that changes immigrants and Scotland, promoted with policies of multiculturalism (Kearns and Whitley 2015; Shubin and Dickey 2013). For example, the 2002 One Scotland, Many Cultures campaign communicated the idea that Scotland is a home to many cultures and that those cultures should be respected and celebrated. The 2014 One Scotland campaign retained this message, and extended it to promote equality across many diversities, including sexuality, disability, gender, religion, and culture. Beyond a general approach, the Scottish government has not developed a national integration strategy for all immigrants, and most services are administered by local authorities. However, the national government has designed a strategy for refugee integration with the New Scots Strategy. The strategy defines integration as a 'two-way process' of positive change, and identifies the Scottish approach as a method of acculturation (Scottish Government 2013a: 9). The strategy uses Ager and Strang's integration framework as the model and it seeks to improve refugee access to services, while noting the importance of 'cohesive, multi-cultural communities' for long-term integration (Scottish Government 2018c: 12; Scottish Government 2013a: 9).

When communities successfully promote acculturation, immigrants have access to resources and services that enable optimal integration outcomes, like language classes, educational opportunities, or employment assistance. Several qualitative and quantitative studies in Scotland affirm the importance of language acquisition for immigrant integration, especially when it comes to accessing information that could assist with integration, like employment opportunities or public services (Kearns and Whitley 2015; Sim and Bowes 2007; Moskal 2014, 2016; Mulvey 2013; Weishaar 2008). Shared language also facilitates social interactions that lead to two-way cultural exchange, which is critical for the development of social cohesion:

> The role of social interaction is crucial to the process of migrant integration into the host society. It is through social contacts and the climate created by the possibility of such contacts that people develop a sense of belonging in a particular social space. (Scottish Government 2016b: 61)

Scotland funds English for Speakers of Other Languages (ESOL) classes for migrants, and though the UK's Home Office sets the rules for the courses, the Scottish government determines the curriculum and how much support to provide.[6]

Failure to learn host country language has consequences for generations of an immigrant's family. Language acquisition leads to increased possibilities for educational qualifications and employment, and both employment and education are empirically associated with positive integration outcomes for migrants in the UK (Cebulla et al. 2010). Immigrants who do not speak English in the UK limit the social and economic mobility of their families because they tend to be underemployed and working in low-skilled jobs (Moskal 2016). Poor host country language skills and underemployment are mutually reinforcing because employment provides a venue and incentives for learning the local language. Employment also leads to a greater sense of belonging and provides migrants with the opportunity to develop important functional skills (Kearns and Whitley 2015; Sim 2009). Language acquisition is critical for different members of an immigrant's family, and is especially important for accessing education services. Success in school is associated with using local amenities and higher degrees of neighbourliness, both of which contribute to social cohesion (Kearns and Whitley 2015).

Some people think migrants should be individually responsible for learning the host country language or getting appropriate qualifications, or that they should provide evidence of integration capacity (language competency and qualifications) before coming to a host country as a signal of their interest in becoming a member of their new community. Over the last decade, many states have written integration requirements into their immigration law as a prerequisite for a visa.[7] While these efforts may be well intended, they impose an unrealistic burden on migrants, especially since some migrants (like refugees) cannot make long-term plans. Furthermore, knowledge or training will always be supplemented with local knowledge or opportunities upon arrival. Communities that willingly provide access to those opportunities are more likely to experience enhanced integration outcomes.

The amount of time a migrant spends in Scotland determines their degree of integration, and migrants who have been in the UK longer demonstrate higher levels of social trust, stronger social relations, and a sense of community

(Kearns and Whitley 2015). Time spent in the UK corresponds with other important facilitators of integration, like higher levels of English proficiency and employment (Office for National Statistics 2014). Refugees exhibit a positive relationship between time spent in the country and community connections only after they receive leave to remain, which illustrates that security of status is required before a migrant can build the connections and attachments that help with integration (Kearns and Whitley 2015). No matter how long a migrant has lived in a state, deep integration begins once migrants move in to a neighbourhood they like, because the neighbourhood is the most important social community (Strang and Ager 2010; Mulvey 2013). No matter how supportive the political elites and national policies are, if migrants encounter hostility in their neighbourhoods, their quality of life will suffer.

Formal exclusion occurs because local service providers lack the necessary experience, skills, and resources to address the requirements of a growing and culturally diverse migrant population. As a representative from the Scottish Refugee Council said with reference to asylum seeker integration:

> A lot of new local authorities had little or no knowledge or experience of doing this . . . I think the Scottish government could put some serious political pressure, and peer pressure amongst local authorities to take part in the programme, but ultimately each local authority is responsible for themselves, and whilst they've done things, I think, reasonably well, issues of longer-term integration aren't necessarily their forte. (Personal interview 3 April 2019)

The Scottish Parliament's Equalities and Human Rights Committee found that local authorities may not be fully informed about what resources are available to an immigrant (Scottish Parliament 2017). Housing is especially problematic:

> Placing people in 'low housing' demand areas seemed counterproductive to the local authority's objective in attracting people to live and work in the area; living in 'low demand housing areas' conflicted with migrant workers' interests in improving their quality of life, while also creating potential areas of conflict with 'local' residents. (De Lima and Wright 2009: 398)

Many migrants in Glasgow live in regeneration areas, which are characterised by low-demand, high-rise estates that are scheduled for demolition and development.[8] Migrants living in these areas display a lower likelihood of engaging in neighbourly exchanges and report lower levels of enjoyment in and satisfaction with their area (Kearns and Whitley 2015).[9] The only reported benefit of living in a regeneration area was better access to financial social support, which speaks to the effectiveness of programmes targeting areas with a concentrated immigrant population.

Efforts to improve integration must target the community structures, and integration must be a collaborative project undertaken by host communities and their migrants. The work must be done locally to have the most positive effects. This is good news for those who want Scotland to have more control over future immigration – it already has control over arguably the most important element of the migrant experience and one that will make the difference between a migrant leaving or staying in the country. However, the importance of the local community means that the desire to welcome and include migrants must have deep roots that spread throughout the whole country. While leadership can be centralised, the motivation and the work must be dispersed. In return, the local communities will feel the main benefits of acculturation, which will improve quality of life for everyone in the neighbourhood. These integration strategies will not be starting with a completely blank slate, however, which means that Scottish elites will need to grapple with the racism that already exists within society in order to ensure a stable foundation for a diverse and cohesive society.

Racism

Though immigrant flows to Scotland have been small compared with other countries, immigrants have always been present in Scottish society. Historical groups of immigrants did not exhibit the racial or cultural diversity associated with immigrants today, but they were perceived as being significantly different from their Scottish hosts, and they were not given a warm welcome into Scottish society. In the mid-1800s, Irish immigrants fleeing famine came to Scotland in large numbers. Irish Catholics were abused and stereotyped by all sections of Scottish society, resulting in the insular Irish communities established around Catholic churches. Irish Protestants fared a bit better, though their Orange traditions (public expressions of Protestant unionism) inflamed sectarian conflict, particularly in the West of Scotland. Signs of sectarianism are still present in Scotland, most virulently and publicly in matches between the Celtic and Rangers football clubs, in political graffiti, and during the summer 'marching season' when the Orange Order marches through cities in Scotland and Northern Ireland.[10] Religious animus formed the basis of most discriminatory behaviour in Scotland at the time, but other migrant groups also experienced xenophobia, including phenotypically white migrants who were racialised and perceived as inferior.[11] Many immigrants experienced targeted discrimination related to the size of the immigrant population (as with the Irish or Russian immigration), or political hostility related to the international climate or political disempowerment (as with German and Lithuanian immigrants) (Braber 2012).

Racism targeting minoritised groups did not manifest as a systemic problem in Scotland before the end of the twentieth century, largely because racial diversification of Scottish society did not begin until the mid-1980s (Penrose and Howard 2008). This does not mean that modern racism was not present in the minds of individual Scots, just that racial difference was not part of the institutional make-up of Scottish society: there was 'not the presence or absence of racism per se, but the absence of a racialization of the political process' (Miles and Dunlop 1986: 23). Even as instances of racism increased, sectarianism occupied the minds of the political elite and 'a political preoccupation between the religious divide between Catholic and Protestant Christians displaced the racism at the centre of English political affairs from Scottish affairs, producing what is now recognized as unwarranted complacency among Scottish decision-makers' (Hopkins and Smith 2008: 105). The neglect allowed racism to take root, and eventually, racism and its attendant social problems were impossible to ignore. Penrose and Howard (2008) summarised early steps leading to the recognition of racism in Scotland. In 1987, a report for the Scottish Ethnic Minorities Research Unit revealed that over 80% of the Indian and Pakistani people living in Glasgow reported experiencing racist abuse, and 20% were physically assaulted. By 1998, the Commission for Racial Equality revealed that Scotland was the site of a disproportionate percentage of the UK's hate crimes, reporting 7.3% of racially motivated incidents in the UK while hosting only 2.1% of the UK's minoritised populations.[12] In 1999, central Scotland recorded the highest rate of racist incidents in the UK, about 15 times higher than London. Many incidents targeted asylum seekers. In 2000, the first year of the refugee resettlement programme in Glasgow, Glasgow City Council housing services recorded 107 instances of racial harassment, of which 96 targeted asylum seekers, and 35 were on a single housing estate (Binns 2002). At the same time, a number of high-profile racist incidents in Scotland were picked up by the mainstream media, including several murders.[13] Lenient sentencing of the murderers raised bigger questions about the extent to which racism was embedded in British/Scottish institutions (Penrose and Howard 2008).

Since the start of the twenty-first century, there have been further disturbing reports of racism directed at immigrants and members of minoritised groups, reaching a peak in 2008/9.[14] Most discrimination occurs in the workplace, the education system, or in the health care system. In 2015, 31% of minoritised residents surveyed in Scotland reported experiencing discrimination within the last five years, and most attributed the discrimination to their race or ethnicity (Meer 2018). Sixty per cent indicated that they did not report their discriminatory treatment to anyone.[15] While many minoritised groups face racism and discrimination in Scotland, three groups merit special attention because of the particular ways that they are believed to challenge Scottish identity: Muslims, Gypsy/Roma communities, and English residents in Scotland are all victims of 'acceptable racism'. None of these groups is a distinct racial group, but they have all been racialised and have experienced racism in Scotland. Racism against members of all three of these groups is justified with claims that they refuse to become Scottish, or that they embody distinctly un-Scottish values.

Islamophobia

The Muslim community in Scotland is small, making up about 1.5% of the population, but this small community has attracted a disproportionate amount of negative attention ever since the 9/11 and 7/7 terrorist attacks fundamentally transformed the experience of Muslims in the UK. Muslims went from being seen as citizens of the Commonwealth to being seen as a potential enemy of the state. According to the 2011 census, 65% of Scotland's Muslims are of Pakistani heritage, but the Muslim community diversified as Muslims from Iraq, Iran, and Afghanistan migrated to the UK as refugees. Ninety-two per cent of the Muslims in Scotland identify as members of a minoritised ethnic group, making the community both religiously and racially distinct. Muslims embody multiple intersecting identities that make it difficult to determine which identity is provoking a particular discriminatory response.

Islamophobia is widespread in Scotland. Hussain and Miller (2006) found that 49% of white Scots hold Islamophobic opinions. When Pakistani Muslims living in Scotland were asked about their experiences, Hussain and Miller found that 87% believed Scots sometimes treat those that they do not see as 'truly Scottish' worse than they treat others, and 51% reported a personal experience with harassment or discrimination that they attributed to their religious or national identity. In 2020, the Scottish Parliament's cross-party group on tackling Islamophobia conducted an inquiry and found that over 83% of participants said they had experienced Islamophobia, most commonly as verbal abuse at work or online. Hussain and Miller (2006) found levels of Islamophobia were lower in Scotland than in England, and unlike in England, street-level nationalism in Scotland does not correlate with Islamophobia. Nevertheless, a large percentage of people express Islamophobic viewpoints, and more worryingly, may feel justified in doing so because they can explain their feelings with Scottish egalitarian values. This is done in two ways. First, people tend to mistakenly equate all Islamic practices with Islamic fundamentalism, and they see fundamentalism and its attendant positions on gender equality and church–state relations as contradicting Scotland's democratic values. Second and relatedly, Scots might see expressions of religiosity, like wearing the headscarf, as a signal that the wearer is choosing to align themselves with an un-Scottish, fundamentalist belief system, and therefore refusing to integrate into Scottish society. Goldie (2018) captured this sentiment in interviews with Scots who identify South Asian Muslims as a 'problem group' in Scotland. They believed Muslims were refusing to conform to national Scottish culture and were choosing to 'stand out' rather than blend in. Hopkins (2010) similarly found that signifiers of 'Muslimness' (dress, skin colour, having a beard) resulted in experiences of exclusion. For Scottish Muslims, 'their birth claims to Scottishness are only deemed "valid" if they are backed up by adherence to perceived cultural norms' (Goldie 2018: 139). Equating Islamic practice with fundamentalism is inaccurate, and religious practices like the headcovering are primarily motivated by personal piety and modesty rather than exclusive loyalty to another culture or political regime (Siraj 2011). These mistakes must be corrected in the public consciousness, and Islamophobia must be given moral weight equivalent to that of racism in policy discussions.

Anti-Roma/Gypsy Sentiment

The Roma/Gypsy population is one of the most systematically oppressed and marginalised populations in Europe. Roma is an umbrella term capturing a wide range of identifications across national, linguistic, cultural, and racial lines. Scotland has an indigenous Gypsy/Traveller population, and migrant Romani communities were established in Scotland after the 2004 and 2007 enlargements of the EU that enabled the Roma populations of East Europe to travel freely. There are no reliable figures on the size of the Roma population in Scotland, but the Scottish government estimated a population of between 3,804 and 4,946 people in 2013 – the real size of the community is likely larger (The Social Marketing Gateway 2013). The majority of the migrant Roma population (around 3,500 people) live in Glasgow, most of whom reside in the Govanhill area, which is Glasgow's most diverse neighbourhood and home to one of the largest Roma communities in Britain.

Scotland was the first nation in the UK to recognise Gypsy/Traveller communities as a racial/ethnic group, which should have provided them protection from discrimination under the 1976 and other subsequent Race Relations Acts. There is evidence of systematic discrimination against Roma populations in Scotland, regardless of whether they are settled or itinerant. Roma populations have faced discrimination in everyday interactions and have been denied their rights to access public services like education and employment assistance (Clark 2018).

Public sentiment responds to local and national press reports on Roma encampments, culture, and behaviours: 'Racialized stereotypes/tropes/fears appear in these reports that feed into and reinforce pre-existing displays of "banal" anti-Gypsyism that runs through society' (Clark 2018: 154). This style of reporting dominates coverage of the Govanhill neighbourhood, where reports of overcrowding and infestation mean that 'place-based racialization has resulted in the problems of an area being attributed to Roma explicitly (and often exclusively) and presented as distinctly "Roma problems" or as symptoms of *The* Roma Problem', rather than being attributed to conditions of economic degradation and predatory landlords (Mullen 2018: 221). The Roma are also stereotyped as a threat to social cohesion, with Govanhill depicted as being 'comprised of separate bounded communities united only in mutual resentment and antagonism' where Roma, and especially Roma men, are disliked and feared (Mullen 2018: 2011). The media hype reached a fever pitch in 2017, with reports 'short on fact and heavy on insinuation', that Roma families were selling their children into prostitution (McKenna 2017). The child sex abuse is presented as the apex of social evils blamed on the Roma, ranging from untidiness to organised crime.

Racism directed at the Roma remains 'acceptable' for two reasons. The first is the way the racialisation of place allowed Roma and the Govanhill community to 'become inextricably linked, to the extent that it has become possible to evoke the Roma "problem" without naming Roma at all' (Mullen 2018: 206). The second reason racism is acceptable is the purported Roma refusal to integrate (evidenced by the maintenance of their language and distinct cultural practices) and their threat to pre-existing social cohesion. By framing the Roma as violating Scotland's social contract, discriminatory attitudes towards the Roma can be justified, while racism against other communities who are more willing to adhere to 'the Scottish way of life' is condemned. This tendency is illustrated by the way Govanhill's Scottish Asian residents are included within the community aggrieved by the presence of the Roma, and are 'often strategically quoted to deflect from allegations of racism' (Mullen 2018: 213). Academic Tom Gallagher (2016) made similar comparisons between the Roma and other foreign-born populations in an editorial in which he asserted that 'Scots, Pakistanis, Bangladeshis and Irish had lived fairly harmoniously together for over a generation. Each community had its quirks but basically nearly everyone adhered to the same rules for living and there were plenty of cross-ethnic friendships' but now 'Roma . . . have so far been unwilling to abide by the rules for amicable urban living.' The euphemistic language and unfavourable comparisons with other minoritised groups within Scotland cover racist sentiments with a veneer of social respectability that allows the speaker to occupy a moral high ground, from whence they can claim to support humane living conditions and community spirit, though the derogatory racist spirit of these statements lies just below the surface. Contrasting attitudes towards immigrant versus other vulnerable groups are even seen among the political elites. A representative from Amnesty International identified the Roma and transgender people as the major targets of discrimination in Scotland and said:

> It's almost political suicide for politicians of Holyrood to get up and give a 'send them home' type speech [about immigrants]. It just wouldn't happen up here . . . We do see quite discriminatory attitudes [towards gypsy travellers and transgender people] in Holyrood which are obviously very disappointing, but kind of highlight how acceptable and widespread [those attitudes] are. (Personal interview 27 March 2019)

Though individual politicians may exhibit derogatory attitudes towards the Roma, the Scottish government recognises disparities in education and social care suffered by the Roma, and in 2017 introduced a Race Equality Plan with a specific section on Gypsy/Travellers (the only group to be singled out in an individual section).[16] The plan is focused on improving outcomes, but it also includes events celebrating Gypsy/Traveller culture and improving community ties. The government established a working group charged with improving the lives of the Roma community members in Scotland. Glasgow City Council is also enforcing compulsory purchase orders to remove properties from the hands of predatory landlords. These steps are overdue and welcome, but it is equally important to confront the pervasive forces in the media and beyond that euphemistically stigmatise the Roma/Gypsy/Traveller communities as 'other' and provide a microphone for the expression of racist sentiments.

Anglophobia

For most of Scottish history, Scotland's defining 'other' has been England, and resentment of the English has provided a unified Scottish social consciousness and identity. Though the political elite have explicitly tried to disassociate Scottish nationalism from antagonistic sentiment, anti-English sentiment (also called Anglophobia) is linked to the rise of Scottish nationalism because Scottishness is defined in part by not being English. Because England is associated with oppression and un-Scottishness, Anglophobia is more socially acceptable than many other phobias or discriminatory attitudes.

Because the English-born are Scotland's largest immigrant group, outnumbering all other first-generation immigrant groups put together, discrimination against them will naturally be pervasive. Hussain and Miller (2006) found Anglophobia is less prevalent than Islamophobia in Scotland, which suggests that English residents are privileged relative to other migrant groups. However, 28% of the English-born participants in their study reported experiencing discrimination for being English. A number of Anglophobic incidents have been covered in the media, and interviews with English-born Scottish residents suggest anti-English banter and abuse is a common occurrence, and 'part of a collective Scottish mentality' (McIntosh et al. 2004: 48). Though English immigrants experience less discrimination than other groups, they 'cope worse with it and react more indignantly to it', which may be a product of their feelings of entitlement to equal treatment within the constituent nations of the UK (Hussain and Miller 2006: 98).

Anglophobia does not look like racism because biological race is not the defining characteristic. The English accent is the most obvious marker of difference, which means that future generations of English-born residents will not necessarily suffer discrimination related to their heritage (McIntosh et al. 2004). However, for the first generation of English transplants, Anglophobia functions much like other phobias and shares many of the same determinants (Hussain and Miller 2006). Furthermore, English residents in Scotland explicitly describe their negative experiences as a form of racism. Anti-English antipathy mimics conventional racism in England in the way it has been politicised: whereas Islamophobia and anti-immigrant sentiment are not associated with national identity or SNP membership, SNP members and those who identify as exclusively Scottish are more likely to be Anglophobic (Hussain and Miller 2006). This raises questions about whether Scottish nationalism and its attendant Anglophobia have displaced more conventional xenophobic attitudes, leading Hussain and Miller to conclude that 'the impact of (Scottish) nationalism is more to redirect phobias than to increase or reduce them' (2006: 83).

The persistent 'acceptable racism' towards Muslims, the Roma/Gypsy communities, and English immigrants reveals blind spots and areas of tension in Scotland's civic nationalism, which highlight the boundaries Scots draw around their concept of Scottishness and point to areas where anti-racism efforts should be increased. Public anti-racism efforts are important, because Hussain and Miller (2006) find that those Muslim and English residents who believe the Scottish Parliament sees their minoritised communities as an asset are much less likely to suspect that Scots are racist. Even if they experience racism, they might be more likely to attribute it to individual ignorance, rather than to a systemic problem, which could help preserve the civic character of Scottish nationalism.

Anti-racism Efforts

Scotland is in an interesting moral position. In some ways, the population should be congratulated – intolerance does not appear to be as widespread in Scotland as it is in the rest of the UK (Pillai et al. 2007; McCollum et al. 2014). For example, Hussain and Miller (2006) found that on comparable indicators, English survey respondents run 14% ahead of Scots in Islamophobia.[17] However, one cannot ignore the persistent hostility towards migrants and minoritised groups, particularly in the urban communities where migrants most often live. Though the challenges of demographic decline and economic growth dominate discussions about the benefits of migration, racism and discrimination must be confronted before immigrants can feel that they are true members of a community. Perhaps racism and discrimination have not been associated with immigration to the same extent in the public eye because the political elite worry that drawing attention to the challenges of diversification risks undermining their arguments about the universal benefits from migration. Work is happening behind the scenes, however. Scottish elites understand that tackling racism is something that must be done actively, based on group-specific instruments to monitor representation and equal treatment. Through their efforts, Scottish elites have developed an approach to race equality that 'can be traced to a distinctly Scottish, rather than UK experience' (Meer 2018: 124). A number of Scottish Acts addressing discrimination offer equivalent protections across a broad array of identity categories, including religion, race, colour, nationality, ethnicity, gender identity, sexual orientation, and disability. Scotland has also sought to mainstream its commitment to race equality across all of its policy domains, while the UK created separate commissions that were more vulnerable to cuts.[18] Meer (2018) argues that the 'Scottish Approach' to race equality has the potential to make a substantial difference, especially when it comes to training public sector staff. He also believes that these efforts could promote more accurate reporting.

Many of these efforts might be invisible to the Scottish public, but the One Scotland, Many Cultures anti-racism campaign included a publicity campaign to raise public awareness of Scotland's cultural diversity and actively celebrate it. The campaign implicitly equated race and culture, and its objective was to change the attitudes and behaviours of Scottish people towards culturally and racially minoritised groups. However, according to Penrose and Howard, the focus on enforcement and individual prejudice was not paired with a clear forward-looking vision of multiculturalism, which demands that an 'individual change their understanding of themselves and of the country that helps define them' rather than merely demanding that they change how they treat others (2008: 129). Multiculturalism requires an active transformation of the individual and the society.

Though the campaign may not have made the direct link between individual and societal transformation, it did have a societal impact by promoting ideas of inclusive, civic nationalism. The campaign challenged the assumption that ethnic or national identities are fixed and unchanging, and rejected the belief that national identities are bestowed by parental inheritance at birth. It established a timeline of Scottish history that highlighted pluralism and transition as central and constant elements of Scottish historical experience. Its objective was to diminish fear and insecurity around the idea of future social change. The campaign portrayed Scottish society as both 'historically rooted and as an evolving social formation' (Penrose and Howard 2008: 121). Furthermore, the campaign deliberately tapped into pre-existing nationalist sentiment and national pride and connected it to an image of a racially diverse and nationally coherent Scotland:

> Slogans such as 'don't let Scotland down' and 'A small country, not a country of small minds', implicitly suggest that individual expressions of racism do a disservice to the country and that a progressive Scotland is one in which cultural diversity thrives. (Penrose and Howard 2008: 124)

Some populations of migrants, like refugees, require special care in fostering social inclusion because the nature of the refugee dispersal programme means that neither the refugee nor the host community has control over where the refugee will end up. This, along with the forced nature of forced migration, means that the refugee does not have time to plan their integration into their new community. In response, Glasgow City Council established a Refugee Support Team, the Scottish government developed a Refugee Integration Action Plan, and the Scottish Refugee Council set up Refugee Integration Networks in key areas of Glasgow. These programmes attempted to smooth the transition process as refugees were integrated into communities. However, as Kearns and Whitley observe, though 'integration projects have been running for over a decade, initially in response to racial tensions and migrant destitution, the challenges to be addressed may have changed but not disappeared' (2015: 2122).

More work must be done to combat prejudice and discrimination in Scotland, especially among Scots at the street level. Scottish elites have sent a consistent message about Scottish multiculturalism and anti-racism, and those efforts have successfully branded Scotland as a place of relative tolerance. However, vulnerable populations continue to experience 'acceptable' racism, which must be identified and repudiated as being inconsistent with Scotland's social norms and national interest.

Conclusion

Evidence from the UK and Europe contradicts the view that increasing ethnic heterogeneity as a result of immigration inherently represents a problematic or corrosive influence on social cohesion. Where acculturation is smooth, discrimination is suppressed, and social connections link members of diverse groups together, community cohesion can be developed and enriched. Furthermore, diverse communities will be more resilient against the inevitable forces of change in this globalised era. Can Scotland achieve these ideal conditions? The Scottish public has to deal with persistent racism, segregated opportunities, and examples of migrant community insularity.[19] Many local stakeholders working with migrants are familiar with best practices, including the development of cross-cutting programmes to simultaneously serve deprived native and immigrant populations, bringing them together to inspire the development of productive social capital. They highlight the importance of community planning to optimise integration, learning from the mistakes of old refugee dispersion programmes. They describe cultural and artistic engagements as especially effective ways to work across divisions because they yield both direct and indirect benefits associated with cultural diversity.

Making these changes requires policy makers to push against cultural headwinds. Some people would prefer to live within homogenous communities and to keep their neighbourhoods exactly the same. Social cohesion is easier to achieve within these homogenous communities. Does that make these communities better? More to the point, is it realistic to expect that societies can remain isolated and homogenous? The international academic consensus suggests that the answer to both questions is no. Political leaders must therefore work to overcome short-term effects of diversification on social cohesion with campaigns to develop bridging social capital, and to lay the cultural groundwork so that demographic, economic, and cultural benefits of migration can come in time.

Laying the groundwork to help local communities develop social cohesion in the presence of diversity is vitally important for the Scottish effort to attract immigrants and should be a top priority for the Scottish government. However, the SNP-led Scottish government may be disincentivised to make integration and community building a central piece of its migration platform because it will not advance its larger ambitions of greater autonomy and independence from the UK. Community cohesion policies are *already* the purview of the Scottish government and there is no political benefit to be gained from highlighting deficiencies in the government's own work. In contrast, government prioritisation of economic and demographic issues is primarily concerned with securing the right to control immigration. A cynic might suggest that the prioritisation of economic and demographic concerns is reflective of the Scottish government's ultimate priority of wresting more political power from Westminster.

The strategy of positioning Scotland against England is demonstrated by the way Scottish elites have advanced a narrative of absent racism in Scotland, because it is able to 'nest so comfortably within the new common sense of Scottish politics, the dominant story that has been forged, by the SNP and others – that the Scots are in some sense different from the English' (Davidson and Virdee 2018: 9). According to this narrative, racism is 'in the heart of English nationalism and in the activities of English right-wing extremism' while Scotland is 'free of racism and its attendant threats' (Hopkins and Smith 2008: 108). Mythologising Scotland is part of the nation-building enterprise, but intrinsic within it is a 'danger of underestimating and thereby disabling the contemporary struggle against racism' that is required to build a truly egalitarian society (Davidson and Virdee 2018: 10). The denial of racism becomes an exclusionary tool as it delegitimises the experience of minoritised Scots who report racism, and it 'indicates a sense of belonging that is qualified or provisional' on the willingness of racial minorities to subscribe to the narrative of absent racism in Scotland (Hopkins and Smith 2008: 108). The lived reality of racialised minorities in Scotland is not seen as a Scottish reality, which removes them from other Scots. The irony of the situation is clear: the political desire to project an image of a racism-free Scotland undermines the political will to work towards combatting racism and building social cohesion in diverse communities in Scotland. As a result, nationalist politics could undermine the political agenda to make Scotland sustainable through migration.

Notes

1. The idea of safely segregated communities somewhat ironically mirrors the native-born defensive withdrawal from diversifying urban centres into gated housing developments or homogenous suburbs.
2. Most of the literature on community cohesion focuses on the impact of diversity, and not immigration. A community can become more diverse without immigration and immigration does not always increase a community's racial, ethnic, or linguistic diversity. It is therefore difficult to make strong claims about the link between immigration and community cohesion.
3. Even though much of this work finds a negative relationship between diversity and generalised trust, the authors admit the relationship is not universal or inevitable. Putnam (2007) theorises that the corrosive effects of ethnic diversity should be evident only in the short to medium turn and admits that some societies have overcome fragmentation by creating cross-cutting forms of social solidarity and more inclusive identities. Stolle et al. (2008) tempered their findings with evidence that the negative effects can be mediated by social ties: those who talk with their neighbours are less influenced by the ethnic and racial make-up of their communities.
4. Gijsberts et al. (2011) tested the effect of diversity on many measures of social cohesion in the Netherlands and found a single relationship similar to that discovered by Laurence (2013): the presence of minoritised groups in a neighbourhood has an adverse influence on neighbourhood contacts, but not on generalised trust/ connectivity, volunteerism, or helping.
5. All residents in Scotland are entitled to health care regardless of their nationality. All children in Scotland are likewise entitled to receive a state school education, though free university education depends on immigration status and length of residency. Refugees are entitled to equal access to further and higher education. The Scottish government has chosen to strongly reinforce the UN's Rights of the Child under the Children (Scotland) Act, and has asserted that migrant, refugee, and asylee children have the same rights as any child under Scottish law.
6. The Scottish ESOL strategy was introduced in 2007, and refreshed in 2015 to account for changes in the migrant population and the policy environment. In 2013, the Home Office required applicants for settlement or citizenship to demonstrate a degree of English language proficiency. In Scotland, ESOL classes are offered by a range of providers including local authorities, colleges, schools, voluntary organisations, universities, and private providers. Funding is usually delivered through partnership with local authorities (Scottish Government 2015).
7. This is often the case with family migration/reunification in Europe, which is protected under European law. States have avoided legal constraints by imposing a set of conditionalities on entry, like compulsory integration courses or integration tests, or additional burdens such as proof of financial or social dependency in the case of children and parents, minimum income requirements, housing conditions, the proof of future cohabitation, or proof of 'active' family ties. These conditions shape the nature of the migrant family to conform with European ideas of a nuclear family (Bonjour and de Hart 2013; Kraler and Bonizzoni 2010; Wray [2011] 2016).
8. Regeneration has not been concluded in most of these communities due to the 2008 financial crisis. As a result, they remain the least desirable areas in Glasgow.

9. Even though migrants in regeneration outcomes report lower levels of satisfaction, forcing them to move to allow for regeneration may damage the integration of migrants living in these areas, as they would be required to move away from the multi-ethnic communities they created. For refugees this would be the second act of involuntary relocation. Deep integration requires both certainty of status and consistency in location.
10. The Orange Order is a fraternity formed in Ulster in 1795 to promote Protestantism and loyalty to the Crown. The marches are part of annual celebrations leading up to 12 July, the anniversary of the Battle of the Boyne of 1690, when William of Orange, a Dutch Protestant, defeated his rival for the English throne, the Catholic King James.
11. Though racism and sectarianism are researched as distinct phenomena, Clayton (2005) remarks on the marked parallels between sectarianism and racism in their underlying determinants and local geographies.
12. Reported crimes do not always represent actual crimes, though they correspond with each other. Higher rates of reporting can signal higher levels of trust or expectation that the authorities will act. It is not clear whether this is the case with hate crimes in Scotland.
13. These include the death of Imran Khan in Glasgow and Surjit Singh Chhokar in Wishaw in 1998.
14. There were 4,564 racially motivated offences recorded by the police in 2008. Since 2008, there has been a year-on-year decline in reported racially motivated offences, down to 1,744 offences in 2018/19 (Crown Office and Procurator Fiscal Service 2019).
15. This underreporting contrasts with 65% of the sample agreeing or strongly agreeing with the statement that 'I have confidence in the laws against discrimination' and 64% agreeing or strongly agreeing they had confidence in the authorities and other organisations to pursue discrimination cases.
16. The 2011 Census reveals that Gypsy/Travellers in Scotland were more likely than the general population to have no qualifications, to be unemployed, to work in low-skilled jobs, and to not own their own home. Their rates of evictions are also very high (Clark 2018).
17. Minoritised and immigrant populations exhibit even lower levels of Islamophobia. Black and Asian people (not all of them Muslim) in England are 21% less Islamophobic, and in Scotland, the English immigrant population is 12% less Islamophobic than majority Scots (Hussain and Miller 2006).
18. In 2012, Scotland placed Scottish Specific Duties on local authorities, requiring each one to publish a mainstreaming report on progress made in integrating the General Equality Duty to eliminate unlawful discrimination, advance equality of opportunity, and foster good relations. Mainstreaming can also be seen in the Race Equality Framework for Scotland (Scottish Government 2016a), which brought stakeholders together to reflect on the successes and failings of Scottish approaches to race equality.
19. The edited volume *No Problem Here* (Davidson et al. 2018) describes historical and modern racism in Scotland; Sime and Fox (2015) describe unequal access to services that are important to children's integration and civic participation; Kay and Morrison (2012) describe the development of minoritised communities in Glasgow.

6

THE POLITICS: PARTY COMPETITION OVER IMMIGRATION IN WESTMINSTER AND HOLYROOD

Immigration may be 'the most toxic issue in British politics for the decade to come' (Shabi 2019). Divisions over immigration cut across party factions, but there is a political trend whereby politicians on the left regularly accuse their right-wing counterparts of using immigrants as a scapegoat for social or economic problems. The reprimands are often accompanied by accusations of racism or bigotry. A classic example is when former Labour Prime Minister Gordon Brown (2007–10) was confronted by a woman complaining about immigrants 'flocking' into the UK. Brown was subsequently caught on a hot microphone calling her a 'bigoted woman':

> Brown's gaffe both consolidated and gave credence to a political coding that would shape everything that came after: the 'hostile environment', the Windrush scandal, the EU referendum and the revival of Britain's far right – deploying a narrative in which sneering, out-of-touch, big-city politicians who favour foreigners and open borders are hopelessly oblivious to the struggles and the so-called 'legitimate concerns' of ordinary working people (who, in this scenario, are always white). (Shabi 2019)[1]

In this environment, immigration became the issue politicians used to signal their stance on a wide range of issues, including nationalism, the EU, labour versus capital, and multiculturalism. When immigration has such symbolic power, it is easy to think about the politics of immigration purely as a feature of party competition. As recent elections have demonstrated, political party members use hard positions on immigration to increase support for their own parties. Partisan politics reflect (and often exaggerate) broader social trends, and the actions and promises of candidates have consequences beyond a single election or re-election. Party competition is therefore a valuable lens through which to understand the prioritisation of immigration and a policy trajectory that shapes everyone's lives. This chapter discusses how that competition has played out in Westminster, the site of the Parliament in the UK, and in Holyrood, the location of the Scottish Parliament. It reviews how party politics have shaped the politics of immigration in Scotland, and the way they have advanced Scottish nation-building. The chapter opens with a brief summary of the general partisan politics of immigration before examining the way Scottish Members of Parliament (MPs) in Westminster discuss immigration in party manifestos, debates, and maiden speeches. It then reviews the more diverse representation of Scottish interests in Holyrood and highlights the political consensus around immigration at the national level. The chapter concludes with a discussion of the strategic and ideological reasons for persistent political consensus about immigration across Scottish politicians from many different political parties.

The Partisan Politics of Immigration

A party's position on immigration can be inferred from the party's ideological placement. Political parties on the left are assumed to favour multicultural and more open immigration policies, while parties on the right are prone to anti-immigrant positions, but this simple left–right dichotomy oversimplifies the issue.[2] On the left, partisans can be divided over immigration based on their relationship with labour. Some support progressive immigration policies and advocate for solidarity with foreign workers, while others see immigration as a threat to the jobs and wages of the working class. Those on the right are also divided. Cultural conservatives might see cultural or ethnic diversity as a threat, while economic conservatives link their free market and pro-business sentiments to the benefits of immigration as a source of labour. It is difficult to pin down a consistent party position on immigration because of immigration's diverse character, but also because it has been a valence issue, in which there is consensus about the general goal of a policy, but parties debate about how to get there. In the UK, common agreement has centred on promoting economically beneficial and high-skilled migration, and carefully controlling all other forms of migration. Party competition develops around which party is best at delivering the objective, and how good the parties are at communicating their positions to the public.

In addition to being a valence issue, immigration has historically been an orthogonal issue for political parties, which means that it has not been central to the party's main position. A party frames immigration so that it fits within its central ideology around which it has the most comparative advantage. For example, a party that occupies a free market position could frame immigration as relating to market forces. A party focused on the working class might discuss migration with reference to whether new migrants compete for jobs or create new opportunities for work. No single party will 'own' the immigration issue in this scenario, but parties will frame the issue differently to support the positions that are more central to their ideologies. This has historically been the case in the UK, especially since the plurality electoral system encourages a move to two catch-all parties.[3] The parties have been oriented by economic class, around capital on the right and labour on the left, which has made immigration a peripheral issue. Things may be changing due to the salience of immigration as one of the main issues driving votes in elections since 2010 (Bale 2014). In addition, populist parties on the far right make immigration a central, rather than orthogonal, issue and their growing appeal motivates other parties to respond by making immigration more central to their platforms.

The party dynamics in the UK take place at national and state levels. Over the last decade, competition over seats at Westminster has driven party positions on immigration. The SNP in Westminster also uses immigration to differentiate itself from the UK-wide parties, but it is concerned about national differentiation, not party competition. Immigration remains an orthogonal issue for political parties in their competition with each other in Holyrood. The rest of this chapter investigates the divergent dynamics of the politics of immigration in Westminster and Holyrood.

WESTMINSTER

Westminster is the site of the Parliament of the UK, which is the supreme legislative body for the whole of the UK and its overseas territories. The way Scottish interests in immigration are presented in Westminster reveals how Scotland situates itself and its interests within the UK, and illuminates areas of convergence with and divergence from other regions in the UK. Divergence has been more common in recent years because since 2015, the Scottish National Party (SNP) consolidated almost all of the Scottish representation, and the ultimate objective of the SNP is to completely revoke Westminster's power over Scotland. Barring that, Westminster has become a site for the political expression of Scottish support for immigration, in opposition to the dominant narrative about immigration control, and this narrative advances the SNP's mission of Scottish nation-building.

The UK Parliament is bicameral, but has three parts including the sovereign, the House of Lords, and the House of Commons. In what follows, 'Parliament' or 'Westminster' refers to the House of Commons, which is an elected chamber representing 650 single member districts. Members of the House of Commons are elected with a plurality electoral system, under which the most natural outcome is for two large centrist parties – the Labour and Conservative Parties – to represent the people of the UK, and whichever party wins a majority of seats forms the government.[4] However, within the last ten years, no party won a majority of the vote in two elections (2010, 2017), resulting in hung elections. Both times, the Conservative Party formed a coalition or governing agreement with another small party. Fears of future electoral losses or another hung parliament made the Conservative majority feel pressured by the increasing success of UK Independence Party (UKIP), a populist party aiming to remove the UK from the EU and, by extension, end free movement. The conflation of EU membership and free movement made the EU synonymous in people's minds with uncontrolled migration. In response, the Conservative Party fought to regain support by picking up immigration as a central party issue and using it as a scapegoat for other policy challenges like pressure on public finances, public services, and the housing shortage. Its hope was to draw the support of those concerned about immigration, but turned off by UKIP's populist tactics. At the same time, the Labour Party realised that its electoral losses to the Conservative Party were partly due to the party's failure to convincingly respond to public concern about immigration.[5] Between 2010 and 2019, the party hardened its stance on immigration, adding to a long history of immigration policy adjustment to compete with the Conservative Party and far right parties, since the populist parties appeal to working-class voters who traditionally support Labour (Bale 2014).[6] The politics of migration in the UK is about party competition, and vice versa.

Scottish constituencies send 59 MPs to Westminster. If Scottish politics resembled those of the rest of the UK, party competition around migration would be echoed in Scottish constituencies. However, Scottish party politics do not resemble those of the UK, even within the halls of Westminster. Before the re-founding of the Scottish Parliament in 1999, political analysis of the UK very rarely distinguished between the regions, and Scottish politics were assumed to be 'British with a difference' since the majority of Scots voted for British political parties and the plurality electoral system encourages two viable party options (McCrone 1992: 146, quoting McAllister and Rose 1984).[7] Regional differences in electoral outcomes were attributed to the socio-economic situation in Scotland, which resembled other parts of the UK. However, McCrone noted political divergence as early as the 1960s, and argued that it 'cannot simply be attributed to quite different social and economic forces impacting on Scotland, but rather their differential political impact north of the border' (1992: 147). The social and economic challenges which Scotland historically shared with other regions of the UK were (and are) refracted through a different political agenda in Scotland.

This different political agenda is illustrated by two major electoral trends in the post-war period: the divergence in the success of the two major political parties north and south of the border, and in the rise and recent success of the SNP. Support for the Conservative Party has held steady in England, but it was halved in Scotland by the 1986 general election.[8] Trends in support for Labour were comparable across the border until the late 70s, at which point Scotland exhibited much higher rates of support for Labour.[9] With the move away from the Conservative Party, most party competition in Scotland took place on the left. By 1970, the combined gap in party vote share between England and Scotland was 11.4%, with 10.3% attributed to Conservative shortfall in Scotland (McCrone 2017). The consequence of this party volatility was that

> Scotland got a government England voted for, as it long had done, but by then, it mattered considerably that the ruling party did not have a political mandate in Scotland. So there entered the political lexicon the 'democratic deficit' whereby the political complexion of the British House of Commons was coloured by an English hue regardless of how Scots voted. (McCrone 2005: 8)

Since the 1970s, the vote share gap between Scotland and England has been in the double digits, averaging 26% and peaking in 2019 at 38%.[10] The propensity for Scots to diverge from English voters in their support for the Conservative and Labour Parties coincides with the rise of the Liberal Party (now the Liberal Democrats) and the SNP, both of which have attracted significant support in Scotland since the 1970s. The rise of the SNP was particularly dramatic, culminating in its success in the 2015 British general election (shortly after the failed independence referendum in 2014), when it won 50% of the Scottish vote and 56 out of 59 seats.[11] This decisive victory in Scotland allowed the SNP to replace the Liberal Party as the third-largest party in the House of Commons. In the 2019 UK general election, the SNP exceeded expectations to win 45% of the Scottish vote, resulting in 48 seats, and maintaining its status as the largest minority party.[12] The dominance of the SNP in the Scottish seats in Westminster hides a more complex political reality on the ground, where Scottish versions of all of the parties compete in the general elections for the right to represent their constituencies. Political competition is an important force driving the politics of migration in Scotland, both in how the parties differentiate themselves from each other and in how the Scottish parties differentiate themselves from the UK-wide parties.

The Scottish Political Parties in Westminster

With the exception of the SNP, the Scottish parties operate as a part of the UK parties. As one SNP MSP explained:

> Some of the parties are all loyal to and controlled by their parent party in Westminster. Therefore, whatever they might want to do, they have to

always think back [to] what comes from Westminster. And if you are the Conservative Party, Labour Party, or Liberal Democrats ... they don't have and are not even seeking the power to overcome that situation, so they do have to maintain those policy standpoints that would be reflective of what's coming from Westminster. (Personal interview 10 June 2016)

Despite their close relationship, the Scottish and UK-wide parties publish their own election manifestos, which are declarations of a party's priorities and intentions. Since the Scottish party manifestos are distinct from the UK party manifestos, they allow for a glimpse at differences between the UK and Scottish parties on issues such as immigration.[13] It is most important to consider the differences for the three largest parties in the House of Commons (the SNP, the Labour Party, and the Conservative Party), which have historically been the major party players in Scotland and now represent 89% of the Scottish constituency.[14]

The Scottish National Party

The main objective of the SNP is for Scotland to gain independence from the UK, though it has taken an ideological stand on a number of other policy issues since the 1970s.[15] Starting with the elections of 1974, the party endorsed a social democratic policy platform and falls on the left side of the ideological spectrum. The party was guided by the ideology of the party elites (especially the leadership of Alex Salmond from 1990 to 2000 and 2004 to 2014), membership preferences, and their main party competition from the Labour Party (Lynch 2009). By establishing an ideological position on the left, the SNP aligned its sympathies with issues such as commitments to full employment, government spending on social services, a living wage, an improved NHS, and opposition to nuclear weapons. Immigration was not a central issue for the SNP until recently, though openness to immigrants was embedded within many policy positions.

The SNP advocates for more open policies to attract both high- and low-skilled workers, and has proposed a devolved immigration policy to allow Scottish government ministers to set a points-based population target. The SNP also wants to extend the Fresh Talent post-study work visa that was introduced by the Labour–Liberal Democrat Scottish coalition government in 2005, which allowed students to be granted a two-year visa extension to find work after graduating from a Scottish university. The SNP justifies these policies with reference to Scottish demographic and economic needs, and describes them as necessary for the development of a multicultural and tolerant Scotland. Hepburn and Rosie (2014) suggest that the SNP is the most pro-immigrant of all of the major parties in the UK.

In its manifestos for the most recent general elections, the SNP's stance on migration consistently orients around advocating for a policy that meets Scotland's particular circumstances. In 2010, immigration did not take up much space, with only one paragraph dedicated to an argument that Scotland should take responsibility for immigration so as to develop a policy that meets national needs, with special emphasis on high-skilled immigration. The 2015 manifesto does not include much detail about immigration policy, either, though it does list immigration as a key policy priority, and specifically mentions the desired reintroduction of the post-study work visa. The 2017 manifesto communicates a much more detailed stance on immigration alongside a positive tone towards immigrants. It pushes for a devolved immigration policy, so that Scotland can meet its economic and humanitarian obligations after Brexit with a more open policy towards labour migrants and refugees. The manifesto advocates for the work-study visa again and mentions the experience of the Brain family, an Australian family threatened with deportation from the Scottish Highlands after the cancellation of the post-study work visa.[16] The 2019 manifesto identifies 'a tailored migration system' as a key pledge of the party. As part of this enhanced focus, the manifesto includes a profile of the work of SNP's immigration spokesperson in Westminster, Stuart McDonald, highlighting his efforts to protect the rights of EU citizens and the ways in which he has championed the benefits of immigration to Scotland within Westminster. The manifesto identifies complete control over immigration as a key feature of the SNP's ambition for independence, but advocates for devolved policy 'in the meantime' (Scottish National Party 2019b: 45). In a section where the achievements of the SNP at Westminster are listed, two relate to migration: the reintroduction of the post-study work visa in 2020/1 and scrapping the Conservative Party proposal of fees for EU citizens applying for settled status.

The SNP manifestos demonstrate that immigration has been a vague policy priority of the SNP for several years and was presented as a relatively minor issue in the general election manifestos until after Brexit, at which point the party took a much stronger position for devolved immigration policy. The politics of Brexit and the likely consequences of ending free movement for Scotland made immigration important in two key ways for the SNP. First, ending free movement between EU countries is likely to create a real problem for the Scottish economy, and as the governing party, the SNP has a responsibility to do whatever it can to rectify the problem. Second, within this context, immigration has been used to demonstrate regional distinctiveness and has become a salient tool of political opposition to UK-wide governance in Westminster, where more anti-immigrant perspectives dominate.

The Labour Party

Until 2005, the most natural ally for the SNP in advancing more pro-immigrant policies would have been the Labour Party. The UK Labour Party has historically been open to immigration, promoting the potential of immigration to address skills shortages and the importance of protecting family migration and human rights, while still acknowledging the need for fair and appropriate controls. However, starting in 2005 under the leadership of Tony Blair (Prime Minister from 1997 to 2007), the party focused on controls and border security. The transition to a securitised approach to migration reflected the changed geopolitical environment after the 9/11 terrorist attacks in the United States and public concern over dramatically increased immigration flows following EU enlargement. In 2010, under the leadership of Gordon Brown (Prime Minister from 2007 to 2010), the approach hardened and the UK Labour manifesto primarily discussed migration under the chapter heading 'Crime and Immigration'. The text acknowledges public pressure on the issue, and reads 'We understand people's concerns about immigration . . . and we have acted' (Labour Party 2010: 5:2). The tone of the manifesto communicates distrust of immigrants and explicitly states that 'coming to Britain is a privilege and not a right' (Labour Party 2010: 5:6). Scottish Labour included the identical language in its 2010 manifesto, but added text about recognising skills shortages with a 'uniformly firm but fair' policy, and the need for a flexible system that is responsive to employers (Scottish Labour 2010: 5:6).

In 2015, under party leader Ed Miliband, the UK-wide Labour Party continued to focus on control, and all paragraphs in the manifesto that discuss immigration are duplicated word for word in the Scottish party manifesto, endorsing a policy that recognises the contribution of immigrants while pushing for enhanced control of immigration 'with fair rules' (Scottish Labour 2015: 54). The Scottish Labour manifesto elaborated on the text of the opening page by emphasising the importance of fairness. The 2015 Scottish manifesto is also reframed to address Scottish interests, instead of the more general British ones.[17]

In 2017, the UK Labour Party manifesto under Jeremy Corbyn continued to acknowledge public anxiety about immigration and used language of control, but the tone towards immigrants softened, with positive statements about the societal and economic contributions of immigrants. Scottish Labour included a unique paragraph in the chapter on negotiating Brexit where it emphasises the importance of immigration for Scotland's economy and asserts Scotland's right to be heard in the development of new immigration policies. In 2019, the tone of the UK Labour Party shifted to more openness, promoting a new and fair immigration system, honouring immigrant workers and students, and committing to protect the rights of migrants. There were no substantive differences in UK and Scottish Labour manifestos in 2019.

The Scottish Labour Party general election manifestos very nearly replicate those of the UK Labour Party.[18] The Scottish branch of the party emphasises principles of fairness, and starting in 2017 the party began to assert Scotland's unique need for immigration. This difference was triggered by Brexit and the loss of free movement. When the UK party moved back to a position of openness in 2019, the Scottish party did not distinguish itself from the UK party on immigration. However, Brexit changed the dynamics of the relationship between Scottish and UK-wide branches of the party. Fractures appeared during the 2019 elections, when there was a possibility that the Labour Party could win and form a government in Westminster with the inherited responsibility to implement Brexit. As 62% of Scottish voters wanted to remain in the EU, the idea that Scottish Labour would be called on to support any form of a Brexit deal did not appeal to prospective Scottish Labour MPs. During the lead-up to the 2019 general election, Labour leader Jeremy Corbyn agreed to allow Scottish Labour to campaign against Brexit, even if Labour won (Carrell 2019). Since Labour did not win the election, different approaches were not necessary. However, the underlying divergence could lead to more distinct preferences for Scottish Labour in the future, especially regarding EU migrants. The extent of divergence depends on the position of the main party and whether it feels the need to compete with the conservative parties in the immigration control policy space.

The Conservative Party and Unionist Party

Considering the visibility and salience of immigration as an issue for conservative voters, the Conservative Party manifestos have referenced it surprisingly infrequently until more recent elections. In 2010, the UK party manifesto under David Cameron (Prime Minister from 2010 to 2016) mentioned immigration only twice. The first mention occurs in a section about attracting the 'brightest and best to our country'. The text acknowledges the positive contributions immigrants have made to Britain, but most of the content is dedicated to describing how the party proposes to limit immigration to 'tens of thousands a year, not hundreds of thousands' (Conservative Party 2010: 21). The second reference links immigration control and crime prevention. The Scottish Conservative manifesto perfectly replicates the positions on immigration in 2010.

Immigration is more dominant in the 2015 manifesto, which includes a detailed plan of action for reducing immigration that covers three full pages. Once again, all content relating to immigration is perfectly replicated in the Scottish Conservative manifesto. Immigration is also mentioned frequently in the 2017 manifesto under Theresa May (Prime Minister from 2016 to 2019), always with reference to control. The section describing immigration controls is less detailed than in 2015, though it reiterates commitments to limiting migration to the tens of thousands. The Scottish Conservatives (under Ruth Davidson) included an extra paragraph in their 2017 manifesto where they emphasise that immigration should remain a reserved policy area under the control of the UK government, but advance the idea that the Scottish government should use its power to attract a higher proportion of the UK's immigrants to Scotland. In 2019, the UK and Scottish Conservative Party manifestos look very different from each other. The UK-wide manifesto (under Boris Johnson) is dedicated to 'getting Brexit done', while the headline of the Scottish Conservative manifesto (under Jackson Carlaw) is 'No to Indyref2', referencing Conservative objections to a second Scottish independence referendum. The opening messages from Boris Johnson are structured to correspond with the different central message of the manifestos. In these manifestos, a new points-based immigration policy is highlighted, though the Scottish manifesto adds a description of a system that 'works for every part of the UK' (Scottish Conservatives 2019). The 2019 Scottish manifesto is tailored to a Scottish audience, with all topics in the table of contents reframed with exclusive reference to Scotland, instead of Britain. Despite these differences, much of the text is duplicated.

In the 2019 UK manifesto, the section heading 'Fix our immigration system' reflects the status quo conservative idea that the immigration system is broken (Conservative Party 2019: 20). The policies include ending free movement, the post-Brexit points-based policy, requirements that immigrants contribute before they withdraw social benefits, privileging high-skilled migration, and an emphasis on integration. The Scottish Conservative manifesto identically reflects all of these policies, but the section is entitled 'An immigration system that works for Scotland and the UK' and opens with a statement about the importance of a consistent UK-wide immigration policy, so as to avoid a 'border at Berwick' (Scottish Conservatives 2019: 23).[19] A second unique paragraph stipulates that Scottish Conservatives will advocate for a system that 'reflects the needs of the places that need migration most – in particular, remote and rural communities and the sectors that are most reliant on migrant labour and where there is no domestic workforce available' (Scottish Conservatives 2019: 23). Rhetoric in the Scottish manifesto is substantially softened in the sub-section 'Contributing to our country'. While the UK manifesto opens with 'It is a basic point of principle – and natural justice – that you should not be able to take out before you have put in' (Conservative Party 2019: 23), the Scottish manifesto opens with 'New arrivals almost always pay the taxes that support our vital services' (Scottish Conservatives 2019: 24).

The Conservative Party manifestos demonstrate how the party emphasised migration as a central policy issue in the 2015 elections and beyond. The manifestos reflect no difference in UK and Scottish party positions on immigration and very little consideration of the Scottish context until 2017, at which point the Scottish Conservatives react to SNP calls for devolved immigration policy with a commitment to maintaining immigration as a reserved issue while acknowledging Scotland's interest in attracting migrants. This shift is a feature of the fallout from Brexit, and the challenges facing Scotland when free movement is stopped. The need to send a different message in Scotland grew stronger in 2019, when for the first time the Scottish manifestos move from a general focus on the interests of Britain to a consideration of the unique situation in Scotland.

Though the Scottish Conservatives endorsed the immigration policies of the UK-wide party, albeit with slightly softer rhetoric, there are signs that the Conservative Parties may diverge. In February of 2020, after Home Secretary Priti Patel published the party's more restrictive post-Brexit points-based system, the Scottish Conservative Party faced pressure to push back. Scottish Conservative Leader Jackson Carlaw said that the policies broke the Scottish party's manifesto pledges, and hinted at plans to lobby for 'a migration system in the final analysis and detail which is appropriate to Scotland' (Carrell 2020). This would bring the Scottish Conservatives more into alignment with the other Scottish parties on immigration than with their own party.[20]

For both the Labour and Conservative Parties, there has been very little difference between the UK-wide and Scottish branches of the parties. However, the aftermath of Brexit represented a moment when the Scottish branches of the parties had to consider whether British interests were too different from Scottish interests concerning migration. Starting in 2017, the Scottish branches of both parties asserted a slightly different position on migration in their manifestos. By 2019, the UK-wide Labour Party moved towards the Scottish position and the language was re-harmonised, while the Scottish Conservative Party became more distinct. Brexit was also the point at which the SNP hardened its stance on migration, recognising it as a salient issue that cleanly demonstrated the distinct interests of Scotland. Immigration became a type of vanguard policy for the SNP in Westminster, where the Scottish constituencies are almost exclusively represented by the SNP.

The SNP's Powers in Westminster

At the time of writing, the SNP provides roughly 80% of Scottish representation in Westminster. The high levels of party representation should provide the SNP with an opportunity to influence state-wide policies, though influence would be facilitated by political alliances or coalitions. Despite its size, the other parties at Westminster do not consider the SNP to be suitable for a governing coalition because it is a regional party with ambitions for Scottish independence.[21] Before the 2015 election, Ed Miliband ruled out the possibility of a governing coalition between Labour and the SNP, saying:

I am not going to sacrifice the future of our country, the unity of our country, I'm not going to give in to SNP demands around Trident [the nuclear programme based on the west coast of Scotland], around the deficit, or anything like that. (Wintour and Watt 2015)

He implied the SNP would make demands on behalf of Scotland to the detriment of the UK, including efforts to break up the UK with Scottish independence.

The Labour and Conservative Parties' unwillingness to work with the SNP is supported by the institutions and customs at Westminster. Parliamentary procedure and the design of the House of Commons privileges the roles of the 'Government' and the 'Official Opposition', which means that discussions and mechanisms of accountability within Parliament function as if there are representatives of only two parties present (Thompson 2018). One manifestation of the privileged status of the two largest parties was the structure of televised debates in 2019, in which only the leaders of the Labour and Conservative Parties engaged in a head-to-head debate.[22] The SNP does not have the power one might expect a sizable third party to possess. Nevertheless, Westminster is a venue for articulation of Scottish preferences, as members of the SNP can be members of committees and introduce and participate in debates. Additionally, as the third-largest party, the SNP formally responds to statements, is given a regular slot at Prime Minister's Question Time, chairs two parliamentary select committees, introduces three opposition day debates, and is provided with funds supporting party activities.[23] However, because preference is given to the government and opposition speakers, it might be two hours between SNP MP speeches during debate, most SNP contributions will be at the end of the debate period, and they will be limited to a small amount of time. Consequently, the SNP MPs in Westminster regularly resort to interventions, where they make a comment during someone else's speech with the permission of the speaker (Thompson 2018).

Under the leadership of SNP Westminster Leader Ian Blackford, SNP MPs made their presence in Westminster impactful. In the first few weeks of the parliamentary session following the 2015 elections, the SNP was visible in the chamber, with 'the heavily populated SNP benches bring[ing] a staggering contrast to the empty Labour and Conservative benches' (Thompson 2018: 453). SNP members were present in the chamber whenever fellow party members were speaking, and the SNP MPs demonstrated party cohesion through social media posts highlighting Commons debates. SNP action was heightened during debates with direct implications for Scotland, like debates on the Scotland Bill, Trident, the changes to the Standing Orders that allowed for English Votes for English Laws, and immigration (Thompson 2018).

In the parliamentary sessions between 2017 and 2019, the SNP introduced four opposition day debates, three of which concerned immigration.[24] The first on 11 November 2017 concerned the rights of EU nationals post-Brexit, proposed by Stephen Gethins of North East Fife, located to the north-east of Edinburgh. His argument centred on the critical reliance of the Scottish economy on migrants from the EU, across industries and sectors. The second opposition debate on 26 June 2019 was introduced by Stuart McDonald of Cumbernauld, Kilsyth and Kirkintilloch East to the north-east of Glasgow. He called for fundamental change in the government's approach to immigration, but focused on the hostile environment created by Right to Rent and its disproportionate impact on immigrant families. Another opposition day debate, introduced by party leader Ian Blackford of Ross, Skye and Lochaber in the north-west of Scotland on 4 July 2018, supported the Claim of Right for Scotland, legislation that acknowledges the sovereign right of the Scottish people to determine the form of government best suited to their needs. Blackford explicitly mentioned immigration when he referred to past Conservative promises to consider devolving power over immigration to Scotland.[25] In the 2020 session, the first opposition day debate introduced by Stuart McDonald on 11 February 2020 argued for a Scottish visa scheme, building on the Scottish government's publication of 27 January 2020 entitled 'Migration: Helping Scotland Prosper'. Opposition day debates are one of the few rights given to the SNP as the largest minority party, and almost all of their speeches discussed immigration. Furthermore, during debates on immigration introduced by others in the House, or during ministerial statements, the SNP will regularly contribute questions, asking about the impact of the policy in Scotland.[26]

Maiden Speeches in Westminster

When a new MP joins the House of Commons, they are given the opportunity to introduce themselves and signal their legislative priorities in a maiden speech.[27] The addition of 57 new SNP MPs since 2015 means that the Scottish voice has been dominated by members of that party, but 12 Scottish Conservatives, 19 Scottish Labour Party members, and 4 Scottish Liberal Democrats gave maiden speeches from 2010 to 2020. A number of MPs discuss or allude to immigration in their maiden speeches in one of four different ways: they link it to the history and character of their constituency, they describe it as part of their personal history and understanding of what it means to be Scottish, they discuss it directly as a policy issue, or they use it to critique the government.

Most of the Scottish MPs who mention immigration or migrants in their maiden speeches connect it to the history or character of their constituency. For example, in her maiden speech during the summer adjournment debate,

SNP MP Marion Fellows of Motherwell and Wishaw (south-east of Glasgow) said:

> my constituency has long taken in folk from afar: Irish refugees after the famine, Lithuanians after the first world war, Congolese refugees more recently, and Polish families, who all add to our society ... My community, my constituency and my country have fantastic assets and attributes. The people are the centre of that. It is not where people are from but where they are going that matters, and our job is to lead the way. (Fellows 2015)

Similarly, SNP MP Chris Law of Dundee West touched on the history of emigration and immigration in his constituency, and connected that history to the character of Scotland:

> The wealth of the city [Dundee] has long been used to reach out to the world, from the Americas to Australia and Asia. There has long been a tradition of welcoming migrants, and in recent years we have built up vibrant Irish, Italian, Polish and Asian communities – something to be proud of and celebrate. This cuts to the heart of who we are in Scotland; we are a' Jock Tamson's bairns. (Law 2015)

SNP MP Kirsten Oswald focused on the diversity of the faith communities in her constituency, which implies a history of migration:

> East Renfrewshire is in many ways a place of contrasts, just like modern Scotland. We are lucky to have active and energetic faith communities playing a full part in local life. This includes being home to Scotland's largest Jewish community, a growing and vibrant Muslim community, and thriving Christian, Hindu and Sikh communities. (Oswald 2015)

Conservative Party MP Paul Masterson, who replaced Oswald in 2017, also spoke on this theme:

> East Renfrewshire is home to Scotland's largest Jewish community. It has a significant Muslim community, a growing Sikh community, and a strong Christian community. It is home to people of all faiths and none – but the key thing is that none of that matters. The constituency is a fine example of everything a modern, open, multicultural and tolerant Britain should be. Testament to that rich diversity and community cohesion is the fact that the constituency will soon be home to the world's first-ever joint Catholic–Jewish school in Newton Mearns. (Masterson 2017)

SNP MP Alison Thewliss (2015) of Glasgow Central similarly emphasised the religious diversity of Glasgow, along with linguistic diversity, noting that her constituents include those born in Glasgow, and those who (like her) chose to make Glasgow their home. All of these statements celebrate the diversity of the Scottish constituencies and advocate for a multicultural understanding of Scottish society.

Others, like SNP Leader Ian Blackford, acknowledge immigrants as important constituents requiring representation. In his maiden speech criticising the EU referendum, Blackford said:

> I was contacted yesterday by a constituent of mine of Dutch origin, who has lived in and contributed to Scotland for 25 years. It is not right that such individuals may be denied a say about our future in Europe. As he said in his letter to me: 'Not being able to vote in the UK election was bad enough, but now being treated like some kind of unwanted foreigner is a real blow.' (Blackford 2015)

Blackford framed the migrant as a participant in the Scottish social contract, someone who has done their part and been betrayed by the UK government. Liberal Democrat Christine Jardine made a similar argument about her constituency of Edinburgh West:

> The constituency is also a key driver of the region's economy, which is dependent on European trade and European citizens who work in the health service and other sectors and who now find that they are under threat from Brexit ... I will work on their behalf for the open, tolerant society I believe in and that offers opportunity for all and protects our human rights. (Jardine 2017)

Labour MP Danielle Rowley (2017) also mentioned the need to protect the rights of EU nationals during the Brexit process. SNP MP Margaret Ferrier of Rutherglen and Hamilton West, near Glasgow, described her personal responsibility to represent refugees as part of her job in Westminster:

> I have been elected to be their voice in Parliament and to speak up for those with no voice: the mother forced to visit the local food bank; the father in low-paid, zero-hours-contract employment; the carer who looks after a family member for no reward; the refugee reaching out for help in their time of need. (Ferrier 2015)

The specific mention of refugees in this 2015 speech is significant because it was the year of Europe's refugee crisis, though Ferrier's comment pre-dates most of the UK's efforts to assist in the situation, and demonstrates an early sensitivity to the vulnerable population. A few years later Conservative MP Stephen Kerr highlighted the contributions of a less vulnerable group of English constituents:

> Frank and Harold Barnwell represent the great things that Britain has achieved – in this case, two English entrepreneurs who moved their

business to Scotland – to create the inventions and businesses that made the modern world. I say to entrepreneurs and innovators across the globe: Stirling is evidently the place to be. (Kerr 2017)

Kerr's statement focuses on migrant contributions to Scotland and the world, while the statements from the SNP MPs focus on what Scotland and the UK owes its community members.

A number of SNP MPs discuss immigration as part of their family experience, describing their families' migration as a formative experience that enables them to empathise with their constituents. For example, Patricia Gibson (2015) from North Ayrshire and Arran described how her life of struggle as a child of poor migrants helps her empathise with her poorer constituents. Dave Doogan of Angus discusses his Irish parentage, linking it to Scotland's history as a

> country that has always looked outward and welcomed others ... My family are indebted to, and a product of, Scotland's hospitality ... Like many children of immigrant parents, I was brought up to appreciate that while no task is beneath me, no target is beyond me, and that though no one is more worthy than I am, I am no better than anyone else. As we say in Scotland, 'We're all Jock Tamson's bairns.' (Doogan 2020)

Stephen Bonnar (2020) of Coatbridge, Chryston and Bellshill discussed the personal impact of the UK's EU referendum, interpreting it as the 'removal of our rights as European citizens'. He is married to a Polish woman and has a daughter that he calls 'half-Polish, fully Scottish', and he expresses a somewhat ironic relief that since his daughter was born in Scotland, he will 'not have to apply for settled status for my own wean' (Bonnar 2020). Bonnar's statement illustrates the fallacy behind the notion that there is a clear 'us' that is distinguishable from the 'them' in debates over immigration, and that the 'us' and 'them' are blended within Scottish families.

Other MPs discuss immigration as a policy priority. SNP MP Stephen Gethins (2015) of North East Fife described the refugee crisis in the Mediterranean as an 'issue for us all'. Relating immigration more specifically to Scotland, SNP MP Drew Hendry from Inverness, Nairn, Badenoch and Strathspey spoke to the need for a devolved immigration policy:

> My constituency is just like others in that it benefits from inward migration. In the highlands, we have suffered for too long a population drain, especially of our young people. A different policy on immigration is needed to address our needs. (Hendry 2015)

SNP MP Tommy Sheppard (2015) of Edinburgh East was much more specific in his maiden speech, which he used to bring up the post-study work visa, calling it 'one of the proverbial babies that has been thrown out with the bathwater in recent immigration reforms' and calling for a replacement mechanism. This mention of the post-study work visa was the only concrete immigration policy raised by any of the SNP MPs in their 2015 maiden speeches.

A few SNP MPs used immigration and diversity as a mechanism by which to criticise Westminster or the Conservative government. Paul Monaghan (2015) from Caithness, Sutherland and Easter Ross in the north of Scotland did not mention immigration in his speech during the debate over the financial statement and budget report, but he did open his speech by mentioning the Clearances and the experience of Scottish emigration as the consequence of prioritising markets over people. His aim is to create a fairer Scotland, a country in which 'no one is left out' (Monaghan 2015). Monaghan's sentiment reinforced that of Philip Boswell (2015) of Coatbridge, Chryston and Bellshill, who interpreted the widespread support for the SNP in Scotland as an endorsement of 'an inclusive, tolerant society that has social and economic justice at its heart, instead of the right-wing neo-liberalism we see from the two main establishment parties of this House'. David Linden from Glasgow East was even more explicit in his maiden speech:

> For too long now, it is the most vulnerable who have felt the sharp end of this Government's austerity programme. Today, sadly, we live in a society in which the middle class are told blame the working class, the working class are told to blame the benefit claimants, and the benefit claimants are told to blame the asylum seekers and refugees ... At a time when hard-hitting decisions are being taken about the nation's finances, and at a time when there is a smokescreen debate raging about immigration, we must consider how we treat others, both as legislators and human beings. (Linden 2017)

SNP MP Hannah Bardell (2015) from Livingston also addressed the Conservative tendency to use immigration as a scapegoat for poor economic rights.

Though few MPs comment on immigration in their maiden speeches, these examples demonstrate that many of them connect immigration to their constituencies, personal histories, or policy priorities, or raise it when criticising the actions of the government.[28] The multidimensional manner in which Scottish MPs invoke immigration reveals the centrality of the issue as a hub around which Scottish MPs think of their communities, themselves, and their relationship with the UK.

Those who do not mention immigration specifically will regularly address issues or principles that are adjacent to immigration. For example, a number of new MPs used their maiden speeches to highlight an image of Scotland as a welcoming place, emphasising themes of openness, tolerance, and diversity acceptance. SNP MP Richard Thomson (2020) describes his constituency of

Gordon as 'a welcoming place that embraces those who come to make their lives there, no matter where in the world they come from and no matter what their circumstances'. Similarly, SNP MP Ronnie Cowan (2015) of Inverclyde articulated his wish that Scotland would 'take our place as a modern, diverse, inclusive and equal nation'.

The idea of a modern, diverse, and inclusive Scottish nation was picked up by SNP MPs who describe Scottish nationalism as civic, with an emphasis on openness and inclusion. Calum Kerr (2015) from Berwickshire, Roxburgh and Selkirk described the SNP's ambition of an 'open, civic, inclusive and aspirational polity that seeks a better Scotland in a better world'. The ambition to be an inclusive and therefore a 'better' nation imbues SNP nationalism with a moral advantage. Tommy Sheppard (2015) set a similar moral tone when he explicitly distinguished between ethnic and civic nationalism in his maiden speech, and said he was offended to see people generalise nationalistic parties and link the SNP to other ethno-nationalist parties responsible for 'the rise of racist and xenophobic organisations throughout this great continent of Europe'. He quotes an earlier maiden speech by Joanna Cherry (2015) of Edinburgh South West in which she describes Scottish nationalism as 'inclusive civic nationalism'. Cherry set up the contrast between ethnic and civic nationalism more aggressively than Sheppard because she implied that the southern constituencies of the UK risk cultivating ethnic nationalism:

> I urge the House not to indulge in the narrow, inward-looking nationalism of withdrawing from the ECHR [European Court of Human Rights] and drawing up its own Bill of Rights ... Look to your consciences and remember that the theatre of the whole world is wider than the kingdom of England. (Cherry 2015)

Cherry's outward-looking sentiment is echoed by a number of other SNP MPs who highlight Scotland's internationalism, and particularly its Europe-facing political culture. In his maiden speech SNP MP Roger Mullin from Kirkaldy and Cowdenbeath invoked the ideas of the 'much misquoted' Scot and economist Adam Smith:

> Adam Smith knew, too, that there is no centre of internationalism. It is something to be sought in the minds and deeds of people; whether you live in a great city of a great land or in a small seaside town on the northern shores of Scotland, you can be international. (Mullin 2015)

SNP MP Stewart McDonald (2015) of Glasgow South identified the place of Scotland in Europe as the reason they were elected: 'I and my 55 colleagues have been sent to this House to argue for Scotland's place in Europe and for the rights of young people and European nationals to have a say on our future in Europe.' McDonald was advocating for the rights of immigrants to vote in the EU referendum. The extension of franchise is a symbol of political acceptance, which connects McDonald's statement to those comments by other MPs who identify immigrants as members of their political constituencies. When Scottish MPs use their maiden speech to emphasise inclusivity, civic nationalism, and internationalism, they demonstrate how politicians can construct an image of a society that is welcoming to and accepting of immigrants without mentioning them specifically.

Reviewing the ways Scottish MPs pursue Scottish interests in Westminster illustrates mechanisms advancing the principles of a distinct immigration policy. The institutions are set up to diminish the impact of any parties beyond the two largest ones, but the SNP has capitalised on the powers and opportunities of the largest minority party, though it does not accept its reduced political status with equanimity. SNP MPs disclaim many of the cultural norms in Westminster, and were strongly rebuked by the speaker for clapping in the chamber (and for refusing to clap after Theresa May's final speech). Thompson recounts how SNP MPs are distinctive in their resistance to institutionalisation in Westminster, and links that resistance to the idea that SNP MPs are less invested in re-election: 'Westminster is not an institution in which the party's MPs want to be for longer than necessary to fulfil their primary policy objective of independence' (2018: 450). This was explicitly expressed in the maiden speech by Dave Doogan:

> While I am here in this place, I must work within the system. I will do so in the service of my constituents and my country. I hope at all times to be collegiate and pragmatic, but do not confuse that with any acceptance of London rule. I will always seek to be constructive and courteous in transacting our business down here, but do not mistake that for submission or fondness for the status quo. I and my SNP colleagues are here to settle up, not settle down. We are here only to help to open the door to a progressive independent future for our country. And when Scotland walks through, into the progressive future of independence and the normality that that brings, the honour will fall to me and my SNP colleagues here gathered to firmly close the door of this place behind us and leave for the last time, taking Scotland's brighter, independent future with us. (Doogan 2020)

This quote reinforces the ultimate agenda of the SNP to be free from Westminster and to have full control over all of its policies. Barring that, the SNP is willing to use the existing institutions to advance its agenda as far as possible. Lynch calls this strategy 'independence by stealth' and argues that devolved powers in taxation and the creation of the Scottish Parliament are examples of incremental policy change moving Scotland towards independence (2002: 253). Based on the way immigration has been raised by the SNP within the chamber, immigration policy is being employed in this way. A member of the SNP leadership expressed this view in an interview, when he suggested that while the SNP had very practical and ideological reasons for supporting devolved immigration policy, it would support any policy that grants more power to Scotland, no matter what the issue is (personal interview 10 June 2016).

The Scottish politics of immigration in Westminster are relatively clean, with most Scottish representatives taking a clear and oppositional stance about immigration being positive for Scotland and the UK. The dominance of SNP means that the party message is consistent and designed to be oppositional to Westminster in general, rather than to one party in particular. The party therefore uses its position and power to push for policies that increase the powers given to Scotland. Of course, the near complete dominance of the SNP and the clarity and consistency of SNP MPs' policy preferences misrepresents the Scottish public. The diversity of the political opinions in Scotland is more likely to be represented in the Scottish Parliament at Holyrood.

HOLYROOD

The devolved Parliament at Holyrood reveals how a different institutional framework creates opportunities for alternative outcomes in the Scottish politics of immigration. The dominance of the SNP has led to strong consensus among the Scottish representatives at Westminster. At Holyrood the more diverse representation of political parties provides opportunities for more policy debate, though there is striking consensus about immigration *across* the Scottish political parties. Previous chapters detail the practical reasons for why Scottish politicians believe immigration is beneficial for Scotland. This section explores some of the institutional reasons for consensus within Holyrood and how the institutions of government reinforce a vision of a multicultural Scotland. It demonstrates consensus in political party documents oriented around the Holyrood elections and how the parties engage with immigration as a national as opposed to a UK-wide policy issue.

The Structure of the Scottish Parliament

The Scottish Parliament building is designed to encourage the exchange of diverse opinions and ideas though constructive and consensual debate. Westminster is adversarial in design, with green benches placed facing each other to facilitate an aggressive partisan debate between the government and the opposition. In contrast, Members of the Scottish Parliament sit in individual seats in a hemicycle arrangement. This seating is modelled on continental European legislatures, and is intended to promote consensus and compromise. The rules governing the behaviour of MSPs also differ from those at Westminster, because the potential for coalition governments and the presence of members from a number of parties change the nature of opposition politics in Holyrood. While there is a lead opposition party, all parties that are not part of the government are part of the opposition, and each has shadow cabinet members.[29] Committees are structured to be representative of the party make-up in the larger chamber.

The institutional contrast between Holyrood and Westminster is deliberate. The communitarian structure of Holyrood was born out of the idea that Scotland has a distinctive identity and political culture, as evidenced by its legal system, educational system, and its social, cultural, and religious traditions (Brown 2000). The final report of the Scottish Constitutional Convention states:

> the coming of a Scottish Parliament will usher in a way of politics that is radically different from the rituals of Westminster: more participative, more creative, less needlessly confrontational . . . a culture of openness which will enable the people of Scotland to see how decisions are being taken in their name, and why. The parliament we propose is much more than a mere institutional adjustment. It is a means, not an end. (Scottish Constitutional Convention 1995)

Asserting that the Parliament is a means rather than an end emphasises the role of the Parliament in improving the lives of the Scottish people, and its importance as a political tool asserting Scotland's right to self-government.

The architecture of the Parliament building makes a statement about Scotland's political character relative to other nations. Architectural studio Miralles Tagliabue EMBT designed the building with a proposal

> that Scotland is a land, not a series of cities. The Parliament should be able to reflect the land it represents . . . not just an 'image' but a physical representation of a participatory attitude to sit together – gathering. Instead of an overwhelming monument, which only relates to dimensions and rhetorical forms, we like to think about it in terms of a psychological approach. (Miralles Tagliabue EMBT 1998: 2)

The appearance of the building therefore incorporates images in 'remembrance of Scotland', of cloisters, overturned boats, water, and mists, with views from the debating chamber of the Burns monument and the profile of Edinburgh, and views from the public gallery of Arthur's Seat. The physical structure of the Parliament building is intended to remind the people of who they were, who they are, and what they can become. It is a deliberate antithesis to the messages sent by the backward-looking classical buildings of other European parliamentary chambers.

By emphasising the connection between the Scottish people and the land, head architect Miralles was asserting a vision of civic Scottish nationalism. As McCrone noted:

this was to be a parliament for all Scots who inhabited the space of Scot-Land. This has older cultural and political resonances, for embedded in Scottish identity is the sense of belonging not to a tribe and ethnic group, but to a place, a territory . . . If you live here, you belong here. (McCrone 2005: 23)

McCrone identified the territorial emphasis as a reflection of a historically diverse country, which used political institutions to achieve consensus and democratic accountability.

The pervasive narrative of consensus and the commitment to representation (bred out of feeling unrepresented in Westminster) explains why the government adopted electoral institutions that guarantee much more diverse representation within the debating chamber. Scotland uses a mixture of plurality and regional-list proportional representation with the alternative member system. Unlike in the UK, where the plurality system tends to result in the election of two large parties, parties in Scotland win seats roughly in proportion to their vote share.[30] As a result, there are five main parties represented in the Scottish Parliament. Appendix B displays the parties achieving representation in the Scottish Parliament after the 2021 elections, along with their general ideological position and the number of seats they occupy. Because most parties are Scottish versions of UK political parties (Scottish Conservative and Unionist Party, Scottish Labour, Scottish Liberal Democrats), many of the dynamics of party competition at the state level have the potential to be re-enacted at the regional level. At the same time, regional pro-independence parties (SNP, The Scottish Green Party) overrepresent national interests and frame them as competing with or at least distinct from English interests. There are therefore two layers of party conversation, and the main party cleavages split along two dimensions: left–right (like in the UK) and constitutional, divided by unionism versus support for Scottish independence (Hepburn 2010b).

The presence of several parties in the Parliament means that one party rarely wins an outright majority. Governments are typically formed by a coalition of more than one party, or the largest party forms a minority government. Both outcomes require compromise on the part of the largest party in order to achieve its legislative goals. Though the SNP won the most votes by far in 2016 and 2021, it fell short of a majority and had to form a minority government. Compared with the complete dominance of the SNP in Westminster, we might expect the ideological diversity in Holyrood to provide space for a more confrontational discussion of immigration, perhaps resembling the competition over the issue in Westminster. Alternatively, we might expect to see a greater willingness on the part of the SNP to compromise and align its position with the other political parties. Given that immigration is a valence issue for the two main UK-wide political parties, with both agreeing that immigration should be controlled and framing it more as a problem or challenge to be overcome, the task of governance might incentivise the SNP to fall in line with their position. Neither of these expectations is borne out in Scotland. The politics of immigration in Holyrood are largely about consensus across parties, compared with the Scottish politics of immigration in Westminster where cohesion is a product of single-party dominance.

Political Parties at Holyrood

The five political parties represented in Holyrood all understand immigration to be an important part of the Scottish economy and society, but they differ in their enthusiasm for making immigration a political issue, and disagree over whether the best approach for policy innovation will be found at the sub-state or state level. The SNP government's framing of immigration as a critical element of Scotland's sustainability has shaped the partisan conversation about it within Scotland:

> If immigration becomes a key concern of [stateless nationalist and regionalist parties] in their development of a nation-building project, then it must also become a concern of sub-state branches of state-wide parties in order to represent regional interests. This dynamic means that party competition over issues such as immigration at the sub-state level may be entirely different from party competition at the state-wide level ... party competition may be consensually in favour of immigration if this is seen as a way to bolster the region's demography and economic growth. (Hepburn and Zapata-Barrero 2014: 8)

Party manifestos for the Holyrood elections reveal the extent of consensus and the degree to which parties prioritise immigration as something they want to take on at the sub-state level. The manifestos reveal that immigration was not as salient for Holyrood elections at it was for Westminster elections in Scotland until after Brexit, when attention to immigration dramatically increased.

The Scottish National Party

As Scotland's governing party, the SNP adopts a positive position towards immigrants and the party leadership goes out of its way to include ethnic minorities in their vision of an independent Scotland. As party leader for over 20 years (1990–2000, 2004–14), Alex Salmond wanted to open Scottish citizenship to everyone living in Scotland, without reference to race or religion, and he clearly endorsed a civic vision for the nation. As a member of the SNP leadership put it:

> We are a civic national party ... we have an approach which suggests that if you want to be Scottish, even if you weren't born here, then you

can be Scottish. And if you want to contribute to this country, and if you want to make your life here and make it a better place for the rest of us, and of course for yourself and your family, that's something that we want to encourage. (Personal interview 10 June 2016)

The endorsement of civic nationalism reflects both values and strategy. The party leadership knows that if it places emphasis on belonging through birth or tradition, it will become vulnerable to accusations of 'ethnic nationalism', which will de-legitimise the party. The vision of civic nationalism is reflected in years of SNP literature and statements from SNP MSPs, who point to non-native Scottish party members as evidence of their inclusiveness. Minoritised groups are typically represented in the party with SNP-affiliated organisations like Scottish Asians for Independence and New Scots for Independence. These affiliated organisations are 'of enormous moral significance for a party that wished to stress its "civic nationalist" credentials' (Hussain and Miller 2006: 34). The SNP leadership is loud in its affirmation of cultural diversity and the conviction that immigrants make Scotland a better place, and it advances policy agendas in alignment with this conviction both in its capacity as the third-largest party in Westminster and as the governing party of Holyrood.[31]

Despite the symbolic and political importance of immigration for the SNP, immigration was not regularly featured in the party manifestos for Scottish elections before Brexit. In 2007, it was introduced in a small section advocating for the Scottish green card, and attracting 'new Scots' is mentioned in a section about economic targets. Immigration is not mentioned at all in the manifestos in 2011 or 2016, but in 2016 a section entitled 'An international Scotland' describes Scotland as a 'diverse, welcoming and outward-looking nation' and discusses the Scottish government's work to support and welcome refugee families (Scottish National Party 2016: 41). In the 2021 manifesto, within a section entitled 'Scotland in the world', Scotland is described as a 'welcoming, outward-looking and inclusive nation' (Scottish National Party 2021: 71). One of the main party commitments is to 'establish a Migration Service for Scotland to help people to settle easily into communities across Scotland and access information on rights and services available to them' (Scottish National Party 2021: 72). A sub-section entitled 'Migration' describes the main arguments for encouraging migration to Scotland, and outlines commitments to a Rural Visa Pilot, easier access to public services for EU citizens, and a refresh of the New Scots Strategy. The section also includes a box entitled 'UK migration policy doesn't work for Scotland', which highlights migration and asylum policy changes that the SNP plans to lobby Westminster for, and outlines the SNP's hopes for devolved immigration policy.

The 2021 manifesto also mentions migrants with reference to improving representation and social inclusion. In a section entitled 'An equal society', the manifesto describes how the SNP-led government extended voting rights for the Scottish Parliament to all foreign nationals with leave to remain and to refugees. The party expresses its intention of extending the right of all eligible voters to stand for election in order to ensure 'a more diverse parliament and local government' (Scottish National Party 2021: 33). Such a proposal will build on Scotland's success in diversifying the Parliament: after the 2011 elections, a quarter of MSPs were born outside Scotland, well above the 17% born outside Scotland in the Scottish population.

The limited discussion of migration in the Scottish election manifestos before 2021 contrasts with the party's manifestos for the Westminster elections, where immigration was explicitly mentioned in every election year. The difference reflects the salience of the issue in the UK versus Scottish context. Because the Scottish Parliament has no power over immigration and because the Scottish public is not as concerned about migration, it was not a persuasive policy agenda for Scottish Parliament elections before Brexit. Things changed after 2016. SNP attention to immigration in its Westminster-facing manifestos increased dramatically in the elections following the EU referendum, and the 2021 Holyrood manifesto demonstrates a similar, even more dramatic shift. Immigration gained salience within Scotland after Brexit as free movement functioned as a proxy for the EU, and the damage of Brexit allows SNP leaders to use immigration as a case in point for why Scotland needs further devolution, and barring that, independence.

The Scottish Labour Party

The SNP cannot claim full credit for forming the Scottish approach to immigration. Positive discourse about immigration began with the Labour–Liberal Democrat coalition during the first two sessions of the Scottish Parliament, lasting from 1999 to 2007. Scottish Labour openly pushed for a distinctive Scottish approach to migration under the Leadership of Jack McConnell (2001–7). The party encouraged the migration of workers from abroad and the diversification of Scotland and in 2004, the executive coalition launched the Fresh Talent Initiative to encourage migration and allow for extended work permits for university graduates.[32] McConnell described the success of the Fresh Talent Initiative as being partly attributable to its place within the One Scotland, Many Cultures campaign, which argued that diversity has positive benefits for Scotland. The clarity of the campaign alongside persuasive evidence demonstrating the advantages of diversity smoothed the way for policy success. According to McConnell, the inclusion of the policy as part of the broader campaign helped 'reduce community tensions, it won support from stakeholders and all of the newspapers (even *The Sun*!) . . . it was a very positive experience' (personal interview 28 June 2016).

In leading Scotland's first government, the Scottish Labour Party promoted an image of an open and multicultural Scotland, though its advocacy was accompanied by a commitment to preserving the union of the UK. During Holyrood elections, the party avoids forcefully advocating for an immigration policy that is wholly distinct from the rest of the UK's. The UK-wide party's restrictiveness from 2010 to 2017 was frustrating to Scottish Labour politicians who believed immigrants are vital contributors to the UK and that immigration should be encouraged. The Scottish Labour strategy has been to advocate for an increased Scottish voice in UK decision making, and pushing for policies that could apply to the whole of the UK and also meet Scotland's needs, like a regional strategy.[33]

The Fresh Talent Initiative was an outlier in this respect. When asked why the policy was successfully launched in 2004 while its reintroduction met so much resistance in 2014, McConnell described the critical importance of strong intra-party leadership coalitions while the party was in government in Holyrood and Westminster. He noted the critical role of Labour MP David Blunkett, who was the Westminster Home Secretary from 2001 to 2005. According to McConnell, Blunkett understood the need for a Home Office policy that met the needs of the different regions of the UK, and was the only Home Secretary to deviate from a one-size-fits-all immigration strategy. As McConnell put it, 'success is a combination of a well thought through proposal, leadership in public and private, and key individuals' (personal interview 28 June 2016). Because the Labour Party was in government in both Westminster and Holyrood, it was possible to make progress on policy without politicising the issue. And, though Fresh Talent advanced a regional approach intended to give Scotland a competitive advantage for immigrants, McConnell stated that he promotes an overarching UK-wide policy that allows for flexibility to meet regional needs.[34]

Given McConnell's enthusiasm and the policy precedent for regional immigration policy, it is surprising that immigration is not mentioned in the 2007, 2011, or the 2016 Scottish Labour manifestos. Both the 2011 and 2016 manifestos include sections on community, within which the party commits to tackle discrimination, celebrate diversity, improve the representation of minoritised groups, and generate movement on the Refugee Integration (Scotland) Bill. In response to the refugee crisis that began in 2015, refugees are emphasised in the 2016 manifesto, with a whole subsection devoted to how the party plans to support refugees in Scotland (Scottish Labour 2016: 44). In the 2021 manifesto, migration is mentioned in passing twice, first as part of a necessary reform agenda post-Brexit – 'we must explore the need to reform our immigration system so that it works for all nations and regions within the UK' (Scottish Labour 2021: 30) – and once as an example of an issue that could be addressed by establishing a

Scottish Council for Global Affairs (Scottish Labour 2021: 114). Within a section entitled 'Social justice' the manifesto describes the Labour Party's commitment to Gypsy/Traveller rights, and its support for the New Scots Strategy and refugee resettlement.

The Scottish Labour Party resembles the SNP in the lack of attention paid to immigration in pre-Brexit Scottish election manifestos, with much less attention paid in its manifestos for Scottish Parliament elections compared with those for the Westminster elections. Nevertheless, Scottish Labour was able to advance a tailored Scottish immigration policy through the Fresh Talent Initiative. Because the Labour Party was simultaneously in government in Westminster and Holyrood from 1999 to 2007, intra-party negotiations made policy movement on immigration at the regional level possible. While other UK-wide parties may someday experience this window of opportunity to advance Scottish interests, because of the resistance to including the SNP in a coalition government in Westminster, the SNP will likely never experience this alignment of power.

The Scottish Conservative and Unionist Party

As the only party on the right side of the political spectrum in Scotland, the Scottish Conservative Party is the only party that has not consistently encouraged migration, though it has not discouraged it, either. The party does not attack its competitors' more progressive immigration policies, and has reacted negatively to the Conservative Party's UK-wide immigration policies. In a speech at Glasgow University, party leader Ruth Davidson criticised Prime Minister Theresa May's immigration target: 'I see neither the sense nor the need to stick to an immigration figure devised nearly a decade ago, which has never been met and does not fit the requirements of the country' (Gordon 2018). Under Davidson's leadership, the Scottish Conservatives urged for Brexit talks to move away from immigration and towards the economy (Reuters 2017). Scottish Conservative leader Jackson Carlaw also lobbied Boris Johnson to rethink the limitations on low-skilled, low-wage immigration under the new points-based system (Carrell 2020).

In its manifestos for Holyrood elections, the Conservative Party did not mention immigration, diversity, or refugees in 2011, 2016, or 2021. Though neither the Scottish Labour Party nor the SNP mention immigration much in their manifestos for the 2011 and 2016 Scottish Parliament elections, the complete neglect of the topics relating to diversity in the Conservative manifestos stands out. Given statements made by Scottish Conservative leadership, and the substantial movement of the party to align with the Scottish government's proposal for a Scottish-specific immigration plan post-Brexit, the failure to mention immigration represents benign neglect.

The Scottish Liberal Democrats

The system of proportional representation in Scotland means that smaller parties have a chance of winning more seats and forming coalition governments, as the Liberal Democrats did with Labour from 1999 to 2007. The Liberal Democrats are positioned in the centre of British politics, with an ideology that draws upon economic liberalism and social democracy. The party is instrumentalist and pro-European. It pushes for greater fiscal autonomy in Scotland and further devolution on a number of key policies, and openly supports immigration, arguing that it is essential to the economy and a benefit to society.

In its manifestos for the Scottish elections, the party advocates strongly for human dignity and human rights. In 2007, the manifesto mentions immigration as a policy area in which the party advocates for improved partnership between the UK and Scotland, and it commits to anti-racism measures. The manifestos do not mention immigration or refugees in 2011 or 2016, though they do advocate for improved treatment of asylum seekers, especially children asylees, in 2007 and 2011. The 2021 manifesto again singles out support for the human rights of refugees and asylum seekers, and mentions taking steps to stop refugee and asylee evictions from temporary housing. The 2021 manifesto only mentions migration with reference to working 'in partnership with the UK Government to ensure that our UK immigration system allows the fishing industry access to the labour that they need to crew their boats' (Scottish Liberal Democrats 2021: 24). The party expresses support for 'tolerance, diversity and human rights at home and abroad' in 2016, and mentions support for refugees as a critical issue (Scottish Liberal Democrats 2016: 20). The 2021 manifesto includes a similar message of putting Scotland forward as a place for 'promoting global issues such as human rights, migration and refugees' (Scottish Liberal Democrats 2021: 52).

As with the other parties, the Scottish Liberal Democrat position on immigration is much more clearly stated in the manifestos for the Westminster elections. The party strongly opposed Brexit, and after the vote, the Scottish Liberal Democrats pushed back against the 'toxic rhetoric on immigration', claiming 'immigration and asylum are under attack' (2017: 7). In its manifestos for the Westminster elections in 2017 and 2019, there is a full section dedicated to 'a compassionate and effective immigration system' and one promoting 'dignity for refugees and asylum seekers' (Scottish Liberal Democrats 2019).

The Scottish Green Party

The Scottish Green Party has environmentalism at its core, but it also supports communitarian economic policies and progressive social policies. It is the only main party other than the SNP to support Scottish independence. The party supports immigration, and the party's voters tend to have the most pro-immigration attitudes. In Westminster manifestos, the party regularly calls for immigration to be celebrated, and pushes back against 'toxic rhetoric' about immigration.

In 2015, its manifesto mentions the reintroduction of the post-study work visa as a policy priority, and during the 2015 Westminster elections, the party's position on immigration became a campaign issue: the party sold mugs with the slogan 'Love immigration, vote Green'. The party is less explicit about immigration in Holyrood elections. While there is no mention of immigration in the 2011 Holyrood manifesto, the party commits to devolved services that will meet the needs of refugees and asylum seekers in a section on 'An internationalist Scotland'. In a section entitled 'Diversity, tolerance and creativity' the party urges multidimensional approaches to equality and the celebration of difference (Scottish Green Party 2011: 19). In 2016, the party restates its commitment to refugees in a section entitled 'Scotland can welcome refugees', in which the party pushes for a bolder strategy for 'new Scots' (Scottish Green Party 2016: 5). It again highlights the importance of promoting equality, this time noting that refugees, migrants, and people from minoritised communities are more likely to experience poverty, unemployment, and political exclusion. Refugee women are named as a group experiencing disproportionately negative social outcomes and needing protection through gender equity measures. Since Brexit, the party has promoted a Scottish immigration policy, which it takes for granted in the 2019 Westminster manifesto, which reads 'Once Scotland has control of its own immigration and asylum system, we will make sure that position is humane and compassionate' (Scottish Green Party 2019: 26). A blog on the Green Party home page calls for a 'concerted, cross-party, pan-institutional campaign FOR immigration . . . our own immigration system based on our humanitarian and welcoming culture and we can build a better society and economy with it' (Chapman 2018). The 2021 Holyrood manifesto reflects this call, and advocates for a full devolution of immigration 'in order to combat the racist consequences of UK Home Office hostile environment policies, for adequate support and an end to destitution in the asylum process, and for asylum seeker accommodation to be in local hands' (Scottish Green Party 2021: 81).

The party also identifies many anti-racist points of action within the Scottish Parliament's devolved powers, and reiterates the need to continue to place pressure on the UK government to support the post-study work visa. The 2021 manifesto includes a full section entitled 'Scotland welcomes refugees', which details policy strategies for how to improve integration, community cohesion, and access to services for refugees and asylum seekers. The manifesto regularly mentions migrants and refugees as important constituents within manifesto sections dedicated to service provision, funding, and decent living and working conditions. In a list of Green Party accomplishments in its equality agenda over the last five years, the party takes credit for winning voting rights for refugees, ending private companies making a profit from housing asylum seekers, and building support for establishing a museum of slavery, colonialism, migration, and empire in Scotland. Before the SNP's detailed plan for immigration in its 2021 manifesto, the Scottish Green Party was the most active in its promotion of pro-immigrant positions within its Holyrood manifestos, by far.

The political parties at Holyrood share their basic immigration and migrant policy preferences. Party consensus centres on the idea that Scotland would benefit from increased migration flows to fill high- and low-skilled jobs and to bolster population growth. The main differences emerge across the old cleavage of unionism versus support for independence, which drives party positions on who should manage immigration. In terms of the partisan approach towards immigration in Holyrood, most parties resembled each other in their near-neglect of immigration in their manifestos before 2021. The partisan consensus made the issue uninteresting during Holyrood elections because it could not be used to attract supporters from other parties. Therefore, differential immigration policy preferences were more clearly stated in other party documents, like the Westminster manifestos, blogs, and party websites. Brexit changed the political landscape. Scottish parties on the ideological left, and especially the SNP, more clearly make the case for devolved or differentiated policy in post-Brexit Holyrood manifestos, and the SNP and Greens use their party platform to argue against the actions of the Westminster government. This shift demonstrates the way Brexit politicised immigration in Scotland. Unlike in Westminster, where the politicisation augments partisan ideological divides, in Holyrood, immigration policy preference is a new manifestation and justification of the cleavage between unionism and independence.

Why Consensus?

Progressive immigration policies built on a foundation of diversity and multicultural initiatives have found widespread support amongst almost all of the main political parties in Scotland. Consensus is a feature of the Scottish approach to governance and the way institutions have been structured, but it is also built on common interests. The findings of the 2001 census predicted a 'population crisis' and motivated political activity to address the issue. Scotland's projected population decline relative to other European countries was attributed to the European countries' ability to make assumptions about future levels of migration, while the Scottish government cannot control or predict immigrant inflows (General Register Office (Scotland) 2002). As one Conservative MSP put it:

> Right across the political spectrum in Holyrood, MSPs from all different parties would say the same thing, or at least would overlap in terms of what they were saying. There's consensus. I think that's also because we are all conscious that we represent a country that, until recently, has had a declining population. We are all conscious of the fact that we represent a country that needs migrant labour in order to make its economy work. We can't afford to be anti-immigrant. (Personal interview 26 March 2019)

Though the population crisis abated over the following decade, Scotland's politicians feel vindicated in their openness to migration, since population growth has been entirely attributable to immigration. Concerns have centred on how to attract and retain migrants to ensure sustained contributions to the country's revenues and the presence of a workforce to support the health and social services required by an ageing population. As an SNP MSP said, 'We don't want to find ourselves attempting to live above our means, we want to increase our means so that we can live that way if we want' (personal interview 10 June 2016). Brexit reanimated the issue of immigration and gave it new political salience, since most of Scotland's immigration is from the countries that joined the EU after 2004. Removing the UK from the EU and stopping freedom of movement will threaten Scotland's source of labour and population support. The urgency of Brexit has once again unified the Scottish political voices on immigration.

Despite the clear importance of immigration to Scottish political actors, the issue has not been as visible in party documents during Scottish elections, though it simultaneously became more prominent in party documents during Westminster elections. Immigration remains a reserved issue and it would be impossible to deliver on any immigration campaign promises made in Scottish elections. Hepburn and Rosie (2014) argue that positive party consensus around immigration may exist precisely because Scotland has little control over immigration. If Scotland achieved some control over immigration, the parties would have to develop specific policies, which would produce more party variance around the details of immigration and integration policy. These differences might make immigration more politically salient in Scotland. However, if we take a hint from trends in Westminster post-Brexit, it is possible that the issue could gain salience in Scotland even before the policy is devolved. Immigration could become a symbolic issue that reinforces the distinct needs and approaches of Scotland, compared with the rest of the UK. Through this frame, the debate over immigration will function as a policy proxy for independence, with pro-independence actors advocating for Scotland's differences to drive policy, while unionists would continue to advocate for a centralised approach.

Scottish politicians may see little benefit to making immigration a policy issue in the Scottish elections. The Scottish public does not overwhelmingly support immigration, and is only slightly less negative about it compared with their counterparts in England (see Chapter 8). The general neutrality of the public is a feature of the low levels of immigration to Scotland, which make it less impactful on people's daily lives. Politicising the issue could threaten the public neutrality and could trigger public opposition to plans to encourage migration.

Another reason for the low salience of immigration in Holyrood elections is the ideological profile of the main political parties. There has been no politically viable right-wing party in recent history, and the Conservative Party's loneliness on the ideological right highlights an important feature of the pro-immigrant political consensus: Scotland has not seen the development of the type of anti-immigrant parties that have flourished south of the border and on the European continent. Hepburn and Rosie (2014) argue that the electoral marginality of the political parties on the right and the tiny distance between the immigration positions of the parties on the left and centre of the ideological spectrum means that immigration has not been used politically in Scotland as a way to determine party fortunes. During the fallout from Brexit, immigration has been politicised in Scotland, but if anything, it has pushed the Scottish political parties towards even greater consensus. The political power of immigration is directed at widening the cleavage between unionists and nationalists, rather than at distinguishing between parties in Scotland. Immigration remains an orthogonal issue in Holyrood, taking a back seat to other issues that drive political conflict. Meanwhile, at Westminster, the Scottish consensus on immigration is represented through the dominance of the SNP as Scotland's representatives. This dominance, combined with the party's commitment to increasing migration to Scotland and the Conservative and Labour commitment to controlling it, has made immigration a powerful symbolic tool that Scottish MPs use to illustrate regional distinctiveness in ideology and interests. This makes it a critical tool for Scottish nation-building within the UK.

Notes

1. The 'hostile environment' policy was implemented by Home Secretary Theresa May in 2012 with the objective to make staying in the UK as difficult as possible, so that people without 'leave to remain' would 'voluntarily' leave. One of the consequences of the policy was the Windrush scandal, which concerned people who were wrongly detained and threatened with deportation (83 were wrongly deported) by the Home Office. Most of the victims were born as British subjects, many were from the Caribbean, and they had been in the UK for over 45 years.
2. Partisan trends are observed at the national level, but also at the European level. Immigration policy preferences of the Members of European Parliament demonstrate that partisans on the left are more likely to support immigration and immigrant rights than their colleagues on the right side of the ideological spectrum

(Lahav 2004). Regionalist parties like the SNP, Sinn Féin (Northern Ireland), or Plaid Cymru (Wales) don't fit nicely on to the left–right dimensions (Hepburn 2009). Because the primary purpose of these parties is regional self-determination, the parties often reject hard ideological positions to gain the greatest possible support.
3. Elections in Westminster are run with a plurality or first past the post electoral system. Prospective Members of Parliament compete for a seat that represents a constituency, and the individual with the most votes wins the seat. A plurality electoral system with district voting results in two main political parties because large parties that appeal to the median voter while maintaining a discrete and distinctive position on policy issues will generally be most competitive (Downs 1957). The districting of the electorate means that where constituent needs are particular, or where the political culture is substantially different (like in Scotland), an alternative political party can win representation.
4. Despite the pressures pushing representation in the UK towards two main parties, ten parties achieved representation in the House of Commons in 2019. Brief descriptions of the parties along with the votes won are listed in Appendix A.
5. Columnist Michael Deacon (2014) described Ed Miliband's immigration policy slogan of 'control immigration fairly' as oxymoronic and part of a contradictory approach to 'placate our working-class voters by sounding tough and severe' and also 'placate our middle-class voters by sounding decent and caring'. Deacon (2014) argues that 'there is no more point in trying to compete with Nigel Farage on immigration than there is in trying to compete with George Osborne on spending cuts; Labour's opponent will always talk tougher'.
6. Bale (2014) suggests that the left has three strategic options for responding to the increasing salience and politicisation of immigration. They can hold on to their liberal-internationalist position by defending migration and making the case for multiculturalism; they can try to defuse the situation by playing down immigration in favour of other issues more favourable to their platform; or they can adopt the issue and limit the extent to which it can be exploited by the other parties. Labour has done all three at different times, but more recently seems to be adopting the third strategy.
7. For much of the nineteenth century, Scotland was a Liberal territory. Between the Great War and the 1950s, Scotland started to resemble the rest of the UK in electoral behaviour, and the Labour and Conservative Parties dominated Westminster elections until 2015 (McCrone 1992).
8. Scottish conservativism prior to the 1980s was rooted in a vision of Toryism linked to Protestantism and Unionism, which placed stress on civic duty and social responsibility. The political ideology of Thatcherism embraced neo-liberal individualism, leading McCrone to assert that 'Thatcherism moved away from its social and ideological base in Scotland [rather] than vice versa' (1992: 158). Subsequent analyses of the effect of Thatcher's policies conclude that 'the Thatcherite choice of post-industrial economy and the deregulation of the market that amplified a process of branch factory economy strongly and negatively impacted Scotland' (Fonteyne and Keating 2015). Persistent Conservative victories in Westminster until 1997 entrenched the economic effects of Conservative rule on Scotland. The governing majority was based on support from the South, which led to an 'Anglicisation' of the Conservative Party. The peripheral regions were underrepresented and as a consequence, political parties were regionalised, making Scotland a Labour (and eventually an SNP) stronghold.
9. Support for Labour would likely have been much higher in Scotland earlier, were it not for the SNP upsurge from 1966 through the mid-70s.

10. The vote share gap in 2010 was 37.3%, in 2015 it was 18.8%, in 2017 it was 31.8%, and in 2019 it was 37.5%.
11. The SNP's previous peak was 11 MPs elected in 1974.
12. Support for the SNP might be wider than indicated by the vote, because the SNP only fields candidates in Scotland. On the night after the 2015 debates, in which SNP Leader Nicola Sturgeon was named the winner by one YouGov poll, the question of whether non-residents of Scotland can vote for the SNP was featured in a list of most searched-for terms on Google (Mason 2015).
13. Immigration-related language in the manifestos includes mention of immigration, migrants, refugees, asylum seekers, diversity, race, and religion.
14. As of the 2019 election, Scottish Liberal Democrats have four seats in Westminster, the Scottish Conservative Party occupy six seats, and the Labour Party one.
15. Before the 1970s, the party tried to remain non-ideological in order to capture as many supporters for independence as possible. Their only objective was to put 'Scotland first', and that meant cutting across the traditional ideological divides.
16. The Brain family entered the UK in 2011 on Mrs Brain's student visa and they planned to stay under the post-study work visa, but the post-study work visa was cancelled by Westminster in 2012. The family tried to apply for other visas, but were threatened with deportation in 2015. The plight of the Brain family was discussed in both Holyrood and Westminster. After two visa extensions, Mrs Brain secured employment that met the requirements for the Tier 2 visa in 2016 (BBC News 2016).
17. The UK manifesto reads 'Britain only succeeds when working people succeed. This is a plan to reward hard work, share prosperity and build a better Britain' (Labour Party 2015). The Scottish manifesto makes the slight adjustment to 'Scotland only succeeds when working people succeed. This is a plan to reward hard work, share prosperity and build a better and fairer Scotland' (Scottish Labour 2015).
18. Scottish party manifestos typically include an additional foreword from the Scottish party leaders and may include or exclude sections and paragraphs, depending on whether they address Scottish interests and Scotland's devolved powers.
19. The 'border at Berwick' is a common catch-phrase for the Conservative Party when discussing Scottish independence or Scottish requests for devolved immigration policy.
20. When Carlaw was asked if he agreed with the SNP's 'Scottish Visa' plans, which were rejected by the Home Office, he said he thought that some of the Scottish government's proposals 'had merit' (Carrell 2020).
21. The SNP's identity as a regional party is a problem for coalition formation because the constituency of the SNP is geographically constrained, meaning the SNP does not represent British people outside Scotland.
22. The UK organised its first debate broadcasts in 2010, and it included the leaders of the Labour Party, the Conservatives, and the Liberal Democrats (the SNP went to court over their exclusion, but the broadcasters argued that the party had insufficient constituencies to form a majority government). Nick Clegg of the Liberal Democrats did very well in the debates, and some credit his performance with substantially influencing the outcome of the 2010 elections, which resulted in a hung parliament. In 2015, there was a seven-way debate between the leaders of all of the parties. In 2019, broadcasters chose a head-to-head format of debate that included only the leaders of the two main parties. In November of 2019, lawyers representing the SNP and the Liberal Democrats brought a case before the High Court in London, claiming that it violated principles of impartiality to restrict the debate programmes to two party leaders. The court decided that broadcasting companies are not subject to judicial review because they do not

exercise a 'public function' and that they were exercising legal editorial judgement.
23. Members of the SNP chaired the Energy and Climate Change Committee and the Scottish Affairs Committee in 2015, and the International Trade and Scottish Affairs Committee in 2017 and 2020.
24. Opposition days are days where the main subject of business is chosen by the opposition parties. Twenty days in each parliamentary session are designated as opposition days, and three of these days are allocated to the leader of the second-largest opposition party, who shares the time with smaller parties.
25. Immigration was brought up two more times in the debate by Labour MPs, who raise it as an important issue that the SNP should be focusing on, if they would give up an obsession with constitutional issues and independence.
26. For example, on 21 January 2019, SNP MP Martyn Day asked for an assessment of the potential effect of the policies outlined in the white paper 'The UK's Future Skills-Based Immigration System' on the Scottish economy. On 20 February 2019, during a debate on the Immigration Bill, Drew Hendry and Stuart McDonald asked about the effects of the bill on Scotland. On 29 April 2019, Martin Day asked about the impact of proposed immigration legislation on tertiary education.
27. When an MP wants to make their first speech in the House, they select the debate, and contact the Speaker with the debate and notification that it will be a maiden speech. The convention is for the speech to relate to the debate, and that it be brief, uncontroversial, contain remarks about the constituency, and pay a tribute to the predecessor. The SNP has not adhered to all of these conventions. For example, one of the most famous maiden speeches during the 2015 session was given by SNP MP Mhairi Black of Paisley and Renfrewshire South, the youngest MP in the House of Commons. In her speech, she sharply attacked the Conservative government's benefit sanctions and called the Labour Party to task, insisting that Labour Members recognise that they are not the only opposition, and that 'in order to be effective, we must oppose, not abstain'. Her fellow SNP MPs clapped enthusiastically at the end of her speech, and were reprimanded by the deputy speaker, as clapping is not permitted in the House (the SNP regularly claps in defiance of this norm). Her speech was shared widely on social media and was viewed more than 10 million times in the first week.
28. Between 2010 and 2020, 16 SNP MPs mentioned migration in their maiden speeches, out of the 58 that gave maiden speeches during this time. Two Conservative MPs out of 12, 1 Labour MP out of 19, and 1 Liberal Democrat MP out of 4 also mentioned migration.
29. Shadow cabinet members form an alternative cabinet out of the opposition, and the shadow ministers mirror the positions of each member of the government's cabinet.
30. Seats roughly correspond to vote share because people vote for both a candidate and a party of their choice. Seventy-three MSPs are elected to represent plurality constituencies, while the remaining 56 are elected with the alternative member system through the party choice vote.
31. The pro-immigrant message from the party leadership has been clear and consistent. However, the messages of party leaders may not be reflected in party members. McCollum et al. (2014) find that those who support independence are more likely to hold anti-immigrant viewpoints. This could be an indication of the split SNP constituency in Scotland, where the party is made up of both ethnic and civic nationalists. Such a split could create an irreconcilable conflict if the SNP achieves its ultimate goal of independence, and could lead to a break-up of the party.
32. The SNP opposition strongly supported the proposal, and also called for further

devolved powers of immigration. SNP Leader John Swinney framed Fresh Talent as Labour's first admission that Scotland requires a distinct immigration policy.
33. Even though the Labour Party achieved the biggest concession towards a regional immigration policy with the Fresh Talent Initiative, the SNP typically has accused the Scottish Labour Party of being too incrementalistic in its immigration approach. The SNP exploits the Scottish–English conflict within Labour and argues that the party is too weak to advance Scotland's national interest.
34. For McConnell, 'overarching' does not mean 'one-size-fits-all'. He believed extending the Fresh Talent Initiative to all of the UK's universities was motivated by a desire to help the English universities and create consistent (i.e. one-size-fits-all) policy. From his perspective, the expansion worked against the original intent of the policy to create a comparative advantage for Scotland that would allow it to attract productive people and diversify the population. The move to create consistency, in his opinion, originated in feelings of jealousy and resentment targeted at the creation of Scotland's comparative advantage (personal interview 28 June 2016).

7

THE PRESS: NEWSPAPER REPORTING ON IMMIGRATION IN THE UK VERSUS SCOTLAND

Creating a community that will attract and retain migrants requires the public to share in the vision of a multicultural Scotland, and political leaders must convincingly frame immigration as an important, relevant, and positive development for the average Scottish person. Framing involves creating a scheme of interpretation: 'To frame is to select some aspects of a perceived reality and make them more salient in a communicating text' (Entman 1993: 52). Successful issue framing includes three phases: the construction of information by political elites, the application of frames by the media, and the impact of frames on political actors and individual opinions (Matthes 2012).[1] Previous chapters have covered the first phase of this process. This chapter focuses on the second phase involving how the media transmits ideas about immigration to the public, and briefly considers the third phase by comparing the opinions of newspaper readers. Research on media framing demonstrates that there is state-level variance in how the media covers immigration (Helbling 2014). Do similar differences manifest across sub-state regions in the UK?

This chapter compares how quality newspapers in the UK and Scotland cover immigration. It determines whether the Scottish public has access to a regional source of information that can impact their opinions about immigration in a meaningful way. This chapter uses a unique dataset of all newspaper articles published between 2013 and 2016 with 'immigration' in the title or keyword in three UK-wide and two Scottish broadsheet newspapers. It evaluates the tone of the articles and the issues and arguments that are associated with immigration in the print media. The chapter begins with a review of the newspaper market in the UK, followed by a discussion about how immigration is framed by the media, before describing the methodology employed in the analysis of 706 UK-wide and Scottish newspaper articles. The analysis explains the nuances in how immigration is framed in the UK-wide and Scottish newspapers to reveal some regional differences, though the biggest differences in framing and tone are attributable to the ideological bias of each newspaper. The chapter considers the implications of the analysis by reviewing how media framing influences the formation of public opinion, and uses survey data to compare the opinions of Scottish people by their preferred newspaper. The chapter concludes by summarising the findings and discussing their implications for Scottish decision makers.

Newspapers in the UK

Europe is a newspaper continent. It has the highest continental newspaper readership and circulation in the world, though there is substantial variation in readership across European states. The UK is one of the top five European states ranked by the amount of time people spend reading papers on an average day (Elvestad and Blekesaune 2008). The UK newspaper market is diverse, made up of quality newspapers (called broadsheets), mid-market papers, popular tabloid papers, and regional papers. Quality papers cover hard news, while tabloids favour sensationalistic stories.[2] Mid-market papers walk the line between the two, including some entertainment pieces alongside coverage of important news events. Regional papers can represent a range of types, but the larger regional papers resemble quality papers with more of a focus on local/regional news.

In 2018, 60% of the UK's adult public (59% of the Scottish public) read at least one quality newspaper at some point in a month, while the monthly readership of the popular/tabloid papers is 65% (71% in Scotland). Forty-one per cent of the Scottish population reads one of the regional news brands (PAMCo 2018). Appendix C provides data on the monthly reach of all the major newspapers: tabloids lead the market, followed by London-based quality broadsheets. Print news producers can reach a wider audience with social media sites, blogs, news sites, and online papers, all of which displace print newspapers in the public's media diet.[3] With all of the print and digital options, news consumption has become complex, dynamic, and highly variable.

Despite the reduced status of the traditional broadsheet newspapers, they are still powerful information transmitters – those who read newspapers are more informed than those who get their news from listening to the radio or watching the television (Holtz-Bacha and Norris 1999; McLeod et al. 1999). The larger size of the quality papers allows for more comprehensive, detailed analysis and original investigative journalism. This chapter capitalises on the power of the broadsheet newspaper and analyses articles on immigration from UK-wide and Scottish quality newspapers to examine whether there are differences in the way they cover immigration.

Framing Immigration

Immigration is an unobtrusive issue, which means that it is not directly observed or experienced by the majority of the population (Zucker 1978). Most people rely on information from others in order to form an opinion about immigration. When journalists frame immigration, they link immigration with something the reader has experienced or something they already hold strong opinions about. For example, a newspaper article might make associations between immigration and increasing house prices, rising crime rates, or ethnic restaurants. Framing is a powerful tool for driving public sentiment, and explains why people with no experience with immigration or immigrants can form very strong opinions about immigration and its potential economic or social impact (Schneider 2008; McLaren 2003).

Journalists are not completely free in their choice of frames and are constrained by their paper's historical or ideological commitments (Sniderman and Theriault 2004). These commitments manifest strongly with coverage on immigration because of the political salience of the issue (Bleich et al. 2015; Kaye 2001). For example, the right-leaning papers *The Times*, *The Telegraph*, and *The Daily Mail* all cover asylum seekers more negatively (Kaye 2001). Furthermore, while British newspapers do not generally portray Muslims in a negative light, the headlines in right-leaning newspapers are consistently more negative than those in left-leaning newspapers (Bleich et al. 2015). The frames associated with immigration also interact with external contexts, like the ideology of the government in power (Bleich et al. 2015; Helbling 2014; Kaye 2001). If the Conservative Party is in power, newspapers will report the government's position more frequently as the status quo, which would lead to overrepresentation of anti-immigrant perspectives or the more frequent use of certain frames. Caviedes (2015) found that immigration is more likely to be framed economically in the UK than in Italy and France, a difference he attributes to the governing Conservative Party's focus on fiscal responsibility. If the government changes, the media framing will also change.

Journalists use specific frames when reporting on certain immigrant groups. In the UK, Baker and colleagues (2008) find that the terms 'migrants' and immigrants' are associated with frames of economic threat (such as competition for jobs), and 'refugees' and 'asylum seekers' are associated with frames of economic burden (such as costs to the welfare regime). Roma are more frequently depicted as an economic threat than other groups, and North Africans are portrayed as a cultural and security threat (Meeusen and Jacobs 2017; van der Linden and Jacobs 2016). The frames used by the British press when referencing intra-EU migration from Bulgaria and Romania relied on a communitarian (as opposed to cosmopolitan) lens, with dominant themes of welfare chauvinism (Balch and Balabanova 2016). Boswell (2007) identifies three central tendencies in the framing of irregular migration in Europe. The first invokes ideas of invasion from 'hoards' of uncontrolled migration, the second centres on social and economic impacts, and the third focuses on criminal networks. Distinct frames are also employed when describing different phases of the migration experience. Helbling (2014) demonstrates how immigration is framed culturally when the integration of immigrants is the subject of the article, while economic frames dominate stories about immigration.

Media framing is complex and contingent upon a number of conditions at the individual, newspaper, and national levels. Because frames are context-sensitive, states vary in the content of their media coverage and the frames employed in their newspapers (Berry et al. 2016; Caviedes 2015; Helbling 2014). Are there similar differences observed in media specific to sub-state nations when compared with state-wide media?

Media Framing in the UK and Scotland

The daily publication of London-based newspapers with state-wide distribution, and those based in Scotland with Scottish distribution, allows for a comparative exploration of whether and how Scottish and UK-wide newspapers frame immigration differently. The quality broadsheet UK-wide newspapers with the largest distribution are *The Guardian*, *The Independent*, and *The Telegraph*, and the Scotland-specific newspapers with the largest distribution are *The Scotsman* and *The Herald*. These newspapers also represent ideological diversity. Of the UK-wide papers, *The Guardian* reflects a centre-left bias, *The Independent* is centrist but with a liberal, pro-market stance, and *The Telegraph* leans to the right of the ideological spectrum.[4] *The Scotsman* and *The Herald* represent a centre-left position, and are differentiated by the location of publication (Edinburgh and Glasgow, respectively). People in Scotland also read UK-wide newspapers, but the Scottish newspapers are intended to approach news from a Scottish perspective and prioritise Scottish issues, making them supplemental to the UK-wide sources.

All articles featuring 'immigration' in the title or keyword were collected from the papers from May 2013 to July 2016, resulting in a dataset of 706 articles published during the years spanning the Scottish independence referendum and the Brexit referendum.[5] Figure 7.1 illustrates the number of stories published by each newspaper, revealing that *The Guardian* and *The Telegraph* published many more articles with 'immigration' in the title than any of the other newspapers. Coverage of immigration has been relatively consistent over time (see Appendix D).

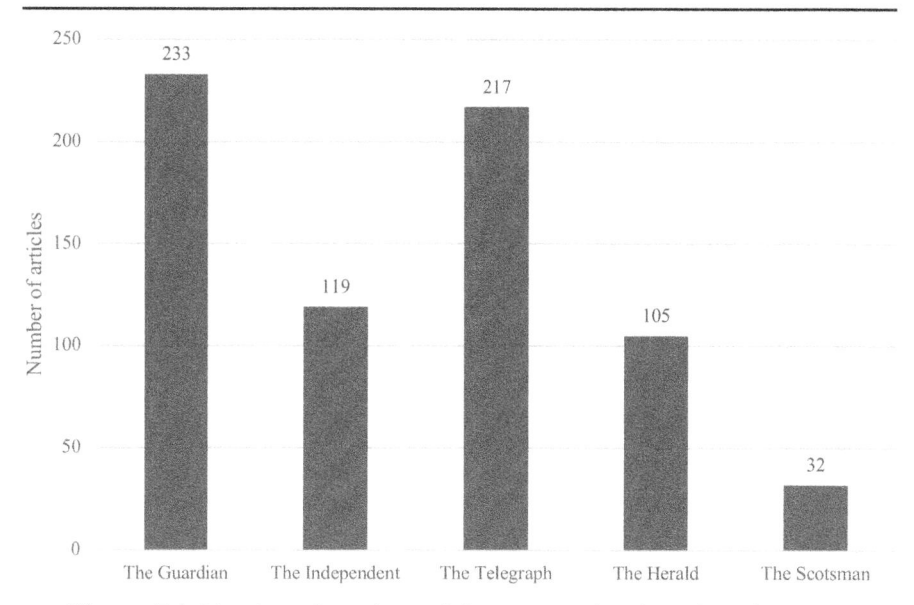

Figure 7.1 Number of articles with 'immigration' in the title or keyword published by newspaper

Coding Article Frames and Arguments

The frequency with which immigration is covered demonstrates its salience, but the nature of the coverage communicates how it is regarded. Each article was labelled (coded) using content analysis software according to the dominant frame(s) employed by the article.[6] The framing labels draw from previous research applying a Habermasian categorisation of identity-related, moral-universal, and utilitarian arguments to explore media and elite discourses (Habermas 1993).[7] Identity frames connect immigration to nationalistic or multicultural concerns, moral frames discuss migration in terms of human rights, equality, or fairness, and utilitarian frames prioritise migration's impact on welfare services, the economy, or national security.

Habermas did not include a political category in his theory of practical discourse, but the comparative literature on the framing of immigration suggests that the political environment directly contributes to positions on immigration (Berry et al. 2016; Caviedes 2015). Articles employing a political frame may not need to appeal to other more substantive frames, and could focus solely on political strategy or partisan politics. For example, in the lead-up to the independence referendum, Scottish elites were accused of using immigration as a political tool to advance claims for independence. During debates about Brexit, many commentators viewed the referendum as a ploy by David

Cameron to pander to anti-immigrant UKIP supporters. Political frames are therefore included in this analysis.

The codes or labels applied to the articles convey the main frame of the article (identity, moral, utilitarian, or political). The articles are also labelled according to arguments employed within the frame. For example, an article with a utilitarian frame will engage with one or more potential arguments about the economy, labour and social security, security, or pragmatic national interests; an article about the fiscal contributions of migrants would be making an economic argument within a utilitarian frame. Multiple labels can be applied to each article if different arguments are used in the body of the piece. The frames, arguments, and examples of related issues are provided in Table 7.1.

It is hypothesised that the ideology of the papers influences frame use. Left-leaning papers should be more likely to employ moral/universalist frames, as the political left aligns with arguments about equality and the implementation of human rights and anti-discrimination legislation. The pro-free market paper *The Independent* might employ utilitarian frames with economic arguments. Right-leaning papers might employ identity and utilitarian frames more frequently, due to their emphasis on fiscal and cultural conservativism. Because the Scottish papers are supplemental to the UK-wide ones with a special focus on Scottish national interests, they should use utilitarian frames with pragmatic arguments more often. These differences aside, framing is not expected to vary by newspaper as much as how the frames are used. For example, all of the newspapers will likely publish articles that frame immigration politically, but they will do it for different purposes. *The Guardian* will use political frames to criticise the Conservative government, while the Scottish papers will also criticise the Conservative government, but for nationalistic rather than partisan reasons.

The percentage of articles employing each of the frames is provided in Figure 7.2.[8] Because more than one frame can be applied to an article, the total percentages for each newspaper add up to more than 100%. The frequency of how often frames are used is consistent across the papers. Identity frames are used about 26% of the time, moral frames about 35% of the time, utilitarian frames about 72% of the time, and political frames about 45% of the time. The Scottish newspapers do not distinguish themselves from the UK-wide papers by the type of frames they used. Across the UK-wide newspapers (*The Guardian*, *The Independent*, *The Telegraph*) the frames employed reflect ideological positioning, with *The Guardian* employing moral frames more often than the other papers, and *The Telegraph* employing identity and utilitarian frames more frequently.

Frames and arguments can be used in different ways. For example, nationalistic arguments under the identity frame could be used to argue for or against

Table 7.1 Frames, arguments, and related issues.

Frame	Identity		Moral	Utilitarian			Pragmatic	Political
Argument	Nationalistic	Multicultural		Economic	Labour and social security	Security		
Related issues	National or community identity	Integration	Fairness	Attract high-skill migrants	Unemployment	Terrorism	National interest	Party competition
	Loss of traditions	Tolerance	Equality	Productivity	Salaries	Criminality	Soft power	Elections
	Islamophobia	Pro-diversity	Discrimination	International competition	Welfare state	Internal security	Globalisation	Political strategy
	National sovereignty	European identity	Human rights		Overcrowding or saturation of benefits	Political stability	Legality	
			Civil liberties			Organised crime		
			Rule of Law					
			Democracy					

Source: Helbling 2014

THE POLITICS OF IMMIGRATION IN SCOTLAND

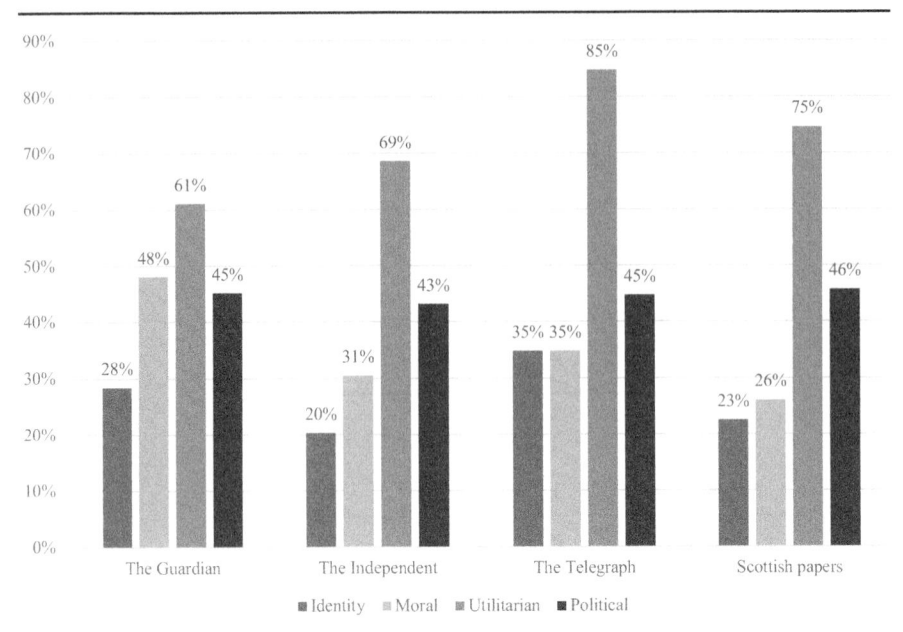

Figure 7.2 Percentage of articles with applied frames by newspaper

increased migration: one could argue that the UK's greatness is a feature of its historical empire that included people of many different cultures, or one could argue that England should be preserved for the English. Both arguments are nationalistic because they discuss community identity, but they convey different messages about the value of immigration for collective identity. Labelling articles with the identity frame and nationalistic argument does not capture intent, which must be communicated through an article's tone towards immigration.

Coding Article Tone

Detecting written tone is difficult because tone is most effectively communicated orally, through patterns of speech and expression. Nevertheless, each article in the sample is coded as either conveying a positive tone about migration (those that are sympathetic to the migrant experience, highlighting the benefits of immigration, or advocating for migration, or adopting a critical tone against those who seek to restrict migration), a negative tone (highlighting the costs of immigration, or advocating for migration restrictions), or a neutral/balanced tone.[9] The assessment of tone considers the focus of the piece (for example, an article about immigration control measures would be coded as conveying a negative tone about immigration), or whether the piece was arguing for or against immigration. Based on the known ideological biases of the newspapers, it is hypothesised that *The Telegraph* will publish articles with a much more negative tone towards immigration than any of the other papers. *The Guardian* is expected to be positive, and given the pro-immigrant signals sent by the Scottish political elites, the Scottish papers are expected to be most positive about immigration.

An example of an article communicating a positive tone is one from *The Guardian* on 5 January 2015 entitled 'Dyson wipes floor with May's student immigration plan'. Though the article discusses May's immigration restrictions, the focus of the piece is on Sir James Dyson's argument that the policy of restricting immigration will hurt the economy. Another example of an article with a positive tone is from *The Telegraph* on 2 January 2014 and is entitled 'Immigration rules are causing a curry crisis'. This article discusses the way immigration has become central to British society through the curry house, and discusses the way the Conservative government's immigration restrictions are threatening the curry houses' ability to attract chefs. An article with a negative code is from *The Independent* on 11 December 2014 entitled 'Foreign killer and criminals "granted British citizenship", damning report reveals'. The article covers a report from John Vince, the Chief Inspector of Borders and Immigration, who found that an overreliance on automated checks meant that immigrants who would have failed 'good character' assessments were allowed to enter the country. Occasionally tone is more ambiguous, as with a story from *The Guardian* on 1 January 2015 entitled 'Paris terror attacks: Far right uses attacks to fuel anti-Islam backlash: Groups claim Paris deaths vindicate prejudices and seek to restrict immigration'. The bulk of the article recounts the anti-immigrant messaging of the far right, though the story opens with quotes from members of Germany's Muslim community who are planning a candlelight vigil for the victims of terrorism and quotes a scholar who warns against an Islamophobic backlash to the terrorist attacks. It was coded as communicating a positive tone about immigrants due to the opening and the closing sentence about prosecuting a mosque vandal.

Figure 7.3 depicts the percentage of the articles about immigration in each paper that communicated a positive, neutral, or negative tone on immigration. *The Telegraph* conveys the least positive image of immigration. Fifty-three per cent of the articles conveying a negative message about immigration were published in *The Telegraph* (105 articles out of a total 230 negative articles). As articles from *The Telegraph* make up 32% of the full sample, negative articles are overrepresented in the conservative paper.[10] As expected, the Scottish papers deploy positive tone most frequently when describing immigration, though *The Guardian* accounts for 42% of all positive immigration stories in the sample (96 out of 239 pro-immigration articles), which suggests that just as negative articles about immigration are overrepresented in *The Telegraph*, positive stories are overrepresented in *The Guardian*.

THE POLITICS OF IMMIGRATION IN SCOTLAND

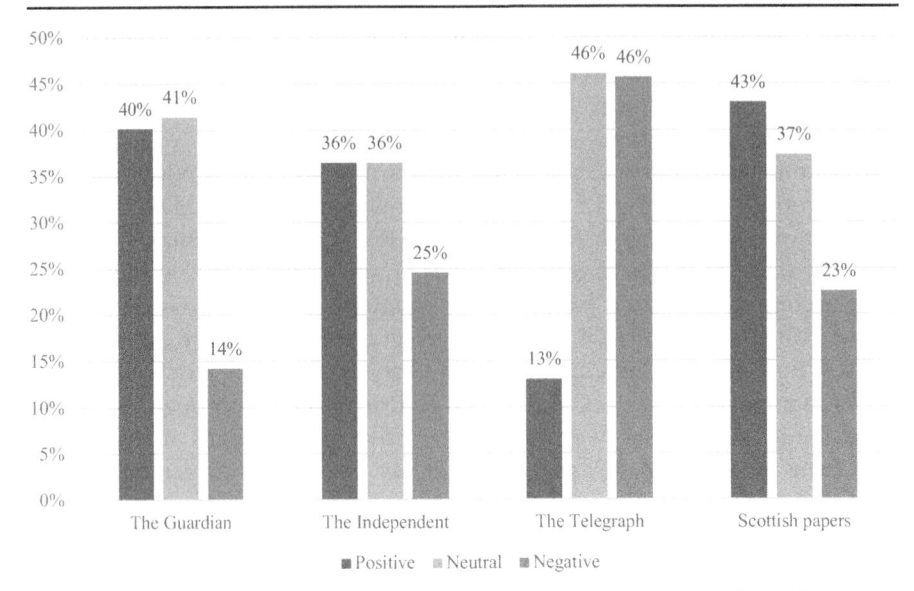

Figure 7.3 Tone of coverage by percentage of 'immigration' articles by newspaper

The distribution of stories by tone confirms the hypothesis that tone is determined by the ideological positions of the papers. Among the UK-wide papers, *The Guardian* and *The Telegraph* are almost mirror images of each other, biased in opposite directions. For both papers, the percentage of stories with a neutral tone just slightly exceeds the percentage of stories with a directed tone. Coverage of immigration in *The Independent* tends to be more positive, though the distribution of positive and negative stories is more equal than in either *The Guardian* or *The Telegraph*. The slight positive skew could be a feature of the paper's leftward lean in political coverage and readership, or it might be attributable to the newspaper's free market stance, which correlates with support for free movement of labour. The Scottish papers communicate a positive tone in the largest percentage of articles, though they also publish a larger percentage of stories with an anti-immigrant tone than *The Guardian*.

Coding Article Type

Newspapers fulfil many functions beyond providing information to their readers. They also help them understand the news and provide a venue for commentary. When reporting the news, reporters attempt to maintain a personal distance, write in the third person, and report on as many aspects of the story as they can, including all sides in a conflict. The reader is left to make up their own mind about the issue. Those who provide commentary (like columnists) provide their perspective on news that has already been reported. Letters

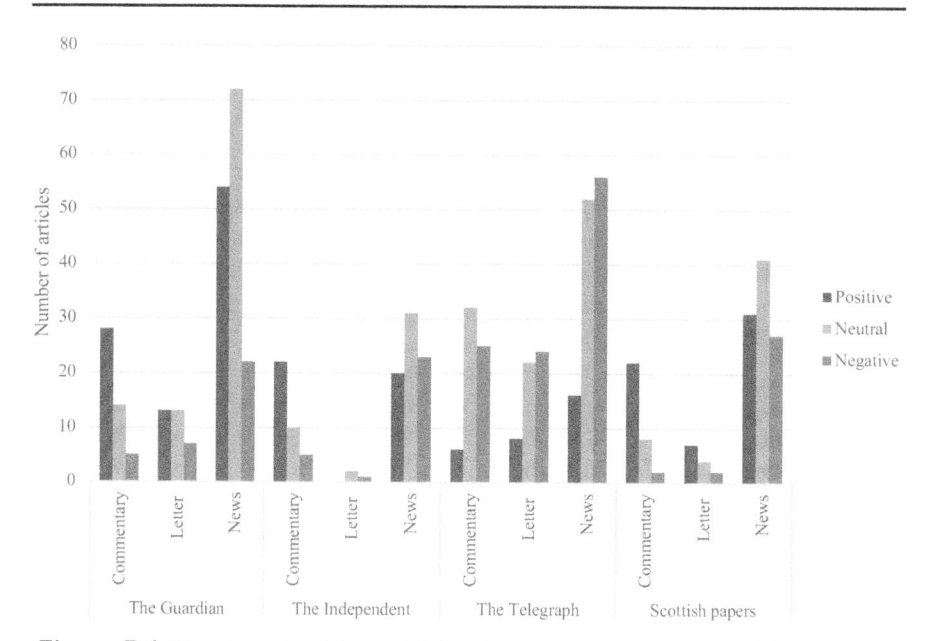

Figure 7.4 Number of articles published by newspaper, type of article, and tone

can come from the political or economic elite or from members of the public. The tone of a piece should be more apparent in pieces providing commentary or in letters to the editor.

Figure 7.4 displays the number of articles published in each newspaper with 'immigration' in the title or keyword, broken down by the tone of coverage and article type. As expected, news articles are more likely than the other types of articles to convey neutral tone, and commentary pieces tend to communicate a distinct tone about immigration in most of the newspapers. The one exception is in *The Telegraph*, where the news stories are more likely to frame immigration negatively, primarily because authors focus on stories about immigration control, which assume immigration is a social problem. With the exception of commentary pieces in *The Telegraph*, the commentary in every other news source overwhelmingly presents immigration in a positive light. *The Telegraph*'s commentary is more likely to be neutral than in other newspapers, and it is also much more likely to convey a negative opinion of immigration.

The Guardian, *The Independent*, and the Scottish papers look very similar in the tone of their coverage across the types of articles and tend to publish more neutral/positive pieces. Forty-five per cent of the news stories in *The Telegraph* convey a negative tone about migrants, while 42% are neutral. *The Guardian* news stories also have a strong slant in a more positive direction, but the slant is not as strong as *The Telegraph*'s negative slant. Thirty-six per cent of news stories in *The Guardian* relay a positive tone and 49% are neutral towards immigration. Bias in news story coverage is problematic because unlike with commentary, where the reader knows they are dealing with a persuasive argument or an individual's opinions, the readers of news articles are not anticipating the need to exercise vigilance in interpreting presumably objective information. Biased news reporting can mislead the public, and negative reporting may contribute to the British public's tendency to grossly overestimate the number and negative social impact of migrants (Duffy and Frere-Smith 2014).

The frame, tone, and type of newspaper articles in the UK-wide and Scottish papers reveal patterns in how the papers report on immigration. The strongest patterns align with the ideological predispositions of the papers, and the ideological differences are clearest in the tone of the commentary pieces. Patterns in the frames applied to articles look remarkably similar across all of the papers, with most articles connecting immigration with utilitarian concerns.

Analysing Frame Application in UK-Wide and Scottish Newspapers

Though UK-wide and Scottish papers frame their stories about immigration in proportionately similar ways, the arguments and tone towards immigration reveal differences in how the frames are used across UK-wide papers and between the Scottish and UK-wide papers. The type of article is also useful for understanding the argument. This section analyses the nuance of the frames, from the most frequently used frames to the least: utilitarian frames, political frames, moral frames, and identity frames.

Utilitarian Frames

Utilitarian frames are the most commonly employed frame by all of the newspapers in their articles about immigration (see Figure 7.2). Utilitarian frames link immigration to practical or pragmatic concerns about the economy, labour and social security, migrant impact on social services and employment, pragmatic arguments about national interest or legal issues, and security. Between 2013 and 2016, *The Telegraph* used utilitarian frames most frequently, in 85% of its articles about immigration, followed closely by the Scottish newspapers, which employed a utilitarian frame in 75% of their articles. Articles in *The Guardian* and *The Independent* include a utilitarian frame between 60% and 70% of the time. Figure 7.5 displays the breakdown of the utilitarian arguments by newspaper.

There are two clear differences between the UK-wide and Scottish newspapers in their use of utilitarian frames. First, mainstream UK-wide newspapers were more likely to employ frames of labour and social security than the Scottish papers, perhaps because concern about social services is strongest in

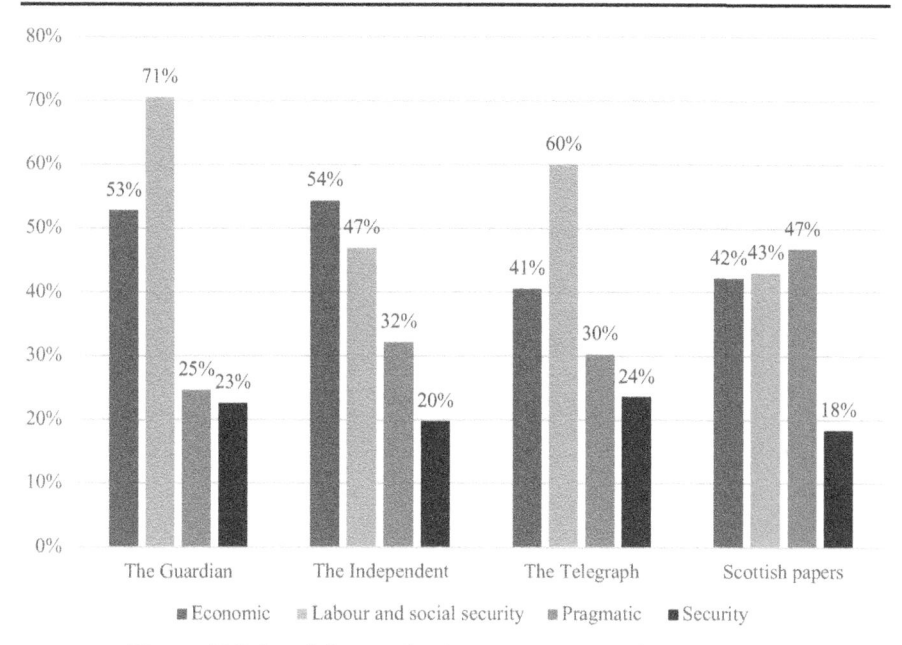

Figure 7.5 Breakdown of utilitarian arguments by newspaper

communities where levels of immigration are the highest and therefore the most likely to be seen as an issue, such as in London. Negative articles framed with labour and social security cover things like David Cameron's 2013 initiatives to restrict benefits to EU workers with a ban on access to housing benefits and a three-month ban on out-of-work benefits. Positive stories focus on migrant contributions to the labour force and to public finances. One commentary piece published on 12 May 2014 in *The Telegraph* entitled 'EU elections 2014: Is immigration good for Britain?' explicitly discussed immigrant utility:

> Settling down may ease social tensions, but ironically, becoming 'normal' Britons will eventually make European immigrants less economically useful to their adopted home. Those that stay will age and require health care and pensions, and have children who must be educated. (Kirkup 2014)

This argument presents immigrants as valuable as long as they can be 'useful' as opposed to a drain on the system, and like most utilitarian arguments, the values conveyed are unidirectional and nationalistic, focused exclusively on how the migrant benefits the UK.

The second noticeable difference between the utilitarian frames used by UK-wide versus Scottish papers is that the Scottish papers employ pragmatic arguments more than the UK-wide newspapers. Pragmatic arguments focus on

THE POLITICS OF IMMIGRATION IN SCOTLAND

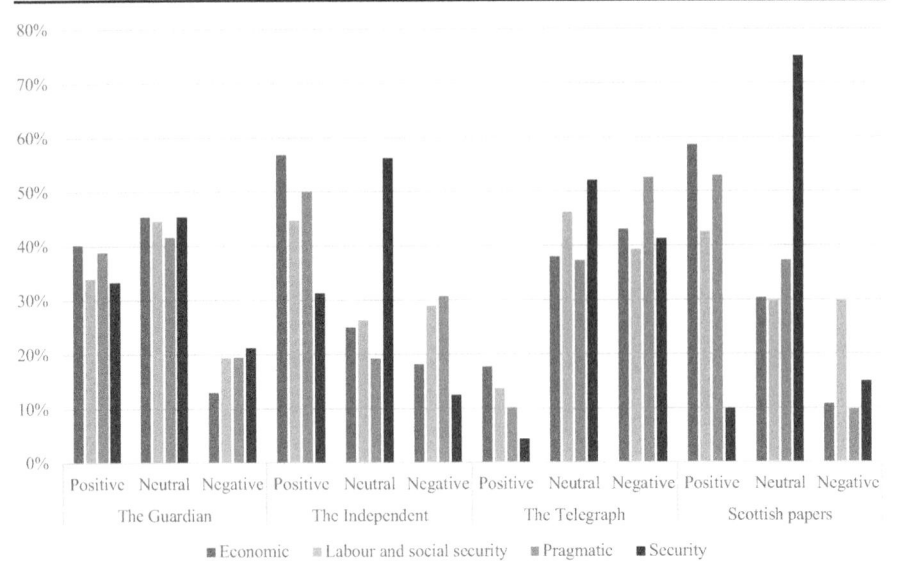

Figure 7.6 Tone of articles employing utilitarian arguments by newspaper

the national interest and the international position of the nation, which is in line with the efforts of the Scottish elites to present openness to immigration as advancing Scotland's national interest and bolstering Scotland's international reputation. An example of an article employing a pragmatic argument was published on 21 November 2014 in *The Herald* entitled 'Demographics show Scotland needs a distinct immigration policy'; another was published in *The Scotsman* on 17 July 2016 with the title 'Immigration reform could hit Scots business post-Brexit'. Both articles emphasise distinct conditions within Scotland that are negatively influenced by Westminster's immigration policy, and argue that a sub-state national immigration policy would yield more favourable demographic and economic outcomes for Scotland.

The breakdown of articles by argument and tone provided in Figure 7.6 communicates the nature of the utilitarian frames. Though the Scottish papers emphasise labour and social security less and pragmatic themes more than the UK-wide papers, the Scottish papers are not outliers in tone. The tone of the stories in the Scottish newspapers most closely resembles the tone of *The Independent*: their stories linking immigration to the economy, labour and social security, and pragmatic themes all convey a more positive tone about immigration and the stories on security issues are predominately neutral. All of the newspapers most frequently report security-related concerns with a neutral tone, though Scottish papers are more neutral when compared with other newspapers. *The Guardian* and *The Independent* lean positive, while

The Telegraph skews negative. The neutral Scottish coverage of immigration with a security frame may relate to Scotland's relative lack of experience with security-related challenges associated with immigration and its lack of control over border security, which is a reserved power. Most of these stories cover irregular migration or potential security threats.

Both Scottish and UK-wide newspapers strongly associate immigration with utilitarian concerns, but there are modest national differences in the choice of utilitarian arguments and the tone of coverage. The Scottish papers emphasise pragmatic arguments and tend to be less negative in their coverage than the other newspapers, though their tone is not very distinguishable from coverage in *The Independent*. The exception is the overwhelmingly neutral tone in the Scottish papers when reporting on immigration and security. The behaviour of the Scottish press seems to mirror the arguments of the Scottish elites, particularly in the overrepresentation of pragmatic arguments with reference to Scottish interests.

Political Frames

Political frames are the second most frequently employed frame in both UK-wide and Scottish newspapers, and they are used in about 40% of the stories in the sample (see Figure 7.2). Political frames discuss the politics associated with immigration, often without discussing immigration or immigration policy substantively. Media providers throughout Europe are crowding out their discussion of policy with coverage of political personalities due to the horse race nature of political elections, especially in polarised political environments like in the UK (Banducci and Hanretty 2014). An example of this tendency comes from a commentary piece by Alan Travis of *The Guardian*:

> With [Cameron's] arbitrary net immigration target now left in tatters, Cameron, like Obama, could have risen to the occasion and tried to change the entire political tone of the debate. Instead, he continued to allow UKIP to frame the debate in terms of narrow party advantage rather than what is good for Britain. It is hardly surprising that the Conservatives, after spending years in opposition claiming loudly that immigration had got out of control, now face the same accusation themselves. (Travis 2014)

Another example comes from a generally pro-immigrant commentary piece by Dan Hodges of *The Telegraph* entitled 'Britons have become scared of the wider world' in which he discusses the political consensus in Westminster around the undesirability of immigration:

> With Clegg's surrender, the final domino has fallen. For the first time in over half a century each of the three major political parties will enter

THE POLITICS OF IMMIGRATION IN SCOTLAND

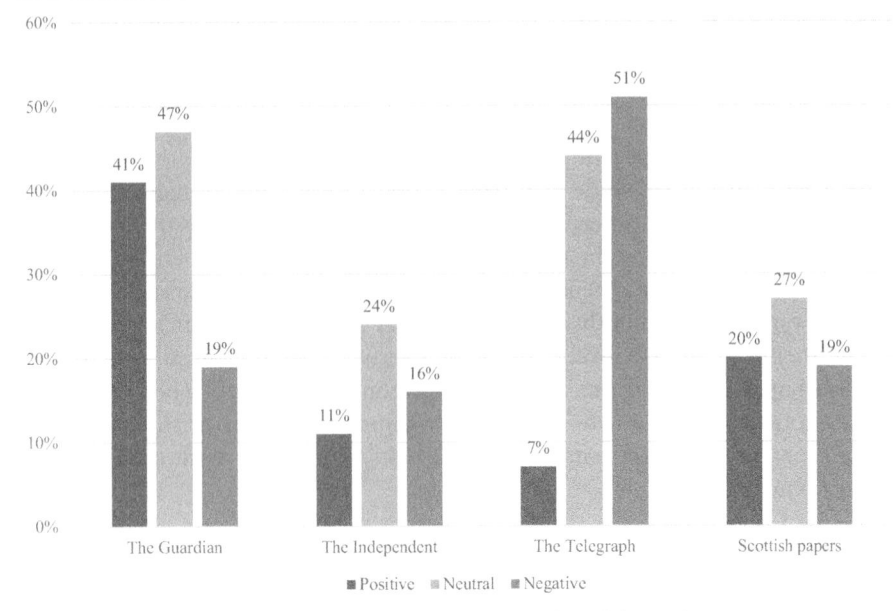

[Bar chart showing tone of articles by newspaper:
- The Guardian: Positive 41%, Neutral 47%, Negative 19%
- The Independent: Positive 11%, Neutral 24%, Negative 16%
- The Telegraph: Positive 7%, Neutral 44%, Negative 51%
- Scottish papers: Positive 20%, Neutral 27%, Negative 19%]

Figure 7.7 Tone of articles employing a political frame by newspaper

the election calling for curbs on immigration. The anti-immigration lobby, which at turns has counted such diverse figures as Enoch Powell, Margaret Thatcher, Frank Field, William Hague, Nick Griffin and Nigel Farage among its number, has won. (Hodges 2014)

And north of the border, a commentary piece by Tom Peterkin in *The Scotsman* critiques the strategy and intent of the Scottish political elites:

> One suspects that [Education Secretary] Russell was deliberately raising the temperature on immigration in the knowledge that this controversial issue is becoming a focal point of the [independence] referendum ... Could it be that SNP politicians are keen to emphasise the idea of differing attitudes to immigration north and south of the Border in an attempt to drown out the practical difficulties of having a distinctive Scottish policy plus an open Border? (Peterkin 2014)

In each example, the authors frame immigration as a political tool, suggesting that the political strategy on immigration is rooted in political competition, rather than what is best for the country.

It is unsurprising, then, that stories employing a political frame tend to be more negative in tone than positive.[11] Figure 7.7 displays the tone of the articles associated with the political frame by newspaper. The tone of the coverage in the UK-wide papers aligns with the ideology of the paper, where *The Guardian* publishes the most articles with a positive tone, followed by *The Independent*, and *The Telegraph* publishes mostly negative articles about the politics of immigration. The political articles with the negative tone mostly cover party competition over controlling immigration, and since the Conservative government was in power during the period of study, the status quo default position is anti-immigrant.

Articles with a political frame and a pro-immigrant tone, like those published in *The Guardian*, still tend to be quite negative about the politics surrounding immigration, but they use a positive argument about immigration to critique the Conservative and anti-immigrant status quo. This perspective is represented by a quote by Alan Travis (2014) in a commentary piece: 'The continuing shambles of the UK immigration system may make it hard to believe, but Britain already has a system of managed immigration largely based on the contribution that those allowed to come can make.' This argument calls the status quo shambolic while simultaneously highlighting how the points-based system implicitly recognises immigrants as having the potential to contribute.

The Scottish papers published a roughly equal number of articles with more negative and positive tone. All but two negative articles discuss UK politics, and all except one report news, meaning that they are written in the third person and dedicated to conveying the message of political actors.[12] For example, a brief news story by David Maddox (2013) in *The Scotsman* covered the Conservative Party's immigration bill, and the heart of the story contains the following quote from Home Secretary Theresa May: 'It is unacceptable that hard-working taxpayers have to compete with people who have no right to be here. This bill will begin to address these absurdities and restore the balance.' This news story does not convey Maddox's personal opinions, but because it focuses on measures to reduce migration it is coded as negative in tone. Many other negative political stories in the Scottish papers similarly focus on the message of the Conservative government or party competition between the Conservatives and UKIP.

Conversely, nearly all of the stories with a positive tone about immigration in the Scottish papers cover the ideological conflict between Holyrood and Westminster over immigration. Over half (11/20) of these positive stories are commentary pieces, like a letter in *The Herald* by Alastair Sim of Universities Scotland:

> We ask the Smith Commission for constitutional recognition of and action to address the fact that Scotland's demographic and economic needs are different to those in the rest of the United Kingdom on the issue of immigration. A successful devolution settlement will be one which allows policy to flex in a way which reflects different economic and demographic circumstances in different parts of the UK but within a

successful Union. It is possible to do this in a way that is highly specific to Scotland and therefore need not affect immigration policy within the rest of the UK. (Sim 2014)[13]

Sim's letter summarises many of the arguments Scottish political elites have used to make the case for devolved control over immigration to allow Scotland to attract more migrants. While highlighting differences between Scotland and the rest of the UK, it suggests the policy can work within the systems and structures of the UK without compromising the Union.

In sum, the UK-wide newspapers differ from each other in their coverage based on the ideological leanings of the papers. *The Guardian* is more likely to use immigration as a reason to critique the Conservative government. *The Telegraph* is more likely to critique the government for its inefficiency in controlling migration and to report on party competition coming from the far right. *The Independent* falls between the two. The Scottish papers are more balanced in articles with a political frame, but the articles with a negative tone are reporting on UK politics. Scottish commentary takes a positive stance towards immigration and focus on national conflicts about immigration.

Moral Frames

Articles with universalist/moral frames connect immigration to concerns about fairness, discrimination, human rights, and democracy. Thirty-six per cent of the total articles in the sample employ moral frames, of which 55% are news articles, 34% are commentary pieces, and 11% are letters to the editor. Looking back at Figure 7.2, *The Guardian* published the most articles with a moral frame (115 articles, or 48% of its stories). *The Telegraph* connects moral concerns to immigration in 35% of its articles and *The Independent* in 31% of its articles. The Scottish newspapers use moral frames in 26% of their stories about immigration. The less frequent use of moral frames by the Scottish newspapers is surprising, since part of Scotland's strategy in using the politics of migration as a tool of nation-building is to place Scotland on a moral pedestal built out of its pro-diversity approach. Figure 7.8 illustrates the tone of articles with a moral frame by newspaper.

Newspapers employ moral frames in a variety of ways. *The Guardian* and the Scottish papers take a positive tone in morally framed articles. Many stories focus on moral obligations towards refugees or those living in inhumane conditions in removal centres or camps. Other stories discuss what a state owes those who have positively contributed to its economy and society. For example, the Archbishop of Canterbury is quoted in *The Herald*:

> But at the heart of Christian teaching about the human being is that all human beings are of absolutely equal and of infinite value and the language we use must reflect the value of the human being and not treat

THE PRESS

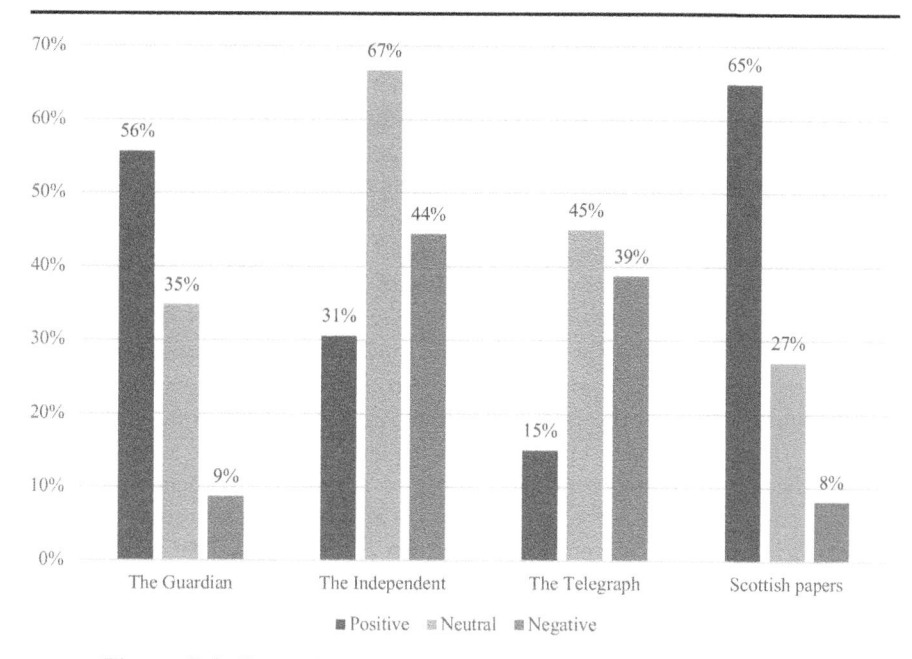

Figure 7.8 Tone of articles employing a moral frame by newspaper

immigration as a deep menace that is somehow going to overwhelm a country that has coped with many waves of immigration and has usually done so with enormous success. It is part of the strength and brilliance of this country that we are so good at this, and I would hate to see us lose that. (Devlin 2014)

This quote eloquently blends moral and identity frames. It praises the strength of the UK (a nationalist identity frame) while pushing for universalist values and targeting ethnocentrism as an internal risk to that strength (a moral frame). It ultimately urges citizens of the UK to return to a value system that willingly includes immigrants.

Contrary to the positive tone of articles in *The Guardian* and the Scottish newspapers, *The Telegraph* and *The Independent* employ moral frames in many stories with a negative tone about migration. Several articles question the fairness of free movement in the EU, which privileges some migrants over others. Some articles focus on the idea of competing or contradictory human rights, asserting that the rights of migrants have been allowed to supersede the rights of UK citizens. A number of articles defend Conservatives against accusations of racism, stating that arguments against migration are not necessarily racist in intent.

Unlike in the analysis of the other frames, where *The Independent* looks more like *The Guardian* than *The Telegraph*, *The Independent* closely resembles *The Telegraph* in its use of the moral frame, and both favour a neutral tone in their articles with a moral frame. The neutral news articles objectively cover asylum politics or document poor conditions in detention or removal centres, while the neutral commentary pieces tend to present arguments both for and against a more liberal approach to immigration. An example of a neutral commentary piece about asylum comes from *The Telegraph* on 30 December 2013 entitled 'Advantage Farage in the immigration debate'. The article discusses a statement made by Farage in which he called for David Cameron to admit Syrian refugees. The piece covers the UK's low acceptance of refugees and argues that the government should do more, though it concludes by arguing that border control must be better managed, noting that Britons favour stronger measures to control EU migration. The focus on asylum and national responsibility applies the moral frame, while juxtaposition arguments for accepting more refugees and tightening the borders make the story balanced in tone. Another prototypical example of a neutral commentary piece with a moral frame comes from *The Guardian* editors on 24 March 2015 entitled '*The Guardian* view on immigration', in which the authors argue:

> It is sometimes claimed that there has been no discussion about immigration. On the contrary, for at least a generation it has been talked about relentlessly. It is just that the conversation has never been very constructive. As a result, it has often resembled a dialogue of the deaf, where the only common factor has been an offhand cruelty to every man or woman who has ever come to the UK to build a better life and finds themselves part of 'them' and not of 'us'. As many of the voices we publish in G2 today show, it is very easy to let even the most talented people making the most prominent contribution feel unwanted. But for some, immigration raises atavistic fears. It challenges identity. With the best of intentions, progressive politicians watching the rise of racist parties elsewhere in Europe long ignored or denied that truth. (The Guardian Editors 2015)

This story is typical of the more neutral commentary pieces in that it pushes back against public perception of migrants, while simultaneously acknowledging the political and social importance of those public perceptions and arguing for the need to address those fears and concerns.

In sum, *The Independent* looks like *The Telegraph* in the tone of articles of moral frames, while it has resembled *The Guardian* or the Scottish papers in their use of political and utilitarian frames. The Scottish papers do not distinguish themselves in their use of moral frames and look like *The Guardian* in the breakdown of articles by tone, though they employed moral frames the least.

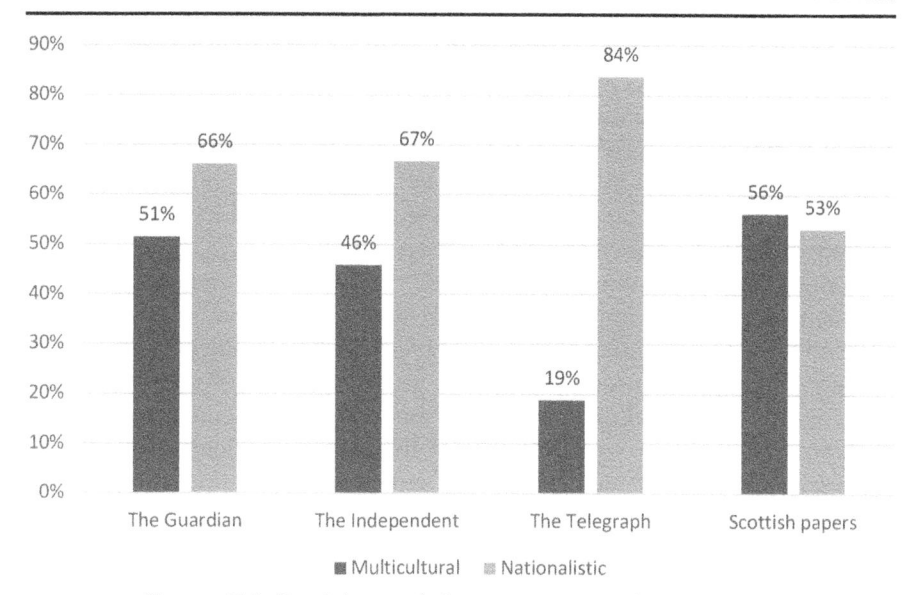

Figure 7.9 Breakdown of identity arguments by newspaper

Identity Frames

Identity frames were employed in roughly 27% of articles across all five newspapers, which, contrary to expectations, makes them the least frequently employed frames.[14] Identity frames are either multicultural or nationalistic in argumentation. Multicultural arguments advocate for greater diversity and tolerance of difference, and promote a more cosmopolitan, and therefore Europe-facing, identity. Nationalistic arguments emphasise the prioritisation of the national community over outsiders and tend to be inherently conservative and often defensive, seeing change introduced by diversity as a threat to common national understandings and values. The relatively low use of identity frames in newspaper articles about immigration is surprising given the regular association between immigration and identity in public discourse, the sensationalistic way instances of ethnic nationalism are discussed in the media, and the way the Scottish political elites have used the politics of immigration to define their civic national identity.

Figure 7.9 displays the percentage of the articles that employ either a multicultural or nationalistic identity frame. All of the UK-wide newspapers employ nationalistic identity frames more often than they employ multicultural identity frames in stories about immigration. Once again, *The Telegraph* stands out from the rest: it employs nationalistic language in 84% of stories with identity frames. The only papers in the sample that employ roughly equal multicultural and nationalistic arguments are the Scottish ones, though the nationalistic stories tend to report on the UK and the politics of UKIP, while the multicultural stories focus more on the Scottish experience. One might expect the nationalistic stories in Scottish papers to focus on the SNP, but given the SNP's leadership, the framing of the party's politics tends towards the utilitarian, rather than culture, tradition, and identity. The split of multicultural and nationalistic arguments therefore reflects the split focus in the Scottish papers on Scottish and UK-wide concerns.

Though they seem mutually exclusive, multicultural and nationalistic arguments occasionally appear within the same article, especially those that advocate for a civic national identity and highlight how multiculturalism and diversity have helped the country achieve greatness. An example is provided by a story by Becky Slack, who published an article on 30 September 2014 in *The Guardian* about a roundtable at the Labour Party Conference discussing whether greater levels of immigration and subsequent ethnic diversity result in more or less social trust and community spirit:

> Ethnic diversity does not come without its challenges, but there is also much to celebrate. One only needs to look to London to see the kind of impact immigration can have, socially and economically. As Prof Shamit Saggar of Essex University said: 'London is an exceptional city. Permanent and temporary influences and identities are all represented there. It doesn't take a huge amount of vision to say that the country as a whole has that kind of future ahead of it' . . . A multicultural, multilingual society would go a long way towards ensuring Britain can maintain its position on the world stage. (Slack 2014)

This quote demonstrates a clear multicultural vision tied to national interest and a desire to see the UK maintain its privileged international status. It also demonstrates that expressions of multicultural nationalism are not exclusively communicated by the Scottish elite.

Figure 7.10 provides the tone breakdown of stories employing multicultural and nationalistic arguments by newspaper. Articles making a nationalistic argument are more likely to be anti-immigrant in tone (except for those published in *The Guardian*), and articles making a multicultural argument are more likely to be positive about immigration. *The Telegraph* displays the cleanest relationship between identity frames and tone – nearly all of the negative stories are nationalistic and nearly all of the more positive stories are multicultural. The neutral stories advance multicultural and nationalistic arguments with equal frequency.

In *The Independent*, multicultural stories are more likely to convey a positive tone towards immigration and nationalistic stories a negative tone, though there are more exceptions than in *The Telegraph*. The tone of the stories balance each other out, reflecting the centrist position of *The Independent* on

THE PRESS

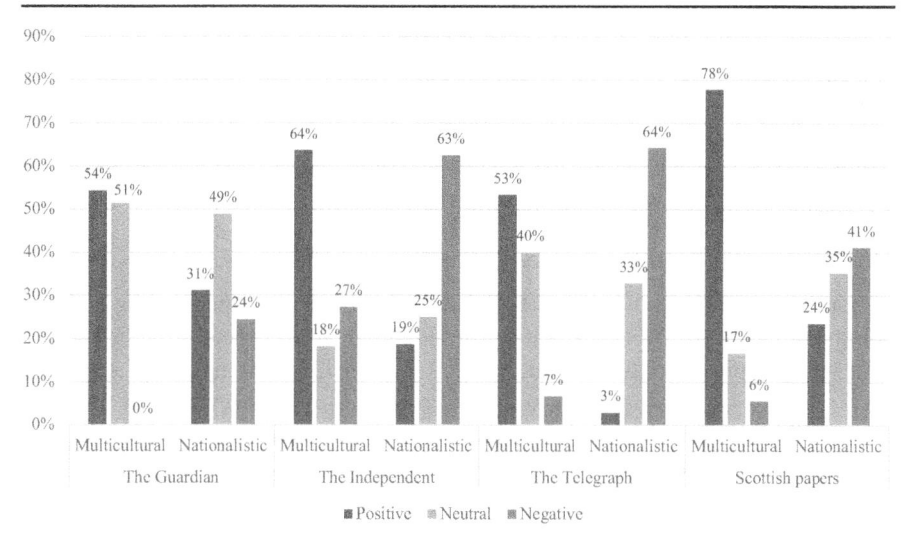

Figure 7.10 Tone of articles employing identity frames by argument and newspaper

social issues. In *The Guardian*, all articles with a negative tone towards immigration are making nationalistic arguments. However, even the nationalistic articles convey neutral or positive tone more often than negative tone. This represents *The Guardian*'s pro-immigrant position, where identity frames are most often employed with a neutral tone, but where tone is employed, articles are more likely to be positive than negative.

In Scotland, the articles with multicultural frames are overwhelmingly pro-immigrant in tone. Stories with a more nationalist frame are more dispersed in their employment of positive, neutral, or negative tones towards migration with a slant towards the more negative tone. The nationalistic stories mostly cover the UK as a whole, though the ones with a pro-immigrant tone all highlight a Scottish contrast to the UK. The results from the Scottish papers suggest that multicultural arguments in Scotland strongly cue pro-immigrant positions

Ultimately, when we consider the difference in coverage across the newspapers, the main difference in the way they employ identity frames is the ideological perspective of the paper. *The Guardian* communicates the most consistent pro-immigrant perspective in articles associating immigration and identity, as the vast majority of articles employing either a multicultural or nationalistic identity frame are neutral or positive in their tone about immigrants. The Scottish papers come next, with a greater proportion of multicultural stories that are overwhelmingly pro-immigrant in tone and tend to speak to the Scottish, rather than the UK, experience. The nationalistic arguments published in the Scottish papers look very much like the arguments published

197

in the UK-wide papers, with a focus on the politics of UKIP and public fear of migrant threat to social cohesion and identity. The distribution of stories in *The Independent* looks like *The Guardian* in the number of articles that were published with identity frames, and much like the Scottish papers in tone. *The Telegraph* is the purist in its association between identity frame and tone, and it leans nationalistic in its argumentation and negative in tone.

THE IMPACT OF MEDIA FRAMING ON POLITICS AND PUBLIC OPINION

The strongest patterns in how the UK-wide and Scottish papers frame articles about immigration are explained by the ideological perspective of the paper, which often predicts the dominant tone of articles, but also predicts how frequently certain frames are used. For example, moral frames and identity frames employing multicultural arguments are used more frequently in papers that lean left ideologically. But do media tone and frame influence political outcomes? Media frames are presumed to impact political outcomes through their ability to alter public opinion or a party's electoral success. For example, when The Sun (a right-leaning tabloid) switched its party endorsement to the Labour Party in 1997, the change altered readers' party preference, but not underlying preferences, to a magnitude of about 2% of the popular vote (Reeves et al. 2016). Media coverage of UKIP has also been found to predict UKIP support (Murphy and Devine 2018). The political impact of the media in the UK is somewhat surprising, since the first-past-the-post electoral system should be least conducive to media effects, compared with the proportional representation systems in the rest of Europe.[15]

Outside election season, the media can influence opinions in ways that impact community cohesion. Most of the UK's reporting on immigration is negative (Esser et al. 2017), and in a comparison of European newspaper coverage of the refugee crisis, British coverage was the most negative towards newcomers (Berry et al. 2016).[16] For example, the rhetoric and symbols that surrounded the UK's asylum policy-making process from 1997 to 2010 depicted asylum seekers as a threat (Mulvey 2010). Threat-based constructions problematise immigration and lead to a sense of political crisis that encourages hostility towards migrants.[17] Based on the tone of articles in the UK-wide and Scottish newspapers (Figure 7.3), we would expect readers of *The Telegraph* to hold the most anti-immigrant perspectives, followed by *The Independent* and the Scottish newspapers. Those who read *The Guardian* should be most positive. Since the comparative research suggests that positive coverage has a stronger effect (van Klingeren et al. 2015), the readers of *The Guardian* and the Scottish papers should have stronger opinions than those who read *The Telegraph*.

While most research on media effects focuses on tone, framing also matters. When the British press emphasised concrete issues like the economy and education (utilitarian frames) with reference to immigration, it was found to increase the public's concern about immigration (McLaren et al. 2017). However, more abstract issues like governmental process or policy-making (political frames) were not associated with a public reaction. Based on the framing patterns across newspapers in articles on immigration, *The Telegraph* is most likely to employ utilitarian frames and labour and social security arguments, and one would expect readers of *The Telegraph* to express more anti-immigrant opinions.

The Scottish Social Attitudes Survey (SSAS) is a probability survey of over 1,000 Scots. It is conducted annually and is one of the few survey instruments that targets an exclusively Scottish sample. The 2015 survey asked whether the respondents regularly read a daily morning newspaper. Thirty-eight per cent of the SSAS respondents reported reading a newspaper daily (487 individuals). This is slightly below the estimate from the brand reach data (Appendix C), which suggests that over half of the British public reads a newspaper. The sample of readers is equally split by gender, even though women are less likely to read print news (Fortunati et al. 2014), but the average age of the readers is much higher (60) than the average age of the non-reader (48). The age profile reflects the reality that newspaper readership is in decline across the UK, as younger generations report reading newspapers much less frequently than previous generations (Thurman and Fletcher 2018). In the SSAS, 62% of those who read newspapers daily read tabloids and not broadsheet papers, which reflects the greater tendency among the Scottish public to read tabloids (71% versus the 59% who read quality papers) (PAMCo 2018). Unfortunately, this leaves a rather small number of people in the sample that read broadsheets (174), and even fewer who read the specific newspapers included in this analysis.[18] Because of the small sample, relationships between newspaper choice and attitudes towards migrants or minorities in the survey cannot be representative, though they hint at whether there are the anticipated differences among Scottish newspaper readers.

Figure 7.11 illustrates mean responses to three questions about whether Scotland would lose its identity with increased immigration by Muslims, East Europeans, or Black and Asian people, broken down by which newspaper the respondents read. Responses could range from disagree strongly (-2) to agree strongly (2), and zero is the neutral position. The patterns confirm expectations, and readers of *The Telegraph* express more negative opinions than any of the readers of other papers. Readers of *The Guardian* express the strongest and most pro-immigrant opinions. The readers of *The Independent*, *The Herald*, and *The Scotsman* express more pro-immigrant positions on average, but are less positive than the readers of *The Guardian*. The figure also compares the opinions of the 174 Scottish people who regularly read broadsheets, the 283 people who regularly read tabloids, and the 801 people who do not read a daily paper. Readers of tabloids exhibit more agreement with the idea that Scotland's identity would be threatened by increased migration, non-readers

THE POLITICS OF IMMIGRATION IN SCOTLAND

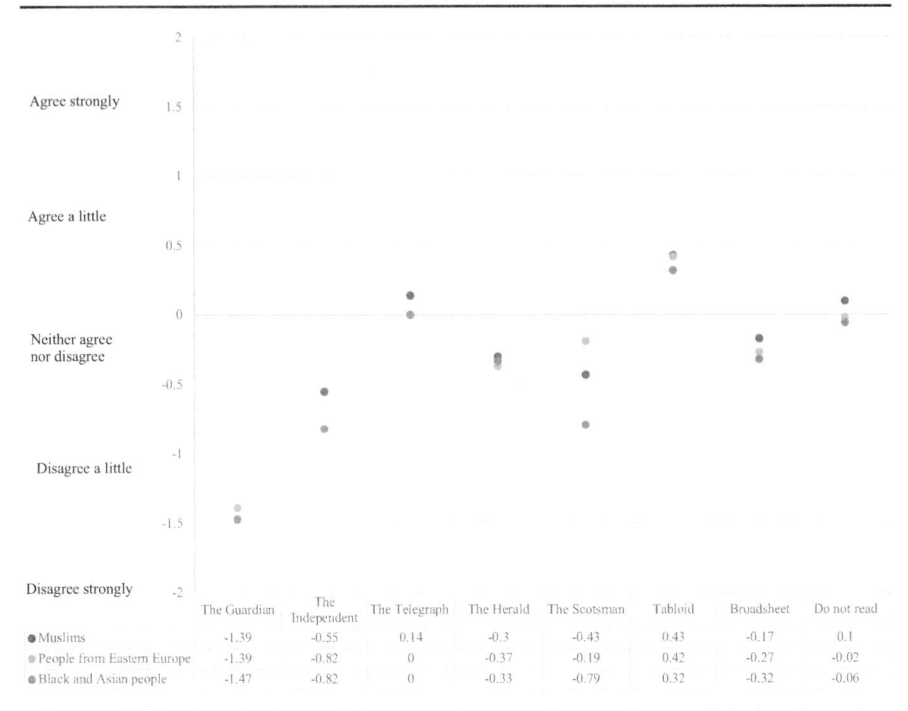

	The Guardian	The Independent	The Telegraph	The Herald	The Scotsman	Tabloid	Broadsheet	Do not read
Muslims	-1.39	-0.55	0.14	-0.3	-0.43	0.43	-0.17	0.1
People from Eastern Europe	-1.39	-0.82	0	-0.37	-0.19	0.42	-0.27	-0.02
Black and Asian people	-1.47	-0.82	0	-0.33	-0.79	0.32	-0.32	-0.06

Figure 7.11 'Scotland would begin to lose its identity if more [Muslims/people from East Europe/Black and Asian people] came to live in Scotland'.
Source: 2015 Scottish Social Attitudes Survey (ScotCen Social Research 2017)

express neutral positions on average, and those who read broadsheets are more likely to disagree that Scotland will lose its identity to immigrants.

Figure 7.12 illustrates the mean responses to two questions asking about whether individuals who are migrants or a member of a minoritised group take jobs from Scottish people. The patterns mimic those from Figure 7.11 in terms of the positions of readers' opinions by paper, though the readers of all papers appear to lean towards disagreeing that migrants and minorities take jobs, as do the non-readers. The only group to express very slight average agreement with the idea that migrants and minorities take jobs are the readers of tabloid newspapers.

Comparing the opinions of Scots who regularly read newspapers by the papers they read reveals expected patterns based on the way those newspapers frame migration and the tone they employ when reporting or commenting on immigration. Readers of all papers express favourable attitudes about the economic impact of migrants on average, and the differences between the readers are smaller. The opinions of the readers of the Scottish newspapers are less pro-immigrant than expected, based on the way *The Guardian* and the

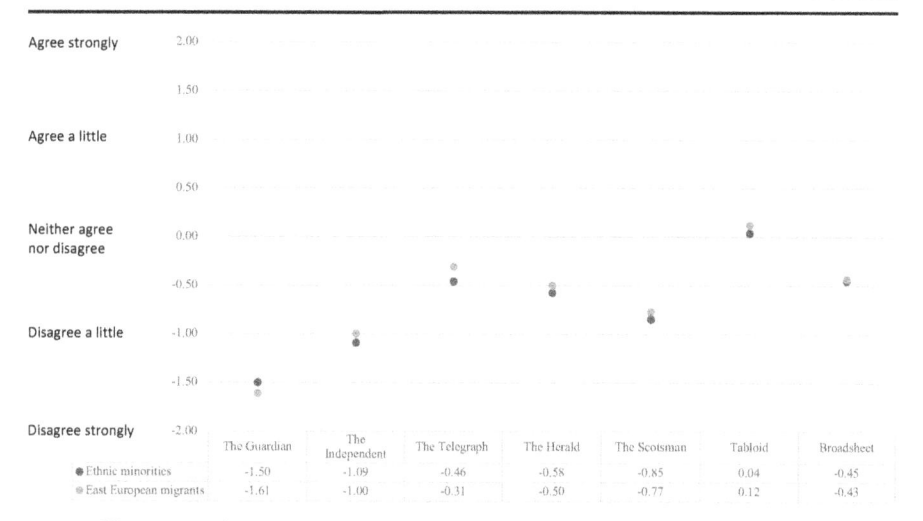

	The Guardian	The Independent	The Telegraph	The Herald	The Scotsman	Tabloid	Broadsheet
Ethnic minorities	-1.50	-1.09	-0.46	-0.58	-0.85	0.04	-0.45
East European migrants	-1.61	-1.00	-0.31	-0.50	-0.77	0.12	-0.43

Figure 7.12 'Ethnic minority/East European migrants take jobs from Scottish people'.
Source: 2015 Scottish Social Attitudes Survey (ScotCen Social Research 2017)

Scottish papers frequently resemble each other in framing. Perhaps the ideological bias of the regional papers does not mirror the ideological profile of their readers, and since there is not great diversity in the ideological bias of Scottish papers, readers who would prefer a more conservative news source must settle for what is available for Scottish-specific news. Though we cannot generalise from these findings due to the small sample size, these averages suggest that media framing and reader opinions about immigration correspond with one another in Scotland.

Conclusion

This chapter explores whether Scottish newspapers differ in meaningful ways from UK-wide papers in the way they cover immigration in order to discover whether Scottish newspaper readers have access to a regional source of information that could impact their views on immigration in a meaningful way. Looking at the aggregate breakdown of frames employed (Figure 7.2), tone (Figure 7.3), and tone by article type (Figure 7.4), the Scottish papers resemble *The Guardian* or *The Independent*, meaning there is little evidence of Scottish distinctiveness in reporting on immigration. Ideology drives framing and tone more than geographic audience. Since Scottish social democracy is a key feature of Scottish nationalism and national identity, the importance of the ideological press is still critical. The press constructs the discursive space in Scotland, and the Scottish newspapers reify social democratic norms. Their coverage resembles that of *The Guardian*, but they face no national-level competitors offering other interpretations, which amplifies the national left-leaning arguments about immigration. Aside from the ideological homogeneity in Scotland, more nuanced analysis of the coverage reveals other areas of Scottish distinctiveness.

The most obvious difference between the UK-wide and the Scottish newspapers is that the Scottish newspapers approach the news from a Scottish perspective. This national focus is reflected in articles with 'immigration' in the title or keyword: 34.6% of the articles in *The Herald* and 53.9% in *The Scotsman* discussed Scotland, versus 3.8% in *The Guardian*, 3.1% in *The Independent*, and 4.7% in *The Telegraph*. This difference should change the way frames are employed if Scottish interests are understood to be distinct from UK interests. A distinct national approach is reflected most markedly in the articles using utilitarian frames, where the Scottish papers are more likely than the UK papers to use pragmatic arguments that make claims about how immigration advances the national interest. The Scottish papers speak to Scottish national interest, while the others focus on the UK. The Scottish papers did not present Scottish nationalistic arguments with an identity frame. Instead, their articles with an identify frame and a nationalistic argument focused more on UK politics. This distinction reinforces the message of the Scottish political elites about Scottish civic nationalism, which they disassociate from ideas of identity, ethnicity, or culture.

The strongest differences in frame and tone are explained by the ideological perspective of the newspaper. For example, moral frames and multicultural arguments of identity frames are used more frequently and associated with positive tone in papers that lean left ideologically. Though *The Guardian* and the Scottish papers are similar ideologically, there are important qualitative differences in how frame and tone are employed in the Scottish newspapers. For example, in the stories employing a political frame, the Scottish papers with a pro-immigrant tone almost exclusively focus on the ideological conflict between Holyrood and Westminster over immigration. The UK-wide papers focus more on partisan conflict. The Scottish papers are also overwhelmingly pro-immigrant in articles employing multicultural arguments within an identity frame, while the UK-wide papers include more neutral multicultural pieces. This reflects the desire of the Scottish elite to link multiculturalism with Scotland's identity and interests.

Comparative research demonstrates the various ways that the media can influence public opinion and political outcomes. Among those Scots who read newspapers regularly, their opinions about immigration correspond with the general tone of their newspaper. However, given how closely the Scottish papers corresponded with the left-leaning UK papers in their use of frames and tone, the opinions of the readers of the Scottish papers should have been closer to the readers of *The Guardian*. Instead, the readers of the Scottish papers are only slightly positive about immigration on average. The disconnect between messaging and opinions resembles the disconnect between the SNP party leadership and the party supporters (see Chapter 8). Those who are interested in Scottish news may not be universally interested in the left-leaning ideology of the paper, just as those who are interested in Scottish independence may not share the SNP's vision of civic nationalism. Still, the newspapers can make a difference in moving opinion, and in order to achieve their objectives for the diversification of Scotland, the Scottish political elites should be unified and loud in their messaging to the media. The Scottish newspapers reflect messaging from the political elites, but the elites should target news providers based in London with pro-immigration material, even if the articles do not explicitly address Scotland's distinct national interest. Journalists should employ frames strategically, and frames that activate negative opinions about immigrants, like welfare, negative economic performance, and security, should be used judiciously, and with a full understanding of their social impacts.

Notes

1. There is a debate in the literature over whether the relationship between political and mass media agendas is top down, with politicians influencing the mass media agenda (Cook 1998), or mediacratic, where political agendas respond to media coverage (Walgrave et al. 2008). The two perspectives are not mutually exclusive. Much of the work on the impact of the media on politics examines the reciprocal relationship between political and media agendas, and investigates the conditions under which the media impacts politics.
2. Tabloid newspapers are smaller than broadsheets, and publish shorter, crisper stories. While some tabloids engage in serious journalism, in the UK, the 'red tops', named for their front-page banners, are sensationalistic.
3. The multiple forms of media impact the way people read the news. For example, online consumption of news is a much faster experience. Thurman (2017) found that a UK national brand gets 40 minutes of reading time with its weekday print edition, but only 30 seconds with its website and apps.
4. A 2010 Ipsos MORI poll estimated that 44% of *The Independent*'s readers voted Liberal Democrat, 32% voted Labour, and 14% voted Conservative, compared with 23%, 29%, and 36% of the electorate. Seventy per cent of *The Telegraph*'s readers voted Conservative, 18% Liberal Democrat, and 7% Labour. Forty-six per cent of *The Guardian*'s readers voted Labour, 37% Liberal Democrat, and 9% Conservative.
5. The International Newsstand database provided the text of all articles from five quality newspapers mentioning the word 'immigration' in the title or keyword from May 2013 to July 2016. Those stories deemed irrelevant (e.g. discussing a movie or celebrity) were removed before the remainder were entered into the database. The search term 'immigration' will not capture all stories about immigration (such as those exclusively discussing refugees, asylum seekers, or international students), but it provides a sample that allows for comparison across newspapers. The independence referendum was on 18 September 2014 and the Brexit referendum was held on 20 June 2016.
6. This approach differs from that of researchers who use newspaper articles to report the positions of political actors by using 'core sentences' to identify the varied

positions of politicians or policy stakeholders presented within the article (Dolezal et al. 2010; Helbling 2012). Labelling the articles as a whole acknowledges that journalists are not merely conveying the positions of policy elites, but that they have control over what kinds of information to report and how to report it.
7. This framing approach has been used to study European integration (Sjursen 2002; Helbling et al. 2010), EU human rights policy (Lerch and Schewllnus 2006), and immigration (Helbling 2014).
8. *The Herald* and *The Scotsman* are combined to ease comparability. The number of stories in *The Scotsman* is much smaller than any of the UK papers, and together *The Scotsman* and *The Herald* report about as many stories on immigration as *The Independent*.
9. There may be a bias towards more negative coverage and frames, because negative coverage has more agenda-setting effects than positive coverage (Baumgartner et al. 1997).
10. Journalists at *The Telegraph* note their minority position in reporting more negative coverage of immigration compared with other mainstream media outlets, and suggest that the positive skew in stories about immigration from other sources represents a political bias in the media. Both *The Telegraph* and *The Guardian* published stories about a pro-immigration bias in the BBC. *The Guardian* cites a review by the BBC Trust which finds an 'overreliance on Westminster voices' on immigration, which tends to be more positive and less concerned about immigration than the wider public (Halliday 2013). This perspective suggests that reporting involves responding to public sentiment, regardless of whether or not that sentiment reflects an empirical reality. *The Telegraph*'s story focuses on a report by Migration Watch, an anti-immigration lobbying organisation, where journalist David Barrett (2015) explicitly outlines the argument that 'The BBC's bias in favour of immigration has been a key block on the Government's ability to tighten control on Britain's borders . . . the BBC was guilty of a "strong bias" and even a reluctance to address issues raised by immigration. The report also warned there was pro-immigration bias in parts of the Civil Service including the Treasury, "irrespective of the impact of immigration on population growth and on the lower paid".'
11. Across all of the newspapers, there were 326 stories employing a political frame, of which 105 convey a negative tone about immigration, 142 a neutral tone, and 79 a positive tone about immigration.
12. The two exceptions include one article discussing the far right in Sweden and one warning that a more open Scottish approach to immigration after independence could face a public backlash.
13. The Smith Commission was charged with making recommendations about what further powers should be devolved to Scotland in the wake of the independence referendum in 2014.
14. The selection mechanism with the keyword 'immigration' may have limited the number with identity frames. 'Immigration' generally refers to the phenomenon of people entering a country, and not the situation of those who are already living in the country, who are usually called 'migrants' or 'immigrants'. Articles with identity frames may be more oriented towards existing minoritised communities and public reactions to them, and would not have necessarily been captured with the keyword 'immigration'.
15. Evidence from Germany indicates that the more the news media reports on immigration, the more people will vote for parties with an anti-immigrant stance (Boomgaarden and Vliegenthart 2007). Vliegenthart et al. (2012) found that the visibility of an anti-immigrant party and especially the party leader in the news

in Belgium, the Netherlands, and Germany correlates with anti-immigrant party success. Using time lags, they confirm that the direction of the relationship proceeds from coverage to success, rather than the other way around. Similarly, Koopmans and Muis (2009) attributed the dramatic rise in support for Pim Fortuyn in the Netherlands to the visibility of the party leader in the media. Walgrave and de Swert (2010) made a similar connection between growing media attention to the issues owned by the Vlaams Blok and support for the party in Belgium.

16. Some of this difference is attributable to the way tabloids regularly use sensationalistic language when reporting on immigration in the UK. Other European states have more homogenous coverage (Eberl et al. 2018).

17. Comparative research reinforces the finding that threat-related media coverage is associated with more negative attitudes towards immigrants (Costello and Hodson 2011; Florack et al. 2003; Schemer 2012). Boomgaarden and Vliegenthart (2009) examine the public impact of the frequency and tone of newspaper coverage of immigrants in Germany and find mixed results, but conclude that positive tone and increased immigrant visibility is associated with a reduction in the perception of problems associated with immigration. They find that the impact of these effects is higher in times when immigration and asylum levels are high. Similarly, van Klingeren et al. (2015) find news coverage with a positive tone about immigration reduces negativity towards immigration in the Netherlands, while a negative tone is not significantly associated with negative perceptions.

18. Eighteen respondents report regularly reading *The Guardian*, 11 read *The Independent*, 13 read *The Telegraph*, 13 read *The Scotsman*, and 24 read *The Herald*.

8

THE PUBLIC: ATTITUDES TOWARDS IMMIGRATION IN SCOTLAND

Between 2001 and 2016, the British public identified immigration as one of the most important issues facing the UK, and in the run-up to the EU referendum in 2015 and 2016, immigration became *the most* important issue for a majority of poll respondents (Blinder and Richards 2020).[1] The salience of immigration reflected its placement at the centre of the Brexit debate, when EU membership was equated with open borders and uncontrolled migration. Attitudes changed after the Brexit referendum, when people reported being more concerned about the EU and the NHS than immigration. Furthermore, while over 70% of respondents in surveys in 2012 and 2013 suggested that immigration should either be reduced a little or reduced a lot, in 2019 that number dropped to 44% (Blinder and Richards 2020).[2] Those who oppose immigration are generally equally concerned about EU and non-EU migration, and often do not distinguish between the two, or between immigration and refugee flows.[3] Anti-immigrant sentiment tends to be directed towards immigrants as a group without differentiating between types of immigrants, purpose of immigration, or the legal regime allowing the migration.

Public sentiment determines which immigration policies are politically viable. The Conservative government in the UK has been sensitive to anti-immigrant public sentiment and has aligned its public policy with public tone. The Conservative Party agenda under David Cameron and Theresa May to reduce net migration to 100,000 without regard for condition of entry mimics the public's insensitivity to differences between groups of immigrants and their reason for entry. Meanwhile, elite rhetoric in Scotland reflects the political consensus that Scotland 'needs' immigration and 'welcomes' immigrants. The implicit assumption of Scottish elites is that the Scottish public is more tolerant of immigration than elsewhere in the UK. One Conservative MSP called this assumption into question:

> I don't buy it. It's one of the things [the SNP] says. I don't actually think public attitudes towards immigration are all that different in Scotland than how they are in England ... But, the political debate about immigration in Scotland has not been anything like as toxic or unpleasant as aspects of the political debate have been in England. I think that's interesting. (Personal interview 26 March 2019)

So, do the views of Scottish elites reflect those of the Scottish public in demonstrating more openness to immigration? How are Scottish public attitudes different from English attitudes? This chapter addresses these questions using survey data to explore Scottish attitudes towards immigrants in order to test elite claims of Scottish exceptionalism in openness to migration.

Scottish Attitudes Towards Migrants

In 2015, the Scottish Social Attitudes Survey (SSAS) included a module focusing on feelings towards migrants and openness to diversity.[4] The first question asks whether the survey respondent believes people coming to Scotland from outside Great Britain make Scotland a better place. Figure 8.1 illustrates the responses to this question. The mode response suggests that Scots are neutral about the positive impact of immigrants, and there is a positive skew (the average response is 0.2 on a scale from -2 to 2 with zero representing neutrality). Forty-one per cent of those surveyed neither agree nor disagree with the statement that migrants make Scotland a better place, though nearly twice as many people agree (39%) compared with those who disagree (20%).

The 2015 SSAS also includes dichotomous questions measuring general appreciation of diversity and tolerance. The first question asks 'would you rather live in an area with different kinds of people or where most people are similar to you?' Forty-three per cent of respondents prefer diverse neighbours, 36% prefer to live with others like themselves, and 21% couldn't decide between the two options. The second question asks whether people agree more with the notion that Scotland should do everything it can to get rid of all kinds of prejudice, or with the idea that sometimes there is a good reason for people to be prejudiced against other people. The strong consensus is that Scotland should make a concerted effort to combat prejudice, with 76% of respondents replying in the affirmative. While it may seem hypocritical for someone who believes Scotland should 'do everything it can to reduce prejudice' to also report a prejudicial preference for a homogenous neighbourhood,

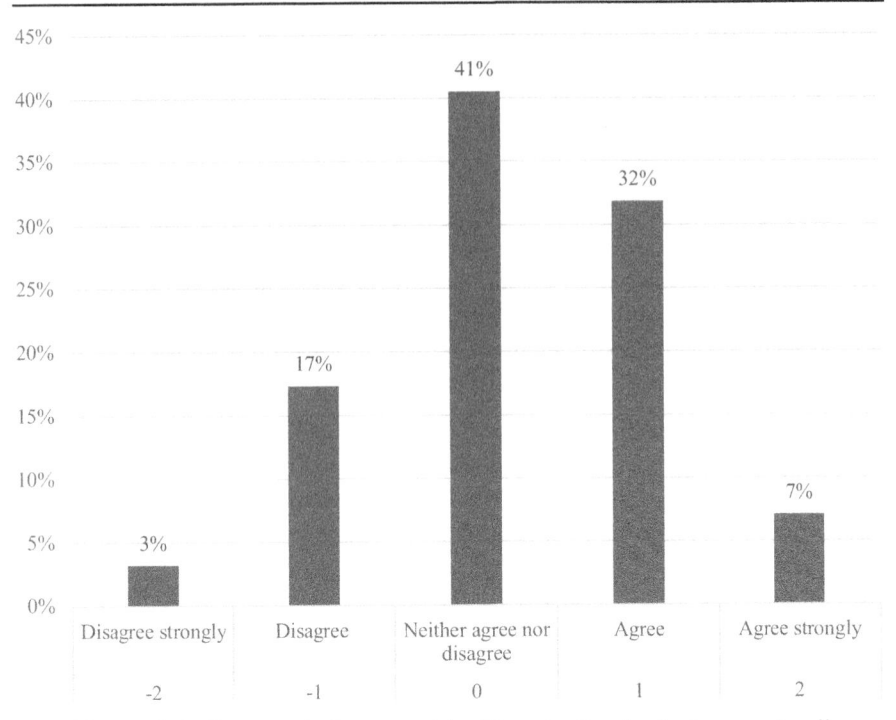

[Bar chart showing responses with values: Disagree strongly (-2) 3%, Disagree (-1) 17%, Neither agree nor disagree (0) 41%, Agree (1) 32%, Agree strongly (2) 7%]

Figure 8.1 'Do people from outside GB make Scotland a better place?'
Source: 2015 Scottish Social Attitudes Survey (ScotCen Social Research 2017)

22% of the total sample holds both opinions.[5] Perhaps people are willing to commit 'Scotland' to something they aren't prepared to do individually. This possibility is reminiscent of Kiely et al.'s (2005) interview with a man who 'deep down' does not believe people from other countries will ever become Scottish, even though he acknowledges that he would never admit to this sentiment to those people. Public versus private commitments to diversity can be disassociated from one another. Further complicating the issue, the 2015 SSAS questions about migrant impact and diversity refer to migrants and minorities very broadly and leave it up to the respondent to determine what a 'better place' might mean. Are Scots thinking about a 'better place' with reference to the economy, or do they understand the question culturally?

Cultural Threat from Migrants

The perception of cultural threat from migrants comes out of a fear of the immigrant 'other', or worries that their presence will dilute the national culture (Fetzer 2000). Threat is most pronounced where the migrant group is noticeably different, such as when they speak another language (Liu et al. 2014), or are racially or culturally distinct (Ford 2011). In their review of the literature on public attitudes towards immigration in North America and Western Europe, Hainmueller and Hopkins (2014) found concerns about group culture were the main drivers of anti-immigrant sentiment. In the UK, perceived threat to British values strongly determined anti-immigration attitudes, and especially attitudes about Muslim immigrants (McLaren and Johnson 2007). Do cultural concerns predict attitudes towards immigration in Scotland?

The 2015 SSAS measures the cultural perception of threat with three questions asking whether the respondent believes increased migration from various immigrant groups (Muslims, East Europeans, Black and Asian people) would pose a threat to Scottish identity. As discussed in Chapter 3, Scottish identity means different things to different people. It can signify membership through ethnic ties, it can be defined by attachment to the nation through residency and civic participation, or it can mean some combination of ethnic and civic ideas. Muslims, East Europeans, and Black and Asian people represent different types of potential cultural threat to these different visions of identity. Muslims may represent a threat to Scottish Presbyterian identity, and potentially to civic values, if people confuse Islamic religiosity with fundamentalism. East Europeans, as the largest group of migrants, could present a threat based on sheer numbers. Black and Asian people represent the possibility of racial threat for those who might adhere to ethnic ideas of Scottishness. These groups should provoke varied perceptions of cultural threat, and based on previous research about Islamophobia in Scotland, Scots might perceive Muslims to be more worrisome than other groups defined by skin colour or nationality (Virdee et al. 2006). As illustrated in Figure 8.2, these expectations are partially confirmed. Forty-three per cent of respondents agree or agree strongly that Muslims pose a threat to Scottish identity. However, an almost equal number are concerned about an identity threat from East Europeans (39%) and Black and Asian people (37%). On a scale from -2 to 2, where zero represents neutrality and the positive numbers represent agreement that there is a threat, the average score of the Muslim variable is 0.12, for the East European variable it is 0.02, and for the Black and Asian racial variable it is -0.03.[6]

The most notable feature of Figure 8.2 is how similar the distribution of responses is: the vast majority of respondents (around 80%) identify threat at the same level across all three groups, meaning that they selected the same answer for all three responses.[7] There are stronger bi-modal tendencies (people are more likely to indicate that they agree or disagree with the statement than to select the neutral response) when compared with the more generic question about migrants making Scotland a 'better place', which suggests that Scottish people, like others in the UK, hold more intense opinions about specific racial or cultural groups (McLaren and Johnson 2007).

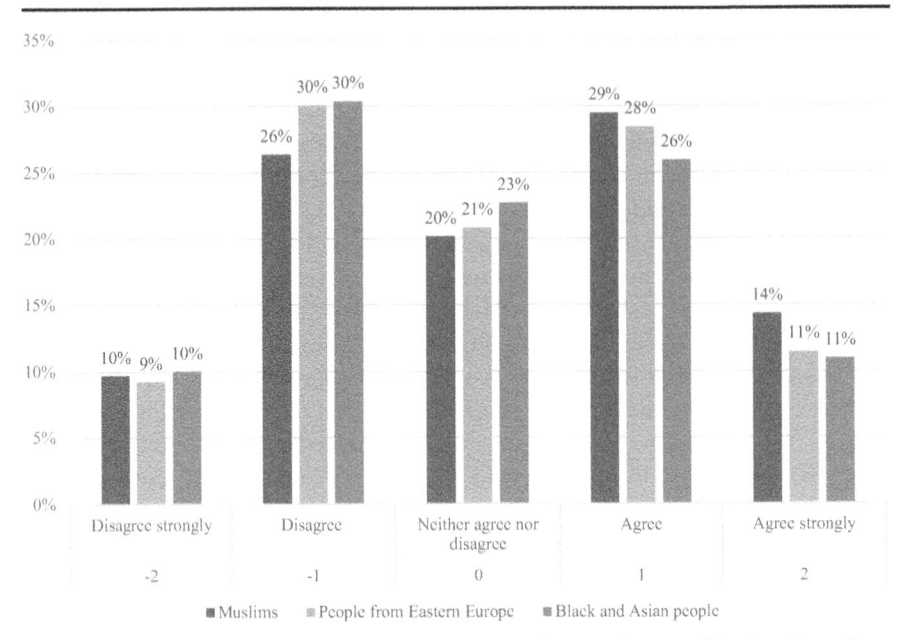

Figure 8.2 'Scotland would begin to lose its identity if more [Muslims/people from East Europe/Black and Asian people] came to live in Scotland'.
Source: 2015 Scottish Social Attitudes Survey (ScotCen Social Research 2017)

Economic Threat from Migrants

Perceptions of economic threat centre on two concerns: whether immigration will alter one's personal financial well-being, and whether immigration impacts the national economy as a whole (Citrin et al. 1997; Mayda 2006). Personal economic concerns involve fears that migrants will create competition for jobs, lower wages, or raise taxes due to increased demand for social services. National economic concerns relate to fears that migrants will create a fiscal burden on public services or otherwise harm the economy. Ample research in the US and Europe reveals that concerns about the national economy are more relevant than individual self-interest in determining attitudes about immigration (Citrin et al. 1997; Dancygier and Donnelly 2013; O'Rourke and Sinnott 2006; McLaren and Johnson 2007). Data from the UK confirm these findings (McLaren and Johnson 2007).

The 2015 SSAS measures the perception of group economic threat with two questions asking whether ethnic minorities or East European migrants take jobs from Scottish people. As with the questions on threats to Scottish identity, these questions should theoretically differentiate between economic threats from different groups, but as illustrated in Figure 8.3, Scots do not distinguish

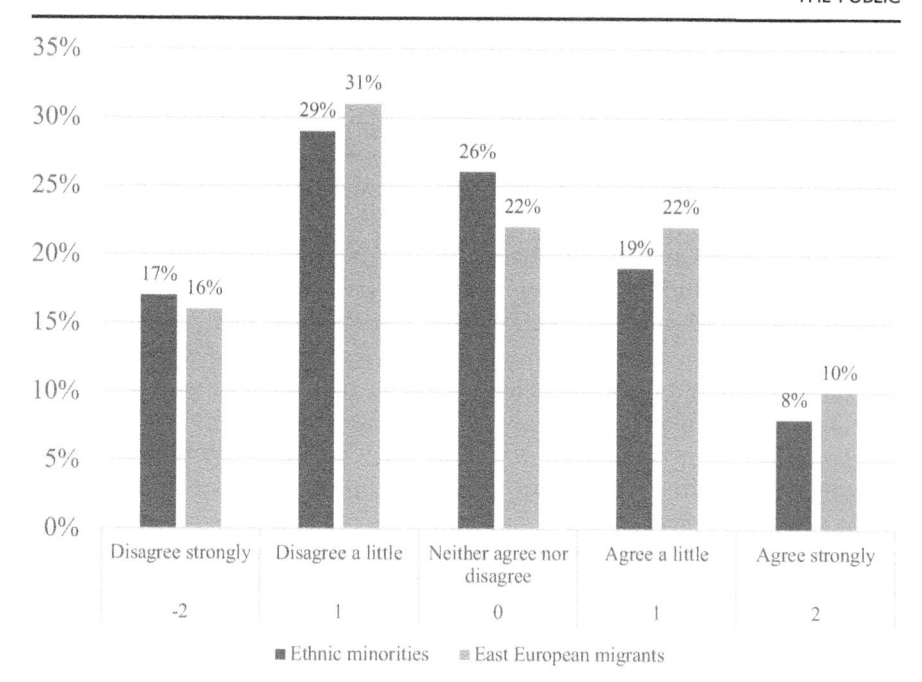

Figure 8.3 'Ethnic minority/East European migrants take jobs from Scottish people.'
Source: 2015 Scottish Social Attitudes Survey (ScotCen Social Research 2017)

much between the subgroups of immigrants with respect to their potential economic threat. Opinions about migrant impact on jobs are less negative than the opinions about cultural impact depicted in Figure 8.2.

The mean score for the question as to whether ethnic minorities take jobs from Scottish people is -0.28 on a scale from -2 to 2, with 2 representing strong agreement. Twenty-seven per cent of respondents agree or strongly agree that minorities take jobs. The mean for whether East European migrants take jobs is -0.21 on a scale from -2 to 2, with 32% of respondents agreeing or strongly agreeing that migrants take jobs.[8] Scots are more likely to perceive an economic threat from East European immigrants, likely because EU free movement permits the unregulated migration of Europeans, leading their migration to be framed as a form of unregulated economic migration. But, as with perceived threat to identity, the most noticeable aspect of Figure 8.3 is the similar distribution in responses, and approximately 80% identified threat at equal levels across both 'non-Scottish' groups.[9]

Scots evaluate migrants more negatively with reference to cultural threat. The stronger reaction could be a product of the groups mentioned in the cultural question (Muslims, East Europeans, Black and Asian people), compared with the more generic reference to ethnic minorities and East European migrants in the economic questions. These differences aside, the identity and economic threat indicators are highly correlated with each other (see Appendix E). These correlations hint at an underlying commonality of responses which suggest that Scots think about hypothetical groups of immigrants in a similar way.

Factor analysis can help researchers understand how similar assessments of economic and cultural threats are. Factor analysis reveals the extent to which groups of variables cling together, based on how similar they are across units of analysis.[10] If the values of a group of variables correspond with one other, the variables should load on a single factor; if the values of variables create two clusters of similarity, there will be two factors, and so on. The researcher can then deduce the underlying commonality between the variables that are clinging together. If people assess immigrant threat to culture and economy in the same way, there would be only one factor. If they differentiate between cultural and economic threat, there would be two factors. If they respond differently based on whether the question refers to immigrants generally, specific groups of immigrants, or racial minorities, there could be three factors.

The factor analysis generated two distinct factors (see Appendix F). The variables loading on the two factors reflect underlying identity and economic dimensions, with some overlap between the two. The indicator of identity threat from East Europe loads on the identity factor and the economic factor, which may reflect the perception that East Europeans are the group representing the greatest number of migrants, thereby posing the largest identity threat, and are also the group with the greatest range of entitlements, rights, and access to many segments of the labour market due to their unregulated ability to migrate. More generic indicators of believing immigrants make Scotland a better place, that Scotland should work to eliminate prejudice, and that it is preferable to live in diverse areas do not strongly load on either of the factors associated with economic or identity threat. These results affirm the correlations shown in Appendix E, which demonstrate that the indicators of economic and cultural threat correlate more highly with each other than they do with the more general indicator capturing the sentiment that immigrants make Scotland a better place. While the factor analysis presents two types of attitudes relating to identity and the economy, the analysis and correlations suggest a slight disassociation of the theoretical consideration of immigration with reference to a generic unlabelled immigrant population from attitudes towards specific groups of people (i.e. Muslims, East Europeans). They could also reflect a desire on the part of survey respondents to respond to general/ generic questions in a socially desirable way, while the questions targeting specific issues associated with identity and the economy evoke greater candour.

Modelling Opinions about Immigrants

Aggregate patterns in Scottish public opinion paint a picture of attitudes towards immigrants with broad strokes, but they cannot reveal what would make an individual Scot feel more or less positive about immigrants. International research suggests that attitudes will depend both on a person's position in the economy and on the economic profile of the prospective immigrant. One cross-national study demonstrated that higher-skilled citizens are less opposed to immigration than their lower-skilled and more economically vulnerable counterparts (Mayda 2006). However, there is ample evidence suggesting that cultural attitudes drive anti-immigrant opinion more than economic threat. Using data from across Europe, Hainmueller and Hiscox (2007) found those with higher levels of education and more advanced civic skills are more likely to favour immigration regardless of immigrant skill level. They attribute the relationship to differences in cultural values and beliefs across education levels, where more educated individuals are more likely to value diversity and less likely to hold discriminatory views. Other European research found that symbolic economic and cultural threat (symbolic threats are anxieties about something that is unlikely to negatively affect a person directly or fear of the unknown) drives attitudes about immigration more than individual self-interest (Card et al. 2012; Hooghe and Marks 2005). Research in the United States and Europe suggests that communities have a general unspoken consensus about who should be admitted into the country, and the consensus is rooted in community-level, norms-based considerations, rather than individual economic status (Bansak et al. 2016; Hainmueller and Hopkins 2015). Comparative research demonstrates the primacy of perceived cultural threat in determining attitudes about immigration, but economic vulnerability and the skills of the prospective immigrant also matter. Do Scots conform with these trends?

Multivariate models test the relative strength of individual attributes on three attitudes about migration: the belief that migrants make Scotland a better place, the perception of a threat to Scottish identity from immigrants, and the perception of a threat to Scottish jobs from immigrants.[11] The results are presented in Appendix G. Based on prior research, the model tests the relative strength of national identities (Hussain and Miller 2006; McCollum et al. 2014), cosmopolitan values (Kentmen-Cin and Erisen 2017; McLaren 2002), political interests and identities (Hepburn 2009), and group and individual economic conditions (Hainmueller and Hopkins 2014; McLaren and Johnson 2007) for predicting attitudes towards immigrants. Summary statistics of all variables included in the models are available in Appendix H.

The results of the models reveal that attitudes towards migrants in Scotland are predicted by a Scot's socio-political values, levels of political information, and economic status: those who endorse progressive values, are highly educated, are knowledgeable about politics, and feel economically secure are most likely to see benefits and reduced threats from immigrants. The results are unpacked in the following sections, which review the ideological and political, the economic, and the sociological determinants of attitudes towards migrants in Scotland.

Ideological and political determinants of attitudes towards migrants

The most consistently significant group of variables in the model predicting attitudes towards migrants are those that capture personal cosmopolitanism, a concept derived from the Greek word *kosmopolitês* (citizen of the world), referring to the idea that all human beings are equal citizens in a global community rather than deriving limited rights from a single state or polity. These ideals transcend parochial attachments to a nation and advocate more for a rights-based, or civic, system of governance.[12] In the Scottish models (see Appendix G), these values are captured with the preferences that Scotland should remain in the EU, that Scotland should fully commit itself to getting rid of prejudice, that institutions should not insist on the removal of religious or cultural articles of clothing, and for living in an area with diverse kinds of people.[13] Most of these variables relate to acceptance of diversity, which is necessary for a fully cosmopolitan perspective. Cosmopolitanism is associated with the EU because it prioritises open borders, multicultural vales, diversity, and an outward-looking inclusive society, all values institutionalised within the mission and treaties of the EU.[14]

Figure 8.4 illustrates the percentage of respondents that perceive immigrants and members of minoritised groups more negatively but who also hold cosmopolitan values, and across the board, they demonstrate lower than average levels of negativity. Those with a preference for living in a diverse neighbourhood are the least negative about the impact of migrant and minoritised populations in Scotland. In the multivariate models, all of these indicators predict a lower likelihood that a Scottish person will perceive either a cultural or economic threat from migrants, and most of them increase the probability that a Scot believes migrants make Scotland a better place (the one exception is the preference for remaining in the EU, which loses statistical significance in the model predicting the belief that migrants make Scotland a better place).

General political dispositions also predict perceptions of migrants. Scots who are interested in politics are less likely to perceive a cultural threat from migrants and are more likely to believe migrants make Scotland a better place. Perhaps those who are interested in politics are more receptive to the messages sent by the political elite. However, following news media does not register as significant in any of the models, despite expectations that exposure to the

THE PUBLIC

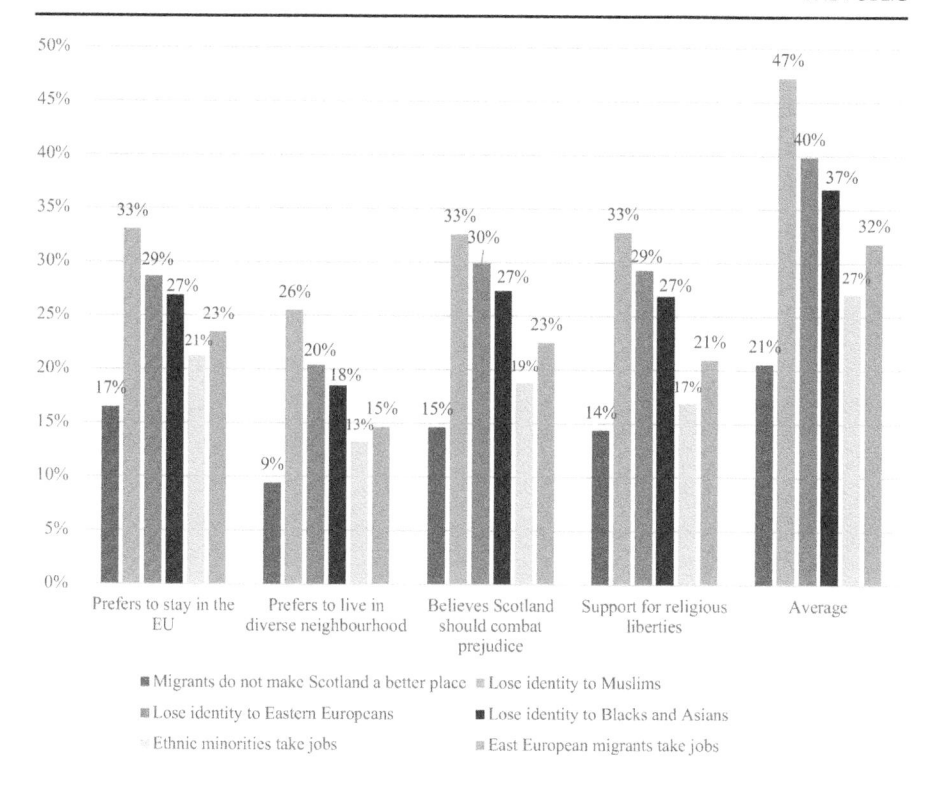

Figure 8.4 Percentage of SSAS respondents agreeing or strongly agreeing with negative attitudes about immigrants by cosmopolitan indicators. *Source*: 2015 Scottish Social Attitudes Survey (ScotCen Social Research 2017)

inclusive elite messaging covered in the media might make Scots more open to immigration (Pillai et al. 2007).[15]

Political party identification is regularly used as a proxy for political ideology, political interest, and exposure to political information. Given the politicisation of immigration in UK elections, Scottish attitudes might correspond with party preferences. However, party rhetoric around immigration is less divisive and less politicised in Scotland – the main political parties share the message that increased immigration to Scotland would be beneficial – so party identity may not be one of the most relevant determinants of attitudes towards migration.[16] Figure 8.5 illustrates the percentage of 2015 SSAS respondents agreeing or strongly agreeing with more negative assessments of migrants, broken down by Scottish political party identification and placed on an ideological spectrum from left to right.

215

THE POLITICS OF IMMIGRATION IN SCOTLAND

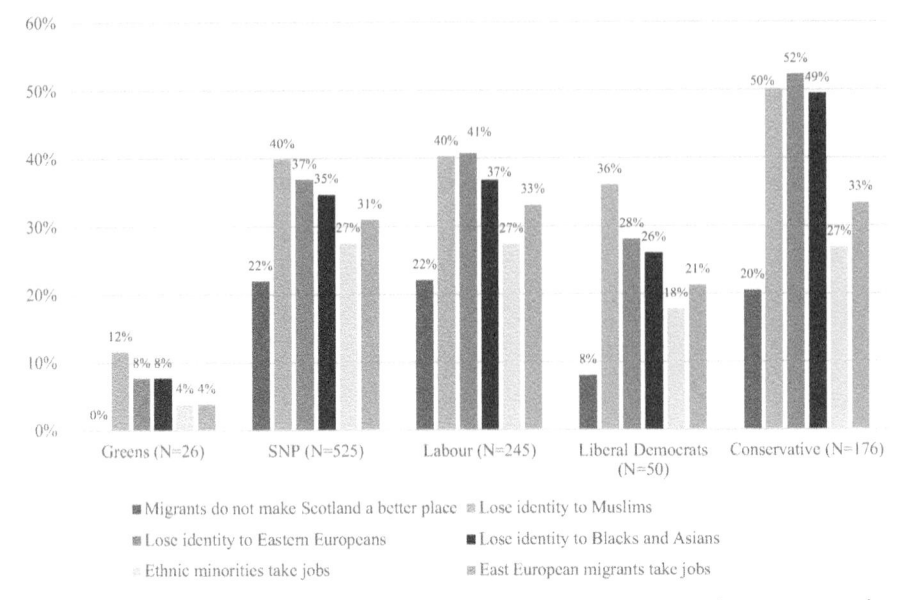

Figure 8.5 Percentage of SSAS respondents agreeing or strongly agreeing with negative attitudes about immigrants by political party.
Source: 2015 Scottish Social Attitudes Survey (ScotCen Social Research 2017)

Conservative Party members are the most likely to express more negative attitudes, but the only substantial differences are in the responses to the questions about identity. This pattern could indicate the resonance of ethno-nationalist messages among Scottish Conservatives. The responses of Conservative Party members do not deviate from the responses of SNP or Labour Party members in the questions about migrant/minority impact on jobs, or in the general assessment of whether migrants make Scotland a better place.[17] Liberal Democrat and especially Green Party members demonstrate significantly less negative attitudes, though the sample of party members is small. These patterns suggest that political party identification could be a salient predictor of attitudes towards immigration, but these differences are not borne out by the results of the statistical models that control for other individual characteristics.[18] The only statistically significant party variable is Green Party support, which is associated with more positive attitudes.[19] This finding echoes the work of Hussain and Miller (2006), who find SNP voting and Scottish identity do not predict any phobias other than Anglophobia. However, when cosmopolitan variables are removed from the model (see Appendix I), identifying with the Labour Party reduces the probability that a Scot will perceive an identity or economic threat from immigrants, and identifying with the SNP reduces the likelihood of believing that immigrants present a threat to Scottish workers.

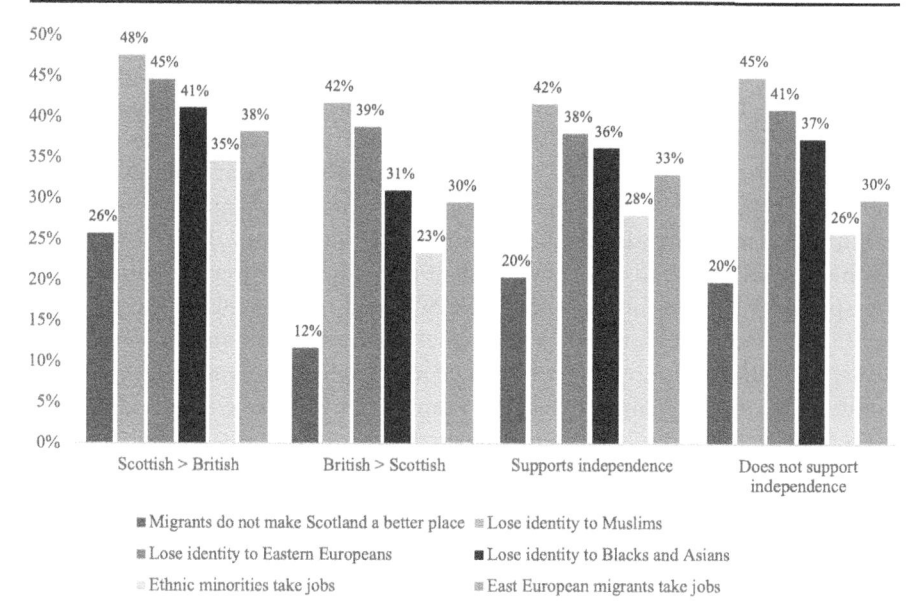

Figure 8.6 Percentage of SSAS respondents agreeing or strongly agreeing with negative attitudes about immigrants by national identity and nationalism.
Source: 2015 Scottish Social Attitudes Survey (ScotCen Social Research 2017)

Figure 8.6 illustrates the frequency of negative perceptions of immigrants broken down by whether a respondent identifies as more Scottish or British. Scottish residents who identify as British generally hold less negative opinions of migrants. Difference of means tests reveal statistically significant differences in disbelieving immigrants make Scotland a better place, and in perceptions that increased migration of Black and Asian people will constitute a threat to Scottish identity. There are also significant differences in the belief that migrants and minorities take jobs from Scottish people. However, in the multivariate models none of these variables retain significance until cosmopolitan variables are removed from the model (see Appendix I). Figure 8.6 also reveals that those who prefer Scottish constitutional independence do not appear to have much less negative attitudes than those who do not want independence, though difference in means tests reveal statistically significant differences across the two groups for perceiving a threat to Scottish identity from Muslims, where those who do not support independence perceive threat more frequently. However, once other variables are controlled for in the multivariate models, a preference for constitutional independence is not a significant predictor of attitudes about immigration until indicators of cosmopolitan values are removed from the model.

The findings from the multivariate models contradict those of McCollum et al. (2014), who found that those who identify as Scottish rather than British are more likely to agree that ethnic minorities threaten Scottish identity and take jobs away from Scottish people. This difference between the previous findings and the results of the models in Appendix G is attributable to the different specification of the models which contain a number of indicators capturing cosmopolitanism. When cosmopolitan indicators are removed from the model (see Appendix I), Scottish identity predicts a lower probability that a respondent believes immigrants make Scotland a better place and a higher probability that a respondent believes that migrants and minorities present a threat to Scotland's identity. A preference for independence increases the probability that a respondent believes that immigrants will make Scotland a better place and reduces the likelihood of perceiving a threat to Scottish identity from migrants and minorities. After controlling for all of the other variables in a model, the effect of cosmopolitanism overwhelms the effect of national identity and political nationalism in driving attitudes towards migrants and minorities.[20]

Economic determinants of attitudes towards migrants

The only other group of indicators registering consistently significant relationships in the multivariate models predicting attitudes towards migrants relate to individual economic status (see Appendix G). A higher income is associated with the perception that migrants make Scotland a better place, but not with either of the threat indices, potentially reflecting the protected status of those with higher incomes from economic competition with migrants. Figure 8.7 demonstrates that those in routine employment are far more likely to perceive a threat from immigrants than those in any other employment classification. The comparison between high- and low-skilled employment (the two largest groups of workers in Scotland) reveal strong differences in opinions, suggesting that there is an association between economic vulnerability and attitudes towards migration.[21] East European migrants are perceived to present a greater threat than ethnic minorities across all of the employment classifications, likely because of different regimes governing EU and non-EU migration and political arguments about free movement. While the points-based immigration system for non-EU migration is designed to tailor migration flows to the economic needs of the UK, EU migration is not subject to any similar considerations. Theoretically, East Europeans could compete with native workers in sectors with no skills shortages, though this does not typically happen (Manacorda et al. 2012).

When occupational status is included in the multivariate model, those in lower supervisory or technical occupations (involving lower-level service positions, or contract workers like tool makers or mechanics) are less likely to see

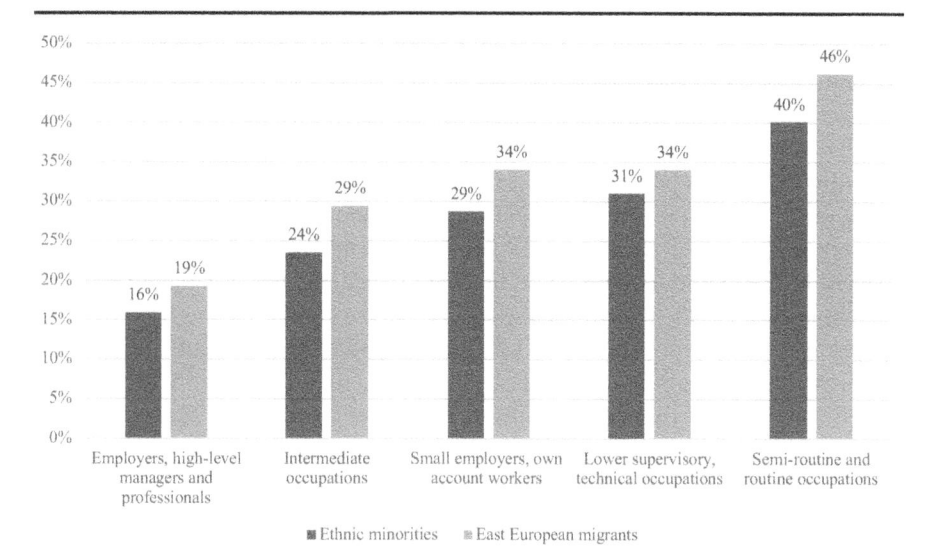

Figure 8.7 Percentage of SSAS respondents agreeing with the notion that migrants/minorities take jobs from Scottish people by socio-economic classification.
Source: 2015 Scottish Social Attitudes Survey (ScotCen Social Research 2017)

a general benefit to Scotland from migration when compared with those in high-level managerial or professional jobs (the excluded category). If income is removed from the model, members of all three of the lower occupational classes are less likely to believe migrants make Scotland a better place, and those in routine occupations are more likely to believe that migrants and minorities take jobs from Scottish workers.[22] When cosmopolitan values are removed from the model, small owners and those in lower supervisory and routine occupations are more likely to hold negative perceptions of immigrants (see Appendix I). These findings suggest that economic status influences general perceptions about the positive impact of migrants. Relationships between the lower occupational statuses and less positive assessments of immigrants indicate that economic vulnerability plays into a perception of threat, affirming previous research findings that high-skilled citizens are less opposed to immigration than their more economically threatened lower-skilled counterparts (Mayda 2006; O'Rourke and Sinnott 2006). Meanwhile, no measures of larger group economic threat, such as perceived status of the economy or the standard of living in Scotland, register as significant in any of the models until the cosmopolitan indicators are removed from the model, at which point positive perceptions of the economy are negatively associated with the perception of economic and cultural threat. These findings contradict literature suggesting that national economic assessments are stronger predictors of attitudes towards immigrants than individual threat (Citrin et al. 1997; Dancygier and Donnelly 2013; O'Rourke and Sinnott 2006).

Sociological determinants of attitudes towards migrants

A number of social conditions provide key explanations for attitudes towards immigration. Education, and especially higher education, reduces parochialism and is associated with cosmopolitan values. In their multiple regression analysis, Hussain and Miller (2006) find that education has the biggest impact on Islamophobic and Anglophobic prejudice in Scotland, and higher levels of education correspond with lower levels of prejudice. Lewis (2006) similarly found that people in Glasgow, Edinburgh, and Dundee with lower levels of education expressed the most hostile attitudes towards asylum seekers. These findings are replicated in the models in Appendix G, which demonstrate a positive association between education and believing immigrants make Scotland a better place, and a lower probability that those with higher levels of education believe immigrants threaten Scottish identity or jobs.

Age is negatively associated with positive perceptions about immigration. Age gaps are generally attributed to generational differences, where younger people tend to be more accepting. Ford (2012) finds that the age divide on attitudes about immigration is much stronger in Britain than in other European and North American countries. The multivariate models in Appendix G reveal inconsistent relationships between age and perceptions of migration, where older people in Scotland have a greater probability of believing that immigrants make Scotland a better place, but also a higher probability of believing that immigrants and members of a minoritised group threaten Scotland's identity and take jobs away from Scottish workers. This inconsistency could be attributable to older people's anxieties about future trends, even as they acknowledge past and current contributions of migrants. Alternatively, while older people may be prepared to acknowledge immigration's positive effects on Scotland as a generic phenomenon, they may have more anxieties associated with particular groups of migrants.

Diverse social networks are critical for developing community cohesion in contexts of racial and ethnic diversity. Hussain and Miller (2006) find that having a Muslim friend reduces Islamophobia, having an English friend reduces Anglophobia, and having a friend of either minoritised group reduces phobias towards both groups. In the 2015 SSAS data, 56% of those who have a close Muslim friend say that immigration makes Scotland a better place, compared with 36% of those who do not have a Muslim friend, and 27% of those with a Muslim friend believe that an influx of more Muslims would threaten Scotland's identity, compared with 46% of those without a Muslim friend, amounting to a 20% difference between the groups. The difference between those who have a close friend of a different ethnic background is around 13%. However, in full the multivariate models, the indicator of diverse friend networks is not a statistically significant predictor of attitudes towards migrants. When the indicators of cosmopolitanism are removed from the model (see Appendix I), having diverse friend networks increases the probability that a respondent believes immigrants make Scotland a better place and reduces the probability that they believe immigrants and ethnic minorities take jobs from Scottish people.

Urban areas are the most ethnically diverse areas of the UK, and in Scotland, the vast majority of immigrants live in the cities of Glasgow and Edinburgh. Urban dwellers may be more likely to interact with and form friendships with diverse people and have a greater opportunity to recognise the benefits that come from migration. Urban dwellers also tend to be younger, more educated, and employed in jobs with higher occupational status, all characteristics associated with greater acceptance of diversity. Appendix J breaks down attitudes by urban/rural classification and suggests that within Scotland, the rural population may be the most acceptant, followed by the urban population. Appendix K lists the Scottish administrative areas, the population density of each area, and the percentage of 2015 SSAS respondents expressing pro-immigrant opinions. There is no discernible pattern. In the multivariate models, living in a small town or rural area does not significantly predict attitudes towards migrants.

The three models in Appendix G suggest individual attitudes towards immigration in Scotland are political but not politicised, in that values and ideology seem to matter but partisan identities do not. Individual economic precarity matters for generic and economic assessments of migrants, but for not the perception of cultural threat. These results confirm the Europe-wide research finding that cultural values and beliefs are the primary drivers of attitudes towards all forms of immigration (Hainmueller and Hiscox 2007). However, comparative work evaluates the relative strength of different economic or identity attributes on a single metric of attitudes about immigration. The models with the 2015 SSAS data are more informative because the different questions about economic and identity threat allow for the assessment of whether there are distinct determinants for different types of feelings about migrants. The results demonstrate that in the Scottish case, the impact of economic vulnerability is limited to assessments of the general and economic impact of immigrants, and does not necessarily extend to a perception of cultural threat. Cosmopolitan values determine attitudes towards immigration more broadly.

Given what is already known about attitudes towards immigrants in the UK and Europe, none of these results are unexpected, though they do offer some interesting and unique insights about how Scottish people differentiate between the types of threats presented by immigrants. This is good news for Scottish political elites, because messaging and policy can be targeted to mitigate anxieties. It is hard to assess the potential uniqueness of the Scottish public without direct comparison with other contexts. Given the political dynamics of Scottish nationalism and the regular comparisons made between Scotland and England in the media, a comparison of public attitudes in Scottish and English populations will be most instructive for determining whether the Scottish public presents a special political opportunity for the development of pro-immigrant policy preferences.

Scottish and English Opinions Compared

A small but important body of research examines Scottish immigration preferences in comparison with other nations within the UK, and the general consensus is that Scottish respondents are more open to and accepting of immigrants than their English counterparts. McCollum et al. (2014) found that with the exception of residents in London, Scots expressed less hostile attitudes towards migration than people in any other UK region.[23] Hussain and Miller (2006) found lower levels of hostility towards Muslims in Scotland relative to England. In logistic regression analysis of the likelihood that someone would regard immigration as one of the two most important problems facing the UK, Ford (2012) found that residency in Scotland was negatively associated with concerns over immigration, compared with the other nations. Qualitative research affirms the prevalence of positive attitudes towards immigrants among Scots. In focus group interviews, Lewis (2006) found relatively high levels of public tolerance for asylum seekers in Scotland. Pillai et al.'s study of migrant reception across ten locations in the UK (two of them in Scotland) leads them to conclude that Scotland 'seems to possess several characteristics that facilitate the reception and integration of new migrants that differ to those observed in England', including elite-level messaging, less sensationalistic newspaper coverage, and socio-demographic features that correlate with openness to migration (2007: 7).[24]

The extant literature suggests that Scots are less pessimistic about immigration and immigrants compared with other national groups in the UK. Data from the British Social Attitudes Survey (BSAS), an annual national survey of about 3,000 participants across England, Wales, and Scotland, provides an opportunity to test the continuity of this trend. The 2015 BSAS contains two general questions about migrants to Britain. The first asks, 'would you say it is generally bad or good for Britain's economy that migrants come to Britain from other countries?' The second asks, 'would you say that Britain's cultural life is generally undermined or enriched by migrants coming to live here from other countries?' Both questions require respondents to rank their response on a ten-point scale, where -5 represents the most negative and 5 the most positive opinion. Frequencies of the responses are illustrated in Figure 8.8.[25]

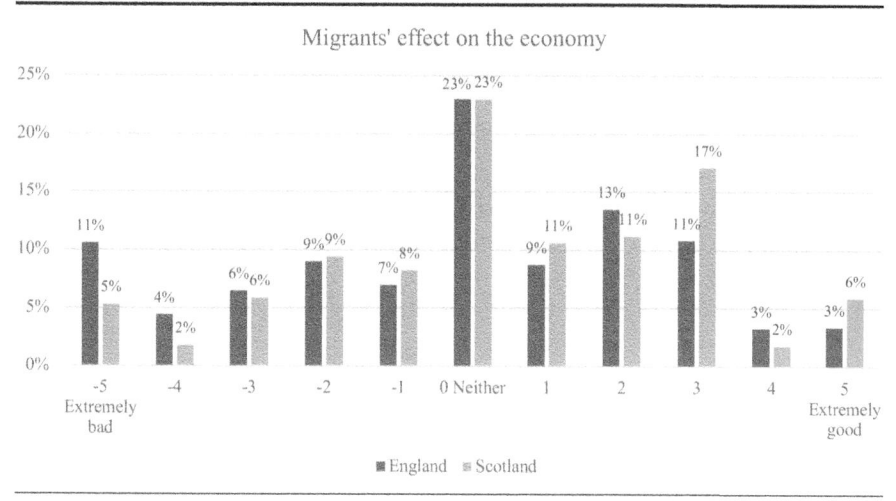

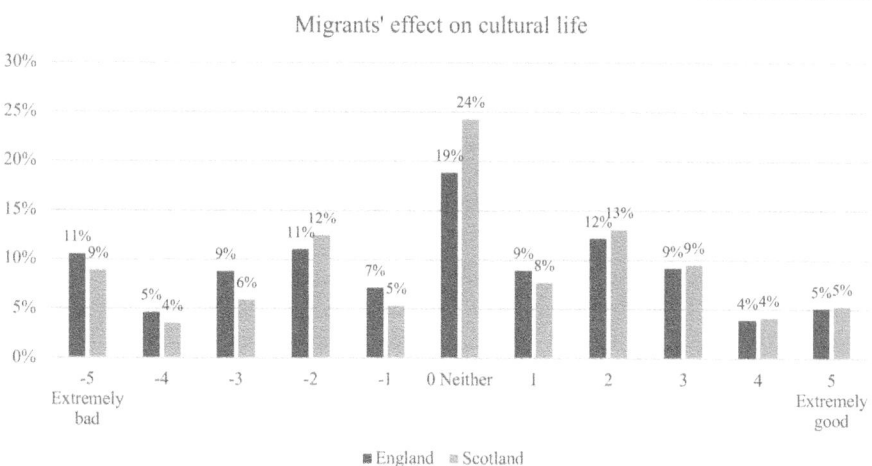

Figure 8.8 Frequency of responses about migrant impact.
Source: 2015 British Social Attitudes Survey (NatCen Social Research 2017)

Scottish respondents are slightly more optimistic (mean score of 0.42 for the economic question and -0.01 for the cultural question) than English respondents (mean score of -0.17 for the economic question and -0.25 for the cultural question) on average, though the mode response for both English and Scottish respondents is zero. Difference of means tests reveal that there is *not* a statistically significant difference between the English and Scottish populations when it comes to their assessment about how migrants influence the cultural life of Britain. Both English and Scottish respondents are more likely to express slightly more optimistic opinions about immigrant impact on the economy than on culture, and there is a statistically significant difference in the Scottish versus English perceptions of the economic contributions of migrants, with Scots having more favourable impressions about migrant contributions to the economy.

The BSAS indicators can each be broken down into two variables ranking from zero to 5, with one variable measuring the strength of positive opinions and the other measuring the strength of negative opinions, and the neutral position coded as zero. Difference of means tests between the Scottish and English samples reveal that within the economy metrics, Scottish respondents are not more likely than the English respondents to say that the migrants are good for the economy, but they are significantly less likely to say they are bad for the economy ($p<0.05$). They are not more likely than the English respondents to say that migrants undermine or enrich the culture. Most of the difference between the UK and Scotland is occurring in the neutral and negative sides of the spectrum. These findings suggest that in the aggregate, Scots are inclined to feel less negatively, though not necessarily more positively, about economic immigration compared with those living in England. It may be more correct to say that in the aggregate, the Scottish population is more ambivalent about economic immigration than the English.

Why is there a difference (no matter how slight) in English and Scottish attitudes towards migration? A multivariate model using the BSAS data tests whether the difference is attributable to a national group effect (see Appendix L). The BSAS model includes Scottish, English, and Welsh respondents, and contains a variable controlling for whether a survey participant lives in Scotland or Wales, with English residency as the category of reference. If the English–Scottish difference in attitudes towards immigration were a national characteristic, the variable for Scotland should be a significant predictor of attitudes after controlling for national identity, and political, economic, and sociological factors. However, it is not a significant predictor of impressions about migrant impact on the national culture or on the economy, suggesting that after controlling for the other individual indicators, there is no significant difference in the opinions of individuals in Scotland versus those in other parts of Britain. In other words, the empirical difference observed between Scotland and England in the comparison of means tests is not a group effect. Rather, the difference must be attributable to the construction of attitudes at the individual level.

Multivariate models of English and Scottish attitudes towards immigrants are presented in Appendix M. The near-identical measurement of variables and the ability to nearly match model specification allows for some comparison of English and Scottish attitudes of migration with the 2015 BSAS and SSAS survey responses.[26] The most important difference between the BSAS and SSAS models is in the measurement of attitudes towards immigrants or minoritised groups. The BSAS asks about the positive impact of immigrants on the culture and the economy, while the SSAS asks about the perception of threat from different migrant groups to Scottish identity and jobs. The BSAS data also unfortunately do not include many measures of cosmopolitan values, which are some of the most important determinants of attitudes towards immigration in the SSAS model. Most other indicators in the models are identical. [27]

Comparing the attitudes represented in the English and Scottish samples reveals more similarities than differences. Across both BSAS and SSAS samples, approval of the UK's place in the EU, level of education, and political interest share significant positive relationships with positive perceptions of immigrants, affirming the link described previously between indicators of cosmopolitan values and openness to immigration. There are a few noticeable differences, however. Prioritising one's national identity (English or Scottish) is associated with a more negative assessment of the cultural impact of immigrants in England but in Scotland there is no impact of national identity on a perceived threat to Scotland's identity. Prioritising Scottish national identity is associated with the likelihood of perceiving an economic threat from immigrants, but there is not a significant relationship between strong English identity and a perceived economic impact of migration. The relationship between Englishness and cultural threat confirms the conceptualisation of Englishness as a more ethnically derived identity that aligns with perceptions that immigration is a threat to a racially defined English culture. Scottishness is defined civically rather than ethnically, which could explain the non-relationship between Scottishness and identity threat. Those who emphasise an exclusively Scottish national identity may be more likely to be concerned with Scotland's relative economic status and the feasibility of a self-sufficient nation, or to feel loyalty to other Scots over migrants.

Political party identification is predictive of attitudes about immigration in England, where support for the Labour Party, Liberal Democrats, or Green Party is associated with more positive perceptions of immigrants. By contrast, in the Scottish sample, only the Green Party is associated with the reduced probability of seeing immigrants as an economic threat. Immigration is more highly politicised in England, and it plays a central role in distinguishing between the parties on the left and right sides of the ideological spectrum, while there is political consensus in Scotland about the general desirability of migration. These elite-level discourses are reflected in the models. Among the sociological determinants, education is associated with more positive perceptions of immigrants across all the models in Scotland and the UK. Older people perceive higher degrees of cultural and economic threat coming from immigration in Scotland, while age is insignificant in the English models.[28]

Scots are quite similar to the English in the way their attitudes towards immigrants work. The opinions of both Scottish and English people average out to be quite neutral, though Scots are slightly less negative about the effect of immigration on the economy. They are not distinctive as a group when controlling for relevant individual-level factors, and many individual ideological characteristics work the same way in both England and Scotland: cosmopolitanism (measured with attitudes about the EU and level of education) and political interest are significant determinants of more favourable attitudes about immigrants in both England and Scotland. However, differences between the two states in the politicisation of the immigrant issue are reflected in individual-level data in the different associations between nationalism and party identification and attitudes towards migrants. This suggests that perhaps the Scottish elites have been successful in their efforts to depoliticise the issue.

CONCLUSION

In the aggregate, Scots are ambivalent about migrants, but the multivariate models in Scotland reveal some unique results that could present a political opportunity to the Scottish elites. Unlike in other contexts, where people conflate different types of migrants and associate threat with any and all migrants, Scots appear to distinguish between the economic and cultural impact of migrants. Conditions of economic vulnerability link only to a perception of economic threat coming from migrants, and do not extend to a perception of cultural threat. Cosmopolitan values determine attitudes towards immigration more broadly. This should allow elites to target policy and rhetoric to alleviate the perception of threat and advance their pro-immigration agenda more easily than elsewhere.

The comparison of Scottish and English attitudes dampens some of this optimism. Compared with the English, Scots hold slightly less negative impressions about migrant impact on the economy, but analysing the determinants of attitudes towards migration reveals there is no statistically significant group-level difference between Scottish and English opinions after controlling for individual-level drivers of immigration opinions. Education, an interest in politics, and pro-EU attitudes drive more positive attitudes in both Scotland and England. The main difference between the two populations is in the nature and degree of politicisation of immigration in England, signalled by how party identification relates to attitudes. There is no such relationship between party identification and attitudes towards immigration in Scotland.

The largely ambivalent public opinion about immigration in Scotland suggests that public attitudes in Scotland are not yet aligned with the pro-immigrant elite discourse. However, immigration has not been politicised in Scotland, which suggests that elites have been successful at demonstrating partisan consensus on the issue. Continued refusal to politicise immigration is critical for those Scottish elites who are promoting an inclusive vision for Scotland. Public ambivalence provides a narrow window of opportunity for advancing a more inclusive agenda, but the tepid feelings Scots have towards migrants should be treated with caution. Recent history in countries like Sweden and Poland demonstrates how a single crisis can quickly turn public opinion against migrants and minorities if multicultural values are not entrenched in the public consciousness. A similar crisis or controversy in Scotland could eliminate Scottish distinctiveness in attitudes towards migrants. For visions of a diverse Scotland to be realised, Scottish elites cannot take public support for granted. They must focus their attention on strengthening the public celebration of (rather than mere acceptance of) diversity within the political culture.

Notes

1. In the 2015 and 2016 Ipsos MORI data, immigration was ranked as more important than the NHS, the EU, the economy, housing, and defence/terrorism.
2. Opposition to immigration has been a consistent feature of British public opinion. Surveys dating back to 1964 also indicate a strong belief that there were too many immigrants in the UK (Blinder and Allen 2016).
3. McLaren and Johnson (2007) highlighted evidence from a Eurobarometer poll in 2000 that suggested Europeans favour identical treatment for labour migrants and asylum seekers. Blinder (2013) found that public perceptions of immigration focus on asylum seekers and permanent arrivals, and that imagining 'immigrants' as asylum seekers or permanent arrivals is associated with a preference for reduced migration.
4. The 2015 survey measured attitudes towards immigration with general questions and cannot address specific issues like preferences for an autonomous immigration policy or attitudes towards particular types of immigrants like foreign students or refugees. The 2015 survey provides the most recent survey data available that includes several questions on migrants.
5. The prejudice question is a forced choice between two options, one of which is a more socially desirable response (that Scotland should get rid of prejudice), leading to social desirability bias. One way to mitigate this bias is through more indirect self-reporting measures, where participants can express prejudicial attitudes, but can justify them with reference to other factors that do not necessarily link to prejudice. The question about living in a diverse area is one such measure, because respondents could justify their answer with reference to social institutions or the economy. However, Axt (2017) finds that direct measures are better predictors of implicit racial attitudes and yield greater differences between racially different populations, which suggests that the best way to know about individual prejudice is to ask about it directly.
6. The differences in means are statistically significant at $p<0.01$.
7. Sequential questions of a similar nature with identical Likert scale responses are vulnerable to response bias in which the respondent defaults to the same response to all of the questions due to expediency or indecision. This is most common with online surveys or scantron surveys where the respondent fills in a circle corresponding with their answer. The SSAS is a face-to-face oral survey, which should reduce this form of bias, but could increase social desirability bias.
8. The difference in means is statistically significant at $p<0.01$.
9. The individual responses of each survey respondent are not perfectly consistent across the dimensions of identity threat and economic threat. Only about 40% of respondents select identical levels of threat across assessments of identity and economic threat.

10. In this instance, our unit of analysis is individuals, and variables are the numeric representations of individual answers to survey questions.
11. Ordered profit models offer the best fit for dependent variables with a natural ordering but where the metric has no linear numeric meaning, such as with variables measuring responses from strongly disagree to strongly agree. The measures of threat perceptions are indices. An index is a compound measure that aggregates multiple indicators into a single variable. Three indicators measuring whether a respondent believes the presence of Muslims, East Europeans, or Black and Asian people presents a threat to Scottish identity are combined into an identity threat index. The index score ranges from 0 to 12. The economic threat index combines the two variables measuring whether a survey respondent believes ethnic minorities or East European migrants take jobs from Scottish people. The resulting index ranges from 0 to 8. Higher scores on the index indicate higher perception of threat.
12. Education levels often correlate with cosmopolitan values, though formal education should not be automatically equated with cosmopolitanism because some types of formal education are disciplinarily narrow and technical.
13. The inclusion of an indicator of respecting religious expression would be considered controversial by cosmopolitan theorists. Some would advocate for an understanding of cosmopolitanism that celebrates diversity, while others would push for a vision of a cosmopolitan ideal that transcends diversity. Both visions of cosmopolitanism push against exclusive individual attachments to a particular culture, and religious garments are often understood to represent cultural, as well as religious, prioritisation and attachment.
14. Support for the EU could also indicate support for free trade, which may or may not link into cosmopolitan values. The variable indicating support for the EU is less correlated with the other indicators of cosmopolitanism.
15. Pillai et al. (2007) note the role of positive media messaging in Scotland in creating an environment more conducive to the development of more inclusive communities. In England, they identify the media as a source of misinformation and fearmongering.
16. See Chapter 7 for a discussion of the party platforms.
17. Difference of means tests confirm there are no statistically significant differences between Conservative Party members and non-Conservative Party members on the indicator of whether a respondent believes immigrants make Scotland a better place, nor on the index measuring economic threat. There is, however, a significant difference between Conservatives and non-Conservatives on the index measuring a threat to Scottish identity.
18. Hussain and Miller (2006) found that if the degree of Scottish identity is removed from their multiple regression models, SNP voting became a significant predictor of Anglophobia, but not Islamophobia. Removing the national identity variables from the models in Appendix G did not change the significance of any of the indicators of political party identification.
19. This significant relationship between Green Party support and positive perceptions of immigration is unsurprising considering the positioning of the Green Party as the most leftist party in Scotland, and the strong and explicit Green Party endorsement of non-discrimination, free movement, and migrant rights (Logan 2017). It would be a mistake to attribute too much to this finding due to the small number of Green Party members in the sample (26).
20. Scottish identity is very weakly correlated with all of the indicators of cosmopolitanism. The correlation coefficients between prioritising Scottish identity over British and indicators of cosmopolitanism is -0.06 with the preference for staying within the EU, 0.08 with the preference for living in diverse communities, 0.08

with believing Scotland should combat prejudice, and 0.05 with the religious tolerance index. Multicollinearity is not driving the result.
21. Thirty-six per cent of Scots in the survey sample are employers, high-level managers, and professionals, and 25% work in semi-routine or routine occupations. Routine or low-skilled occupations include waiters and waitresses, machinists, sorters, packers, railway station staff, road construction workers, building labourers, dockers, couriers, refuse collectors, car park attendants, and cleaners. Twelve per cent of Scots are in lower supervisory technical occupations, 10% are in intermediate occupations, and 8% are small employers or own account workers.
22. Removing income from the models predicting perceptions of identity and economic threat does not change the significance of the occupational status variables.
23. McCollum et al. (2014) also found that those who identify as Scottish rather than British are more likely to agree that ethnic minorities threaten Scottish identity and take jobs away from Scottish people, and that a preference for independence rather than further devolution is associated with the perception that ethnic minorities present threats to Scottish workers.
24. Pillai et al. (2007) note that positivity towards immigrants is not uniform across Scotland, and that hostility towards immigrants in Scotland varies with the immigrant's race.
25. The 2015 BSAS includes 1,868 English respondents and 170 Scottish respondents.
26. Previous work demonstrating that Scots are comparatively open to immigration generally derived their findings from comparisons of aggregate data and simple descriptive statistics (e.g. McCollum et al. 2014). Where statistical models are used to describe attitudes towards immigration in the existing research, the analysis is often built around an exploration about how individual-level demographic characteristics determine immigration attitudes in either the UK or Scotland, without considering comparative data.
27. The differences between the BSAS and SSAS models in Appendix M and the SSAS models in Appendix G are the measurement of the dependent variables, the exclusion of many of the cosmopolitan variables in the BSAS (especially questions about whether the government should work to eliminate prejudice, the question about whether it is preferable to live in diverse areas, and questions about religious tolerance), the exclusion of questions about constitutional preference, the exclusion of large group economic assessments about relative economic threat and quality of life, the exclusion of an indicator of whether the respondent is friends with Muslims or people with a different ethnicity, and the inclusion of an additional question about TV news consumption. The two surveys yield roughly comparable numbers in the models, with 615 English respondents and 660 Scottish respondents. There is also a Scottish sample in the BSAS, which would allow for more direct comparisons with identical specifications. Once all the variables are included in the model, the Scottish sample in the BSAS drops to only 57 from a total sample of 335. As Scotland has only 8% of the UK's population, the proportion of Scots to English in the BSAS is representatively appropriate. However, for comparing the power of individual determinants, it is much more useful to compare the roughly equal samples of the BSAS and the SSAS.
28. The age effect disappears in the extended Scottish models in Appendix G when more expansive indicators of cosmopolitan values and constitutional preference are included in the models.

9

THE PROJECTIONS: ALTERNATIVE FUTURES FOR THE POLITICS OF IMMIGRATION IN SCOTLAND

Political philosopher Hannah Arendt wrote 'sovereignty is nowhere more absolute than in matters of emigration, naturalization, nationality, and expulsion' (1973: 278). Much of this book is dedicated to describing the way Scottish political elites attempt to alter and reverse this relationship, and use the politics of migration, membership, and inclusion to assert their sovereignty. Since Scotland is part of the UK and the assertion of Scotland's sovereignty requires the UK to relinquish it, much of the nationalist discourse is dedicated to establishing enough differences between Scotland and England to justify secession, or at least further devolution as a compromise solution. Any plan for political autonomy must be accompanied by a vision of what will happen after autonomy is achieved. What will the relationship between Scotland and their previous supreme government look like? How many institutions will be maintained and shared between Scotland and the UK and how many will be changed? How has Scotland's relationship with the EU as a region of the UK primed it for EU membership? What are the prospects for the new state in the international arena? Who would be Scotland's allies? The answers to these questions are inherently unknowable, but that has not stopped speculation. The political elite in Scotland must balance potentially competing visions of a future Scotland: as a minority claimant within a larger state, as a state-like actor in Europe, and as a member of the international community. Though state, European, and international policy audiences call for contradictory things, they mutually reinforce the nation-building process by forcing Scotland to define its identity and activity in each political sphere.

Immigration has become a symbol of Scotland's ambitions. Previous chapters document the way the Scottish political elites use the politics of immigration to demonstrate their multicultural interests and ideologies. Openness to immigrants signals their acceptance of the idea that people from international communities can become part of Scotland. For example, while questioning the economic impact of the post-study work visa, a Liberal Democrat MSP admitted its power as an international symbol:

> It's kind of totemic in that sense rather than being a fundamental pillar of a more productive economy, but on the other hand, it sends out a big international signal that Scotland's open for business, that we like and want people from different walks of life, from different industries, from different countries, to be part of Scotland. I think that's quite important as well. (Personal interview 22 June 2016)

Scots are also proud of the impact their emigrants have had all over the world, which makes them a part of foreign systems and societies.[1]

This chapter begins with a discussion of how the Scottish elite has used immigration to frame the nation's possible future with England. The England-facing politics of immigration centre on contrasting national approaches to immigration and multiculturalism and how the contrast is used to advocate for independence. Independence and its implications for immigration would profoundly impact English–Scottish relations, due to the potential construction of a border and the creation of Scottish citizenship law. The discussion of English–Scottish relations then reviews the implications of the oppositional national stance towards England for English people living in Scotland, and considers what it means for Scotland's ambition to be an inclusive, multicultural state. The next section of the chapter explores the way the Scottish leadership uses migration to position itself within the institutions and ideology of the EU. It explores how the EU has legitimised Scotland's political personality and how Scotland has used the organisation to advance its interests. It also discusses the way the EU incentivises free movement and pro-immigration policies among its regions and prospective states. The final section of the chapter looks at the role immigration and emigration plays in developing Scotland's international reputation and examines the way Scotland's public diplomacy promotes positive contributions of immigrants and internationalism. The chapter concludes by considering how a sustained focus on immigration functions as a mechanism for defining Scotland's future, regardless of whether Scotland achieves independence.

ENGLAND-FACING POLITICS OF IMMIGRATION

The England-facing politics of immigration in Scotland involve a direct national comparison of migrant and minority-related policies and opinions. Scottish nationalism makes the comparison oppositional, charging Westminster with failing to protect Scottish national interests, valorising Scotland relative to England, and justifying Scottish independence (Hepburn 2009). The resurgence of the far right in England facilitates accusations of English ethnic nationalism and racism. Scottish ministers and pro-independence groups use growing support of right-wing populism as proof of a general rightward drift in English politics while Scotland remains on the left (Carrell 2014a). The Scottish leadership describes Scotland as being more democratic (in listening to their electorate and advocating for their interests) and more progressive (in pushing for a cosmopolitan vision of their nation) than the UK government and the English nation. The claims of ideological difference and unmet national interest, coupled with arguments that Scotland is underrepresented while England is overrepresented in Westminster, feed calls for devolution and independence.

Researchers have tested claims of difference between England and Scotland that would warrant a region-focused immigration system. One body of work empirically assesses whether Scotland has a special need for immigration because of Scotland's demographic and economic challenges. These researchers conclude that in the aggregate, Scotland and England look quite different, but that Scotland does not face unique challenges compared with regions in England and in Wales (Migration Advisory Committee 2018b). Rather, Scotland's social and economic structures have become *more* like those in the rest of the UK over the twentieth century (Paterson et al. 2004).[2]

A second body of work examines ideological claims that there is a different socio-political culture and therefore different political constituencies in Scotland, where xenophobia supposedly has no purchase:

> This narrative of absent racism in Scottish history has become even more entrenched in the course of recent developments . . . because it is able to nest so comfortably within the new common sense of Scottish politics, the dominant story that has been forged, by the SNP and others – that the Scots are in some sense different from the English – more egalitarian, more likely to place an emphasis on collectivism over individualism and on government intervention over self-reliance. (Davidson and Virdee 2018: 9)

The supposed differences are layered on top of mistaken understandings that while 'race relations' are an obvious and ongoing problem in England, racism has no relevance in Scotland.[3] These differences support the government's description of immigrants and ethnic minorities as 'new Scots', a position that provokes further contrast with the UK's Conservative government's 'hostile environment' for immigrants.

Davidson and Virdee (2018) argue that these contrasts oversimplify the issue and provide incentives for people to take Scotland's diversity-acceptant rhetoric at face value, without properly interrogating whether the myths are grounded in truth. The historical role Scotland played in the British Empire and colonial conquest and the Scottish participation in the Atlantic slave trade provide a strong foundation for the development of racial hierarchies in Scotland, and as Hopkins (2008) notes, there are continuities in England and Scotland in the racial constructs and the processes that racialise people. Hopkins demonstrates that the minoritised groups that experience racism in England also experience similar forms of racism in Scotland. He further argues that the same impulses to marginalise those who are perceived to be different because of their skin colour, body markings, adornment, and behaviour are at work in both countries. While he acknowledges the continuities, Hopkins maintains that there are discontinuities between Scotland and England. He suggests that while most analysis on race and racism takes a British perspective, and assumes the whole of the UK experienced identical forces, the particularities of the Scottish context have yielded unique outcomes. In particular, he highlights how the ethnic composition, geographical distribution, and socio-economic class of migrant communities in Scotland have structured race relations differently.

Both Hopkins (2008) and Penrose and Howard (2008) attribute Scottish–English differences to politics and the politicisation of race, rather than to a fundamental difference in the underlying social issues: 'political processes were radicalized in England in a way that they were not in Scotland' (Hopkins 2008: 138). Hopkins highlights several political features of Scotland that create a contrast with England: the near absence of explicitly racist or fascist political organisations in Scotland, the promotion of civic nationalism in Scotland, and the different legislative environment with the devolution of powers. These things create a different climate for racially minoritised groups in Scotland. Furthermore, members of minoritised groups recognise and replicate the idea that the experience for members of the minoritised groups is different, and superior, in Scotland. This final point manifests in the ways minoritised groups relate to the construction and contestation of Scottish national identity and how that identity operates as an alternative to British identity (Chapter 3).

Scots frame their tolerance towards minoritised groups as a response to their own oppression at the hands of the English (again, conveniently overlooking Scottish participation in the expansion and maintenance of the British Empire). This perspective allows Scots to see themselves as members of an oppressed community alongside minoritised groups, with a common English oppressor

(Penrose and Howard 2008). Hopkins (2008) notes acceptance of this idea among young Scottish Muslim men who support the SNP, who discuss their support with reference to the North–South/Scottish–English contrast. They describe Scotland as marginalised within the UK and worthy of empathy from other similarly oppressed peoples.

When it comes to justifying more liberal immigration policies, ideology and perception are perhaps more important than empirical claims of difference. Northern England and Scotland face similar challenges, but the prevailing ideology in Scotland provides Scottish decision makers with the political opportunity to do something about them, if they had the power. However, Hepburn argues:

> the most important reason why Scotland has escaped the anti-immigration hysteria that peppers political debates in England/UK is due to its lack of power on the issue. Scotland's lack of competence over immigration policy allows it to subdue political mobilisation, to avert responsibility – and culpability – to the UK Government on unpopular aspects of immigration, and to avoid the glare of media attention on rising numbers. (Hepburn 2014: 11)

Hepburn's comments highlight how independence will change the dynamics of the politics of immigration, and will transition it from a tool of political differentiation to a policy area over which Scotland must claim full responsibility. What Scotland would do with its new competencies over immigration will greatly impact the relationship between an independent Scotland and the rest of the UK.

The UK and an Independent Scotland

There are a number of thorny constitutional and practical challenges that come with splitting the state, and Hepburn (2014) suggests that immigration will cause the greatest tension between an independent Scotland and the rest of the UK. Independence means Scotland would have the right to determine its own migration policies, along with the management and control of borders. The SNP-led Scottish government asserts that upon independence it will create a Scottish points-based immigration system aimed at increasing net migration into Scotland, coupled with a more humane refugee and asylum policy (Scottish Government 2013b). This policy proposal prompted a hostile response in London, where government politicians argued that the plan would threaten years of UK-wide policy dedicated to controlling and reducing the number of migrants. UK government officials used colourful imagery of border posts and defensive fortifications along the Scottish border, arguing that two contiguous nations with markedly different immigration policies require extensive border checks (Carrell 2014c). They also warned that independence will require Scotland to absorb all the costs of border defence to discourage illegal immigration and terrorism.

Concerns about the border gained additional traction after Brexit, as Scotland's pro-Europe position led UK officials to fear an independent Scotland would seek EU membership, and potentially inclusion within the Schengen Agreement, which allows for free movement of residents of the 26 European countries in the Schengen Area with no internal borders between them (the UK is not a member of the Schengen Area). The UK is concerned that a Scotland within the EU's Schengen Area and attracting immigrants will become a site of departure for EU migrants to cross irregularly into the UK. With Scotland in the EU, Scotland's border with the rest of the UK would also be an external border for the EU. The Schengen Border Code details requirements for when a Schengen country borders a non-Schengen country: checkpoints and border guards, patrolling the border, document checks, and potentially the construction of a hard border. Scotland would have to apply these rules to the Scottish–English border and to a sea border with Northern Ireland. The border challenges facing Scotland and England will resemble those facing Northern Ireland and Ireland, which was one of the greatest obstacles in negotiating a workable Brexit deal.[4]

Another option is for Scotland to opt out of the Schengen Agreement to be part of the Common Travel Area (CTA), which allows British and Irish citizens to travel freely between and reside in both countries.[5] This CTA will be critical in any divorce talks because it will govern movement between Scotland and the rest of the UK, which in 2018 amounted to an average of about 51,000 border crossings per day (Transport Scotland 2018; White 2020). The UK government insists that if Scotland were to remain part of the CTA, their external immigration policy would have to be coordinated, even though up to this point, the UK and Ireland have maintained their own visa and immigration policies. While the Scottish government has argued that Schengen and the CTA are not mutually incompatible, the UK government, recognising the greater relative importance of the CTA for Scotland, insisted in 2014 that Scotland could not join both agreements. Some analysts argue that the most likely outcome will be for the EU to require Scotland to join the Schengen Area and leave the CTA in return for EU membership, though they could agree upon a model of deferred participation (Wright 2013). Others suggest there is little reason for other EU member states to object if Scotland remains in the CTA, as long as the UK wants to avoid a border, which would be in both Scotland's and the UK's best interests (Keating 2017).

Citizenship policies will also need to be resolved upon independence. Around 9% of Scotland's population was born in England, and there are over 850,000 Scottish-born people living elsewhere in the UK, equivalent to about 16% of Scotland's population. In the lead-up to the Brexit referendum, the

Scottish government proposed an inclusive model of citizenship that replicates or is more liberal than the policies governing UK citizenship. All British citizens habitually residing in Scotland would be considered Scottish citizens, as would Scottish-born British citizens living outside of Scotland. Others could apply, including immigrants with qualifying visas, those with a Scottish parent or grandparent, and those who spent ten years living in Scotland at some point in their lives (Scottish Government 2013b). The UK allows dual or multiple citizenships, and so would Scotland. The Scottish government admits that the UK is empowered to decide whether to allow for dual Scottish/UK citizenship, but assumes the usual rules would apply so as to allow for continued patterns of residency and movement across the border for citizens of both nations. The Scottish citizenship policy represents a standard mix of citizenship policies, combining birth in the country with descent/ancestry criteria. However, there are many gaps that could impact the relationship between Scotland and the UK, the lives of citizens living in other nations, and immigrants, depending on how the policy is implemented.[6]

The spectre of independence, potential Scottish control over immigration policy, and the porous land border between Scotland and the UK deeply impacts Scottish–English relations and the way the politics of immigration are developed in both contexts. While much of the tension is limited by the hypothetical future of Scottish independence, there are consequences playing out in real time, with implications for people in both Scotland and the UK.

Consequences of England–Scotland Contrasts

Scottish claims for independence require Scottish nationalists to make the argument that Scotland is distinct from the rest of the UK. The Scottish nationalist political elite make two critical points. First, that the differences are insurmountable and require a complete political split. Second, that the difference is between the nations, and is not translatable to individuals. However, daily encounters between Scottish and English people demonstrate persistent perceptions of individual difference tied to nationality. Instances of hate against English-born people in Scotland (captured with the term 'Anglophobia') are difficult to reconcile with the narrative of Scottish openness and multiculturalism.

Hussain and Miller's work on Scotland's multicultural nationalism suggests that the existence of England as a 'common, external, and very significant other' may have displaced the antipathies that might have been directed at other outsiders, such as Muslims (2006: 66).[7] Bond (2006) discovers a similar contradiction in a greater reluctance among Scots to see an English-born resident as Scottish than to see a minoritised resident with a Scottish accent as Scottish. These contradictions lead to an uncomfortable truth: a benign Scottish nationalism welcomes foreign-born residents of Scotland, but the same acceptance is not extended to English-born residents. This discrimination towards English people, despite substantial shared history, cultural similarities, and shared ethnicity, gives weight to Hussain and Miller's argument that the differential treatment of English people is the product of the oppositional politics of Scottish nationalism.

Anglophobia is the most serious consequence of the England-facing politics of nationalism, as it represents an internal contradiction in the vision of the nation. The English born are the largest group of people born outside Scotland, with a population doubling that of all other immigrant groups combined, and Scotland cannot afford to alienate its English-born residents. Should Scotland achieve independence, all English people within Scotland will become either Scottish citizens or legal immigrants. This will substantially change the dynamics of the politics of immigration and who is considered an immigrant in Scotland. It will be a challenge for Scotland to move from framing England as the main foil in its national ambitions to incorporating English people into the vision of the 'new Scots' that will determine the viability and the direction of the nation.

Europe-Facing Politics of Immigration

The politics surrounding immigration in Scotland involve stakeholders beyond the UK. The EU is critical to Scotland's experience with migration because its members have been the primary sending states of migrants in Scotland. The EU is also a resource for Scottish nationalists in their efforts to advance their interests and their agenda of independence, which would come with full autonomy over immigration. This section describes the way Scottish elites, especially those in the SNP, have activated pro-European politics in pursuit of their political agenda, alongside the way the EU has legitimised and institutionalised Scotland's place in Europe. The EU delivers benefits to Scotland by advancing their cause for greater national autonomy, pushing Scotland towards diversity and multiculturalism, and providing a legal structure for an independent Scotland's immigration policy.

Advancing Scottish Independence with the EU

Sub-state nationalist parties and the EU are strange bedfellows. While sub-state nationalist parties advocate for increased sovereignty and sometimes full political independence, the EU weakens the relevance of traditional state sovereignty in the international system. A sub-state nationalist party with ambitions for political independence that also supports European integration, such as the SNP, would appear to be a contradiction: it is difficult to imagine why a country that is resisting a centralised state would be in favour of subordination to another supranational foreign authority. Facing increasing globalisation and greater European integration, many nationalists feel strong pressure to valorise and protect their cultures, which leads many nationalist parties on the European continent to adopt an anti-EU and anti-immigration stance (Hepburn 2009).

Under the SNP's leadership, the Scottish government has advanced a vision of Scotland within Europe.[8] As early as the 1990s, the SNP's 'Independence in Europe' policy framed Scotland's future as an independent member of the European Community. Scotland is not the only region to see a brighter future in Europe. Many regionalist political parties are more supportive of European integration precisely because EU integration threatens state sovereignty (Marks and Wilson 2000).[9] Regionalist nationalist arguments have historically been rejected with claims that it would be impractical and self-defeating to upset political traditions based on centralised administrative structures, but underneath the umbrella of EU institutions, many critical institutions (i.e. trade, financial, and banking regulations; human rights; environmental policy) remain intact. Furthermore, smaller states gain enhanced opportunities to promote their interests through free trade within a regionalised Europe (Jolly 2015). As one leading member of the SNP put it:

> We believe that an independent Scotland in the European Union would be able to influence and negotiate in a stronger position for the direction we, as a nation, broadly speaking, would like to go down, and we're also very, very aware that Westminster, in particular the Conservative elite, are very much more inclined to a different political standpoint. (Personal interview 10 June 2016)

The UK is Scotland's biggest trading partner. Will enhanced opportunities offered by the EU be enough to support Scotland? Before Brexit, independence did not present as big a risk, because if Scotland and the rest of the UK were members of the EU, free trade between the two countries could continue. With Brexit, Scotland must choose between the UK and the EU. It will have to join the CTA or make another agreement to maintain a free trade relationship with the UK, and it is not clear that the EU will allow Scotland the legal exemptions required for those agreements. Those who support a vision of Scotland in Europe argue that if Scotland were to choose the EU, EU membership would provide an external support framework that could replace those formerly provided by the UK state.

The EU Promoting Scotland's National Interest

European integration rescales political authority. It weakens regions' ties to central states and encourages the empowerment of smaller levels of governance, like cities and regions, because they represent a closer link with the grassroots sites of policy implementation (Keating 2009). This engagement creates new opportunities for sub-state actors to pursue their interests (Lynch 1996; Keating and McGarry 2001). Regions and nationalist parties can pursue forms of influence within their states and in Europe. As a country with devolved powers and a democratically elected regional government with a political party system and civic institutional structures for policy implementation, Scotland has legitimacy as a political actor within the EU.

In return, the EU offers several advantages to regions like Scotland, including representation through the Committee of the Regions; access to the core European institutions like the Council of Ministers, the Commission, and the European Parliament; involvement in lobbying organisations and European political parties through regional offices in Brussels; and access to special rights, funding, and minority protections under European law (Tatham 2008).

EU-level policies initially provoked a protectionist reaction from many regions worried that the supranational institutions would ignore their interests (Hepburn and McLoughlin 2011). Regional actors established offices in Brussels to lobby EU institutions and they demanded the creation of the Committee of the Regions (CoR) in 1994 (Tatham 2008). The CoR is an advisory body through which regional representatives can share opinions on legislation impacting regions and cities. It is consulted on most policy domains, and has been a forum for discussing sub-state competencies over immigration. For example, the committee repeats the following in a number of legal opinions:

> local and regional authorities play a decisive role in creating the right conditions for third-country nationals to have access to information and services relating to employment, education, healthcare, housing, culture and other public goods, giving them the opportunity to build a strong link with their host society. (Committee of the Regions 2009)

The committee argues for multi-level governance for the successful integration of immigrants and requests better support for regions to implement integration initiatives. The creation of institutions like the CoR, where regional interests are paramount, provides a venue for advocacy and encourages the development of regionalism within member states.[10]

Examples from the central EU institutions demonstrate other ways the EU gives regions a voice and reinforces regional political movements. Since devolution in 1999, Scottish ministers have attended the Council of the European Union (also called the Council of Ministers) when devolved issues are under discussion.[11] Since immigration is a reserved power, Scottish ministers would not be involved in discussions about free movement or immigration.

The European Commission has a monopoly on initiative in most EU policy fields. It consults widely and is open to parties interested in a policy. Regions have enthusiastically provided opinions, especially when they diverge from their state government, as is sometimes the case with Scotland and England. The Commission occasionally exploits heterogeneity of preferences within member states to buttress its position at the expense of the state government. This strategy is not always received favourably within the UK. Tatham quotes a UK official:

> if the Commission think [sic] that they can weaken the UK's position by exploiting links with Scotland for instance, I don't criticize the Commission for that, I admire them for having spotted the opportunity and I see it as our job as the national authority to make sure that it does not undermine us. (Tatham 2008: 503)

The Commission and the devolved Scottish government can therefore occasionally form an alliance against the UK state to advance common interests.

European Parliament elections have provided an opportunity for regional interests to gain a political foothold and have a voice on the international scene. Scotland occupies six seats in the European Parliament, and in 2019, the SNP won three seats.[12] Once representatives of a party are elected, the European Parliament provides parties with the opportunity to collaborate in a party family. The SNP belongs to a regionalist party family, though the differences between regionalist parties across Europe make collaboration difficult.[13] Members of the European Parliament (MEPs) are charged with representing their party family and legislating for Europe rather than for their states or regions, but 'MEPs who are sensitive to regional concerns can be a very effective way for regions to promote their particular interests, bypass their member-state's tutelage, gain direct access to the Commission's hierarchy and directly influence EU legislation' (Tatham 2008: 506).

European-level political opportunities have fundamentally altered the political objectives of regional governments and parties. While the SNP clings to its ambitions for full independent statehood, other regionalist parties have used the opportunities to moderate their demands and pursue a post-nationalist strategy that does not require traditionally defined political sovereignty. Incrementalists, who are happy to increase regional autonomy through less radical forms of constitutional change, can be found within the ranks of the SNP. Even pro-independence advocates argue for independence within a post-national context, where conventional states are disempowered relative to local and international and supranational entities.

In sum, European-level representation does not provide an opportunity for Scottish representatives to influence immigration policy directly. However, Scottish elites unequivocally believe increased immigration is in the national interest, and moves towards enhanced regional power indirectly impact the politics of immigration. Furthermore, deeper integration at the European level is associated with greater electoral support for regionalist parties, which empowers them to more effectively pursue their interests (Jolly 2007).

The EU Promoting Diversity
The EU is a helpful ally for regionalists, but it is only willing to work with state and national/regional actors who conform with its standards and expectations. When it comes to immigration, EU membership comes with three expectations. The first is ideological, related to the character of the EU as an amalgamation of many different states, cultures, languages, and traditions, giving rise to the EU motto 'united in diversity'. Participating in such a union requires respect for diversity and an underlying belief in cultural equality that supports equal participation.[14] The second expectation is rights-based, requiring member states to demonstrate a commitment to human rights, and respect for and protection of minoritised groups. The third expectation anticipates that EU members will endorse and participate in the Schengen Agreement. The commitment to free movement is at the heart of European integration, and preferences for immigration and European integration are closely linked in the minds of the European public (Lahav 2004).[15] To be perceived as legitimate actors within the EU, sub-state nationalists must adopt civic and inclusive criteria for national membership.

Conformance to the EU's expectations is evaluated when a state seeks to join the EU. Membership is conditional upon a state's ability to meet the Copenhagen Criteria and the terms of the acquis communautaire.[16] They include economic and political dimensions, but the political criteria are unevenly applied. For example, the required protection of minority rights has not been prioritised or equally enforced. Nevertheless, the EU's commitment to respect and protect minorities has inspired policy change in European countries. Smith (2015) uses the case of Estonia to explore the tensions between ethnic nationalism and the pursuit of EU membership. He demonstrates that EU conditionality around the humane and fair treatment of minoritised groups imposed constraints over state-building policies like naturalisation, which resulted in a new discourse of 'emerging multicultural democracy' in Estonia that was consistent with EU norms.

Because Scotland was already in the EU through its subordinate status within the UK, pressures of ascension to the EU do not apply to Scotland like they did to Estonia. However, during the lead-up to the independence referendum, there was debate over whether Scotland could become a member of the EU immediately upon achieving independence. British unionists argued that it could not, and the European Commission confirmed that an independent Scotland must apply for membership.[17] To ensure a speedy application process, pro-independence Scots were incentivised to demonstrate their compliance with European standards, and in the case of minority protections, to show themselves to be more deserving of EU membership than the rest of the UK. With Brexit, Scotland was forced out of the EU against the will of the

Scottish people, and demonstrations of Scotland's European-ness were even more noticeable. The Scotland Is Now campaign released a video in which a Scottish man stands on the beach facing Europe and yells that the Scottish people, universities, and businesses are open to Europeans. He declares, 'our arms are open, our minds are open', and he urges Europe to 'continue our love affair'.[18] Nicola Sturgeon wrote an open letter to EU citizens living in Scotland in 2016 and 2019 reinforcing the Scottish government's desire for EU migrants to stay in Scotland, and in 2019 she committed government resources to help European immigrants apply for settled status.

In order to receive the benefits of continued inclusion within EU institutions, nationalistic political parties face European pressure to de-ethnicise nation-building projects in order to be seen as legitimate and as sharing values of democracy, diversity, and human rights. Parties presenting themselves as Europe-facing and welcoming of immigrants, like the SNP and the Convergència i Unió in Catalonia, are welcomed into European networks, while those that are explicitly against European integration and immigration, like the Lega Nord in Italy, are excluded (Hepburn 2009). In the case of the Lega Nord, its anti-immigrant stance preceded its anti-European stance. The party originally saw the EU as presenting an opportunity for the advancement of regional interests, but when it was criticised and excluded from EU institutions because of its position on immigration, it started to change its position on the EU.

In sum, the EU has influence over the politics of immigration in Scotland through the expectation that members will conform with a pro-diversity ideology. The possibilities introduced by the independence and Brexit referenda motivated decision makers in Scotland to demonstrate conformance with those expectations. Though Scotland might have independently taken the multicultural, pro-immigrant path for all the reasons addressed in other chapters of this book, the turn towards Europe pre-dates an agenda on immigration, which suggests some influence of the EU on policy preferences in Scotland.

EU Law on Immigration

If an independent Scotland joins the EU, which is the stated objective of the SNP-led Scottish government, EU legislation will directly impact Scotland's immigration policy. As a new member state, Scotland would have to, at a minimum, adopt all provisions of the acquis communautaire, including those that pertain to immigration. EU member states are entitled to have a national system of visas, residence permits, and work permits, meaning that most control over economic and student migration remains in the state. However, an EU directive governs family reunification, which determines the minimum conditions under which family reunification is granted, establishes procedural guarantees, and provides rights for the family members concerned. A significant body of EU legislation pertains to asylum seekers and especially the minimum standards by which those seeking asylum should be treated. While the UK has opted out of a number of the specific requirements relating to asylum and family reunification, general practice in the UK meets the minimum standards, meaning Scotland could maintain the status quo upon independence (Wright 2013).

Scotland might be expected to join the EU's Blue Card Network, which promotes high-skilled migration and fills gaps in the labour markets of participating states where those gaps cannot be filled by native-born workers or other legal EU citizens/residents. Once a state grants a Blue Card to an immigrant at an employer's request, the immigrant is entitled to move to another EU state for work after two years. The UK currently opts out of this system, but given the objectives of the Scottish government, it would likely participate in this programme.

The most significant EU requirement with the potential to influence Scotland's immigration is the Schengen Agreement. Joining the Schengen Agreement is the norm for EU member states. Even though Scotland has stated its desire to remain in the CTA, there is little reason to think that the EU would see that as preferable to a Scotland in the Schengen Area. Scotland's negotiation position is weak compared with that of the Commission, especially in the post-Brexit context. Only two EU countries – the UK and the Republic of Ireland – have been able to opt out of the Schengen Agreement. Scotland in the Schengen Area would dramatically reshape Scottish–UK relations. However, 'the benefit to Scotland of being in the Schengen Area – and out of the CTA – is thus a trade-off for Scotland between making *one* border less transparent and *twenty-six* other borders more transparent' (Wright 2013: 52, italics original). The question is whether flows from the Schengen Area would make up for a hard border with England, and how open Scotland's immigration policy would be towards workers and students from the UK.

Global-Facing Politics of Immigration

Though the EU is Scotland's aspirational international partner, Scotland's leadership also wants Scotland to be a legitimate independent actor on the world stage with an enviable country brand. A strong country brand yields a number of benefits including increased exports, tourism, and investment, and immigration plays a key role in forming Scotland's international reputation. Scottish elites use their pro-diversity and welcoming political ethos to court positive perceptions of the country, and to draw people to live, work, invest, and do business in Scotland. As such, Scotland's ability to attract migrants is both cause and effect of the nation's international reputation.

The Scottish government evaluates its own performance in order to identify where the country's reputation is at risk.[19] The Anholt Ipsos Nation Brands Index (NBI) asks a random sample of people in 20 countries what they think about the culture, exports, governance, investment and immigration, people, and tourism of 50 countries (see Appendix N). The data provide a snapshot of attitudes towards and perceptions of Scotland, and measure and rank the country's international reputation, which allows for comparison over time and relative to other countries. Scotland's scores have been stable since it began measuring reputation with the NBI in 2008, and in 2018, its overall score on the NBI was 62.7 out of 100, the highest score since the baseline study in 2008 (60.2). Scotland places 16th out of 50 evaluated countries around the world.

The NBI measures public impressions about Scotland's openness towards immigrants, and Scotland is ranked 11th in how welcoming its people are. There is also a full multi-indicator dimension evaluating whether respondents perceive Scotland to be a good place in which to live, work, study and invest. Scotland ranks 17th on this dimension. In individual metrics that make up the dimension, Scotland ranks 13th in the perception that the country cares about equality, and 14th in whether the respondent would be willing to live and work in the country.

The NBI survey polled 500 respondents from Scotland about their opinions of the 50 countries in the survey including Scotland. Scots usually rank themselves first, and they gave their country its highest recorded score of 75.7 out of 100 in 2014, the year of the independence referendum. The top three groups of attributes that Scots rank Scotland most highly on are tourism, people, and 'immigration and investment', all three of which measure how welcoming Scotland is to outsiders. Self-assessment may yield inflated data, but variance in Scottish responses about Scotland shows that Scots can be discriminating and critical of their own country. Furthermore, when it comes to political culture, what a country's people believe about their country's reputation might be more important than the perception of others. The One Scotland, Many Cultures campaign recognised the cultural weight of Scotland's international reputation for Scots, and used it for political purposes: one of the public service announcements to increase awareness of casual racism in Scotland contrasted the positive international reputation of Scots with their culturally insensitive behaviour and demanded that Scots 'Live up to your reputation.' The campaign assumed that Scots believe they have a favourable reputation of equality and have an interest in maintaining it.

How does a country enhance its international reputation? The NBI demonstrates that higher scores are correlated with familiarity and exposure through visits or virtual contact. Part of an effort to improve an international reputation must involve outreach to increase exposure. The Scottish government supports the international activity of Scottish bodies, notably through the Executive's International Strategy and European Strategy, both launched in 2004. The government also began campaigns of public diplomacy, which involves cultivating positive public opinion in other countries and international organisations.[20] When Scotland provides development assistance to a country, those contributions allow Scotland to participate in implementing global policies like those affiliated with the Sustainable Development Goals, even without being a member of the relevant international organisations.[21] These activities give Scotland international prestige and legitimacy as a global actor. Scotland relies heavily on public diplomacy because Scotland does not have the right to engage in official independent international political partnership without the involvement of the UK government. Fortunately, cultural agreements between Scotland and other international actors are seen by the UK government as being relatively benign, even though the agreements align with Scottish desires to foster independent relations away from the influence of the UK Parliament.[22]

Public diplomacy campaigns often relate to historical Scottish emigration as a foundation for a positive diplomatic relationship. For example, Clarke (2014) describes a number of projects undertaken by the Scottish government in Kolkata, India in 2008, most notably the conservation of a decaying Scottish cemetery and buildings with an important Scottish cultural legacy, like Duff College and Roxburgh Building.[23] Clarke notes the meaning behind the selection of these educational buildings rather than other structures with more negative connotations, like the Scottish-owned jute mills that exploited local labour and entrenched inequalities:

> The Scottish cemetery seems unthreatening because the people interred there have long since faded from local memory. The buildings of Roxburgh and Duff offer a relatively benign account of Scottish involvement in the British Empire and in the colonization of India – highlighting the positives rather than the negatives of this period. (Clarke 2014: 240)

In addition to building a positive narrative about Scotland's involvement in India, these artefacts make important symbolic connections to the positive contributions of emigrant Scots in India during British rule.

Scottish development assistance to Malawi is similarly negotiated with reference to Scotland's emigrant history. Malawi's development assistance programme was unveiled in 2005 as the first international agreement for the Scottish government (Alexander 2014).[24] The link between the two countries is attributed to the welcome that the famous Scot Dr David Livingstone received when he entered what is now Malawi in 1859. The Scottish government has enthusiastically used Livingstone as the symbolic figurehead of Scotland's interaction with the sub-Saharan region, and through emigrant symbolism, the Scottish–Malawian partnership can 'reassure the Scottish people of their perceived heritage of having made a positive impact on the world' (Alexander 2014: 81).

Cultural diplomacy contributes to Scottish nation-building in two critical ways. First, the diplomatic effort promotes a coherent national brand. Second, developing a Scottish reputation requires Scotland to differentiate itself from the rest of the UK. This is especially important when Scotland engages in diplomacy with former British colonies. Scotland occupied a privileged position in the British Empire and the Scottish people disproportionately benefited from opportunities in Britain's colonial territories.[25] As such, Scottish involvement in cultural preservation in places like India runs the risk of attracting charges of neo-colonialism. Scotland seems to have avoided this, and has successfully negotiated its involvement in the same places where British attempts at cultural diplomacy have failed.[26] Clarke (2014) attributes Scottish success to a reframing of Scottish involvement in India, where the projects

> frame the Scotland–India relationship as one typified by a shared belief in equality, freedom of government and the ability of humanity to drive positive change. These values, expressed through carefully selected heritage sites and cultural events, promote the perception of Scotland and India occupying similar positions within the British Empire, rather than being on opposing sides of the colonial system. (Clarke 2014: 244)

With this new frame, the two nations can be united against the imperial tendencies of the UK. This underdog positioning allows Scotland to accept sympathy rather than censure in the international context, and allows it to weave a narrative about mutually beneficial Scottish involvement in India.

Though Scottish public diplomacy may yield positive results for the countries receiving aid and assistance, Scotland gains the most from its international involvement. First Minister Jack McConnell described the motivations for Scotland's public diplomacy as rooted in Scotland's economic interest, and 'promoting Scotland as a location for investment, for work, for education and for goods and services' (Alexander 2014: 76). In an interview with Colin Alexander, he described development assistance as part of a larger strategy to promote Scottish interests:

> Between 2001 and 2004 there were three main elements to the development of this strategy. The first was the launch of the Fresh Talent Initiative in 2003 where I was determined to increase immigration to Scotland and we agreed, for example, a specific visa regime with the UK government for those who wanted to live and work in Scotland. The second was the development of a new international image for Scotland based on extensive research, putting the Saltire flag and a series of modern images centre stage, and using the theme 'Now is the time' and 'Scotland is the place'. This linked the drive for immigration with an expansion of our promotion of tourism, exports, education and inward investment. (Alexander 2014: 76)

McConnell explicitly connects Scotland's modern efforts to promote immigration, and international outreach built on relationships formed through Scottish emigration, and he ties both to Scotland's economic success.

Scotland has a comparatively strong and consistent international reputation, and migration has been a central element in developing Scotland's reputation. Scottish emigration laid the foundation for international relationships, and Scotland has framed that foundation with the positive contribution of immigrants to host societies. Scotland's international brand has revolved around its welcoming and open people, and its reputation has been deliberately developed through public diplomacy, with actions intended to draw people to Scotland and ensure its future as a stable country.

Conclusion

Scotland's future will be driven by its politics of immigration. If Scotland remains a region of the UK, the regional attidudes towards migration and the EU's policy of free movement will still draw a stark line between the political cultures of Scotland and England. The differences will be used to garner sympathy for a Scotland that wants to be international and multicultural, but is held back by an isolationist and nationalistic England. While the institutions of the EU are less available to Scotland after Brexit, Scotland will use public diplomacy to build an international reputation and to pursue international relationships, and Scotland's history of emigration and immigration will play a role in those efforts.

If Scotland achieves independence, it will gain power over immigration and its own diplomatic relationships. Independence will profoundly change the relationship between Scotland and the UK, not least because Scotland will have to negotiate all of the policies that regulate relationships between two contiguous and interdependent states. English residents in Scotland would become either Scottish citizens or official immigrants, which would reframe who Scottish elites are talking about when they talk about immigrants. Independence will also provide an opportunity to test the follow-through of Scottish politicians, and reveal the extent of their pro-EU and pro-immigrant positions. Regardless of which path Scotland takes, its approach to immigration will remain a central political tool that the Scottish elite will use to define Scotland's relationships with its neighbours, its region, and the world.

Notes

1. The second part of Arthur Herman's *How the Scots Invented the Modern World: The True Story of How Western Europe's Poorest Nation Created Our World & Everything in It* (2001) is dedicated to the Scottish diaspora and its role in the development of the modern state system and capitalism, art, literature, and science.
2. McCrone (1992) analysed the industrial, occupational, and sectoral changes in

Scotland compared with changes in England and Wales from 1851 to 1981. He finds the similarities north and south of the border are much greater than the differences: 'Far from being a specialized "region" of Britain, however, Scotland throughout its industrial history has had a very similar profile to Britain as a whole, while containing considerable internal specialization, reflecting its position as a distinct country within the United Kingdom' (74).

3. Penrose and Howard (2008) argue that this perspective of a Scottish difference in racism was founded on the three beliefs: 1) that the presence of racial minorities is a prerequisite for racism, 2) that the degree of racism is proportional to the size of the minoritised communities, and 3) that Scots are inherently more tolerant. They argue that the real difference is that the racialisation of Scottish politics and society was substantially delayed compared with England. This should not be confused with an absence of racism in the form of interpersonal and systemic discrimination, abuse, and violence (see Chapter 5).

4. An independent Scotland in the EU would further complicate the situation of Northern Ireland, which would then be sandwiched between two EU states with Scotland to the north-east and Ireland to the south-west.

5. The CTA agreement dates back to the creation of the Irish Free State (1922), pre-dating the Schengen Agreement (1985). In effect, it functions like the Schengen Area, allowing freedom of movement between the UK, the Republic of Ireland, the Isle of Man, and the Channel Islands.

6. For example, it is not clear what specific rules and procedures would be implemented (naturalisation tests, record of character, etc.), whether the process will be discretionary, and what appeals process would be in place (see Shaw 2013).

7. Hussain and Miller (2006) find higher level levels of Islamophobia than Anglophobia among Scottish survey respondents. However, they find that having a strong sense of Scottish national identity and being an SNP voter are associated with higher levels of Anglophobia, but not Islamophobia.

8. The SNP has not always been a strong supporter of the EU. It opposed European integration until the 1980s, when the new social and political dimensions of integration emerged, at which point SNP leadership could envision the EU as an arena in which to advance the party's social-democratic ideology (Hepburn and McLoughlin 2011).

9. Regionalist parties are geographically concentrated within a region, like Catalonia, the Basque country, Scotland, or Wales. Jolly (2007) examines the party manifestos of regionalist political parties in Belgium, Finland, Ireland, Italy, Spain, and the UK, and finds regionalist parties are more pro-EU than other small parties and nearly as favourable as mainstream political parties.

10. This dynamic is seen in the transformation of the principle of subsidiarity, which was intended to regulate the division of competencies between the states and the European level. The Committee of the Regions has seized and extended subsidiarity to the division of competencies between the EU, the states, and the regions.

11. The Scottish ministers are not entirely free in the Council of Ministers. The negotiation line must be agreed upon in advance, the UK has the last word, and Scottish ministers may not dissent.

12. Before 2015, the SNP outperformed its UK electoral successes at the European level, and the party's successes were accompanied by EU-facing policy development within the party (Lynch 2009).

13. There are big disparities across regionalist parties in traditional ideology (left vs right) and in their constitutional ambitions (autonomy vs independence) (De Winter and Türsan 1998). They also vary widely in their attitudes towards the EU.

14. Many critics suggest the commitment to diversity is rhetorical, as racial and ethnic minorities are underrepresented in the EU institutions. Racial and ethnic minorities make up roughly 10% of the European population, but only 5% of the members of the Parliament come from similar backgrounds. The underrepresentation is even lower in the Commission and Council, where it is estimated to be around 1%.
15. Expectations of openness to free movement and open immigration are limited to movement within the member states only. When it comes to migrants from outside the EU, there is no common policy. Some suggest that the result of greater EU integration has been a generally restrictive turn away from extra-EU migration, creating an image of a 'fortress Europe' with borders that must be protected (Lahav 2004).
16. The Copenhagen Criteria are the rules determining whether a country is eligible to join the EU. States must have institutions to ensure democratic governance and human rights, have a functioning market economy, and agree to the obligations and intent of the EU. The acquis communautaire is the cumulative body of EU laws comprising the EU's objectives, substantive rules, policies, and primary and secondary legislation and case law. It includes treaties, regulations, and directives passed by the EU institutions, and judgments from the European Court of Justice. All prospective EU member states must adopt and implement all of the acquis to join the EU.
17. The President of the European Commission, José Manuel Barroso, discouraged the independence vote by insisting that Scotland, once independent from the UK, would have to apply for membership. Leaders of the No campaign seized on this issue and used it to mobilise voters, arguing that a vote to remain within the UK was a vote to remain within the EU. When the EU referendum resulted in the decision to remove the whole of the UK from the EU, Scottish voters felt that they had been misled.
18. A representative of the Scottish Refugee Council noted the objective of the Scotland Is Now campaign as identity promotion: 'Obviously we're trying to promote this Scottishness identity – ok it's a bit romantic – but you know the Scots like a bit of romanticism' (personal interview 3 April 2019).
19. See 'National Performance Framework' at <https://nationalperformance.gov.scot/>.
20. Public diplomacy includes governments speaking directly to foreign publics. It often uses cultural exchange to foster positive opinions. It falls within the realm of 'soft power' which uses cultural and ideological attraction between countries to accomplish international goals, rather than the 'hard power' of economic or military coercion.
21. Official development assistance is beyond Scotland's legal mandate and is a matter reserved to the UK. As a result, Scottish aid money is not given to governments, but is distributed to Scottish awardees that undertake projects abroad.
22. Past experience demonstrates that the articulation of Scottish interests with international partners like the EU strengthens the UK's position, because Scottish and UK interests are similar. Policy differences between the UK and Scotland are more about prioritisation, rather than being of a fundamental nature (Imrie 2006).
23. Duff College belonged to Scottish missionary Alexander Duff and was constructed in the 1840s to house a Scottish Presbyterian school that educated British, European, and Indian students. The Roxburgh Building was owned by William Roxburgh, who worked under the East India Company and was superintendent of the Calcutta Botanic Gardens. In that capacity he made a significant contribution to botany on the Indian subcontinent (Clarke 2014).

24. Scotland developed a broad international development assistance programme in 2008, but Malawi remains a development priority.
25. For example, in the most profitable parts of the East India Trading Company, nearly half of the accountants and officer cadets were Scottish (Devine 2003).
26. Clarke (2014) discusses the way British cultural interventions in Kolkata in India were halted by local heritage practitioners who accused the project of cultural colonialism. Meanwhile, Scottish commitments to the conservation of Scottish sites in Kolkata were celebrated with a 2009 Protocol of Cooperation.

CONCLUSION:
THE PROSPECTS FOR ATTRACTING AND RETAINING MIGRANTS IN SCOTLAND

When SNP First Minister Nicola Sturgeon opened the Scottish Parliament in 2016, she described the Scottish people:

> We're the grandchildren and the great grandchildren of the thousands who came from Ireland to work in our shipyards and in our factories. We are the 80,000 Polish people, the 8,000 Lithuanians, the 7,000 each from France, Spain, Germany, Italy and Latvia, who are among the many from countries beyond our shores that we are so privileged to have living here amongst us. We are the more than half a million people born in England, Wales and Northern Ireland who have chosen to live here in Scotland. We are the thousands of European students studying at our universities and our colleges, and we are the doctors and nurses from all across our continent and beyond, who care for us daily in our National Health Service. Whether we have lived here for generations, or are new Scots from Europe, India, Pakistan, Africa and countries across the globe we are all of this and more. We are so much stronger for the diversity that shapes us. We are one Scotland. We are simply home to all those who have chosen to live here. That is who and what we are. (Scottish Government 2016c)

Sturgeon and the rest of the political elite class in Scotland embrace a civically defined Scottish national identity that celebrates diversity and promotes pluralism. They are not content to allow Scotland to passively diversify – they actively encourage immigration, even to the point of hosting twice as many Syrian refugees as the UK average.

The clear messaging from the Scottish political elites demonstrates that the Scottish politics of immigration have become a central tool of Scottish ideological and practical nation-building. Ideologically, the Scottish position on immigration heightens the conflict between the forces of English conservativism and Scottish social democracy, and the geographic boundedness of the dominant ideologies bolsters the nationalistic claims of the SNP. Practically, immigration literally builds the Scottish nation through its contribution to Scotland's population and economic growth. Because the nation-building politics of immigration involve both Scottish identity and interests, the politics of immigration have become the vanguard of Scotland's national ambitions.

Four circumstances have allowed immigration to occupy uncontroversial space in Scotland's politics of nation-building, The first is that most political competition occurs on the political left, and there are as yet no challenges to the SNP's vision of civic nationalism. This allows the SNP-led government to advance the association between immigration and uniquely Scottish national identities and interests without substantial pushback. Second, Scotland has experienced rather low levels of immigration, and most of its immigration is made up of phenotypically white people from the rest of the UK, Europe, or North America. Scotland has therefore avoided many of the tensions that came with rapid and visible diversification in other contexts. Relatedly, because Scotland cannot control immigration, it is able to deflect responsibility for any unpopular elements associated with migration on to the UK government. Finally, the Scottish and English votes on the Brexit referendum highlighted the different political environments north and south of the border and reinforced the international outlook of Scotland against the populist narrative of 'taking back control' in England. The prospect of ending free movement and the implications for Scottish businesses and the nation's population growth were especially troubling to the Scottish political elites and emphasised the divergent national interests of England and Scotland.

The Scottish political elits class exploited these circumstances to describe immigration as the key to Scotland's sustainable future. The Scottish government must therefore make every effort to attract and retain immigrants. Nationalists find it politically useful to focus their attention on the campaign to achieve Scottish control over immigration and to highlight English–Scottish difference, but much can be achieved through Scotland's devolved competencies. The following recommendations for how to attract more migrants and maintain a pro-diversity political culture build on the powers that the Scottish Parliament and local authorities already have, followed by additional recommendations for if Scotland achieves independent control over immigration.

The final section argues that many of these recommendations and lessons from the Scottish case can be applied in multiple country contexts and at different levels of government.

Attracting Immigrants

The Scottish government is devoted to making Scotland a welcoming place for immigrants. There are positive externalities of this work in the form of a coherent civic national identity, a political case for independence, and a favourable international reputation, even if immigration cannot be increased. However, given the support immigration would provide to Scotland's demography and economy, it is fair to assume the elite-level interest in immigration is genuine. What can Scotland do to attract more immigrants? There is evidence that innovation-enhancing social conditions, such as favourable educational environments and opportunities to develop rich social capital, enhance a region's attractiveness to migrants (Rodríguez-Pose and Ketterer 2012).[1] However, most migrants prioritise economic opportunities as a prerequisite of a decision to move (Findlay et al. 2003; Houston et al. 2008). There are some migrants who select a destination before finding work, particularly those who are self-employed, but these migrants are a small percentage of the workforce. Creating a welcoming environment is not enough; strategies to attract immigrants with vibrant and cosmopolitan communities must be matched with suitable economic opportunities.

At the moment Scotland does not stand out as a land of economic opportunity. In the National Brands Index, Scotland is ranked 14th out of 50 countries in terms of whether a survey respondent would like to live and work there. It ranks 18th in the attractiveness of the Scottish business investment opportunities and the dimension on exports yields Scotland's weakest ranking in the whole survey (21st). These rankings reflect and perhaps reify a perception that 'Scotland is a place to be educated in and possibly to retire to (if you can stand the weather) but too parochial in its ambitions to work in' (Imrie 2006: 72).

Scotland must create more economic opportunities for migrants. Where there are labour and skills shortages, the government should continue its efforts to incentivise recruiters to look beyond Scotland for talent, and to provide wages that correspond with the requirements of the UK's immigration system. Many areas with shortages are rural, small communities. In order to convince migrants to move, the local and national government must make those areas attractive. Reliable broadband and public transportation could help migrants in rural areas feel connected to their communities locally and abroad, and affordable housing would offset costs associated with relocation. Intentional social engineering with housing aimed at diversifying residential areas could create neighbourhoods more likely to interest migrants. Britain's minoritised populations are more comfortable living in diverse areas, even if the diversity of the community includes the presence of groups other than one's own (Fieldhouse and Cutts 2010).

Attracting immigrants will be difficult in areas without significant labour shortages or skills gaps. If immigrants are lured with employment under these conditions, immigrants could displace Scottish workers, which would have negative social and political effects. Such regions could focus on the recruitment and support of immigrant and non-immigrant entrepreneurs to establish businesses and increase employment. Such a scheme will require investment in infrastructure to promote business innovation, such as access to broadband and a map of entrepreneur service organisations (universities, libraries, government offices, events) to promote business innovation. Targeted entrepreneurial strategies are unlikely to draw the numbers needed to sustain population growth, but they are an important first step. Until Scotland achieves control over immigration policy, it will not be able to draw large numbers from abroad, but if it creates attractive opportunities, it could draw foreign and UK-born people from other areas of the UK, which may achieve the same goals.

Maintaining a Pro-diversity and Anti-racist Political Culture

Scotland is distinctive in its progressive approach to immigration paired with low barriers for inclusion and access to public services. The lack of politicisation on the issue and public ambivalence about immigration presents a window of opportunity for political elites to build a multicultural nation without much social or political opposition. However, public sentiment changes quickly, and elites are concerned that immigration could be rapidly politicised, as was the case in Sweden and Poland during and after the Syrian refugee crisis. Scottish exceptionalism does not stretch to the belief that the Scottish people are any less racist or that they will react any differently than other people under the same conditions, and anti-immigrant movements have grown across the European continent in response to growing diversification. The pro-immigrant position of the political elite likewise cannot be taken for granted. As a Conservative MSP said:

> We can't afford to be anti-immigrant. And you know, hand on heart, if we could afford to be anti-immigrant, am I confident that we wouldn't be? I don't mean 'we' the Tories, I mean 'we' the Scottish political class. I don't have that confidence at all. (Personal interview 26 March 2019)

The Scottish leadership must take advantage of the post-Brexit moment of consensus to establish social norms and values that will withstand change.

All politicians and especially the party leaders must make a commitment to avoid politicising immigration, no matter what happens in the broader political environment. Hepburn and Rosie (2014) suggest independence will likely result in politicisation and polarisation over immigration, as the Scottish government will have to accept responsibility for immigration and the political parties will take concrete and competing policy positions. The temptation to use the different approaches to immigration to build support for the party during elections will be strong, but must be resisted. If not, Scotland will lose its distinctiveness, to the detriment of resident immigrant communities. As journalist Joyce McMillan said:

> The Scottish parties' decision to lead from the liberal centre-left on race and migration, and not to feed the rhetoric of fear and xenophobia that so often shapes the immigration debate at UK level, has had an almost entirely positive effect, particularly in enabling us to keep untangling this fierce knot of related issues, and to think relatively clearly about the race laws we want, the immigration we need, and the EU membership we would probably still choose. (McMillan 2015)

A move away from political consensus on race and immigration will re-tie the knot and choke progress. Systems of party discipline allow party leaders to hold members accountable, which allows for a coordinated effort to avoid politicising immigration. It is perhaps more important to use community management to direct public opinion and thereby temper the impulse to use immigration politically. Scottish elites have an opportunity to make a significant difference, since Scottish opinions are largely ambivalent in the post-Brexit context.

Many people are concerned about immigration because they believe diversification negatively effects community cohesion, anticipating that people who are different will not be trusted by the wider community. Research demonstrates that there can be a relationship between diversity and distrust, but that most of the effect is attributable to economic deprivation. In deprived contexts, the introduction of a new population could be seen as competition for scarce resources, and may produce resentment. The government should closely monitor the settlement of migrants and refugees in regeneration or other deprived areas, and should target investment in these areas. First, the government and local authorities should clearly signal the advantages of population growth for public services that are accessible to everyone. Second, the government should be careful to invest in the whole community, avoiding the perception that refugees or immigrants are receiving targeted assistance. Infrastructure investments should be designed to promote positive interactions in a structured environment to help develop productive social capital. Controlled environments are vital for developing productive diverse social interactions because they allow for codes of conduct, and expulsion or punishment if the code is violated. Schools are the most obvious structured and prejudice-free environment, but the development of community centres or sport and leisure facilities could reach a larger demographic, structuring interactions through clubs or classes that bring people with similar interests together. There is evidence of xenophobia and racism among the Scottish public, and structured contact helps ensure that racist expression will not be tolerated or permitted to undermine the value of the social interaction. Local authorities and organisations should prioritise the value of these contacts in their mission and should ensure that anyone in a leadership position (instructors, coaches, etc.) engages with the mission of multiculturalism and anti-racism and is prepared to enforce it.

The effectiveness of these strategies will depend on early intervention. Signs of prejudice emerge early and peak in mid-childhood (five to seven years old) (Raabe and Beelman 2011). Prejudices are more entrenched in adults, which makes it difficult to quickly change the social culture to be more accepting of diversity. Anecdotally, within structured activities of sports clubs, children do not display negative behaviour nearly as often as their parents, and parental examples can socialise children much more effectively than social programming. Efforts must target people at all points in the lifecycle to have an effect, though adults are harder to reach due to their home and work obligations.

The workplace is a structured environment that can lead to productive social interactions for adults. Many workplaces attempt to address prejudice through diversity training, but research on the programmes shows that diversity training can be more harmful than helpful. Workers respond to 'force fed' trainings with anger and resistance, and in some cases, express more negative opinions and biases afterward. 'The most effective programs engage people in working for diversity, increase their contact with women and minorities, and tap into their desire to look good to others' (Dobbin and Khalev 2016). This can be done though engaging people in a project to recruit promising minoritised employees, or through mentoring relationships. Increased contact with minoritised co-workers helps people recognise discrimination and racism as a real problem, and through an empathetic response, provokes an increased desire to commit to anti-racism. Social accountability and positive affirmation encourage people to participate in voluntary programmes or to develop and implement programmes.

Efforts must be designed and administered locally. The example of diversity training demonstrates that people do not like feeling preached at or compelled to do things, especially if the body issuing the mandate appears to be elitist or out of touch. Programmes must appear to be organic and designed to meet local needs. The role of the Scottish government must therefore be limited to providing incentives and support for local authorities and community organisations, using the tactics of the more successful corporate diversity programmes to engage local authorities in working to improve social environments for their constituencies. The central government should also continue to require mainstreaming reports on equality promotion from the local authorities so that it can assess performance, and with the help of the Convention of Scottish Local Authorities (COSLA), it can identify areas of improvement and connect local authorities to the appropriate resources. Anti-racism efforts must also be infused across all of the devolved policy areas – employment, health, housing, education, social security – at the national and local levels. It cannot be limited to one department or unit.

The Scottish government's most visibly active role will continue to involve clear public messaging about anti-racism and the benefits of diversity and immigration. Government messaging normalises values and activates a sense of duty and deference to authority among the general population. More importantly, minoritised and migrant groups hear and interpret government messaging. Hussain and Miller (2006) found that Muslim and English residents who believe that the government regards them as an asset are much less likely to suspect other Scots of racism. It could be that the Parliament's multicultural campaigns shape the minoritised and immigrant perspectives more than they impact the prejudices themselves, but even so, that effect is critical for creating a community where diverse groups feel welcomed.

Finally, the pro-immigrant stakeholders should develop a coherent media campaign. Most members of minoritised groups believe that the media worsens perceptions of minoritised persons and provokes instances of discrimination against them. As Eberl and colleagues observe:

> The fact that there is generally a limited framing repertoire when it comes to the debate about migration, perhaps due to time and resource constraints, results in journalistic reporting that consciously or unconsciously reproduces and reinforces dominant, mostly negative frames, in the debate about immigration ... potentially legitimizing ethnocentric and nationalist rhetoric, or undermining policy efforts concerning long-term integration of migrants and refugees. (Eberl et al. 2018: 212)

Stakeholders must target both Scottish and UK-wide media sources with positive messaging about immigrants, immigration, and diversity, since the Scottish public consumes both. News and entertainment media should be encouraged to depict immigrant and minoritised Scots as regular members of society, being careful not to depict them in stereotyped roles. Casting minoritised Scots with a Scottish accent could start the process of mainstreaming, since research suggests that the accent is the most critical marker of Scottishness. Persistent images of a diverse Scotland will help normalise differences.

Implementing an Independent Immigration Policy

The Scottish government has articulated a feasible points-based immigration policy that could function within the devolved or independent context, and the policy would be ideally paired with free movement in the Schengen Area.

As Scotland transitions into implementing its policy, the government must manage migration flows to reduce the possibility of social conflict. A representative from the Scottish Refugee Council made this point very clearly:

> [Migration] needs to be managed, and part of the argument around having more local and Scottish control is around being able to manage some of these tensions – so we fought really hard, and the Home Office are now committed to it – we are in a partnership board at a local authority level, which will allow the local authority to have more say in where people are going to be accommodated in Glasgow. Social engineering is not done by a multinational company, but in discussion with local authorities and communities – who knows the community better than the communities and the local authority? – and [resettlement] shouldn't just be where you can get the cheapest accommodation. If asylum seekers are going to be put into that community, then the community should benefit from it in different ways, and [asylum seekers should] not just be seen as a drain. (Personal interview 3 April 2019)

Building on the experience of receiving asylum seekers and refugees, economic and family migration should be increased gradually, to allow communities time to adjust to new residents. The Scottish government could translate its regional differentiation plans for the UK system into a system that awards more points for settlement in remote and underpopulated areas within Scotland. The Rural Visa Pilot proposed by the SNP would be a good start. Based on visa applications, social funding could anticipate population change, rather than reacting to it, in order to give local authorities time to invest in the housing and infrastructure required to host new populations. A priority of any independent or highly devolved system should be avoiding the conditions in other European states that have mobilised publics against immigration and migrants. Change must be gradual and anticipated with appropriate resources and services.

What Can Be Learned from the Scottish Experience?

Some elements of the Scottish experience will not be replicated anywhere else, but identical conditions are not necessary to translate important lessons from Scotland. First, the Scottish case clearly demonstrates the power of an elite-led marriage of national and cosmopolitan identities. Defining national identity with reference to political values and avoiding ethnic- or conflict-oriented identities allows a political community to be diversity-acceptant. Defining the national interest as requiring the participation of immigrants and other international actors reinforces an outward-looking cosmopolitanism. It also allows for the development of political consensus that avoids the politicisation of immigration and the xenophobic attitudes that accompany politicisation. Relatedly, the civic nationalism advanced by the SNP illustrates that nationalism can be leveraged to promote modern democratic values and should not automatically be rejected as parochial.

The way Scottish political actors have pursued their interest in immigration demonstrates the power sub-state political entities can have, even when their interests challenge some of the most fundamental tenets of state sovereignty. Though the Scottish government has not yet achieved its ultimate goal of control over immigrant entry, it has worked within its existing powers to make substantial progress towards developing an international reputation and articulating policy objectives to make Scotland an attractive destination. At a time when many state governments suffer from political sclerosis, Scotland's successes endorse alternative sites of governance beyond and within the state as productive areas for policy advocacy, development, and implementation. The sites that could follow Scotland's example need not be nations, and could be any community with a unique political system, including states in a federal system, cities, regions, international organisations, or corporations.

Finally, this chapter's recommendations for attracting migrants and maintaining a diversity-acceptant culture can be implemented anywhere. Scotland has an advantage in that it is just starting to diversify, which means it can pre-empt many of the social conflicts about immigration. However, even where anti-immigrant sentiment is pervasive, each generation provides a new opportunity to engineer a social context that welcomes those who will make the community more acceptant, resilient, and successful.

Note

1. Unfortunately for Scotland, climate also plays a role in attracting migrants, and regions with mild winters exercise a pull effect (Rodríguez-Pose and Ketterer 2012).

APPENDICES

Appendix A
Parties represented in Westminster's House of Commons in 2019

Party	Ideological positioning	Seats	% seats	Vote share
Conservative Party	Centre-right	365	56.1	43.6
Labour Party	Centre-left	203	31.2	32.2
Scottish National Party	Centre-left/catch-all	48	7.4	3.9
Liberal Democrats	Centre/centre-left	11	1.7	11.5
Democratic Unionist Party	Centre-right/right-wing	8	1.2	0.8
Sinn Féin	Centre-left/left-wing	7	1.1	0.6
Plaid Cymru	Centre-left/left-wing	4	1	0.5
Social Democratic and Labour Party	Centre-left	2		0.4
Green Party	Left-wing	1		2.7
Alliance Party	Centre/centre-left	1		0.4

Appendix B
Parties Represented in Holyrood in 2021

Party	Ideological positioning	Constitutional position	Ideology	Total seats	% seats	% constituency and regional vote
Scottish National Party	Centre-left/catch-all	Scottish independence	Independence within the EU; socially democratic; progressive personal taxation; pro-European	64	49.6	47.7 40.3
Scottish Conservative and Unionist Party	Centre-right	Unionist	Economic liberalism; opposed to a second independence referendum; advocates for strong but limited government and less governmental interference and more personal responsibility in decision making; advocates localism and low taxation	31	24.0	21.9 23.5
Scottish Labour	Centre-left	Unionist	Social democracy; democratic socialism; opposed to a second independence referendum; £10 real living wage; increase public services, protect small businesses; increase funding for the National Health Service in Scotland through taxing the richest; focus on diplomacy and peaceful solutions to global conflicts	22	17.1	21.6 17.9
Scottish Green Party	Centre-left/left-wing	Scottish independence	Scottish independence; pro-European; environmentalism; support for communitarian economic policies; support for proportional representation; progressive on social policies; opposed to nuclear power	8	6.2	1.3 8.1
Scottish Liberal Democrats	Centre/centre-left	Unionist	Believes the Scottish Parliament should exercise greater responsibility on fiscal matters; tolerance of social diversity; supports proportional representation for public election; internationalism; greater involvement in the EU; supports more power for the Scottish Parliament within a federal Britain; pro-European	4	3.1	6.9 5.1

Appendix C
Monthly brand reach of newspapers in Great Britain, October–September 2018

Newspaper	Circulation
Qualities	
The Guardian	23,473
The Telegraph	22,539
The Independent	18,493
The Times	8,250
i	4,764
Mid-market	
The Mail	26,766
The Express	14,281
Popular/Tabloids	
The Sun	29,488
The Mirror	21,992
Metro	21,464
The Evening Standard	13,397
The Daily Star	6,700
The Daily Record	4,296
Regional	
The Scotsman (Scotland)	2,317
The Yorkshire Post	1,211
The Herald (Scotland)	910
The Press and Journal (northern Scotland)	689
The Courier (Dundee, Scotland)	580
The Sunday Post (Scotland)	547

Source: PAMCo 2018

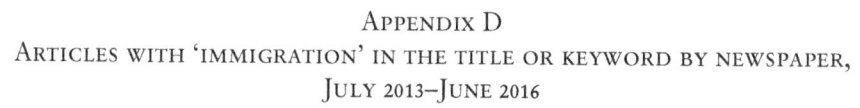

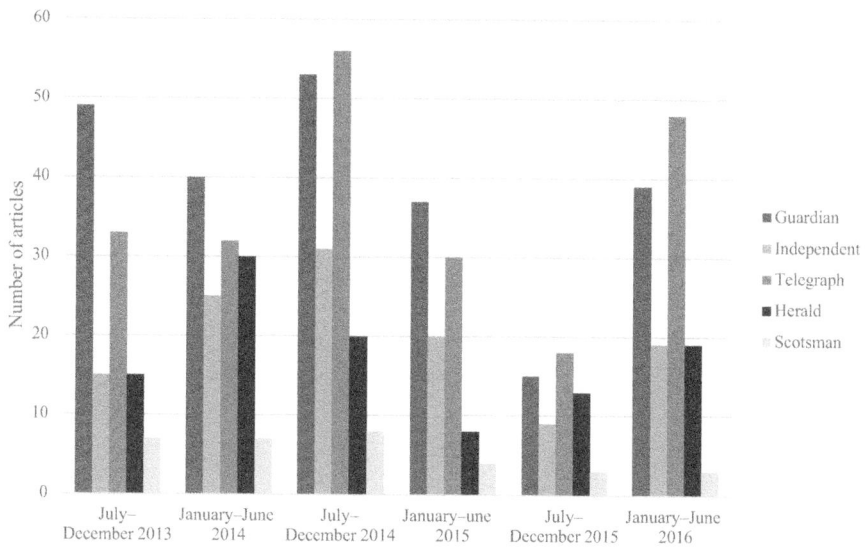

Appendix D
Articles with 'immigration' in the title or keyword by newspaper, July 2013–June 2016

Appendix E
Correlation table of attitudes towards minoritised groups and diversity

	1	2	3	4	5	6	7
1 Immigrants make Scotland better	1						
2 Identity threat – Muslims	−0.50	1					
3 Identity threat – East Europeans	−0.52	0.87	1				
4 Identity threat – Blacks and Asians	−0.50	0.87	0.90	1			
5 Minorities take jobs	−0.54	0.60	0.62	0.61	1		
6 Migrants take jobs	−0.51	0.57	0.62	0.58	0.89	1	
7 Live in diversity	0.37	−0.41	−0.42	−0.41	−0.39	−0.42	1
8 Combat prejudice	0.33	−0.37	−0.37	−0.35	−0.36	−0.35	0.29

Source: 2015 Scottish Social Attitudes Survey (ScotCen Social Research 2017)

Appendix F
Principle component factor analysis of attitudes towards minoritised groups and diversity in Scotland (varimax rotation)

	1 Factor loading	2 Factor loading
Immigrants make Scotland better	0.403	−0.420
Identity threat – Muslims	**0.851**	0.308
Identity threat – East Europeans	**0.865**	0.344
Identity threat – Blacks and Asians	**0.879**	0.316
Minorities take jobs	0.387	**0.835**
Migrants take jobs	0.365	**0.837**
Live in diversity	−0.332	−0.213
Combat prejudice	−0.294	−0.264

Appendix G
Ordered probit model of Scottish attitudes towards immigrants and minoritised groups

	People from outside GB make Scotland a better place	Identity threat index	Economic threat index
Nationalism			
Scottish ID > British ID	−0.113 (0.124)	0.057 (0.119)	0.096 (0.120)
British ID > Scottish ID	−0.001 (0.167)	−0.029 (0.158)	0.114 (0.162)
Scottish independence	−0.002 (0.125)	−0.085 (0.119)	−0.083 (0.121)
Cosmopolitan values			
Stay in EU	0.136 (0.115)	−0.507 (0.111)*	−0.325 (0.111)*
Live in diversity	0.283 (0.063)*	−0.326 (0.060)*	−0.327 (0.061)*
Religious liberties	0.112 (0.019)*	−0.072 (0.018)*	−0.108 (0.018)*
No prejudice	0.552 (0.132)*	−0.560 (0.125)*	−0.571 (0.126)*
Political determinants			
Political interest	0.178 (0.048)*	−0.132 (0.046)*	0.044 (0.046)
Conservative Party	−0.001 (0.224)	0.139 (0.214)	−0.179 (0.218)
Labour Party	0.171 (0.203)	−0.153 (0.194)	−0.127 (0.198)
Liberal Democrats	−0.014 (0.301)	−0.042 (0.285)	−0.021 (0.297)
Green Party	1.241 (0.196)*	−0.655 (0.360)	−0.847 (0.372)*
SNP	0.241 (0.196)	−0.188 (0.186)	−0.229 (0.192)
Media consumption			
Newspaper readership	−0.030 (0.106)	0.012 (0.101)	−0.110 (0.103)
Internet news	−0.034 (0.021)	0.024 (0.020)	0.021 (0.021)
Economic determinants			
Income	0.025 (0.010)*	−0.006 (0.010)	−0.013 (0.010)
Intermediate occupation†	0.136 (0.182)	−0.155 (0.174)	−0.033 (0.177)

	People from outside GB make Scotland a better place	Identity threat index	Economic threat index
Small owner†	−0.432 (0.205)*	0.084 (0.195)	0.148 (0.197)
Lower occupation†	−0.573 (0.172)*	−0.001 (0.165)	0.136 (0.165)
Routine occupation†	−0.221 (0.151)	0.195 (0.145)	0.332 (0.147)*
Scottish standard of life	−0.028 (0.050)	−0.033 (0.047)	0.054 (0.048)
Scottish economy	−0.004 (0.053)	−0.056 (0.051)	−0.011 (0.052)
Sociological determinants			
Education	0.075 (0.035)*	−0.085 (0.034)*	−0.071 (0.035)*
Female	−0.127 (0.102)	−0.029 (0.097)	−0.042 (0.099)
Age	0.076 (0.033)*	0.065 (0.032)*	0.068 (0.032)*
Diverse friends	0.088 (0.071)	0.020 (0.067)	−0.020 (0.069)
Small town‡	−0.087 (0.126)	0.073 (0.120)	0.002 (0.122)
Rural‡	0.238 (0.136)	−0.042 (0.129)	−0.090 (0.131)
N	519	520	514
Pseudo R^2	0.20	0.12	0.14

Notes: * $p<0.05$
† Reference categories: employers/managers/professional
‡ Reference category: urban

Appendix H
Survey variable descriptions

	Variable	Coding	N UK Scotland	Mean (SD) UK Scotland
Dependent variables	Migrants have positive impact on culture (BSAS only)	*Does migration generally undermine/enrich British cultural life?* 0=Cultural life undermined 5=Neither 10=Cultural life enriched	2,144	4.72 (2.81)
	Migrants have positive impact on economy (BSAS only)	*Is migration generally good/bad for the economy?* 0=Extremely bad for the economy 5=Neither 10=Extremely good for the economy	2,148	4.85 (2.69)
	People from outside GB make Scotland a better place (SSAS only)	0=Disagree strongly 1=Disagree 2=Neither agree nor disagree 3=Agree 4=Agree strongly	1,275	2.22 (0.92)
	Identity threat index (SSAS only)	Index of three variables: 'Scotland would begin to lose its identity if more [Muslims/people from East Europe/Black and Asian people] came to live in Scotland' 0=Disagree strongly 1=Disagree 2=Neither agree nor disagree 3=Agree 4=Agree strongly x 3, resulting in an index from 0 to 12	1,272	6.12 (3.44)
	Economic threat index (SSAS only)	Index of two variables: '[Ethnic minorities/East European migrants] take jobs from Scottish people' 0=Disagree strongly 1=Disagree 2=Neither agree nor disagree 3=Agree 4=Agree strongly x2, resulting in an index from 0 to 8	1,213	3.51 (2.35)

APPENDICES

National identity/Nationalism	Scottish ID > British ID	Identification of the respondent's national identity as 1=Scottish not British 1=More Scottish than British 0=Equally Scottish and British 0=More British than Scottish 0=British not Scottish	1,213	0.55 (0.50)
	British ID > Scottish ID	Identification of the respondent's national identity as 0=Scottish not British 0=More Scottish than British 0=Equally Scottish and British 1=More British than Scottish 1=British not Scottish	1,213	0.12 (0.33)
	Exclusive national identity (BSAS only)	Identification of the respondent's national identity as 1=Scottish/English/Welsh not British 0=More Scottish/English/Welsh than British 0=Equally Scottish/English/Welsh and British 0=More British than Scottish/English/Welsh 0=British nor Scottish/English/Welsh	3,934	0.21 (0.41)
	Exclusive British identity	Identification of the respondent's national identity as 0=Scottish not British 0=More Scottish than British 0=Equally Scottish and British 0=More British than Scottish 1=British not Scottish	3,934 1,213	0.09 (0.29) 0.07 (0.25)
	Scottish independence (SSAS only)	What is your view on how to rule Scotland? 0=Scotland should remain part of the UK without an elected parliament OR Scotland should remain part of the UK with its own elected parliament 1=Scotland should become independent	1,208	1.34 (0.60)

APPENDIX H
(CONTINUED)

Variable	Coding	N UK Scotland	Mean (SD) UK Scotland
Stay in EU	*Should Britain continue EU membership?* 0=Withdraw 1=Remain	979 1,050	0.64 (0.48) 0.71 (0.46)
Live in diversity (SSAS only)	*Would you rather live in an area with different kinds of people?* 0=Where most people are similar to you 1=Can't choose 2=With lots of different kinds of people	1,231	1.07 (0.89)
Religious liberties (SSAS only)	Index of four variables: 'Should the bank be able to insist that the employee take off his/her [turban, crucifix, veil, headscarf] while he/she is at work?' 0=Yes, definitely should 1=Yes, probably should 2=No, probably should not 3=No, probably should not (coding reversed in index)	1,213	7.52 (2.96)
No prejudice (SSAS only)	*Scotland should get rid of prejudice or not* 0=Sometimes there is good reason for people to be prejudiced against certain groups 1=Scotland should do everything it can to get rid of all kinds of prejudice	1,180	0.76 (0.43)

Cosmopolitanism

	Political interest	How much interest do you generally have in what is going on in politics? 0=None at all 1=Not very much 2=Some 3=Quite a lot 4=A great deal	4,326 1,288	2.02 (1.17) 2.17 (1.21)
Political determinants	Conservative Party	Respondent's political party identity 1=Conservative 0=All other parties	4,101 1,178	0.35 (0.48) 0.15 (0.36)
	Labour Party	Respondent's political party identity 1=Labour 0=All other parties	4,101 1,178	0.30 (0.46) 0.21 (0.41)
	Liberal Democrats	Respondent's political party identity 1=Liberal Democrats 0=All other parties	4,101 1,178	0.05 (0.22) 0.04 (0.20)
	Green Party	Respondent's political party identity 1=Green Party 0=All other parties	4,101 1,178	0.03 (0.18) 0.02 (0.15)
	SNP	Respondent's political party identity 1=Scottish National Party 0=All other parties	4,101 1,178	0.03 (0.18) 0.45 (0.50)

Appendix H
(Continued)

<table>
<tr><th colspan="2"></th><th>Variable</th><th>Coding</th><th>N
UK
Scotland</th><th>Mean (SD)
UK
Scotland</th></tr>
<tr><td rowspan="3">Media consumption</td><td></td><td>Newspaper readership</td><td>Do you regularly read one or more daily morning newspaper?
0=No
1=Yes</td><td>4,328

1,288</td><td>0.31
(0.46)
0.38
(0.49)</td></tr>
<tr><td></td><td>TV news
(BSAS only)</td><td>How often do you watch all or part of a news programme on television?
0=Never
1=Less often than once a month
2=Once a month
3=A couple of times a month
4=At least once a week
5=Several times a week
6=Every day
7=Several times a day</td><td>4,328</td><td>5.04
(1.94)</td></tr>
<tr><td></td><td>Web news</td><td>How often, it at all, do you look online at a news or newspaper website?
0=Never
1=Less often than once a month
2=Once a month
3=A couple of times a month
4=At least once a week
5=Several times a week
6=Every day
7=Several times a day</td><td>4,328

1,288</td><td>2.91
(2.81)
3.21
(2.83)</td></tr>
</table>

APPENDICES

Economic determinants	Income	Income of your household from all sources before tax, including benefits and savings – ordinal variable	3,582	9.63 (5.99)
	Intermediate occupation	0=All other occupational status	1,070	9.39 (5.78)
		1=Intermediate occupational status	4,164	0.13 (0.33)
			1,204	0.10 (0.30)
	Small owner	0=All other occupational status	4,164	0.09 (0.29)
		1=Small owner occupational status	1,204	0.09 (0.29)
	Lower occupation	0=All other occupational status	4,164	0.13 (0.33)
		1=Lower supervisory or technical occupational status	1,204	0.13 (0.33)
	Routine occupation	0=All other occupational status	4,164	0.30 (0.46)
		1=Routine occupational status	1,204	0.30 (0.46)
	Scottish standard of life (SSAS only)	Has the standard of living in Scotland increased or fallen in the last 12 months? 0=Fallen a lot 1=Fallen a little 2=Stayed the same 3=Increased a little 4=Increased a lot	1,147	3.03 (1.04)
	Scottish economy (SSAS only)	Has Scotland's economy got stronger or weaker in the last 12 months? 0=A lot weaker 1=A little weaker 2=Stayed the same 3=A little stronger 4=A lot stronger	1,153	1.85 (0.95)

APPENDIX H
(CONTINUED)

	Variable	Coding	N UK Scotland	Mean (SD) UK Scotland
Sociological determinants	Education	*Highest educational qualification obtained* 0=No qualification 1=Standard grades 4–7 2=Standard grades 1–3 3=Highers/A levels or equivalent 4=Higher educ below degree 5=First degree 6=Postgraduate degree	4,225 1,260	2.67 (1.93) *2.76 (1.92)*
	Female	0=Not female 1=Female	4,328 1,288	0.56 (0.50) *0.55 (0.50)*
	Age	*Age in years, categorised* <=34 35–44 45–54 55–60 60–64 >=65	4,328 1,288	2.49 (1.92) *2.63 (1.89)*
	Diverse friends (SSAS only)	0=No Muslim or ethnically different friends 1=Either Muslim or ethnically different friends 2=Both Muslim and ethnically different friends	1,231	0.51 (0.70)
	Small town	0=All other settlements 1=Settlements of between 3,000 and 10,000 people	1,126	0.21 (0.41)
	Rural	0=All other settlements 1=Settlements of fewer than 3,000 people	1,126	0.17 (0.37)

Source: 2015 British Social Attitudes Survey (NatCen Social Research 2017); 2015 Scottish Social Attitudes Survey (ScotCen Social Research 2017)

Appendix I
Truncated ordered probit model of Scottish attitudes towards immigrants and minorities

	People from outside GB make Scotland a better place	Identity threat index	Economic threat index
Nationalism			
Scottish ID > British ID	−0.276 (0.105)*	0.256 (0.102)*	0.185 (0.103)
British ID > Scottish ID	−0.004 (0.149)	0.025 (0.143)	0.089 (0.145)
Scottish independence	0.210 (0.107)*	−0.222 (0.103)*	−0.145 (0.105)
Political determinants			
Political interest	0.200 (0.042)*	−0.133 (0.040)*	−0.078 (0.040)
Conservative Party	−0.023 (0.190)	0.206 (0.184)	−0.148 (0.185)
Labour Party	0.287 (0.169)	−0.321 (0.163)*	−0.417 (0.165)*
Liberal Democrats	0.279 (0.272)	−0.260 (0.260)	−0.422 (0.269)
Green Party	1.412 (0.343)*	−0.938 (0.329)*	−1.354 (0.349)*
SNP	0.244 (0.161)	−0.223 (0.155)	−0.326 (0.158)*
Media consumption			
Newspaper readership	0.025 (0.093)	−0.111 (0.089)	−0.094 (0.091)
Internet news	−0.012 (0.018)	0.003 (0.018)	−0.002 (0.018)
Economic determinants[†]			
Income	0.013 (0.009)	−0.009 (0.009)	−0.009 (0.009)
Intermediate occupation	0.085 (0.160)	−0.186 (0.155)	−0.028 (0.156)
Small owner	−0.552 (0.173)*	0.348 (0.165)*	0.397 (0.166)*
Lower occupation	−0.647 (0.151)*	0.243 (0.145)	0.309 (0.145)*
Routine occupation	−0.227 (0.131)	0.307 (0.127)*	0.402 (0.128)*
Scottish standard of life	−0.024 (0.043)	−0.025 (0.041)	0.029 (0.042)
Scottish economy	0.083 (0.046)	−0.120 (0.044)*	−0.106 (0.045)*
Sociological determinants			
Education	0.120 (0.032)*	−0.104 (0.031)*	−0.093 (0.031)*
Female	−0.036 (0.089)	−0.105 (0.086)	−0.099 (0.087)
Age	0.059 (0.029)*	0.050 (0.027)	0.052 (0.028)
Diverse friends	0.190 (0.062)*	−0.103 (0.059)	−0.173 (0.060)*
Small town	−0.143 (0.109)	0.023 (0.105)	−0.027 (0.106)
Rural	0.157 (0.120)	−0.063 (0.115)	−0.058 (0.116)
N	644	643	639
Pseudo R^2	0.11	0.06	0.06

Notes: * $p<0.05$
[†] Reference categories: employers/managers/professional/urban

Appendix J
Percentage of pro-immigrant responses by urban/rural classification

	% agreeing or strongly agreeing that immigrants make Scotland a better place	% disagreeing or strongly disagreeing that Scotland would lose its identity if more Muslims, East Europeans, and Black and Asian people came to live in Scotland	% disagreeing or strongly disagreeing that ethnic minorities and East European migrants take jobs from Scottish people
Large urban areas	40	35	47
Other urban areas	40	33	40
Accessible small town	36	36	38
Remote small town	30	34	41
Accessible rural	47	39	45
Remote rural	39	34	38

Source: 2015 Scottish Social Attitudes Survey (ScotCen Social Research 2017)

Appendix K
Percentage of pro-immigrant responses by Scottish administrative area

	Persons per square km	Number of 2015 SSAS participants	% agreeing or strongly agreeing that immigrants make Scotland a better place	% disagreeing or strongly disagreeing that Scotland would lose its identity if more Muslims, East Europeans, and Black and Asian people came to live in Scotland	% disagreeing or strongly disagreeing that ethnic minorities and East European migrants take jobs from Scottish people
Aberdeen City	1,240	46	39	41	57
Aberdeenshire	41	98	28	21	33
Angus	54	49	59	27	33
Argyll and Bute	13	40	15	38	41
Clackmannanshire	323	11	36	9	36
Dumfries and Galloway	23	41	46	44	51
Dundee City	2,477	23	13	17	27
East Ayrshire	97	50	20	22	24
East Dunbartonshire	613	43	40	37	53
East Lothian	152	42	45	29	44
East Renfrewshire	533	9	44	33	56
Edinburgh, City of	1,894	60	59	43	54
Eilean Siar	9	23	27	17	20
Falkirk	533	39	53	38	49
Fife	278	51	39	35	35
Glasgow City	3,471	71	35	34	50
Highland	9	86	39	29	45
Inverclyde	495				
Midlothian	247	41	34	41	38
Moray	43	15	53	40	47
North Ayrshire	154	22	50	41	45
North Lanarkshire	720	101	32	34	32
Orkney Islands	22				
Perth and Kinross	28	58	32	36	48
Renfrewshire	668	17	53	59	60
Scottish Borders	24	31	52	39	57
Shetland Islands	16	15	53	53	57
South Ayrshire	92	40	38	23	32
South Lanarkshire	178	118	42	38	44
Stirling	42				
West Dunbartonshire	564	13	25	31	50
West Lothian	417	11	64	82	80
Average			39	34	42

Note: Bold numbers indicate percentages above the average
Source: 2015 Scottish Social Attitudes Survey (ScotCen Social Research 2017)

Appendix L
Ordered probit model of attitudes towards immigrants and minoritised groups in the UK

	BSAS Migrants have positive impact on culture	BSAS Migrants have positive impact on economy
National identity		
Exclusively English identity	−0.327 (0.101)*	−0.182 (0.101)
Exclusively British identity	0.106 (0.125)	0.241 (0.126)
Political determinants		
Stay in EU	0.495 (0.088)*	0.460 (0.089)*
Political Interest	0.221 (0.043)*	0.281 (0.043)*
Conservative Party	0.148 (0.140)	0.139 (0.141)
Labour Party	0.303 (0.141)*	0.323 (0.141)*
Liberal Democrats	0.779 (0.219)*	0.755 (0.221)*
Green Party	0.369 (0.233)	0.676 (0.239)*
UKIP	−0.341 (0.193)	−0.081 (0.192)
SNP	0.647 (0.307)*	0.531 (0.308)
Media consumption		
Newspaper readership	0.119 (0.086)	0.141 (0.087)
TV news	−0.068 (0.024)*	−0.053 (0.024)*
Internet news	−0.008 (0.017)	−0.004 (0.017)
Economic determinants		
Income	0.001 (0.009)	0.014 (0.009)
Intermediate occupation†	−0.171 (0.134)	−0.139 (0.134)
Small owner†	0.279 (0.148)	0.258 (0.149)
Lower supervisory/technical occupation†	−0.154 (0.135)	−0.232 (0.135)
Routine occupation†	−0.184 (0.126)	−0.167 (0.127)
Sociological determinants		
Education	0.044 (0.028)	0.064 (0.029)*
Female	0.040 (0.082)	−0.090 (0.083)
Age	−0.039 (0.027)	−0.005 (0.027)
Region		
Scotland	−0.101 (0.184)	0.078 (0.185)
Wales	−0.279 (0.184)	−0.306 (0.185)
N	701	698
Pseudo R^2	0.06	0.08

Notes: * $p<0.05$
 † Reference categories: employers/managers/professional

Source: 2015 British Social Attitudes Survey (NatCen Social Research 2017)

Appendix M
Ordered Probit Model of Attitudes towards Immigrants and Minoritised Groups in England and Scotland

	BSAS Migrants have positive impact on culture (English)	SSAS Identity threat index	BSAS Migrants have positive impact on economy (English)	SSAS Economic threat index
National identity				
Exclusive national identity	−0.358 (0.109)*	0.094 (0.095)	−0.120 (0.109)	0.236 (0.098)*
Exclusive British identity	0.119 (0.131)	−0.200 (0.152)	0.227 (0.132)	−0.289 (0.157)
Political determinants				
Stay in EU	0.526 (0.092)*	−0.647 (0.090)*	0.514 (0.093)*	−0.453 (0.091)*
Political Interest	0.222 (0.046)*	−0.191 (0.037)*	0.291 (0.046)*	−0.137 (0.038)*
Conservative Party	0.161 (0.148)	0.263 (0.165)	0.124 (0.149)	−0.060 (0.171)
Labour Party	0.312 (0.152)*	−0.109 (0.157)	0.320 (0.153)*	−0.147 (0.164)
Liberal Democrats	0.791 (0.231)*	−0.162 (0.225)	0.665 (0.232)*	−0.146 (0.233)
Green Party	0.322 (0.246)	−0.456 (0.289)	0.577 (0.251)*	−0.852 (0.301)*
UKIP	−0.332 (0.203)	−0.201 (0.142)	−0.105 (0.202)	−0.250 (0.149)
SNP		−0.201 (0.142)		−0.250 (0.149)
Media consumption				
Newspaper readership	0.117 (0.092)	−0.047 (0.085)	0.190 (0.093)*	−0.086 (0.088)
TV news	−0.050 (0.026)*		−0.048 (0.026)	
Internet news	−0.014 (0.018)	0.0004 (0.02)	−0.008 (0.018)	−0.003 (0.017)
Economic determinants				
Income	−0.003 (0.010)	−0.001 (0.008)	0.011 (0.010)	−0.010 (0.009)
Intermediate occupation†	−0.180 (0.144)	−0.137 (0.147)	−0.190 (0.144)	0.077 (0.148)
Small owner†	0.304 (0.155)	0.261 (0.149)	0.252 (0.156)	0.237 (0.152)
Lower occupation†	−0.157 (0.146)	0.172 (0.136)	−0.157 (0.147)	0.225 (0.138)
Routine occupation†	−0.166 (0.135)	0.215 (0.118)	−0.114 (0.135)	0.282 (0.121)*
Sociological determinants				
Education	0.061 (0.030)*	−0.084 (0.027)*	0.091 (0.031)*	−0.084 (0.028)*
Female	0.041 (0.089)	−0.098 (0.080)	−0.049 (0.089)	−0.095 (0.082)
Age	−0.042 (0.029)	0.072 (0.025)*	−0.008 (0.029)	0.077 (0.026)*
N	610	723	607	695
Pseudo R^2	0.07	0.07	0.08	0.07

Notes: * $p<0.05$
† Reference categories: employers/managers/professional

Source: 2015 British Social Attitudes Survey (NatCen Social Research 2017); 2015 Scottish Social Attitudes Survey (ScotCen Social Research 2017)

Appendix N
The Anholt Ipsos Nation Brands Index

The NBI examines the images of around 50 nations each year, by conducting online interviews with 20,000 adults aged 18 and over, in 20 core panel countries (1,000 per panel country).

Nation branding is evaluated along the following dimensions:

- **Exports:** The public's image of products and services from each country and the extent to which consumers proactively seek or avoid products from each country of origin.
- **Governance:** Public opinion about national government competency and fairness, as well as its perceived commitment to global issues such as peace and security, justice, poverty, and the environment.
- **Culture and heritage:** Global perceptions of each nation's heritage and appreciation for its contemporary culture, including film, music, art, sport, and literature.
- **People:** The population's reputation for competence, openness and friendliness, and other qualities such as tolerance.
- **Tourism:** The level of interest in visiting a country and the draw of natural and man-made tourist attractions.
- **Investment and immigration:** The power to attract people to live, work, or study in each country and how people perceive a country's quality of life and business environment.

For 2018, the measured nations were:

- **North America:** Canada, the US
- **Western Europe:** Austria, Belgium, Denmark, Finland, France, Germany, Greece, Ireland, Italy, the Netherlands, Northern Ireland, Norway, Scotland, Spain, Sweden, Switzerland, Belgium, the UK
- **Central/Eastern Europe:** Croatia, Czech Republic, Hungary, Poland, Russia, Turkey, Ukraine
- **Asia-Pacific:** Australia, China, India, Indonesia, Japan, New Zealand, Singapore, South Korea, Taiwan, Thailand
- **Latin America/Caribbean:** Argentina, Brazil, Chile, Colombia, Jamaica, Mexico, Peru
- **Middle East/Africa:** Egypt, Kenya, Nigeria, Qatar, Saudi Arabia, South Africa, United Arab Emirates

The core panel countries were:

- **North America:** Canada, the US
- **Western Europe:** France, Germany, Italy, Sweden, the UK, Scotland (additional country – 500 interviews)
- **Central/Eastern Europe:** Poland, Russia, Turkey
- **Asia-Pacific:** Australia, China, India, Japan, South Korea
- **Latin America/Caribbean:** Argentina, Brazil, Mexico
- **Middle East/Africa:** Egypt, South Africa

BIBLIOGRAPHY

Ager, Alastair, and Alison Strang. 2008. 'Understanding Integration: A Conceptual Framework.' *Journal of Refugee Studies* 21, no. 2 (June): 166–91. <https://doi.org/10.1093/jrs/fen016>.

Alesina, Alberto, Edward Glaeser, and Bruce Sacerdote. 2001. 'Why Doesn't the US Have a European-Style Welfare System?' Working Paper. Working Paper Series. National Bureau of Economic Research, October. <https://doi.org/10.3386/w8524>.

Alexander, Colin. 2014. 'Sub-state Public Diplomacy in Africa: The Case of the Scottish Government's Engagement with Malawi.' *Place Branding and Public Diplomacy* 10, no. 1 (February): 70–86. <https://doi.org/10.1057/pb.2013.29>.

Alfano, Marco, Christian Dustmann, and Tommaso Frattini. 2016. 'Immigration and the UK: Reflections after Brexit.' *SSRN Electronic Journal*. <https://doi.org/10.2139/ssrn.2900373>.

Allport, Gordon Willard. 1954. *The Nature of Prejudice.* New York: Doubleday.

Anderson, Benedict. 2006. *Imagined Communities: Reflections on the Origin and Spread of Nationalism.* London: Verso Books.

Anderson, Bridget. 2015. '"Heads I Win. Tails You Lose." Migration and the Worker Citizen.' *Current Legal Problems* 68, no. 1 (January): 179–96. <https://doi.org/10.1093/clp/cuv012>.

Anderson, Christopher J., and Aida Paskeviciute. 2006. 'How Ethnic and Linguistic Heterogeneity Influence the Prospects for Civil Society: A Comparative Study of Citizenship Behavior.' *The Journal of Politics* 68, no. 4 (November): 783–802. <https://doi.org/10.1111/j.1468-2508.2006.00470.x>.

Anderson, Kirsten. 2013. 'Education, Immigration and Integration in Scotland.' *Policy Scotland* (blog). <https://policyscotland.gla.ac.uk/education-immigration-integration/>.

Anderson, Michael. 2018. *Scotland's Populations from the 1850s to Today.* Oxford: Oxford University Press. <http://www.oxfordscholarship.com.ezproxy.is.ed.ac.uk/view/10.1093/oso/9780198805830.001.0001/oso-9780198805830>.

Arendt, Hannah. 1973. *The Origins of Totalitarianism*. New York: Harcourt Brace Jovanovich.

Arrighi de Casanova, Jean-Thomas. 2014. 'Managing Immigration in a Multinational Context. Border Struggles and Nation-Building in Contemporary Scotland and Catalonia.' In *The Politics of Immigration in Multi-level States: Governance and Political Parties*, edited by Eve Hepburn and Ricard Zapata-Barrero, 108–29. Palgrave Politics of Identity and Citizenship Series. London: Palgrave Macmillan. <https://doi.org/10.1057/9781137358530_6>.

Asari, Eva-Maria, Daphne Halikiopoulou, and Steven Mock. 2008. 'British National Identity and the Dilemmas of Multiculturalism.' *Nationalism and Ethnic Politics* 14, no. 1 (March): 1–28. <https://doi.org/10.1080/13537110701872444>.

Axt, Jordan R. 2017. 'The Best Way to Measure Explicit Racial Attitudes Is to Ask about Them:' *Social Psychological and Personality Science*, 4 October. <https://doi.org/10.1177/1948550617728995>.

Baker, Paul, Costas Gabrielatos, Majid KhosraviNik, Michał Krzyżanowski, Tony McEnery, Ruth Wodak. 2008. 'A Useful Methodological Synergy? Combining Critical Discourse Analysis and Corpus Linguistics to Examine Discourses of Refugees and Asylum Seekers in the UK Press.' *Discourse & Society* 19, no. 3: 273–306. <https://doi.org/10.1177/0957926508088962>.

Balch, Alex, and Ekaterina Balabanova. 2016. 'Ethics, Politics and Migration: Public Debates on the Free Movement of Romanians and Bulgarians in the UK, 2006–2013.' *Politics* 36, no. 1 (February): 19–35. <https://doi.org/10.1111/1467-9256.12082>.

Bale, Tim. 2014. 'Putting It Right? The Labour Party's Big Shift on Immigration since 2010.' *The Political Quarterly* 85, no. 3: 296–303. <https://doi.org/10.1111/1467-923X.12091>.

Bale, Tim. 2018. 'Who Leads and Who Follows? The Symbiotic Relationship between UKIP and the Conservatives – and Populism and Euroscepticism.' *Politics* 38, no. 3 (1 August): 263–77. <https://doi.org/10.1177/0263395718754718>.

Banducci, Susan, and Chris Hanretty. 2014. 'Comparative Determinants of Horse-Race Coverage.' *European Political Science Review* 6, no. 4 (November): 621–40. <https://doi.org/10.1017/S1755773913000271>.

Bansak, Kirk, Jens Hainmueller, and Dominik Hangartner. 2016. 'How Economic, Humanitarian, and Religious Concerns Shape European Attitudes toward Asylum Seekers.' *Science*, 22 September, aag2147. <https://doi.org/10.1126/science.aag2147>.

Barclay, Andrew, Robert Ford, and Maria Sobolewska. 2019. 'The 2010 Ethnic Minority British Election Study.' Mendeley Data, Version 1, 2 August. doi: 10.17632/kzj2c23frp.1.

Bardell, Hannah. 2015. 'Maiden Speech.' Presented at the Scotland Bill (Second Reading), 6 August. <https://publications.parliament.uk/pa/cm201516/cmhansrdcm150608/debtext/150608-0003.htm#15060821000110>.

Barklay, Nicola, and Tammy Swift-Adams. 2018. 'Delivering More Homes for Scotland: Barriers and Solutions.' Homes for Scotland. <https://www.homesforscotland.com/Portals/HomesForScotland/Publications/HFS%20Solutions%20Paper.pdf>.

Barrett, David. 2015. 'BBC "Bias" Hinders Immigration Crackdown, Says Report.' *The Telegraph*, 12 February. <https://www.telegraph.co.uk/news/uknews/immigration/11406531/BBC-bias-hinders-immigration-crackdown-says-report.html>.

Barrio, Astrid, Oscar Barberà, and Juan Rodríguez-Teruel. 2018. '"Spain Steals from Us!" The "Populist Drift" of Catalan Regionalism.' *Comparative European Politics* 16, no. 6 (1 November): 993–1011. <https://doi.org/10.1057/s41295-018-0140-3>.

Baumgartner, Frank, Brian Jones, and Beth Leech. 1997. 'Media Attention and Congressional Agendas.' In *Do the Media Govern? Politicians, Voters and Reporters in America*, edited by Shanto Iyengar and Richard Reeves, 349–63. Thousand Oaks, CA: SAGE.

BBC News. 2004. 'McConnell's Legislative Speech.' *BBC News*, 7 September, sec. Scotland. <http://news.bbc.co.uk/2/hi/uk_news/scotland/3634150.stm>.

BBC News. 2014. 'Scottish Referendum: Scotland Votes "No" to Independence.' *BBC News*, 19 September, sec. Scotland. <https://www.bbc.com/news/uk-scotland-29270441>.

BBC News. 2015a. 'Nicola Sturgeon: Scotland Ready to Take 1,000 Refugees.' *BBC News*, 4 September, sec. Scotland Politics. <https://www.bbc.com/news/uk-scotland-scotland-politics-34146653>.

BBC News. 2015b. 'Theresa May Pledges Asylum Reform and Immigration Crackdown.' *BBC News*, 6 October, sec. Politics. <https://www.bbc.com/news/uk-politics-34450887>.

BBC News. 2016. 'Brain Family Can Stay in UK Says Home Office.' *BBC News*, 21 September, sec. Highlands & Islands. <https://www.bbc.com/news/uk-scotland-highlands-islands-37421599>.

BBC News. 2017. 'Global Search to Tackle Teacher Shortage.' *BBC News*, 4 February, sec. Scotland. <https://www.bbc.com/news/uk-scotland-38867669>.

BBC News. 2018a. 'Fruit "Left to Rot" Due to Labour Shortages.' *BBC News*, 20 July, sec. Tayside & Central. <https://www.bbc.com/news/uk-scotland-tayside-central-44884882>.

BBC News. 2018b. 'New Strategy for Helping Refugees.' *BBC News*, 10 January, sec. Scotland. <https://www.bbc.co.uk/news/uk-scotland-glasgow-west-42612226>.

BBC News. 2019. 'European Elections 2019: Nicola Sturgeon Says Scotland Can Stay in EU.' *BBC News*, 17 May, sec. Scotland Politics. <https://www.bbc.com/news/uk-scotland-scotland-politics-48307775>.
BBC News. 2020. '"Empathy" for Scotland Joining the EU, Says Tusk.' *BBC News*, 2 February, sec. Scotland Politics. <https://www.bbc.com/news/uk-scotland-scotland-politics-51342714>.
Bechhofer, Frank, David McCrone, Richard Kiely, and Robert Stewart. 1999. 'Constructing National Identity: Arts and Landed Elites in Scotland.' *Sociology* 33, no. 3: 515–34. <http://www.jstor.org/stable/42857960>.
Berry, John W. 1997. 'Immigration, Acculturation, and Adaptation.' *Applied Psychology* 46, no. 1: 5–34. <https://doi.org/10.1111/j.1464-0597.1997.tb01087.x>.
Berry, M., I. Garcia-Blanco, and K. Moore. 2016. 'Press Coverage of the Refugee and Migrant Crisis in the EU: A Content Analysis of Five European Countries.' Geneva: United Nations High Commissioner for Refugees. <https://www.unhcr.org/56bb369c9.html>.
Bhandari, Kalyan. 2016. 'Imagining the Scottish Nation: Tourism and Homeland Nationalism in Scotland.' *Current Issues in Tourism* 19, no. 9 (28 July): 913–29. <https://doi.org/10.1080/13683500.2013.789005>.
Binns, Craig. 2002. 'Topic Paper: Ethnic Minorities, Asylum Seekers and Refugees.' Glasgow: GCC Housing Services.
Blackford, Ian. 2015. 'Maiden Speech.' Presented at the Debate on the Address (2nd Day), 28 May. <https://publications.parliament.uk/pa/cm201516/cmhansrd/cm150528/debtext/150528-0003.htm#15052828000923>.
Blanchflower, David G., Jumana Saleheen, and Chris Shadforth. 2007. 'The Impact of the Recent Migration from Eastern Europe on the UK Economy.' SSRN Scholarly Paper. Rochester, NY: Social Science Research Network, 1 February. <https://papers.ssrn.com/abstract=969406>.
Bleich, Erik, Hannah Stonebraker, Hasher Nisar, and Rana Abdelhamid. 2015. 'Media Portrayals of Minorities: Muslims in British Newspaper Headlines, 2001–2012.' *Journal of Ethnic and Migration Studies* 41, no. 6 (12 May): 942–62. <https://doi.org/10.1080/1369183X.2014.1002200>.
Blinder, Scott. 2013. 'Imagined Immigration: The Impact of Different Meanings of "Immigrants" in Public Opinion and Policy Debates in Britain.' *Political Studies* 63, no. 1: 80–100. <https://doi.org/10.1111/1467-9248.12053>.
Blinder, Scott, and William L. Allen. 2016. 'UK Public Opinion toward Immigration: Overall Attitudes and Level of Concern.' Oxford: Centre on Migration, Policy and Society, 28 November. <http://www.mig rationobservatory.ox.ac.uk/wp-content/uploads/2016/04 / Briefing-Public_Opinion_Immigration_Attitudes_Concern.pdf>.

Blinder, Scott, Martin Rhus, and Carlos Vargas-Silva. 2011. 'Top Ten Problems in the Evidence Base for Public Debate and Policy-Making on Immigration in the UK.' Migration Observatory. <https://migrationobservatory.ox.ac.uk/resources/reports/top-ten-problems-in-the-evidence-base-for-public-debate-and-policy-making-on-immigration-in-the-uk/>.

Blinder, Scott, and Lindsay Richards. 2020. 'UK Public Opinion toward Immigration: Overall Attitudes and Level of Concern.' Migration Observatory. <https://migrationobservatory.ox.ac.uk/resources/briefings/uk-public-opinion-toward-immigration-overall-attitudes-and-level-of-concern/>.

Bond, Ross. 2006. 'Belonging and Becoming: National Identity and Exclusion.' *Sociology* 40, no. 4 (1 August): 609–26. <https://doi.org/10.1177/0038038506065149>.

Bond, Ross. 2017a. 'Minorities and Diversity in Scotland: Evidence from the 2011 Census.' *Scottish Affairs* 26, no. 1: 23–47. <https://doi.org/10.3366/scot.2017.0162>.

Bond, Ross. 2017b. 'Multicultural Nationalism? National Identities among Minority Groups in Scotland's Census.' *Journal of Ethnic and Migration Studies* 43, no. 7 (19 May): 1121–40. <https://doi.org/10.1080/1369183X.2016.1232162>.

Bond, Ross. 2017c. 'Sub-state National Identities among Minority Groups in Britain: A Comparative Analysis of 2011 Census Data.' *Nations and Nationalism* 23, no. 3: 524–46. <https://doi.org/10.1111/nana.12253>.

Bonino, Stefano. 2018. 'The Migration and Settlement of Pakistanis and Indians.' In *New Scots: Scotland's Immigrant Communities since 1945*, edited by T. M. Devine and Angela McCarthy, 75–103. Edinburgh: Edinburgh University Press.

Bonjour, Saskia, and Betty de Hart. 2013. 'A Proper Wife, a Proper Marriage: Constructions of "Us" and "Them" in Dutch Family Migration Policy.' *European Journal of Women's Studies* 20, no. 1 (1 February): 61–76. <https://doi.org/10.1177/1350506812456459>.

Bonnar, Steven. 2020. 'Maiden Speech.' Presented at the Agriculture Bill, 2 March. <https://hansard.parliament.uk/Commons/2020-02-03/debates/CD69351D-4AAC-4DAF-AF3F-911152D8C582/AgricultureBill#contribution-BFF6891D-3338-449A-86B5-0D07D9111DB4>.

Boomgaarden, Hajo G., and Rens Vliegenthart. 2009. 'How News Content Influences Anti-immigration Attitudes: Germany, 1993–2005.' *European Journal of Political Research* 48, no. 4 (June): 516–42. <https://doi.org/10.1111/j.1475-6765.2009.01831.x>.

Boomgaarden, Hajo, and R. Vliegenthart. 2007. 'Explaining the Rise of Anti-immigrant Parties: The Role of News Media Content in the Netherlands.' *Tijdschrift Voor Communicatiewetenschappen* 26 (1 January): 404–17.

Boswell, Christina. 2007. 'Migration Control in Europe after 9/11: Explaining the Absence of Securitization.' *JCMS: Journal of Common Market Studies* 45, no. 3: 589–610. <https://doi.org/10.1111/j.1468-5965.2007.00722.x>.

Boswell, Philip. 2015. 'Maiden Speech.' Presented at the Financial Statement, and Budget Report, 7 August. <https://publications.parliament.uk/pa/cm201516/cmhansrd/cm150708/debtext/150708-0002.htm#15070837000953>.

Botterill, Kate, Peter Hopkins, Gurchathen Sanghera, and Rowena Arshad. 2016. 'Securing Disunion: Young People's Nationalism, Identities and (In)Securities in the Campaign for an Independent Scotland.' *Political Geography* 55: 124–34.

Braber, Ben. 2012. 'Immigrants.' In *The Oxford Handbook of Modern Scottish History*, edited by T. M. Devine and Jenny Wormald, 491–509. Oxford: Oxford University Press.

Brooks, Libby. 2016. 'Scotland Welcomes 1,000th Syrian Refugee.' *The Guardian*, 1 September, sec. Scotland. <https://www.theguardian.com/uk-news/2016/sep/01/scotland-celebrates-arrival-of-1000th-syrian-refugee>.

Brown, A. 2000. 'Designing the Scottish Parliament.' *Parliamentary Affairs* 53, no. 3 (1 July): 542–56. <https://doi.org/10.1093/pa/53.3.542>.

Brown, Stewart J. 1991. '"Outside the Covenant": The Scottish Presbyterian Churches and Irish Immigration, 1922–1938.' *The Innes Review* 42, no. 1: 19–45.

Brubaker, Rogers. 1992. *Citizenship and Nationhood in France and Germany*. Cambridge, MA: Harvard University Press.

Brubaker, Rogers. 1996. *Nationalism Reframed: Nationhood and the National Question in the New Europe*. Cambridge: Cambridge University Press.

Bulman, May. 2019. 'Boris Johnson Faces Accusations of Racism after Saying Migrants Should Not "Treat UK as Their Own".' *The Independent*, 9 December, sec. Home News. <https://www.independent.co.uk/news/uk/home-news/boris-johnson-eu-migrants-immigration-britain-general-election-a9238941.html>.

Cairney, Paul, Siabhainn Russell, and Emily St Denny. 2016. 'The "Scottish Approach" to Policy and Policymaking: What Issues Are Territorial and What Are Universal?' *Policy & Politics* 44, no. 3 (8 July): 333–50. <https://doi.org/10.1332/030557315X14353331264538>.

Campbell, Glenn. 2019. 'Brexit "Has Changed EU View of Scotland".' *BBC News*, 15 September, sec. Scotland Politics. <https://www.bbc.com/news/uk-scotland-scotland-politics-49690513>.

CAQ. 2020. 'Identity and Culture.' *Coalition Avenir Québec* (blog). <https://coalitionavenirquebec.org/en/blog/enjeux/identity-and-culture/>.

Card, David, Christian Dustmann, and Ian Preston. 2012. 'Immigration, Wages, and Compositional Amenities.' *Journal of the European Economic Association* 10, no. 1 (1 February): 78–119. <https://doi.org/10.1111/j.1542-4774.2011.01051.x>.

Carrell, Severin. 2012. 'Scotland's Population at a Record High.' *The Guardian*, 17 December. <https://www.theguardian.com/uk/2012/dec/17/scotland-population-record-high>.

Carrell, Severin. 2013. 'Nigel Farage Flees Barrage of Abuse from Edinburgh Protesters.' *The Guardian*, 16 May, sec. Politics. <https://www.theguardian.com/politics/2013/may/16/nigel-farage-edinburgh-protesters-van>.

Carrell, Severin. 2014a. 'Scottish Independence: Plans to Loosen Immigration Controls "Need Debate".' *The Guardian*, 24 April, sec. Politics. <https://www.theguardian.com/politics/2014/apr/24/scottish-independence-loosen-immigration-debate>.

Carrell, Severin. 2014b. 'SNP under Fire after Ukip Secures First Scottish Seat in European Parliament.' *The Guardian*, 26 May, sec. Politics. <http://www.theguardian.com/politics/2014/may/26/ukip-first-scottish-seat-european-elections>.

Carrell, Severin. 2014c. 'Theresa May Would Seek Passport Checks between Scotland and England.' *The Guardian*, 14 March. <http://www.theguardian.com/uk-news/2014/mar/14/passport-checks-needed-between-independent-scotland-and-england>.

Carrell, Severin. 2016. 'Sturgeon Accuses Gove of Lying over Scottish Immigration Quotas.' *The Guardian*, 13 June, sec. Europe. <https://www.theguardian.com/politics/2016/jun/13/nicola-sturgeon-michael-gove-scottish-immigration-quotas-snp-scottish-independence>.

Carrell, Severin. 2019. 'Scottish Labour Is Free to Campaign against Brexit, Says Corbyn.' *The Guardian*, 22 November, sec. Politics. <https://www.theguardian.com/politics/2019/nov/22/scottish-labour-free-campaign-against-brexit-jeremy-corbyn>.

Carrell, Severin. 2020. 'Scottish Tories Urge Rethink over Points-Based Immigration.' *The Guardian*, 20 February, sec. UK News. <http://www.theguardian.com/uk-news/2020/feb/20/scottish-tories-urge-rethink-over-points-based-immigration>.

Carrell, Severin, and James McEnaney. 2019. 'Housing Crisis on Arran Leaves Hundreds of Islanders without Homes.' *The Guardian*, 22 April, sec. Society. <https://www.theguardian.com/society/2019/apr/22/housing-crisis-on-arran-leaves-hundreds-of-islanders-without-homes>.

Castle, Stephen. 2020. 'U.K.'s New Immigration Rules Will Restrict Low-Skilled Workers.' *The New York Times*, 19 February, sec. World. <https://www.nytimes.com/2020/02/19/world/europe/uk-immigration-low-skilled-workers.html>.

Cavanagh, Luke, Franca Eirich, and John-Glyn McLaren. 2008. *Fresh Talent: Working in Scotland Scheme: An Evidence Review*. Edinburgh: Scottish Government.

Caviedes, Alexander. 2015. 'An Emerging "European" News Portrayal of Immigration?' *Journal of Ethnic and Migration Studies* 41, no. 6 (12 May): 897–917. <https://doi.org/10.1080/1369183X.2014.1002199>.

Cebulla, A., M. Daniel, and A. Zurawan. 2010. 'Spotlight on Refugee Integration: Findings from the Survey of New Refugees in the United Kingdom.' Report. UK Home Office. <https://digital.library.adelaide.edu.au/dspace/handle/2440/98498>.

Chapman, Maggie. 2018. 'We Need a Scottish Immigration Policy Based on Our Humanitarian & Welcoming Culture.' Scottish Greens, 28 September. <https://greens.scot/blog/we-need-a-scottish-immigration-policy-based-on-our-humanitarian-welcoming-culture>.

Cherry, Joanna. 2015. 'Maiden Speech.' Presented at the Debate on the Address (2nd Day), 28 May. <https://publications.parliament.uk/pa/cm201516/cmhansrd/cm150528/debtext/150528-0002.htm#15052828000901>.

Citrin, Jack, Donald P. Green, Christopher Muste, and Cara Wong. 1997. 'Public Opinion toward Immigration Reform: The Role of Economic Motivations.' *The Journal of Politics* 59, no. 3 (1 August): 858–81. <https://doi.org/10.2307/2998640>.

Clark, Colin. 2018. 'Sites, Welfare, and "Barefoot Begging": Roma and Gypsy/Traveller Experiences of Racism in Scotland.' In *No Problem Here: Understanding Racism in Scotland*, edited by Neil Davidson, Minna Liinpää, Maureen McBride, and Satnam Virdee, 145–61. Edinburgh: Luath Press.

Clarke, Amy. 2014. 'Scotland's Heritage Investments in India: Acts of Cultural Diplomacy and Identity Building.' *Scottish Affairs* 23, no. 2 (22 April): 234–49. <https://doi.org/10.3366/scot.2014.0019>.

Clayton, Tristan. 2005. '"Diasporic Otherness": Racism, Sectarianism and "National Exteriority" in Modern Scotland.' *Social & Cultural Geography* 6, no. 1 (1 February): 99–116. <https://doi.org/10.1080/1464936052000335991>.

Committee of the Regions. 2009. 'Own-Initiative Opinion of the Committee of the Regions on Local and Regional Authorities at the Forefront of Integration Policies.' *Official Journal of the European Union*, 28 May. <https://eur-lex.europa.eu/legal-content/EN/TXT/HTML/?uri=CELEX:52008IR0212&from=EN>.

Conservative Party. 2005. 'It's Time for Action: Conservative Election Manifesto 2005.' Conservative Party.

Conservative Party. 2010. 'Invitation to Join the Government of Britain: The Conservative Manifesto 2010.' Conservative Party.

Conservative Party. 2015. 'Strong Leadership. A Clear Economic Plan. A Brighter, More Secure Future: The Conservative Manifesto 2015.' Conservative Party.

Conservative Party. 2017. 'Forward, Together: Our Plan for a Stronger Britain and a Prosperous Future: The Conservative and Unionist Party Manifesto 2017.' Conservative Party.

Conservative Party. 2019. 'Get Brexit Done, Unleash Britain's Potential: The Conservative and Unionist Party Manifesto 2019.' Conservative Party.

Cook, Timothy E. 1998. *Governing with the News: The News Media as a Political Institution*. Chicago: University of Chicago Press.

Copus, Andrew. 2018. 'Demographic Projections for the Scottish Sparsely Populated Area (SPA) 2011–2046.' Aberdeen: The James Hutton Institute.

Costello, Kimberly, and Gordon Hodson. 2011. 'Social Dominance-Based Threat Reactions to Immigrants in Need of Assistance.' *European Journal of Social Psychology* 41, no. 2: 220–31. <https://doi.org/10.1002/ejsp.769>.

Cowan, Edward J. 2003. *'For Freedom Alone': The Declaration of Arbroath, 1320*. East Linton: Tuckwell Press.

Cowan, Ronnie. 2015. 'Maiden Speech.' Presented at the Equal Pay and The Gender Pay Gap (Opposition Debate), 7 January. <https://publications.parliament.uk/pa/cm201516/cmhansrd/cm150701/debtext/150701-0003.htm#15070135001344>.

Crew, Jemma. 2019. 'ONS Figures Show Heavy Reliance of NHS on Foreign-Born Workers.' *The Sunday Post* (blog). <https://www.sundaypost.com/fp/ons-figures-show-heavy-reliance-of-nhs-on-foreign-born-workers/>.

Crown Office and Procurator Fiscal Service. 2019. 'Hate Crime in Scotland.' <https://www.copfs.gov.uk/publications/equality-and-diversity>.

Cruz, Alicia, Rosa M. Batista-Canino, and Esther Hormiga. 2014. 'Differences in the Perception and Exploitation of Entrepreneurial Opportunities by Immigrants.' *Journal of Business Venturing Insights* 1–2 (1 December): 31–6. <https://doi.org/10.1016/j.jbvi.2014.09.005>.

Curtice, John. 2014. 'It All Depends on Your Perspective: Economic Perceptions and the Demography of Voting in the Scottish Independence Referendum.' *Fraser of Allander Economic Commentary* 38 (12 November): 147–52. <https://strathprints.strath.ac.uk/50290/>.

Curtice, John. 2018. 'Just 15 Months to Go: What Scotland Is Making of Brexit.' January. <http://natcen.ac.uk/our-research/research/just-15-months-to-go-what-scotland-is-making-of-brexit/>.

Dancygier, Rafaela M., and Michael J. Donnelly. 2013. 'Sectoral Economies, Economic Contexts, and Attitudes toward Immigration.' *The Journal of Politics* 75, no. 1 (1 January): 17–35. <https://doi.org/10.1017/S0022381612000849>.

Davidson, Neil, Minna Liinpää, Maureen McBride, and Satnam Virdee, eds. 2018. *No Problem Here: Understanding Racism in Scotland*. Edinburgh: Luath Press.
Davidson, Neil, and Satnam Virdee. 2018. 'Introduction: Understanding Racism in Scotland.' In *No Problem Here: Understanding Racism in Scotland*, edited by Neil Davidson, Minna Liinpää, Maureen McBride, and Satnam Virdee, 9–12. Edinburgh: Luath Press.
de Lima, Philomena, and Sharon Wright. 2009. 'Welcoming Migrants? Migrant Labour in Rural Scotland.' *Social Policy and Society* 8, no. 3 (July): 391. <https://doi.org/10.1017/S1474746409004941>.
De Winter, Lieven, and Huri Türsan. 1998. *Regionalist Parties in the European Union*. London: Routledge.
Deacon, Michael. 2014. 'Sketch: Ed Miliband Talks about Immigration (for Seven Minutes and 25 Seconds).' *The Telegraph*, 16 December. <https://www.telegraph.co.uk/news/politics/ed-miliband/11295853/Sketch-Ed-Miliband-talks-about-immigration-for-seven-minutes-and-25-seconds.html>.
Dearden, Lizzie. 2014. 'Scottish Independence: Young Ethnic Minority Scots Concerned About.' *The Independent*, 17 September . <http://www.independent.co.uk/news/uk/scottish-independence/scottish-independence-young-ethnic-minority-scots-concerned-about-division-amid-growing-nationalism-9738039.html>.
Delhey, Jan, and Kenneth Newton. 2005. 'Predicting Cross-National Levels of Social Trust: Global Pattern or Nordic Exceptionalism?' *European Sociological Review* 21, no. 4 (1 September): 311–27. <https://doi.org/10.1093/esr/jci022>.
Dennison, James, and Matthew Goodwin. 2015. 'Immigration, Issue Ownership and the Rise of UKIP.' *Parliamentary Affairs* 68, no. suppl_1 (1 September): 168–87. <https://doi.org/10.1093/pa/gsv034>.
Devine, T. M. 2003. *Scotland's Empire, 1600–1815*. London: Allen Lane.
Devine, T. M. 2012a. 'A Global Diaspora.' In *The Oxford Handbook of Modern Scottish History*, edited by T. M. Devine and Jenny Wormald, 159–82. Oxford: Oxford University Press.
Devine, T. M. 2012b. *Scotland's Empire: The Origins of the Global Diaspora*. London: Penguin Books.
Devine, T. M. 2017. 'The End of Disadvantage? The Descendants of Irish-Catholic Immigrants in Modern Scotland since 1945.' In *New Perspectives on The Irish in Scotland*, edited by Martin J. Mitchell, 191–207. Edinburgh: John Donald.
Devine, T. M. 2018. 'Invisible Migrants? English People in Modern Scotland.' In *New Scots: Scotland's Immigrant Communities since 1945*, edited

by T. M. Devine and Angela McCarthy, 21–49. Edinburgh: Edinburgh University Press.

Devine, T. M., and Angela McCarthy. 2018. 'Introduction: The Historical and Contemporary Context of Immigration to Scotland since 1945.' In *New Scots: Scotland's Immigrant Communities since 1945*, edited by T. M. Devine and Angela McCarthy, 1–20. Edinburgh: Edinburgh University Press.

Devlin, Kate. 2014. 'Archbishop Takes Swipe at Politicians over Immigration.' *Herald Scotland*, 27 October. <https://www.heraldscotland.com/news/13186692.archbishop-takes-swipe-at-politicians-over-immigration/>.

Dickie, Mure. 2018. 'Scotland Faces Five Years of Anaemic Economic Growth.' *Financial Times*, 31 May. <https://www.ft.com/content/4afca46a-64e2-11e8-90c2-9563a0613e56>.

Dillon, Stephen. 2013. 'The Impact of Migrant Children in Glasgow Schools.' Glasgow: University of Glasgow. <http://www.migrationscotland.org.uk/uploads/files/documents/stephen_dillon_research_report_final_0.pdf>.

Dobbin, Frank, and Alexandra Kalev. 2016. 'Why Diversity Programs Fail.' *Harvard Business Review* (July–August): 10.

Dodd, Vikram. 2016. 'Police Blame Worst Rise in Recorded Hate Crime on EU Referendum.' *The Guardian*, 11 July, sec. Society. <https://www.theguardian.com/society/2016/jul/11/police-blame-worst-rise-in-recorded-hate-on-eu-referendum>.

Dolezal, Martin, Marc Helbling, and Swen Hutter. 2010. 'Debating Islam in Austria, Germany and Switzerland: Ethnic Citizenship, Church–State Relations and Right-Wing Populism.' *West European Politics* 33, no. 2 (March): 171–90. <https://doi.org/10.1080/01402380903538773>.

Doogan, Dave. 2020. 'Maiden Speech.' Presented at the Direct Payments to Farmers (Legislative Continuity) Bill, 21 January. <https://hansard.parliament.uk/Commons/2020-01-21/debates/35DD1ED8-A9B2-47CB-B7F8-5C335D63D5ED/DirectPaymentsToFarmers(LegislativeContinuity)Bill#contribution-99F3D8DD-F77B-4121-AACE-A27724B5BA9C>.

Downs, Anthony. 1957. 'An Economic Theory of Democracy.' In *Democracy: A Reader*, edited by Ricardo Blaug and John J. Schwarzmantel, 260–76. New York: Harper.

Dubuc, Sylvie. 2012. 'Immigration to the UK from High-Fertility Countries: Intergenerational Adaptation and Fertility Convergence.' *Population and Development Review* 38, no. 2: 353–68. <https://doi.org/10.1111/j.1728-4457.2012.00496.x>.

Duffy, Bobby, and Tom Frere-Smith. 2014. 'Perceptions and Reality: Ten Things We Should Know about Attitudes to Immigration in the UK.' *The Political Quarterly* 85, no. 3: 259–66. <https://doi.org/10.1111/1467-923X.12096>.

Dupré, Jean-François. 2012. 'Intercultural Citizenship, Civic Nationalism, and Nation Building in Québec: From Common Public Language to *Laïcité*.' *Studies in Ethnicity and Nationalism* 12, no. 2: 227–48. <https://doi.org/10.1111/j.1754-9469.2011.01132.x>.

Dustmann, Christian, Francesca Fabbri, and Ian Preston. 2005. 'The Impact of Immigration on the British Labour Market.' *The Economic Journal* 115, no. 507 (1 November): F324–41. <https://doi.org/10.1111/j.1468-0297.2005.01038.x>.

Dustmann, Christian, and Tommaso Frattini. 2014. 'The Fiscal Effects of Immigration to the UK.' *The Economic Journal* 124, no. 580 (1 November): F593–643. <https://doi.org/10.1111/ecoj.12181>.

Dustmann, Christian, Tommaso Frattini, and Ian P. Preston. 2013. 'The Effect of Immigration along the Distribution of Wages.' *The Review of Economic Studies* 80, no. 1 (1 January): 145–73. <https://doi.org/10.1093/restud/rds019>.

Dustmann, Christian, and Ian P. Preston. 2007. 'Racial and Economic Factors in Attitudes to Immigration.' *The B.E. Journal of Economic Analysis & Policy* 7, no. 1. <https://doi.org/10.2202/1935-1682.1655>.

Easton, Mark, and Ben Butcher. 2018. 'Where Have the UK's 10,000 Syrian Refugees Gone?' *BBC News*, 24 April. <https://www.bbc.com/news/uk-43826163>.

Eberl, Jakob-Moritz, Christine E. Meltzer, Tobias Heidenreich, Beatrice Herrero, Nora Theorin, Fabienne Lind, Rosa Berganza, Hajo G. Boomgaarden, Christian Schemer, and Jesper Strömbäck. 2018. 'The European Media Discourse on Immigration and Its Effects: A Literature Review.' *Annals of the International Communication Association* 42, no. 3 (3 July): 207–23. <https://doi.org/10.1080/23808985.2018.1497452>.

Efendic, Adnan, Tomasz Mickiewicz, and Anna Rebmann. 2015. 'Growth Aspirations and Social Capital: Young Firms in a Post-Conflict Environment.' *International Small Business Journal* 33, no. 5 (1 August): 537–61. <https://doi.org/10.1177/0266242613516987>.

Elgot, Jessica. 2014. 'Why Are So Many Scots from Ethnic Minorities Voting Yes?' *HuffPost UK*, 14 June. <https://www.huffingtonpost.co.uk/2014/06/12/scotland-independence-referendum_n_5488582.html>.

Elvestad, Eiri, and Arild Blekesaune. 2008. 'Newspaper Readers in Europe: A Multilevel Study of Individual and National Differences.' *European Journal of Communication* 23, no. 4 (1 December): 425–47. <https://doi.org/10.1177/0267323108096993>.

Entman, Robert M. 1993. 'Framing: Toward Clarification of a Fractured Paradigm.' *Journal of Communication* 43, no. 4 (December): 51–8. <https://doi.org/10.1111/j.1460-2466.1993.tb01304.x>.

Equality and Human Rights Commission. 2018. 'Is Scotland Fairer?' London:

Equality and Human Rights Commission. <https://www.equalityhumanrights.com/sites/default/files/is-britain-fairer-2018-is-scotland-fairer_0.pdf>.

Esser, F., S. Engesser, J. Matthes, and R. Berganza. 2017. 'Negativity.' In *Comparing Political Journalism*, edited by Claes de Vreese, Frank Esser, and David Nicolas Hopmann, 71–91. London: Routledge.

Esses, Victoria M., Lynne M. Jackson, and Tamara L. Armstrong. 1998. 'Intergroup Competition and Attitudes toward Immigrants and Immigration: An Instrumental Model of Group Conflict.' *Journal of Social Issues* 54, no. 4: 699–724. <https://doi.org/10.1111/j.1540-4560.1998.tb01244.x>.

European Commission. 2006. 'Communication from the Commission to the Council, the European Parliament, the European Economic and Social Committee and the Committee of the Regions – Report on the Functioning of the Transitional Arrangements Set out in the 2003 Accession Treaty.' EMPL, 8 February. <https://eur-lex.europa.eu/legal-content/GA/ALL/?uri=CELEX:52006DC0048>.

European Council on Refugees and Exiles. 2018. 'Scotland Leads the Way on Refugee Integration.' *ECRE Weekly Bulletin*, 19 January. <https://mailchi.mp/ecre/ecre-weekly-bulletin-19012018#Scotland>.

Evans, Nicholas J., and Angela McCarthy. 2018. '"New" Jews in Scotland since 1945.' In *New Scots: Scotland's Immigrant Communities since 1945*, edited by T. M. Devine and Angela McCarthy, 50–74. Edinburgh: Edinburgh University Press.

Fellows, Marion. 2015. 'Maiden Speech.' Presented at the Summer Adjournment, 16 July. <https://publications.parliament.uk/pa/cm201516/cmhansrd/cm150716/debtext/150716-0003.htm#15071648000289>.

Ferguson, Lisa. 2015. 'Nicola Sturgeon "Happy" to Give Refugees a Home.' *The Scotsman*, 6 September. <https://www.scotsman.com/news/politics/nicola-sturgeon-happy-to-give-refugees-a-home-1-3879126>.

Ferrier, Margaret. 2015. 'Maiden Speech.' Presented at the Scotland Bill (2nd Reading), 6 August. <https://publications.parliament.uk/pa/cm201516/cmhansrd/cm150608/debtext/150608-0002.htm#15060817000137>.

Fetzer, Joel S. 2000. 'Economic Self-Interest or Cultural Marginality? Anti-immigration Sentiment and Nativist Political Movements in France, Germany and the USA.' *Journal of Ethnic and Migration Studies* 26, no. 1 (1 January): 5–23. <https://doi.org/10.1080/136918300115615>.

Fieldhouse, Edward, and David Cutts. 2010. 'Does Diversity Damage Social Capital? A Comparative Study of Neighbourhood Diversity and Social Capital in the US and Britain.' *Canadian Journal of Political Science/Revue Canadienne de Science Politique* 43, no. 2: 289–318. <https://www.jstor.org/stable/20743151>.

Fieschi, Catherine. 2019. 'Why Europe's New Populists Tell so Many Lies – and Do It so Shamelessly.' *The Guardian*, 30 September. <http://www.theguardian.com/commentisfree/2019/sep/30/europe-populist-lie-shamelessly-salvini-johnson>.

Figueira, Catarina, Giorgio Caselli, and Nicholas Theodorakopoulos. 2016. 'Migrant Entrepreneurs as Cosmopolitan Change Agents: A Bourdieuian Perspective on Capital Accumulation.' *Society and Business Review* 11, no. 3 (1 January): 297–312. <https://doi.org/10.1108/SBR-10-2015-0064>.

Findlay, Allan M., Aileen Stockdale, Caroline Hoy, and Cassie Higgins. 2003. 'The Structuring of Service-Class Migration: English Migration to Scottish Cities.' *Urban Studies*, 1 September. <https://journals.sagepub.com/doi/abs/10.1080/0042098032000116112>.

Finlay, Richard J. 2004. *Modern Scotland 1914–2000*. London: Profile Books.

Florack, Arnd, Ursula Piontkowski, Anette Rohmann, Tanja Balzer, and Steffi Perzig. 2003. 'Perceived Intergroup Threat and Attitudes of Host Community Members toward Immigrant Acculturation.' *The Journal of Social Psychology* 143, no. 5 (1 October): 633–48. <https://doi.org/10.1080/00224540309598468>.

Fonteyne, Bruno, and Michael Keating. 2015. 'Thatcher's Legacy in Scotland.' Université Catholique de Louvain. <https://s3.amazonaws.com/academia.edu.documents/39832848/Fonteyne_B_THATCHERS_LEGACY_IN_SCOTLAND-5-2015.pdf?response-content-disposition=inline%3B%20filename%3DFonteyne_B_THATCHER_S_LEGACY_IN_SCOTLAND.pdf&X-Amz-Algorithm=AWS4-HMAC-SHA256&X-Amz-Credential=AKIAIWOWYYGZ2Y53UL3A%2F20200225%2Fus-east-1%2Fs3%2Faws4_request&X-Amz-Date=20200225T150253Z&X-Amz-Expires=3600&X-Amz-SignedHeaders=host&X-Amz-Signature=16b748359f106fcff3cbcb748b8b501a1a3225edd7bc034a3f002ff9c826f918>.

Ford, Robert. 2011. 'Acceptable and Unacceptable Immigrants: How Opposition to Immigration in Britain Is Affected by Migrants' Region of Origin.' *Journal of Ethnic and Migration Studies* 37, no. 7 (1 August): 1017–37. <https://doi.org/10.1080/1369183X.2011.572423>.

Ford, Robert. 2012. 'Parochial and Cosmopolitan Britain: Examining the Social Divide in Reactions to Immigration.' The German Marshall Fund of the United States, 13 June. <https://www.gmfus.org/publications/parochial-and-cosmopolitan-britain-examining-social-divide-reactions-immigration>.

Ford, Robert, and Matthew Goodwin. 2014. 'Understanding UKIP: Identity, Social Change and the Left Behind.' *The Political Quarterly* 85, no. 3: 277–84. <https://doi.org/10.1111/1467-923X.12099>.

Fortunati, Leopoldina, Mark Deuze, and Federico de Luca. 2014. 'The New

about News: How Print, Online, Free, and Mobile Coconstruct New Audiences in Italy, France, Spain, the UK, and Germany.' *Journal of Computer-Mediated Communication* 19, no. 2: 121–40.
Fox, Jon E., and Cynthia Miller-Idriss. 2008. 'Everyday Nationhood.' *Ethnicities* 8, no. 4 (1 December): 536–63. <https://doi.org/10.1177/1468796808088925>.
Friedberg, Rachel M., and Jennifer Hunt. 1995. 'The Impact of Immigrants on Host Country Wages, Employment and Growth.' *Journal of Economic Perspectives* 9, no. 2 (June): 23–44. <https://doi.org/10.1257/jep.9.2.23>.
Friedman, Vanessa. 2019. 'Boris Johnson and the Rise of Silly Style.' *The New York Times*, 23 July, sec. Style. <https://www.nytimes.com/2019/07/23/style/boris-johnson-and-the-rise-of-silly-style.html>.
Fry, Michael. 2001. *The Scottish Empire*. Edinburgh: Birlinn.
Gallagher, Tom. 2016. 'Tom Gallagher: Hubristic Sturgeon Turns a Blind Eye to the Turmoil in Her Own Backyard.' *The Conservative Woman* (blog). <https://conservativewoman.co.uk/tom-gallagher-hubristic-sturgeon-turns-a-blind-eye-to-the-turmoil-in-her-own-backyard/>.
Geertz, Clifford. 1963. 'The Integrative Revolution: Primordial Sentiments and Civil Politics in the New States.' In *Old Societies and New States: The Quest for Modernity in Asia and Africa*, edited by Clifford Geertz, 105–19. New York: Free Press of Glencoe.
Gellner, Ernest. 1983. *Nations and Nationalism*. 2nd edn. Ithaca, NY: Cornell University Press.
General Register Office (Scotland). 2002. 'Scotland's Population 2001: The Registrar General's Annual Review of Demographic Trends.' Edinburgh: General Register Office for Scotland.
Gesthuizen, Maurice, Tom van der Meer, and Peer Scheepers. 2008. 'Education and Dimensions of Social Capital: Do Educational Effects Differ Due to Educational Expansion and Social Security Expenditure?' *European Sociological Review* 24, no. 5 (1 December): 617–32. <https://doi.org/10.1093/esr/jcn021>.
Gethins, Steven. 2015. 'Maiden Speech.' Presented at the Debate on the Address (1st Day), 27 May. <https://publications.parliament.uk/pa/cm201516/cmhansrd/cm150527/debtext/150527-0003.htm#1505281000159>.
Gibson, Patricia. 2015. 'Maiden Speech.' Presented at the Scotland Bill (2nd Reading), 8 June. <https://publications.parliament.uk/pa/cm201516/cmhansrd/cm150608/debtext/150608-0003.htm#15060818000026>.
Gijsberts, Mérove, Tom van der Meer, and Jaco Dagevos. 2011. '"Hunkering Down" in Multi-ethnic Neighbourhoods? The Effects of Ethnic Diversity on Dimensions of Social Cohesion.' *European Sociological Review* 28, no. 4 (26 March): 527–37. <https://doi.org/10.1093/esr/jcr022>.

Gilpin, Nicola, Matthew Henty, Sara Lemos, Jonathan Portes, and Chris Bullen. 2006. 'The Impact of Free Movement of Workers from Central and Eastern Europe on the UK Labour Market.' Department for Work and Pensions Working Paper no. 29. <http://conference.iza.org/conferen ce_files/amm2006/lemos_s1613.pdf>.

Giordani, Paolo E., and Michele Ruta. 2011. 'The Immigration Policy Puzzle.' *Review of International Economics* 19, no. 5: 922–35. <https://doi.org /10.1111/j.1467-9396.2011.00995.x>.

Goldie, Paul. 2018. 'Cultural Racism and Islamophobia in Glasgow.' In *No Problem Here: Understanding Racism in Scotland*, edited by Neil Davidson, Minna Liinpää, Maureen McBride, and Satnam Virdee, 128–44. Edinburgh: Luath Press.

Goodhart, David. 2004. 'Too Diverse?' *Prospect* (February): 32–7.

Gordon, Tom. 2018. 'Ruth Davidson Throws Down Gauntlet to May on Immigration, NHS and Tax.' *The Herald*. <https://www.heraldscotland .com/news/16256703.ruth-davidson-throws-gauntlet-may-immigration -nhs-tax/>.

Gouriévidis, Laurence. 2000. 'Representing the Disputed Past of Northern Scotland: The Highland Clearances in Museums.' *History & Memory* 12, no. 2 (1 December): 122–41. <https://doi.org/10.1353/ham.2000. 0014>.

Gourtsoyannis, Paris. 2020. 'Boris Johnson Blasts SNP's Scottish Visa Plan as "Deranged" at PMQs.' *The Scotsman*, 29 January. <https://www.scotsm an.com/news/scottish-news/boris-johnson-blasts-snps-scottish-visa-plan -deranged-pmqs-1395752>.

Green, Anne E., Maria De Hoyos, Paul Jones, and David Owen. 2008. 'Rural Development and Labour Supply Challenges in the UK: The Role of Non-UK Migrants.' *Regional Studies* 43, no. 10: 1261–73. <https://doi .org/10.1080/00343400801932318>.

Green, Chris. 2018. 'Refugees and Asylum Seekers Could Be Given the Right to Vote in Scotland.' *The Scotsman*, 5 January. <https://www.scotsman .com/news/refugees-and-asylum-seekers-could-be-given-right-to-vote-in -scotland-1-4654555>.

Green Party. 2015. 'For the Common Good: General Election Manifesto 2015.' Green Party.

Green Party. 2019. 'If Not Now, When? Manifesto 2019.' Green Party.

Guentner, Simon, Sue Lukes, Richard Stanton, Bastian A. Vollmer, and Jo Wilding. 2016. 'Bordering Practices in the UK Welfare System.' *Critical Social Policy* 36, no. 3 (1 August): 391–411. <https://doi.org/10.1177/02 61018315622609>.

Gulliver, Kevin. 2016. 'Forty Years of Struggle: A Window and Race and Housing, Disadvantage and Exclusion.' Human City Institute.

<https:// humancityinstitute.files.wordpress.com/2017/01/forty-years-of-struggle.pdf>.
Habermas, Jürgen. 1993. *Justification and Application. Remarks on Discourse Ethics*. Cambridge: Polity Press.
Hainmueller, Jens, and Michael J. Hiscox. 2007. 'Educated Preferences: Explaining Attitudes toward Immigration in Europe.' *International Organization* 61, no. 2: 399–442.
Hainmueller, Jens, and Daniel J. Hopkins. 2014. 'Public Attitudes toward Immigration.' *Annual Review of Political Science* 17: 225–49.
Hainmueller, Jens, and Daniel J. Hopkins. 2015. 'The Hidden American Immigration Consensus: A Conjoint Analysis of Attitudes toward Immigrants.' *American Journal of Political Science* 59, no. 3 (1 July): 529–48. <https://doi.org/10.1111/ajps.12138>.
Halliday, Josh. 2013. 'BBC Had "Deep Liberal Bias" over Immigration, Says Former News Chief.' *The Guardian*, 3 July. <http://www.theguardian.com/media/2013/jul/03/bbc-deep-liberal-bias-immigration>.
Hampshire, James. 2005. *Citizenship and Belonging: Immigration and the Politics of Demographic Governance in Postwar Britain*. Basingstoke: Palgrave Macmillan.
Hansen, Randall. 2000. *Citizenship and Immigration in Postwar Britain*. Oxford: Oxford University Press.
Harper, Marjory. 2012. *Scotland No More?: Emigration from Scotland in the Twentieth Century*. Edinburgh: Luath Press.
Harper, Marjory. [1998] 2017. *Emigration from Scotland between the Wars: Opportunity or Exile?* Manchester: Manchester University Press. <https://www.manchesterhive.com/view/9781526119667/9781526119667.xml>.
Harper, Sarah. 2016. 'The Important Role of Migration for an Ageing Nation.' *Journal of Population Ageing* 9, no. 3 (1 September): 183–89. <https://doi.org/10.1007/s12062-016-9152-4>.
Hassan, Gerry, and Chris Warhurst. 2002a. *Anatomy of the New Scotland*. Edinburgh: Mainstream. <https://strathprints.strath.ac.uk/7705/.
Hassan, Gerry, and Chris Warhurst. 2002b. 'New Scotland? Policy, Parties and Institutions.' *The Political Quarterly* 72, no. 2: 213–26. <https://doi.org/10.1111/1467-923X.00360>.
Hatton, Timothy J., and Massimiliano Tani. 2005. 'Immigration and Inter-regional Mobility in the UK, 1982–2000.' *The Economic Journal* 115, no. 507 (1 November): F342–58. <https://doi.org/10.1111/j.1468-0297.2005.01039.x>.
Hearn, Jonathan. 2000. *Claiming Scotland: National Identity and Liberal Culture*. Edinburgh: Edinburgh University Press.
Heath, Anthony, Jean Martin, and Gabriella Elgenius. 2007. 'Who Do We

Think We Are? The Decline of Traditional Social Identities.' In *British Social Attitudes Survey: British Social Attitudes: The 23rd Report*, edited by John Curtice, Katarina Thompson, Miranda Phillips, and Mark Johnson, 2–34. London: SAGE Publications.

Hechter, Michael. 1975. *Internal Colonialism: The Celtic Fringe in British National Development*. Berkeley, CA: University of California Press.

Heinisch, Reinhard, Emanuele Massetti, and Oscar Mazzoleni. 2018. 'Populism and Ethno-territorial Politics in European Multi-level Systems.' *Comparative European Politics* 16, no. 6 (1 November): 923–36. <https://doi.org/10.1057/s41295-018-0142-1>.

Heinz, Frigyes Ferdinand, and Melanie E. Ward-Warmedinger. 2006. 'Cross-Border Labour Mobility within an Enlarged EU.' SSRN Scholarly Paper. Rochester, NY: Social Science Research Network, 1 October. <https://papers.ssrn.com/abstract=923371>.

Helbling, Marc. 2012. *Islamophobia in the West: Measuring and Explaining Individual Attitudes*. London: Routledge.

Helbling, Marc. 2014. 'Framing Immigration in Western Europe.' *Journal of Ethnic and Migration Studies* 40, no. 1: 21–41. <https://doi.org/10.1080/1369183X.2013.830888>.

Helbling, Marc, Dominic Hoeglinger, and Bruno Wüest. 2010. 'How Political Parties Frame European Integration.' *European Journal of Political Research* 49, no. 4: 495–521. <https://doi.org/10.1111/j.1475-6765.2009.01908.x>.

Henderson, Ailsa, Chris Carman, Robert Johns, and James Mitchell. 2018. 'Migration, Engagement and Constitutional Preferences: Evidence from the 2014 Scottish Independence Referendum.' In *New Scots: Scotland's Immigrant Communities since 1945*, edited by T. M. Devine and Angela McCarthy, 252–62. Edinburgh: Edinburgh University Press.

Henderson, Ailsa, Charlie Jeffery, Robert Liñeira, Roger Scully, Daniel Wincott, and Richard Wyn Jones. 2016. 'England, Englishness and Brexit.' *The Political Quarterly* 87, no. 2: 187–99. <https://doi.org/10.1111/1467-923X.12262>.

Hendry, Drew. 2015. 'Maiden Speech.' Presented at the European Union Referendum Bill (Second Reading), 6 September. <https://publications.parliament.uk/pa/cm201516/cmhansrd/cm150609/debtext/150609-0003.htm#15060939001075>.

Hepburn, Eve. 2009. 'Regionalist Party Mobilisation on Immigration.' *West European Politics* 32, no. 3 (May): 514–35. <https://doi.org/10.1080/01402380902779071>.

Hepburn, Eve. 2010a. '"Citizens of the Region": Party Conceptions of Regional Citizenship and Immigrant Integration.' *European Journal of*

Political Research 50, no. 4: 504–29. <https://doi.org/10.1111/j.1475-67 65.2010.01940.x>.
Hepburn, Eve. 2010b. 'Small Worlds in Canada and Europe: A Comparison of Regional Party Systems in Quebec, Bavaria and Scotland.' *Regional & Federal Studies* 20, no. 4–5 (1 December): 527–44. <https://doi.org/10 .1080/13597566.2010.523637>.
Hepburn, Eve. 2014. 'Independence and the Immigration Debate in Scotland.' *British Politics Review* 9, no. 2: 10–12.
Hepburn, Eve. 2020. 'Migrant Integration in Scotland: Challenges and Opportunities.' Iriss, 4 June. <https://www.iriss.org.uk/resources/insigh ts/migrant-integration-scotland-challenges-and-opportunities>.
Hepburn, Eve, and P. J. McLoughlin. 2011. 'Celtic Nationalism and Supranationalism: Comparing Scottish and Northern Ireland Party Responses to Europe.' *British Journal of Politics & International Relations* 13, no. 3 (August): 383–99. <https://doi.org/10.1111/j.1467 -856X.2010.00426.x>.
Hepburn, Eve, and Michael Rosie. 2014. 'Immigration, Nationalism, and Politics in Scotland.' In *The Politics of Immigration in Multi-level States: Governance and Political Parties*, edited by Michael Rosie and Eve Hepburn, 241–60. Palgrave Politics of Identity and Citizenship Series. London: Palgrave Macmillan. <https://doi.org/10.1057/9781137358530_12>.
Hepburn, Eve, and Ricard Zapata-Barrero. 2014. 'Introduction: Immigration Policies in Multi-Level States.' In *The Politics of Immigration in Multi-Level States: Governance and Political Parties*, edited by Michael Rosie and Eve Hepburn, 3–18. Palgrave Politics of Identity and Citizenship Series. London: Palgrave Macmillan. <https://doi.org/10.1057/9781137 358530_12>.
Herman, Arthur. 2001. *How the Scots Invented the Modern World: The True Story of How Western Europe's Poorest Nation Created Our World & Everything in It*. London: Fourth Estate.
Hirschi, Caspar. 2012. *The Origins of Nationalism: An Alternative History from Ancient Rome to Early Modern Germany*. Cambridge: Cambridge University Press.
HM Treasury. 2019. 'Country and Regional Analysis November 2019.' National Statistics. <https://assets.publishing.service.gov.uk/government /uploads/system/uploads/attachment_data/file/847025/CRA_2019_-_ma in_text.pdf>.
Hodges, Dan. 2014. 'Britons Have Become Scared of the Wider World.' *The Daily Telegraph*, 5 August.
Holtz-Bacha, Christina, and Pippa Norris. 1999. '"To Entertain, Inform, and Educate": Still the Role of Public Television.' *Political Communication* 18, no. 2: 123–40. <https://doi.org/10.1080/105846001750322943>.

Hooghe, Liesbet, and Gary Marks. 2005. 'Calculation, Community and Cues: Public Opinion on European Integration.' *European Union Politics* 6, no. 4 (1 December): 419–43. <https://doi.org/10.1177/1465116505057816>.

Hopkins, Peter. 2008. 'Politics, Race, and Nation: The Difference that Scotland Makes.' In *New Geographies of Race and Racism*, edited by Claire Dwyer and Caroline Bressey, 113–24. London: Routledge.

Hopkins, Peter E. 2010. 'Young Muslim Men in Scotland: Inclusions and Exclusions.' *Children's Geographies* 2, no. 2: 257–72. <https://doi.org/10.1080/14733280410001720548>.

Hopkins, Peter, and Malcolm Hill. 2006. 'This Is a Good Place to Live and Think about the Future... The Needs and Experiences of Unaccompanied Asylum-Seeking Children in Scotland.' Scottish Refugee Council. <https://www.scottishrefugeecouncil.org.uk/wp-content/uploads/2019/10/This-is-a-good-place-to-live-and-think-about-the-future-The-needs-and-experiences-of-unaccompanied-asylum-seeking-children-in-Scotland.pdf>.

Hopkins, Peter, and Susan J. Smith. 2008. 'Scaling Segregation; Racialising Fear.' In *Fear: Critical Geopolitics and Everyday Life*, edited by Rachel Pain and Susan J. Smith, 103–16. London: Routledge.

Horne, Marc. 2016. 'EU Diplomats Praise Scotland as "Haven" in Wake of Brexit.' *The Times*, 27 October, sec. Scotland. <https://www.thetimes.co.uk/article/eu-diplomats-praise-scotland-as-haven-in-wake-of-brexit-hqn659r2x>.

House of Commons. 2005. 'Minutes of Evidence Taken Before Home Affairs Committee – Terrorism and Other Home Office Issues.' 8 February, question 61. <https://publications.parliament.uk/pa/cm200405/cmselect/cmhaff/321/5020805.htm>.

Houston, Donald, Allan Findlay, Richard Harrison, and Colin Mason. 2008. 'Will Attracting the "Creative Class" Boost Economic Growth in Old Industrial Regions? A Case Study of Scotland.' *Geografiska Annaler: Series B, Human Geography* 90, no. 2: 133–49. <https://doi.org/10.1111/j.1468-0467.2008.00283.x>.

Hudson, Nicola, and Andrew Aiton. 2016. 'Financial Scrutiny Unit Briefing: EU Nationals Living in Scotland.' Financial Scrutiny Unit, 3 November.

Hughes, Kirsty. 2020. 'Brexit, Scotland and Europe.' Scottish Centre on European Relations, 6 February. <https://www.scer.scot/database/ident-12382>.

Hussain, Asifa M., and William L. Miller. 2006. *Multicultural Nationalism*. Oxford: Oxford University Press. <https://doi.org/10.1093/0199280711.001.0001>.

Imrie, Colin. 2006. 'Internationalising Scotland: Making Scotland Global and International in Its Outlook.' *Scottish Affairs* 54 (First Series), no. 1 (1 February): 68–90. <https://doi.org/10.3366/scot.2006.0005>.

International Organization for Migration. 2005. *Costs and Benefits of International Migration*. World Migration 2005. Geneva: International Organization for Migration. <https://publications.iom.int/books/world-migration-report-2005-costs-and-benefits-international-migration>.

Irwin, Neil. 2014. 'Why Does Scotland Want Independence? It's Culture vs. Economics.' *The New York Times*, 9 September. <https://www.nytimes.com/2014/09/10/upshot/why-does-scotland-want-independence-its-culture-vs-economics.html>.

Jackson, Ben. 2014. 'The Political Thought of Scottish Nationalism.' *The Political Quarterly* 85, no. 1 (1 January): 50–6. <https://doi.org/10.1111/j.1467-923X.2014.12058.x>.

Jackson, Debbie. 2020. '"You Can't Close the Border – We Live on Both Sides".' *BBC News*, 14 July, sec. South Scotland. <https://www.bbc.com/news/uk-scotland-south-scotland-53390872>.

Jardine, Christine. 2017. 'Maiden Speech.' Presented at the Health, Social Care and Security, 28 June. <https://hansard.parliament.uk/Commons2017-06-28/debates/BC4CBE6F-0750-4939-A277-0745C918E944/HealthSocialCareAndSecurity#contribution-49C69CD9-8568-4DCE-AF19-FAD9E83E499C>.

Jolly, Seth Kincaid. 2007. 'The Europhile Fringe?: Regionalist Party Support for European Integration.' *European Union Politics* 8, no. 1 (1 March): 109–30. <https://doi.org/10.1177/1465116507073290>.

Jolly, Seth K. 2015. *The European Union and the Rise of Regionalist Parties*. Ann Arbor: University of Michigan Press.

Jones, Huw. 1970. 'Migration to and from Scotland Since 1961.' *The Royal Geographical Society* 49 (March).

Jones, Siân. 2013. '"Thrown Like Chaff in the Wind": Excavation, Memory and the Negotiation of Loss in the Scottish Highlands.' *International Journal of Historical Archaeology* 16, no. 2 (1 June): 346–66. <https://doi.org/10.1007/s10761-012-0181-2>.

Joppke, Christian. 1999. *Immigration and the Nation-State*. Oxford: Oxford University Press. <https://doi.org/10.1093/0198295405.001.0001>.

Kay, Rebecca, and Andrew Morrison. 2012. 'Evidencing the Social and Cultural Benefits and Costs of Migration in Scotland.' <http://www.migrationscotland.org.uk/our-research/social-and-cultural-impacts-of-migration>.

Kaye, Ronald. 2001. 'Blaming the Victim: An Analysis of Press Representation of Refugees and Asylum Seekers in the United Kingdom in the 1990s.' In *Media and Migration: Constructions of Mobility and Difference*, edited by R. King and N. Wood, 53–70. London: Routledge.

Kearns, Ade, and Elise Whitley. 2015. 'Getting There? The Effects of Functional Factors, Time and Place on the Social Integration of Migrants.' *Journal of Ethnic and Migration Studies* 41, no. 13 (10 November): 2105–29. <https://doi.org/10.1080/1369183X.2015.1030374>.

Kearton, Antonia. 2005. 'Imagining the "Mongrel Nation": Political Uses of History in the Recent Scottish Nationalist Movement.' *National Identities* 7, no. 1 (1 March): 23–50. <https://doi.org/10.1080/14608940500072933>.

Keating, Michael. 2001a. *Nations against the State: The New Politics of Nationalism in Quebec, Catalonia and Scotland.* 2nd edn. London: Palgrave Macmillan.

Keating, Michael. 2001b. *Plurinational Democracy: Stateless Nations in a Post-Sovereignty Era.* Oxford: Oxford University Press.

Keating, Michael. 2004. 'European Integration and the Nationalities Question.' *Politics & Society* 32, no. 3 (1 September): 367–88. <https://doi.org/10.1177/0032329204267295>.

Keating, Michael. 2009. *The Independence of Scotland: Self-Government and the Shifting Politics of Union.* Oxford: Oxford University Press.

Keating, Michael. 2017. 'The European Question.' In *Debating Scotland: Issues of Independence and Union in the 2014 Referendum*, 102–18. Oxford: Oxford University Press.

Keating, Michael, and Paul Cairney. 2015. 'A New Elite? Politicians and Civil Servants in Scotland after Devolution.' *Parliamentary Affairs* 59, no. 1: 43–59. <https://doi.org/10.1093/pa/gsj009>.

Keating, Michael, and Nicola McEwen. 2017. 'The Scottish Independence Debate.' In *Debating Scotland: Issues of Independence and Union in the 2014 Referendum*, edited by Michael Keating, 1–26. Oxford: Oxford University Press.

Keating, Michael, and John McGarry. 2001. *Minority Nationalism and the Changing International Order.* Oxford: Oxford University Press.

Kenny, Michael. 2016. 'The Genesis of English Nationalism.' *Political Insight* 7, no. 2 (1 September): 8–11. <https://doi.org/10.1177/2041905816666124>.

Kentmen-Cin, Cigdem, and Cengiz Erisen. 2017. 'Anti-immigration Attitudes and the Opposition to European Integration: A Critical Assessment.' *European Union Politics* 18, no. 1 (1 March): 3–25. <https://doi.org/10.1177/1465116516680762>.

Kerr, Calum. 2015. 'Maiden Speech.' Presented at the Financial Statement and Budget Report, 7 September. <https://publications.parliament.uk/pa/cm201516/cmhansrd/cm150709/debtext/150709-0003.htm#15070966000442>.

Kerr, Stephen. 2017. 'Maiden Speech.' Presented at the Air Travel Organisers' Licensing Bill, 7 March. <https://hansard.parliament.uk/Commons/2017-07-03/debates/B5BEA920-847D-4AD9-85E0-D44CE6337399/AirTra

velOrganisers%E2%80%99LicensingBill#contribution-D55B624D-FB39-4D96-8847-76320217492F>.
Kessel, Stijn van. 2015. 'Populist Parties in the United Kingdom.' In *Populist Parties in Europe: Agents of Discontent?*, 114–68. Basingstoke: Palgrave Macmillan.
Kiely, Richard, Frank Bechhofer, and David McCrone. 2005. 'Birth, Blood and Belonging: Identity Claims in Post-Devolution Scotland.' *The Sociological Review* 53, no. 1: 150–71. <https://doi.org/10.1111/j.1467-954X.2005.00507.x>.
Kiely, Richard, Frank Bechhofer, Robert Stewart, and David McCrone. 2001. 'The Markers and Rules of Scottish National Identity.' *The Sociological Review* 49, no. 1 (1 February): 33–55. <https://doi.org/10.1111/1467-954X.00243>.
Kirkup, James. 2014. 'EU Elections 2014: Is Immigration Good for Britain?' *The Telegraph*, 12 May. <https://www.telegraph.co.uk/news/worldnews/europe/eu/ 10822956/EU-elections-2014-Is-immigration-good-for-Britain.html>.
Kitschelt, Herbert, and Anthony J. McGann. 1995. *The Radical Right in Western Europe: A Comparative Analysis*. Ann Arbor: University of Michigan Press.
Koopmans, Ruud, and Jasper Muis. 2009. 'The Rise of Right-Wing Populist Pim Fortuyn in the Netherlands: A Discursive Opportunity Approach.' *European Journal of Political Research* 48, no. 5: 642–64. <https://doi.org/10.1111/j.1475-6765.2009.00846.x>.
Kraler, Albert, and Paola Bonizzoni. 2010. 'Gender, Civic Stratification and the Right to Family Life: Problematising Immigrants' Integration in the EU.' *International Review of Sociology* 20, no. 1 (1 March): 181–7. <https://doi.org/10.1080/03906700903525792>.
Kumar, Krishan. 2010. 'Negotiating English Identity: Englishness, Britishness and the Future of the United Kingdom.' *Nations and Nationalism* 16, no. 3: 469–87. <https://doi.org/10.1111/j.1469-8129.2010.00442.x>.
Kuzio, Taras. 2002. 'The Myth of the Civic State: A Critical Survey of Hans Kohn's Framework for Understanding Nationalism.' *Ethnic and Racial Studies* 25, no. 1 (1 January): 20–39. <https://doi.org/10.1080/01419870120112049>.
Kuznetsov, Yevgeny. 2008. 'Mobilizing Intellectual Capital of Diasporas: From First Movers to a Virtuous Cycle.' *Journal of Intellectual Capital* 9, no. 2 (18 April): 264–82. <https://doi.org/10.1108/14691930810870337>.
Kymlicka, Will. 2000. 'Nation-Building and Minority Rights: Comparing West and East.' *Journal of Ethnic and Migration Studies* 26, no. 2 (1 April): 183–212. <https://doi.org/10.1080/13691830050022767>.

Kymlicka, Will. 2001. *Politics in the Vernacular: Nationalism, Multiculturalism, and Citizenship*. Oxford: Oxford University Press.
Kymlicka, Will. 2011. 'Multicultural Citizenship within Multination States.' *Ethnicities* 11, no. 3 (1 September): 281–302. <https://doi.org/10.1177/1468796811407813>.
Labour Party. 2010. 'A Future Fair for All: The Labour Party Manifesto 2010.' Labour Party.
Labour Party. 2015. 'Britain Can Be Better: The Labour Party Manifesto 2015.' Labour Party.
Labour Party. 2017. 'For the Many Not the Few: The Labour Party Manifesto 2017.' Labour Party.
Labour Party. 2019. 'It's Time for Real Change: The Labour Party Manifesto 2019.' Labour Party.
Lahav, Gallya. 2004. *Immigration and Politics in the New Europe: Reinventing Borders*. Cambridge: Cambridge University Press.
Lancee, Bram. 2010. 'The Economic Returns of Immigrants' Bonding and Bridging Social Capital: The Case of the Netherlands.' *International Migration Review* 44, no. 1: 202–26. <https://doi.org/10.1111/j.1747-7379.2009.00803.x>.
Lane, Alasdair. 2020. 'Scotland's Slave Trade History in the Spotlight amid Global Anger at Racial Injustice.' *NBC News*, 13 June. <https://www.nbcnews.com/news/world/calls-grow-scotland-reckon-its-slave-owning-past-n1230406>.
Laurence, James. 2013. '"Hunkering Down or Hunkering Away?" The Effect of Community Ethnic Diversity on Residents' Social Networks.' *Journal of Elections, Public Opinion & Parties* 23, no. 3 (August): 255–78. <https://doi.org/10.1080/17457289.2013.808641>.
Laurence, James, and Anthony Heath. 2008. 'Predictors of Community Cohesion: Multi-level Modelling of the 2005 Citizenship Survey.' Communities and Local Government. <https://webarchive.nationalarchives.gov.uk/20120920045003/http://www.communities.gov.uk/documents/communities/pdf/681539.pdf>.
Law, Alex. 2018. 'The Trouble with Sectarianism.' In *No Problem Here: Understanding Racism in Scotland*, edited by Neil Davidson, Minna Liinpää, Maureen McBride, and Satnam Virdee, 90–112. Edinburgh: Luath Press.
Law, Chris. 2015. 'Maiden Speech.' Presented at the Britain and International Security, 7 February. <https://publications.parliament.uk/pa/cm201516/cmhansrd/cm150702/debtext/150702-0003.htm#15070238000522>.
Layton-Henry, Zig. 1992. *The Politics of Immigration: Immigration, Race and Race Relations in Post-War Britain*. Oxford: Wiley-Blackwell.
Leahy, Sharon, Kim McKee, and Joe Crawford. 2017. 'Generating Confusion,

Concern, and Precarity through the Right to Rent Scheme in Scotland.' *Antipode* 50, no. 3: 604–20. <https://doi.org/10.1111/anti.12369>.

Leith, Murray Stewart. 2012. 'The View from above: Scottish National Identity as an Elite Concept.' *National Identities* 14, no. 1 (1 March): 39–51. <https://doi.org/10.1080/14608944.2012.657081>.

Leith, Murray Stewart, and Duncan Sim. 2012. 'Second Generation Identities: The Scottish Diaspora in England.' *Sociological Research Online* 17, no. 3 (1 August): 1–12. <https://doi.org/10.5153/sro.2628>.

Leith, Murray Stewart, and Duncan Sim. 2017. 'The Scots in England – a Different Kind of Diaspora?' *National Identities* 21, no. 2 (27 November): 119–34. <https://doi.org/10.1080/14608944.2017.1397617>.

Leith, Murray Stewart, and Daniel P. J. Soule. 2011. *Political Discourse and National Identity in Scotland*. Edinburgh: Edinburgh University Press.

Lemos, Sara, and Jonathan Portes. 2008. 'New Labour? The Impact of Migration from Central and Eastern European Countries on the UK Labour Market.' SSRN Scholarly Paper. Rochester, NY: Social Science Research Network, 19 October. <https://papers.ssrn.com/abstract=1286694>.

Lerch, Marika, and Guido Schwellnus. 2006. 'Normative by Nature? The Role of Coherence in Justifying the EU's External Human Rights Policy.' *Journal of European Public Policy* 13, no. 2: 304–21. <https://doi.org/10.1080/13501760500452665>.

Leung, Angela Ka-yee, William W. Maddux, Adam D. Galinsky, and Chi-yue Chiu. 2008. 'Multicultural Experience Enhances Creativity: The When and How.' *American Psychologist* 63, no. 3: 169–81. <https://doi.org/10.1037/0003-066X.63.3.169>.

Levie, Jonathan. 2007. 'Immigration, In-migration, Ethnicity and Entrepreneurship in the United Kingdom.' *Small Business Economics* 28, no. 2 (1 March): 143–69. <https://doi.org/10.1007/s11187-006-9013-2>.

Levin, Eric, Alberto Montagnoli, and Robert E. Wright. 2009. 'Demographic Change and the Housing Market: Evidence from a Comparison of Scotland and England.' *Urban Studies* 46, no. 1 (1 January): 27–43. <https://doi.org/10.1177/0042098008098635>.

Lewis, Miranda. 2006. 'Warm Welcome: Understanding Public Attitudes to Asylum Seekers in Scotland.' London: Institute for Public Policy Research, June. <http://www.ippr.org/files/images/media/files/publication/2011/05/warm_welcome_1518.pdf>.

Liberal Democrats. 2010. 'Liberal Democrat Manifesto 2010.' Liberal Democrats.

Liberal Democrats. 2015. 'Manifesto 2015: Liberal Democrats.' Liberal Democrats.

Liinpää, Minna. 2019. 'Scotland, SNP and the Push for Independence: Ethnic Minorities and National Imagination.' *The Sociological Review* (blog). <https://www.thesociologicalreview.com/scotland-snp-and-the-push-for-independence-ethnic-minorities-and-national-imagination/>.

Liinpää, Minna, Maureen McBride, Neil Davidson, and Satnam Virdee. 2014. '"Racism: From the Labour Movement to the Far-Right".' *Ethnic and Racial Studies* 38, no. 3: 446–51. <https://doi.org/10.1080/01419870.2015.974645>.

Linden, David. 2017. 'Maiden Speech.' Presented at the Education and Local Services, 27 June. <https://hansard.parliament.uk /Commons/2017-06-27/debates/ ACC3BDDE-6E2A-444B-9C6A-EA71C0530F77/EducationAndLocalServices#contribution-0CFEB383-480D-4355-9205-BA5B78D7D3FD>.

Liphshiz, Cnaan. 2016. 'In Post-Brexit Scotland, Jews Warm Up to Leaving UK.' *The Times of Israel*, 8 July. <http://www.timesofisrael.com/in-post-brexit-scotland-jews-warm-up-to-leaving-uk/>.

Liu, Amy H., Anand Edward Sokhey, Joshua B. Kennedy, and Annie Miller. 2014. 'Immigrant Threat and National Salience: Understanding the "English Official" Movement in the United States.' *Research & Politics* 1, no. 1 (13 May): 2053168014531926. <https://doi.org/10.1177/2053168014531926>.

Logan, Caitlin. 2017. 'Scottish Greens Say Immigration Must Be Devolved to Protect Migrant Rights Post-EU.' CommonSpace, 4 October. <https://www.commonspace.scot/articles/11813/scottish-greens-say-immigration-must-be-devolved-protect-migrant-rights-post-eu>.

Longhi, Simonetta, Peter Nijkamp, and Jacques Poot. 2005. 'A Meta-analytic Assessment of the Effect of Immigration on Wages.' *Journal of Economic Surveys* 19, no. 3: 451–77. <https://doi.org/10.1111/j.0950-0804.2005.00255.x>.

Lucchino, Paolo, Chiara Rosazza Bondibene, and Jonathan Portes. 2012. 'Examining the Relationship between Immigration and Unemployment Using National Insurance Number Registration Data.' *National Institute of Economic and Social Research (NIESR) Discussion Papers*, no. 386. London: National Institute of Economic and Social Research.

Lukes, Sue, Nigel de Noronha, and Nissa Finney. 2018. 'Slippery Discrimination: A Review of the Drivers of Migrant and Minority Housing Disadvantage.' *Journal of Ethnic and Migration Studies* 45, no. 17 (18 July): 3188–206. <https://doi.org/10.1080/1369183X.2018.1480996>.

Lynch, Peter. 1996. *Minority Nationalism and European Integration*. Cardiff: University of Wales Press.

Lynch, Peter. 2002. *SNP: The History of the Scottish National Party*. Cardiff: Welsh Academic Press.

Lynch, Peter. 2009. 'From Social Democracy Back to No Ideology? – The Scottish National Party and Ideological Change in a Multi-level Electoral Setting.' *Regional & Federal Studies* 19, no. 4–5 (1 December): 619–37. <https://doi.org/10.1080/13597560903310402>.

McAllister, Ian, and Richard Rose. 1984. *The Nationwide Competition for Votes: The 1983 British Election*. London: Frances Pinter.

McCall, Chris. 2018. 'Will Scotland's Population Shrink without Its Own Migration System?' *The Scotsman*, 28 March. <https://www.scotsman.com/news/politics/will-scotland-s-population-shrink-without-its-own-migration-system-1-4714313>.

McCollum, David, Beata Nowok, and Scott Tindal. 2014. 'Public Attitudes towards Migration in Scotland: Exceptionality and Possible Policy Implications.' *Scottish Affairs* 23, no. 1 (February): 79–102. <https://doi.org/10.3366/scot.2014.0006>.

McCrone, David. 1992. *Understanding Scotland: The Sociology of a Stateless Nation*. London: Routledge.

McCrone, David. 2002. 'Who Do You Say You Are? Making Sense of National Identities in Britain.' *Ethnicities* 2, no. 3: 301–20.

McCrone, David. 2005. 'A Parliament for a People: Holyrood in an Understated Nation.' *Scottish Affairs* 50 (First Series), no. 1 (1 February): 1–25. <https://doi.org/10.3366/scot.2005.0002>.

McCrone, David. 2017. *The New Sociology of Scotland*. Thousand Oaks, CA: SAGE.

McCrone, David, and Richard Kiely. 2000. 'Nationalism and Citizenship.' *Sociology* 34, no. 1: 19–34. <https://www.cambridge.org/core/journals/sociology/article/nationalism-and-citizenship/F2091D104772D9C8E8B68704DA974B0E>.

Macdonald, Catriona M. M. 2009. *Whaur Extremes Meet: Scotland's Twentieth Century*. Edinburgh: John Donald.

McDonald, Stewart. 2015. 'Maiden Speech.' Presented at the European Union Referendum Bill (2nd Reading), 6 September. <https://publications.parliament.uk/pa/cm201516/cmhansrd/cm150609/debtext/150609-0003.htm#15060950001354>.

Macdonell, Hamish. 2017. 'Post-Study Work Visas Are Dead, Declares London.' *The Times*, 4 July. <http://link.galegroup.com/apps/doc/A497680061/AONE?u=mlin_s_wheaton&sid=AONE&xid=01f03145>.

McIntosh, Ian, Duncan Sim, and Douglas Robertson. 2004. '"It's as If You're Some Alien . . ." Exploring Anti-English Attitudes in Scotland.' *Sociological Research Online* 9, no. 2 (1 May): 46–56. <https://doi.org/10.5153/sro.922>.

McIntyre, Fiona. 2020. 'Double Post-Study Visa to Four Years, Says Ex-minister.' *Research Professional News* (blog), 15 June. <https://www

.researchprofessionalnews.com/rr-he-government-home-office-2020-6-double-post-study-visa-to-four-years-says-ex-minister/>.
McKenna, Kevin. 2017. 'The Roma Are Yet again Scapegoats for Society's Ills.' *The Guardian*, 10 December. <http://www.theguardian.com/commentisfree/2017/dec/10/roma-again-scapegoats-for-ills-of-society>.
MacKenzie, John M., and T. M. Devine. 2011. *Scotland and the British Empire*. Oxford: Oxford University Press.
McKinney, Stephen J., and James C. Conroy. 2015. 'The Continued Existence of State-Funded Catholic Schools in Scotland.' *Comparative Education* 51, no. 1 (2 January): 105–17. <https://doi.org/10.1080/03050068.2014.935579>.
McLaren, Lauren M. 2002. 'Public Support for the European Union: Cost/Benefit Analysis or Perceived Cultural Threat?' *The Journal of Politics* 64, no. 2 (1 May): 551–66. <https://doi.org/10.1111/1468-2508.00139>.
McLaren, Lauren. 2003. 'Anti-immigrant Prejudice in Europe: Contact, Threat Perception, and Preferences for the Exclusion of Migrants.' *Social Forces* 81, no. 3 (1 March): 909–36. <https://doi.org/10.1353/sof.2003.0038>.
McLaren, Lauren, Hajo Boomgaarden, and Rens Vliegenthart. 2017. 'News Coverage and Public Concern about Immigration in Britain.' *International Journal of Public Opinion Research* 30, no. 2 (7 January): 173–93. <https://doi.org/10.1093/ijpor/edw033>.
McLaren, Lauren, and Mark Johnson. 2007. 'Resources, Group Conflict and Symbols: Explaining Anti-immigration Hostility in Britain.' *Political Studies* 55, no. 4 (December): 709–32. <https://doi.org/10.1111/j.1467-9248.2007.00680.x>.
McLaughlin, Mark. 2020. 'Half-Empty Schools at Risk as Populations Fall.' *The Times*, 10 January, sec. Scotland. <https://www.thetimes.co.uk/article/half-empty-schools-at-risk-as-populations-fall-qttk0cnr6>.
McLeod, Jack M., Dietram A. Scheufele, and Patricia Moy. 1999. 'Community, Communication, and Participation: The Role of Mass Media and Interpersonal Discussion in Local Political Participation.' *Political Communication* 16, no. 3 (1 July): 315–36. <https://doi.org/10.1080/105846099198659>.
McMillan, Joyce. 2015. 'Scots Stand Apart on Immigration.' <https://www.scotsman.com/news/opinion/columnists/joyce-mcmillan-scots-stand-apart-immigration-1510365>.
MacNab, Scott. 2014. 'Immigrants "Not the Answer" for Scotland's Economy.' *The Scotsman*, 16 May. <https://www.scotsman.com/news/politics/immigrants-not-the- answer-for-scotland-s-economy-1-3413055>.
McNeil, Rob. 2014. 'The Scottish Diaspora and Scottish Independence.'

Migration Observatory, 24 June. <https://migrationobservatory.ox.ac.uk/resources/commentaries/the-scottish-diaspora-and-scottish-independence/>.

Maddox, David. 2013. 'Immigration Bill Passes First Hurdle in Commons.' *The Scotsman*, 23 October. <https://www.scotsman.com/news/uk-news/immigration- bill-passes-first-hurdle-commons-1557114>.

Malchow-Møller, Nikolaj, Jakob Roland Munch, Sanne Schroll, and Jan Rose Skaksen. 2008. 'Attitudes towards Immigration – Perceived Consequences and Economic Self-Interest.' *Economics Letters* 100, no. 2 (1 August): 254–7. <https://doi.org/10.1016/j.econlet.2008.02.003>.

Manacorda, Marco, Alan Manning, and Jonathan Wadsworth. 2012. 'The Impact of Immigration on the Structure of Wages: Theory and Evidence from Britain.' *Journal of the European Economic Association* 10, no. 1 (1 February): 120–51. <https://doi.org/10.1111/j.1542-4774.2011.01049.x>.

Marks, Gary, and Carole J. Wilson. 2000. 'The Past in the Present: A Cleavage Theory of Party Response to European Integration.' *British Journal of Political Science* 30, no. 3 (July): 433–59. <https://www.jstor.org/stable/194003>.

Marlborough, Conor. 2020. 'Boris Johnson Has "Hostile Agenda" on Devolution, SNP's Ian Blackford Claims.' *The Scotsman*, 15 July. <https://www.scotsman.com/news/politics/boris-johnson-has-hostile-agenda-devolution-snps-ian-blackford-claims-2914366>.

Marsh, Sarah, and Niamh McIntyre. 2020. 'Six in 10 UK Health Workers Killed by Covid-19 Are BAME.' *The Guardian*, 25 May. <https://www.theguardian.com/world/2020/may/25/six-in-10-uk-health-workers-killed-by-covid-19-are-bame>.

Mason, Rowena. 2015. 'Can I Vote for the SNP If I Live in England?' *The Guardian*, 3 April, sec. Politics. <https://www.theguardian.com/politics/2015/apr/03/can-voters-outside-scotland-vote-snp>.

Mason, Rowena. 2016. 'Gove: EU Immigrant Influx Will Make NHS Unsustainable by 2030.' *The Guardian*, 20 May. <https://www.theguardian.com/politics/2016/may/20/eu-immigrant-influx-michael-gove-nhs-unsustainable>.

Massetti, Emanuele. 2018. 'Left-Wing Regionalist Populism in the "Celtic" Peripheries: Plaid Cymru and the Scottish National Party's Anti-austerity Challenge against the British Elites.' *Comparative European Politics* 16, no. 6 (1 November): 937–53. <https://doi.org/10.1057/s41295-018-0136-z>.

Masterson, Paul. 2017. 'Maiden Speech.' Presented at the Air Travel Organisers' Licensing Bill, 7 March. <https://hansard.parliament.uk/Commons/2017-07-03/debates/B5BEA920-847D-4AD9-85E0-D44CE6337399/AirTra

velOrganisers%E2%80%99LicensingBill#contribution-250478F5-6522-4C06-9190-1C70B6305908>.
Matthes, Jörg. 2012. 'Framing Politics: An Integrative Approach.' *American Behavioral Scientist* 56, no. 3 (March): 247–59. <https://doi.org/10.1177/0002764211426324>.
May, Theresa. 2011. 'Foreign Student Visas: Home Secretary's Statement.' GOV.UK, May. <https://www.gov.uk/government/speeches/foreign-student-visas-home-secretarys-statement>.
Mayda, Anna Maria. 2006. 'Who Is against Immigration? A Cross-Country Investigation of Individual Attitudes toward Immigrants.' *The Review of Economics and Statistics* 88, no. 3 (1 August): 510–30. <https://doi.org/10.1162/rest.88.3.510>.
Meer, Nasar. 2015. 'Looking up in Scotland? Multinationalism, Multiculturalism and Political Elites.' *Ethnic and Racial Studies* 38, no. 9 (15 July): 1477–96. <https://doi.org/10.1080/01419870.2015.1005642>.
Meer, Nasar. 2018. 'What Do We Know about BAME Self-Reported Racial Discrimination in Scotland?' In *No Problem Here: Understanding Racism in Scotland*, edited by Neil Davidson, Minna Liinpää, Maureen McBride, and Satnam Virdee, 114–27. Edinburgh: Luath Press.
Meeusen, Cecil, and Laura Jacobs. 2017. 'Television News Content of Minority Groups as an Intergroup Context Indicator of Differences between Target-Specific Prejudices.' *Mass Communication and Society* 20, no. 2 (4 March): 213–40. <https://doi.org/10.1080/15205436.2016.1233438>.
Meredith, Ian. 2017. 'Irish Migrants in the Scottish Episcopal Church in the Nineteenth Century.' In *New Perspectives on the Irish in Scotland*, edited by Martin J. Mitchell, 44–64. Edinburgh: John Donald.
Mickiewicz, Tomasz, Frederick Wedzerai Nyakudya, Nicholas Theodorakopoulos, and Mark Hart. 2017. 'Resource Endowment and Opportunity Cost Effects along the Stages of Entrepreneurship.' *Small Business Economics* 48, no. 4 (April): 953–76. <https://doi.org/10.1007/s11187-016-9806-x>.
Mickiewicz, Tomasz, Mark Hart, Frederick Nyakudya, and Nicholas Theodorakopoulos. 2019. 'Ethnic Pluralism, Immigration and Entrepreneurship.' *Regional Studies* 53, no. 1: 80–94. <https://doi.org/10.1080/00343404.2017.1405157>.
Migration Advisory Committee. 2012. 'Analysis of the Impacts of Migration.' January. <https://assets.publishing.service.gov.uk/government/uploads/system/uploads/attachment_data/file/257235/analysis-of-the-impacts.pdf>.
Migration Advisory Committee. 2018a. 'EEA Migration in the UK: Final

Report.' September. <https://assets.publishing.service.gov.uk/government/uploads/system/uploads/attachment_data/file/741926/Final_EEA_report.PDF>.
Migration Advisory Committee. 2018b. 'EEA-Workers in the UK Labour Market: Interim Update.' March. <https://assets.publishing.service.gov.uk/government/uploads/system/uploads/attachment_data/file/694494/eea-workers-uk-labour-market-interim-update.pdf>.
Migration Advisory Committee. 2020. 'Migration Advisory Committee (MAC) Report: Points-Based System and Salary Thresholds.' January. <https://www.gov.uk/government/publications/migration-advisory-committee-mac-report-points-based-system-and-salary-thresholds>.
Miles, Robert, and Anne Dunlop. 1986. 'The Racialization of Politics in Britain: Why Scotland Is Different.' *Patterns of Prejudice* 20, no. 1 (1 January): 23–33. <https://doi.org/10.1080/0031322X.1986.9969845>.
Ministry of Housing, Communities and Local Government. 2020. 'Social Housing Lettings: April 2018 to March 2019, England.' Ministry of Housing, Communities and Local Government, 28 January. <https://assets.publishing.service.gov.uk/government/uploads/system/uploads/attachment_data/file/861471/Social_Housing_Lettings_in_England_April_2018_to_March_2019.pdf>.
Miralles Tagliabue EMBT. 1998. 'Scottish Parliament Concept Design.' <https://www.parliament.scot/VisitorInformation/4.Enric_Miralles_Moya.pdf>.
Mitchell, James. 2015. 'Sea Change in Scotland.' *Parliamentary Affairs* 68, no. suppl_1 (1 September): 88–100. <https://doi.org/10.1093/pa/gsv029>.
Mitchell, James, and Arno van der Zwet. 2010. 'A Catenaccio Game: The 2010 Election in Scotland.' *Parliamentary Affairs* 63, no. 4 (1 October): 708–25. <https://doi.org/10.1093/pa/gsq019>.
Mitchell, Martin J. 1998. *The Irish in the West of Scotland 1797–1848: Trade Unions, Strikes and Political Movements*. Edinburgh: John Donald.
Mitchell, Martin J. 2017. 'Irish Catholics in the West of Scotland in the Nineteenth Century: Despised by Scottish Workers and Controlled by the Church?' In *New Perspectives on The Irish in Scotland*, edited by Martin J. Mitchell, 1–19. Edinburgh: John Donald.
Miyares, J. Rubén Valdés. 2017. 'On the Trail of the Highland Clearances: The Clearances Metanarrative in Scottish Historical Fiction.' *English Studies* 98, no. 6 (18 August): 585–97. <https://doi.org/10.1080/0013838X.2017.1322384>.
Modood, Tariq, Richard Berthoud, Jane Lakey, James Nazroo, Patten Smith, Satnam Virdee, and Sharon Beishon. 1997. *Ethnic Minorities in Britain: Diversity and Disadvantage*. London: Policy Studies Institute. <http://www.psi.org.uk/site/publication_detail/694>.

Monaghan, Paul. 2015. 'Maiden Speech.' Presented at the Financial Statement and Budget Report, 7 September. <https://publications.parliament.uk/pa/cm201516/cmhansrd/cm150709/debtext/150709-0003.htm#15070966000444>.

Moreno, Luis. 2006. 'Scotland, Catalonia, Europeanization and the "Moreno Question".' *Scottish Affairs* 54 (First Series), no. 1 (February): 1–21. <https://doi.org/10.3366/scot.2006.0002>.

Moskal, Marta. 2014. 'Polish Migrant Youth in Scottish Schools: Conflicted Identity and Family Capital.' *Journal of Youth Studies* 17, no. 2 (7 February): 279–91. <https://doi.org/10.1080/13676261.2013.815705>.

Moskal, Marta. 2016. 'Language and Cultural Capital in School Experience of Polish Children in Scotland.' *Race Ethnicity and Education* 19, no. 1 (2 January): 141–60. <https://doi.org/10.1080/13613324.2014.911167>.

Mudde, Cas. 2004. 'The Populist Zeitgeist.' *Government and Opposition* 39, no. 4: 541–63. <https://doi.org/10.1111/j.1477-7053.2004.00135.x>.

Mudde, Cas, and Cristóbal Rovira Kaltwasser. 2017. *Populism: A Very Short Introduction.* Oxford: Oxford University Press.

Mullen, Ashli. 2018. '"Race", Place and Territorial Stigmatization: The Construction of Roma Migrants in and through Govanhill, Scotland.' In *New Scots: Scotland's Immigrant Communities since 1945*, edited by T. M. Devine and Angela McCarthy, 205–31. Edinburgh: Edinburgh University Press.

Mullin, Roger. 2015. 'Maiden Speech.' Presented at the Debate on the Address (6th Day), 6 April. <https://publications.parliament.uk/pa/cm201516/cmhansrd/cm150604/debtext/150604-0003.htm#15060445002595>.

Mulvey, Gareth. 2010. 'When Policy Creates Politics: The Problematizing of Immigration and the Consequences for Refugee Integration in the UK.' *Journal of Refugee Studies* 23, no. 4 (1 December): 437–62. <https://doi.org/10.1093/jrs/feq045>.

Mulvey, Gareth. 2013. 'In Search of Normality: Refugee Integration in Scotland.' Scottish Refugee Council. <https://www.scottishrefugeecouncil.org.uk/wp-content/uploads/2019/10/In-search-of-normality-Refugee-Integration-in-Scotland-PDF.pdf>.

Murphy, Justin, and Daniel Devine. 2018. 'Does Media Coverage Drive Public Support for UKIP or Does Public Support for UKIP Drive Media Coverage?' *British Journal of Political Science* 50, no. 3 (July): 1–18. <https://doi.org/10.1017/S0007123418000145>.

NatCen Social Research. 2017. *British Social Attitudes Survey, 2015.* [data collection]. 3rd edn. UK Data Service. SN: 8116. <http://doi.org/10.5255/UKDA-SN-8116-3>.

National Records of Scotland. 2018a. 'Scotland's Population 2017 – The

Registrar General's Annual Review of Demographic Trends.' National Records of Scotland. <https://webarchive.nrscotland.gov.uk/20210315222159/https://www.nrscotland.gov.uk/statistics-and-data/statistics/stats-at-a-glance/registrar-generals-annual-review/2017>.
National Records of Scotland. 2018b. 'Scotland's Population Continues to Increase.' National Records of Scotland. <https://www.nrscotland.gov.uk/news/2018/scotlands-population-continues-to-increase>.
National Records of Scotland. 2018c. 'Total Migration to or from Scotland.' National Records of Scotland. <https://www.nrscotland.gov.uk/statistics-and-data/statistics/statistics-by-theme/migration/migration-statistics/migration-flows/total-migration-to-or-from-scotland>.
National Records of Scotland. 2019. 'Scotland's Population 2019 – The Registrar General's Annual Review of Demographic Trends.' National Records of Scotland. https://www.nrscotland.gov.uk/statistics-and-data/statistics/stats-at-a-glance/registrar-generals-annual-review/2019
NHS. 2018. 'Specified Staff by Nationality Grouping March 2018, July 2018.' NHS Digital, 7 November. <https://digital.nhs.uk/data-and-information/find-data-and-publications/supplementary-information/2018-supplementary-information-files/staff-numbers/specified-staff-by-nationality-grouping-march-2018-july-2018>.
North Star. 2017. 'Syrian Refugees to Be Housed in Dingwall.' *North Star*, 2 November. <https://www.north-star-news.co.uk/News/Syrian-refugees-to-be-housed-in-Dingwall-02112017.htm>.
OECD. 2019. 'Programme for International Student Assessment (PISA): Results from PISA 2018, United Kingdom.' <https://www.oecd.org/pisa/publications/PISA2018_CN_GBR.pdf>.
Office for National Statistics. 2011. '2011 Census: Key Statistics and Quick Statistics for Local Authorities in the United Kingdom.' Office for National Statistics, 11 October. <https://www.ons.gov.uk/peoplepopulationandcommunity/populationandmigration/populationestimates/bulletins/keystatisticsandquickstatisticsforlocalauthoritiesintheunitedkingdom/2013-10-11#population>.
Office for National Statistics. 2014. '2011 Census Analysis: Social and Economic Characteristics by Length of Residence of Migrant Populations in England and Wales.' Office for National Statistics, 4 November. <https://www.ons.gov.uk/peoplepopulationandcommunity/populationandmigration/internationalmigration/articles/2011censusanalysissocialandeconomiccharacteristicsbylengthofresidenceofmigrantpopulationsinenglandandwales/2014-11-04>.
Office for National Statistics. 2018. 'Provisional Long-Term International Migration Estimates.' Office for National Statistics, 27 August. <https://www.ons.gov.uk/peoplepopulationandcommunity/populationandmigra

tion/internationalmigration/datasets/migrationstatisticsquarterlyreportprovisionallongterminternationalmigrationltimestimates/current>.
Ohinata, Asako, and Jan C. van Ours. 2013. 'How Immigrant Children Affect the Academic Achievement of Native Dutch Children.' *The Economic Journal* 123, no. 570 (1 August): F308–31. <https://doi.org/10.1111/ecoj.12052>.
Omi, Michael, and Howard Winant. 2015. *Racial Formation in the United States*. New York: Routledge.
O'Rourke, Kevin H., and Richard Sinnott. 2006. 'The Determinants of Individual Attitudes towards Immigration.' *European Journal of Political Economy* 22, no. 4 (1 December): 838–61. <https://doi.org/10.1016/j.ejpoleco.2005.10.005>.
Oskooii, Kassra A. R., and Karam Dana. 2017. 'Muslims in Great Britain: The Impact of Mosque Attendance on Political Behaviour and Civic Engagement.' *Journal of Ethnic and Migration Studies* 44, no. 9 (31 May): 1479–505. <https://doi.org/10.1080/1369183X.2017.1330652>.
Oswald, Kirsten. 2015. 'Maiden Speech.' Presented at the Scotland Bill (2nd Reading), 6 August. <https://publications.parliament.uk/pa/cm201516 /cmhansrd/cm150608/debtext/150608-0003.htm#15060821000112>.
Oxford Economics. 2018. 'The Fiscal Impact of Immigration to the UK: A Report for the Migration Advisory Committee.' <https://www.oxfordeconomics.com/recent-releases/8747673d-3b26-439b-9693-0e250df6dbba>.
PAMCo. 2018. 'Newsbrands: Total Brand Reach.' 17 October–18 September 18. <https://pamco.co.uk/wp-content/uploads/2018/11/Newsbrands-PAMCo-4-2018.zip>
Parker, Simon. 2009. *The Economics of Entrepreneurship*. Cambridge: Cambridge University Press.
Pasini, Elisabetta. 2018. 'Migration and Competition for Schools: Evidence from Primary Education in England.' <https://conference.iza.org/conference_files/AMM_2018/pasini_e26726.pdf>.
Paterson, Lindsay, Frank Bechhofer, and David McCrone. 2004. *Living in Scotland: Social and Economic Change since 1980*. Edinburgh: Edinburgh University Press. <https://edinburghuniversitypress.com/book-living-in-scotland-pb.html>.
Paterson, Lindsay, Alice Brown, John Curtice, and Kerstin Hinds. 2001. *New Scotland, New Politics?: Are Social and Political Ties Fragmenting?* Edinburgh: Polygon.
Peev, Gerri. 2012. 'Revealed: How HALF of All Social Housing in Parts of England Goes to People Born Abroad.' *Daily Mail*, 15 April. <https://www.dailymail.co.uk/news/article-2130095/Calls-British-people-given

-priority-social-housing-queue-revealed-foreigners-HALF-properties.html>.
Pehrson, Samuel, Vivian L. Vignoles, and Rupert Brown. 2009. 'National Identification and Anti-immigrant Prejudice: Individual and Contextual Effects of National Definitions.' *Social Psychology Quarterly* 72, no. 1 (1 March): 24–38. <https://doi.org/10.1177/019027250907200104>.
Pellew, Jill. 1989. 'The Home Office and the Aliens Act, 1905.' *The Historical Journal* 32, no. 2 (June): 369–85. <https://doi.org/10.1017/S0018246X00012206>.
Penrose, Jan, and David Howard. 2008. 'One Scotland, Many Cultures: The Mutual Constitution of Anti-racism and Place.' In *New Geographies of Race and Racism*, edited by Claire Dwyer and Caroline Bressey, 95–112. London: Routledge.
Peterkin, Tom. 2014. 'Tom Peterkin: Russell Fans Flames over Immigration.' *The Scotsman*, 30 January. <https://www.scotsman.com/news/opinion/columnists/tom-peterkin-russell-fans-flames-over-immigration-1546464>.
Pettigrew, Thomas F. 1997. 'Generalized Intergroup Contact Effects on Prejudice.' *Personality and Social Psychology Bulletin* 23, no. 2 (1 February): 173–85. <https://doi.org/10.1177/0146167297232006>.
Pettigrew, Thomas F. 1998. 'Intergroup Contact Theory.' *Annual Review of Psychology* 49, no. 1: 65–85. <https://doi.org/10.1146/annurev.psych.49.1.65>.
Pettigrew, Thomas F., and Linda R. Tropp. 2006. 'A Meta-analytic Test of Intergroup Contact Theory.' *Journal of Personality and Social Psychology* 90, no. 5: 751–83. <https://psycnet.apa.org/record/2006-07099-004>.
Piacentini, Teresa. 2018. 'African Migrants, Asylum Seekers and Refugees: Tales of Settling in Scotland.' In *New Scots: Scotland's Immigrant Communities since 1945*, edited by T. M. Devine and Angela McCarthy, 176–204. Edinburgh: Edinburgh University Press.
Piętka-Nykaza, Emilia. 2018. 'Polish Diaspora or Polish Migrant Communities? Polish Migrants in Scotland, 1945–2015.' In *New Scots: Scotland's Immigrant Communities since 1945*, edited by T. M. Devine and Angela McCarthy, 126–49. Edinburgh: Edinburgh University Press.
Pillai, Rachel, Sarah Kyambi, Keiko Nowacka, and Dhananjayan Sriskandarajah. 2007. 'The Reception and Integration of New Migrant Communities.' London: Institute for Public Policy Research, 29 March. <https://www.ippr.org/files/images/media/files/publication/2011/05/new_migrant_communities_1572.pdf>.
Pittock, Murray. 2012. 'Scottish Sovereignty and the Union of 1707: Then and Now.' *National Identities* 14, no. 1 (1 March): 11–21. <https://doi.org/10.1080/14608944.2012.657082>.

Pittock, Murray. 2014. *The Road to Independence?: Scotland in the Balance*. Revised and expanded 2nd edn. London: Reaktion Books.

Pocock, J. G. A. 1982. 'The Limits and Divisions of British History: In Search of the Unknown Subject.' *The American Historical Review* 87, no. 2: 311–36.

Portillo, Michael. 2016. 'Cameron's Blunder and the Conservative Party Leadership.' Portland, 8 July. <https://portland-communications.com/uk-politics/camerons-blunder-and-the-conservative-party-leadership/>.

Pouliakas, Konstantinos, Deborah Roberts, Eudokia Balamou, and Dimitris Psaltopoulos. 2014. 'Modelling the Effects of Immigration on Regional Economic Performance and Wage Distribution: A Computable General Equilibrium (CGE) Analysis of Three European Union Regions.' *Regional Studies* 48, no. 2 (1 February): 318–38. <https://doi.org/10.1080/00343404.2011.653332>.

Putnam, Robert D. 2000. 'Bowling Alone: America's Declining Social Capital.' In *Culture and Politics: A Reader*, edited by Lane Crothers and Charles Lockhart, 223–34. New York: Palgrave Macmillan. <https://doi.org/10.1007/978-1-349-62965-7_12>.

Putnam, Robert D. 2007. '*E Pluribus Unum*: Diversity and Community in the Twenty-First Century: The 2006 Johan Skytte Prize Lecture.' *Scandinavian Political Studies* 30, no. 2: 137–74. <https://doi.org/10.1111/j.1467-9477.2007.00176.x>.

Raab, Gillian, and Chris Holligan. 2012. 'Sectarianism: Myth or Social Reality? Inter-sectarian Partnerships in Scotland, Evidence from the Scottish Longitudinal Study.' *Ethnic and Racial Studies* 35, no. 11 (1 November): 1934–54. <https://doi.org/10.1080/01419870.2011.607506>.

Raabe, Tobias, and Andreas Beelmann. 2011. 'Development of Ethnic, Racial, and National Prejudice in Childhood and Adolescence: A Multinational Meta-analysis of Age Differences.' *Child Development* 82, no. 6: 1715–37. <https://doi.org/10.1111/j.1467-8624.2011.01668.x>.

Ray, Celeste. 2001. *Highland Heritage: Scottish Americans in the American South*. Chapel Hill, NC: University of North Carolina Press.

Read, Bridget. 2019. 'Real Equality Is When We Can Elect a Female Slob.' *The Cut*, 24 July. <https://www.thecut.com/2019/07/boris-johnsons-sloppy-appearance-would-never-work-for-women.html>.

Record Reporter. 2018. 'Catholic Church Blasts "Intimidating" Orange Marches as Glasgow Priest Spat On.' *Daily Record*, 8 July. <https://www.dailyrecord.co.uk/news/scottish-news/catholic-church-blasts-intimidating-orange-12879258>.

Reeves, Aaron, Martin McKee, and David Stuckler. 2016. '"It's The Sun Wot Won It": Evidence of Media Influence on Political Attitudes and Voting from a UK Quasi-natural Experiment.' *Social Science Research* 56 (1 March): 44–57. <https://doi.org/10.1016/j.ssresearch.2015.11.002>.

Rendall, Michael S., and Deborah J. Ball. 2004. 'Immigration, Emigration and the Ageing of the Overseas-Born Population in the United Kingdom.' *Population Trends*, no. 116: 18–27.

Reuters. 2017. 'Scottish Conservatives Want Emphasis off Immigration and on Economy.' *Reuters*, 12 June. <https://br.reuters.com/article/uk-britain-election-scotland-immigration-idUKKBN1931AB>.

Rodríguez-Pose, Andrés, and Tobias D. Ketterer. 2012. 'Do Local Amenities Affect the Appeal of Regions in Europe for Migrants?' *Journal of Regional Science* 52, no. 4: 535–61. <https://doi.org/10.1111/j.1467-9787.2012.00779.x>.

Rosie, Michael. 2017. 'Protestant Action and the Edinburgh Irish.' In *Irish Catholics in the West of Scotland in the Nineteenth Century: Despised by Scottish Workers and Controlled by the Church?*, 145–58. Edinburgh: John Donald.

Rosie, Michael, and Eve Hepburn. 2014. '"The Essence of the Union . . .": Unionism, Nationalism and Identity on These Disconnected Islands.' *Scottish Affairs* 24, no. 2 (August): 141–62. <https://doi.org/10.3366/scot.2015.0064>.

Ross, Nicola J., Malcolm Hill, and Anita Shelton. 2008. '"One Scotland. Many Cultures": The Views of Young People from White Ethnic Backgrounds on Multiculturalism in Scotland.' *Scottish Affairs* 64 (First Series), no. 1 (1 August): 97–116. <https://doi.org/10.3366/scot.2008.0038>.

Rowley, Danielle. 2017. 'Maiden Speech.' Presented at the Exiting the European Union and Global Trade, 6 July. <https://hansard.parliament.uk/Commons/2017-07-06/debates/B1351616-A3BA-4A62-AEA7-7A77F80D733B/ExitingTheEuropeanUnionAndGlobalTrade#contribution-DDDA1B93-0F78-4EC2-BFBF-4DCCF4D7456B>.

Roxburgh, Angus. 2014. 'Letter from Edinburgh: What It Really Means to Be Scottish.' *The New Statesman*, 4 September.

Sá, Filipa. 2015. 'Immigration and House Prices in the UK.' *The Economic Journal* 125, no. 587 (1 September): 1393–424. <https://doi.org/10.1111/ecoj.12158>.

Saeed, Amir, Neil Blain, and Douglas Forbes. 1999. 'New Ethnic and National Questions in Scotland: Post-British Identities among Glasgow Pakistani Teenagers.' *Ethnic and Racial Studies* 22, no. 5: 821–44.

Sales, Ben. 2014. 'Many Scottish Jews Wary of Independence.' *The Jewish Press*, 16 September. <https://www.jewishomaha.org/jewish-press/2014/09/many-scottish-jews-wary-of-independence/>.

Salmond, Alex. 2014. 'Scotland's Place in Europe.' Bruges, 28 April. <https://news.gov.scot/speeches-and-briefings/scotlands-place-in-europe-2>.

Sarrouh, Beesan T. 2018. 'Elusive Inclusion: Comparing the Counter-intuitive Accommodation Policies of Islamic Schools in Scotland and Quebec.' *Journal of Ethnic and Migration Studies* 47, no. 7 (8 October): 1667–85. <https://doi.org/10.1080/1369183X.2018.1528868>.

Schain, M. 2008. *The Politics of Immigration in France, Britain, and the United States: A Comparative Study*. Basingstoke: Palgrave Macmillan.

Schemer, Christian. 2012. 'The Influence of News Media on Stereotypic Attitudes toward Immigrants in a Political Campaign.' *Journal of Communication* 62, no. 5 (1 October): 739–57. <https://doi.org/10.1111/j.1460-2466.2012.01672.x>.

Schneider, S. L. 2008. 'Anti-immigrant Attitudes in Europe: Outgroup Size and Perceived Ethnic Threat.' *European Sociological Review* 24, no. 1 (1 February): 53–67. <https://doi.org/10.1093/esr/jcm034>.

ScotCen Social Research. 2010. *Scottish Social Attitudes Survey, 2009*. [data collection]. UK Data Service. SN: 6638. <http://doi.org/10.5255/UKDA-SN-6638-1>.

ScotCen Social Research. 2013. *Scottish Social Attitudes Survey, 2011*. [data collection]. UK Data Service. SN: 7228. <http://doi.org/10.5255/UKDA-SN-7228-1>.

ScotCen Social Research. 2017. *Scottish Social Attitudes Survey, 2015*. [data collection]. 2nd edn. UK Data Service. SN: 8188. <http://doi.org/10.5255/UKDA-SN-8188-2>.

Scottish Affairs Committee. 2018. 'Scotland's Immigration Needs.' <https://publications.parliament.uk/pa/cm201719/cmselect/cmscotaf/488/48804.htm#footnote-167>.

Scottish Conservatives. 2010. 'Invitation to Join the Government of Britain: The Conservative Manifesto for Scotland 2010.' Scottish Conservatives.

Scottish Conservatives. 2011. 'Common Sense for Scotland.' Scottish Conservatives.

Scottish Conservatives. 2015. 'Strong Leadership: A Brighter, More Secure Future: The Scottish Conservative and Unionist Party Manifesto 2015.' Scottish Conservatives.

Scottish Conservatives. 2016. 'A Stronger Opposition, A Stronger Scotland: The Scottish Conservative and Unionist Party Manifesto 2016.' Scottish Conservatives.

Scottish Conservatives. 2017. 'Forward, Together: Our Plan for a Stronger Scotland, a Stronger Britain and a Prosperous Future: The Scottish Conservative and Unionist Party Manifesto 2017.' Scottish Conservatives.

Scottish Conservatives. 2019. 'No to IndyRef2: The Scottish Conservative and Unionist Party Manifesto 2019.' Scottish Conservatives.

Scottish Constitutional Convention. 1995. 'Scotland's Parliament: Scotland's

Right.' Edinburgh: Convention of Scottish Local Authorities. <https://paulcairney.files.wordpress.com/2015/09/scc-1995.pdf>.

Scottish Executive. 2004. 'New Scots: Attracting Fresh Talent to Meet the Challenge of Growth.' Scottish Executive. <https://www.webarchive.org.uk/wayback/archive/20180519032825/http://www.gov.scot/Publications/2004/02/18984/33676>.

Scottish Faiths Action for Refugees. 2017. 'Sanctuary in Scotland: Information on Refugee Issues for Faith Groups in Scotland.' Scottish Faiths Action for Refugees. <http://www.sfar.org.uk/wp-content/uploads/2016/04/Sanctuary-in-Scotland.pdf>.

Scottish Fiscal Commission. 2018. 'Scotland's Economic and Fiscal Forecasts.' Edinburgh: Scottish Fiscal Commission, May. <https://www.fiscalcommission.scot/wp-content/uploads/2019/11/Scotlands-Economic-and-Fiscal-Forecasts-May-2018-FINAL-web-version.pdf>.

Scottish Government. 2013a. 'New Scots: Integrating Refugees in Scotland's Communities, 2014–2017.' <https://core.ac.uk/download/pdf/82919095.pdf>.

Scottish Government. 2013b. 'Scotland's Future: Your Guide to an Independent Scotland.' <https://www2.gov.scot/resource/0043/00439021.pdf>.

Scottish Government. 2015. 'Welcoming Our Learners: Scotland's ESOL Strategy 2015–2020 The English for Speakers of Other Languages (ESOL Strategy for Adults in Scotland 2015.' <https://education.gov.scot/Documents/ESOLStrategy2015to2020.pdf>.

Scottish Government. 2016a. 'Race Equality Framework for Scotland 2016 to 2030.' 21 March. <https://www.gov.scot/publications/race-equality-framework-scotland-2016-2030/>.

Scottish Government. 2016b. 'The Impacts of Migrants and Migration into Scotland.' Research, 28 October. <https://www.gov.scot/publications/impacts-migrants-migration-scotland/pages/9/>.

Scottish Government. 2016c. 'Official Opening of the Scottish Parliament.' 2 July. <https://www.gov.scot/publications/official-opening-scottish-parliament/>.

Scottish Government. 2016d. 'Scottish Social Attitudes 2015: Attitudes to Discrimination and Positive Action.' 30 September. <https://www.gov.scot/publications/scottish-social-attitudes-2015-attitudes-discrimination-positive-action/>.

Scottish Government. 2017. 'The Contribution of EEA Citizens to Scotland: Response to the Migration Advisory Committee Call for Evidence.' <https://www.gov.scot/publications/contribution-eea-citizens-scotland-scottish-governments-response-migration-advisory-committee-9781788514057/pages/7/>.

Scottish Government. 2018a. 'EU Workers in Scotland's Social Care

Workforce: Contribution Assessment.' Research. Health and Social Care Integration Directorate, 9 July. <https://www.gov.scot/publications/contribution-non-uk-eu-workers-social-care-workforce-scotland/pages/2/>.
Scottish Government. 2018b. 'Global Campaign Takes Scotland to the World.' 11 April. <https://www.gov.scot/news/global-campaign-takes-scotland-to-the-world/>.
Scottish Government. 2018c. 'New Scots: Refugee Integration Strategy 2018 to 2022.' 10 January. <https://www.gov.scot/publications/new-scots-refugee-integration-strategy-2018-2022/>.
Scottish Government. 2018d. 'Non-UK Nationals in Scotland's Workforce: Statistics from the Annual Population Survey 2018.' 29 May. <https://www2.gov.scot/Resource/0054/00547429.pdf>.
Scottish Government. 2018e. 'Religiously Aggravated Offending in Scotland 2017–2018: Analysis of Charges.' 15 June. <https://www.gov.scot/publications/religiously-aggravated-offending-scotland-2017-18/pages/4/>.
Scottish Government. 2018f. 'Scotland's Place in Europe: People, Jobs and Investment.' <https://www.gov.scot/publications/scotlands-place-europe-people-jobs-investment/>.
Scottish Government. 2018g. 'Scotland's Population Needs and Migration Policy: Discussion Paper.' External Affairs Directorate, 7 February. <https://www.gov.scot/publications/scotlands-population-needs-migration-policy/>.
Scottish Government. 2019a. 'Post-Study Work.' 4 August. <https://www.gov.scot/news/post-study-work/>.
Scottish Government. 2019b. 'Response to UK Government Announcement of New Immigration Route for International Students.' <https://www.gov.scot/news/response-to-uk-government-announcement-of-new-immigration-route-for-international-students/>.
Scottish Green Party. 2011. 'Scottish Parliament Manifesto 2011.' Scottish Green Party.
Scottish Green Party. 2015. 'Manifesto 2015: An Economy for the People, A Society for All: Scottish Greens 2015 Manifesto.' Scottish Green Party.
Scottish Green Party. 2016. 'A Better Scotland Needs a Bolder Holyrood: Scottish Greens Manifesto 2016.' Scottish Green Party.
Scottish Green Party. 2019. 'Demand Climate Action: Scottish Greens Manifesto 2019.' Scottish Green Party.
Scottish Green Party. 2021. 'Our Common Future: Scottish Greens Manifesto 2021.' Scottish Green Party.
Scottish Labour. 2010. 'A Fair Future for All: The Scottish Labour Manifesto 2010.' Scottish Labour.
Scottish Labour. 2011. 'Fighting for What Really Matters: The Scottish Labour Party Manifesto 2011.' Scottish Labour.

Scottish Labour. 2015. 'The Scottish Labour Manifesto 2015.' Scottish Labour.
Scottish Labour. 2016. 'Invest in Scotland's Future: Both Votes Labour.' Scottish Labour.
Scottish Labour. 2017. 'Together We're Stronger: The Scottish Labour Party Manifesto 2017.' Scottish Labour.
Scottish Labour. 2019. 'Real Change for the Many Not the Few: Scottish Labour Manifesto 2019.' Scottish Labour.
Scottish Labour. 2021. 'Scottish Labour's National Recovery Plan.' Scottish Labour.
Scottish Liberal Democrats. 2007. 'We Think Scotland Has a Bright Future: Scottish Liberal Democrats 2007 Manifesto.' Scottish Liberal Democrats.
Scottish Liberal Democrats. 2011. 'Scottish Liberal Democrats Manifesto 2011.' Scottish Liberal Democrats.
Scottish Liberal Democrats. 2016. 'Be the Best Again: Scottish Parliament 2016 Manifesto.' Scottish Liberal Democrats.
Scottish Liberal Democrats. 2017. 'Change Britain's Future: Scottish Liberal Democrat Manifesto 2017.' Scottish Liberal Democrats.
Scottish Liberal Democrats. 2019. 'Stop Brexit, Stop Independence, Build a Brighter Future: Scottish Liberal Democrat Election Manifesto 2019.' Scottish Liberal Democrats.
Scottish Liberal Democrats. 2021. 'Put Recovery First: Scottish Liberal Democrat Manifesto 2021.' Scottish Liberal Democrats.
Scottish National Party. 2007. 'SNP Manifesto 2007.' Scottish National Party.
Scottish National Party. 2010. 'Elect a Local Champion: SNP Manifesto 2010.' Scottish National Party.
Scottish National Party. 2011. 'Re-elect a Scottish Government Working for Scotland: Scottish National Party Manifesto 2011.' Scottish National Party.
Scottish National Party. 2015. 'Stronger for Scotland: SNP Manifesto 2015.' Scottish National Party.
Scottish National Party. 2016. 'Re-elect: SNP Manifesto 2016.' Scottish National Party.
Scottish National Party. 2017. 'Stronger for Scotland: SNP Manifesto 2017.' Scottish National Party.
Scottish National Party. 2019a. 'Scotland's for Europe: 2019 European Election Manifesto.' Scottish National Party.
Scottish National Party. 2019b. 'Stronger for Scotland: SNP Manifesto 2019.' Scottish National Party.
Scottish National Party. 2021. 'Scotland's Future: SNP Manifesto 2021.' Scottish National Party.
Scottish Parliament. 2010. 'Inquiry into Migration and Trafficking.' Equal

Opportunities Committee, 14 December. <https://www.parliament.scot/parliamentarybusiness/PreviousCommittees/23830.aspx>.
Scottish Parliament. 2017. 'Hidden Lives – New Beginnings: Destitution, Asylum and Insecure Immigration Status in Scotland.' The Equalities and Human Rights Committee. <http://www.parliament.scot/S5_Equal_Ops/Reports/EHRiC_3rd_Report_2017.pdf>.
Scottish Parliament. 2018. 'Migration Advisory Committee Report – in the Scottish Parliament on 18th September 2018.' Scottish Parliament. <https://www.theyworkforyou.com/sp/?id=2018-09-18.2.0&p=14062>.
Sebesta, Edward H. 2000. 'The Confederate Memorial Tartan: Officially Approved by the Scottish Tartan Authority.' *Scottish Affairs* 31 (First Series), no. 1 (1 May): 55–84. <https://doi.org/10.3366/scot.2000.0019>.
Seymour, Michel. 2000. 'Quebec and Canada at the Crossroads: A Nation within a Nation.' *Nations and Nationalism* 6, no. 2: 227–55. <https://doi.org/10.1111/j.1354-5078.2000.00227.x>.
Shabi, Rachel. 2019. 'How Immigration Became Britain's Most Toxic Political Issue.' *The Guardian*, 15 November, sec. Politics. <https://www.theguardian.com/politics/2019/nov/15/how-immigration-became-britains-most-toxic-political-issue>.
Sharp, J., A. Cumbers, J. Painter, and N. Wood. 2014. 'Deciding Whose Future? Challenges and Opportunities of the Scottish Independence Referendum 2014 for Scotland and Beyond.' *Political Geography* 41: 32–42.
Shaw, Jo. 2009. 'Political Rights and Multilevel Citizenship in Europe.' In *Illiberal Liberal States: Immigration, Citizenship, and Integration in the EU*, edited by Elspeth Guild, Kees Groenendijk, and Sergio Carrera, 29–49. London: Routledge.
Shaw, Jo. 2013. 'Citizenship in Scotland's Future.' Centre on Constitutional Change. <https://www.centreonconstitutionalchange.ac.uk/opinions/citizenship-scotlands-future>.
Shedden, Sam. 2018. 'Refugees in Scotland to Be Given Right to Vote.' *The Scotsman*, 24 May. <https://www.scotsman.com/news/politics/refugees-in-scotland-to-be-given-right-to-vote-1-4744219>.
Sheppard, Tommy. 2015. 'Maiden Speech.' Presented at the Debate on the Address (2nd Day), 28 May. <https://publications.parliament.uk/pa/cm201516/cmhansrd/cm150528/debtext/150528-0003.htm#15052828000937>.
Shubin, Sergei, and Heather Dickey. 2013. 'Integration and Mobility of Eastern European Migrants in Scotland.' *Environment and Planning A: Economy and Space* 45, no. 12 (1 December): 2959–79. <https://doi.org/10.1068/a45533>.
Shutes, Isabel. 2011. 'Policy Primer: Social Care for Older People and Demand for Migrant Workers.' Migration Observatory. <https://migrationobser

vatory.ox.ac.uk/wp-content/uploads/2016/04/Policy-Primer-Social-Care.pdf>.
Sim, Alastair. 2014. 'Letters.' *The Herald*, 20 November.
Sim, Duncan. 2009. '"This Is My Village Now": Post-Status Refugee Needs and Experiences in Glasgow.' Glasgow Campaign to Welcome Refugees. Paisley: University of West of Scotland.
Sim, Duncan. 2012. 'Scottish Devolution and the Scottish Diaspora.' *National Identities* 14, no. 1 (1 March): 99–114. <https://doi.org/10.1080/14608944.2012.657084>.
Sim, Duncan, and Alison Bowes. 2007. 'Asylum Seekers in Scotland: The Accommodation of Diversity.' *Social Policy & Administration* 41, no. 7 (1 December): 729–46. <https://doi.org/10.1111/j.1467-9515.2007.00582.x>.
Sime, Daniela, and Rachael Fox. 2015. 'Migrant Children, Social Capital and Access to Services Post-Migration: Transitions, Negotiations and Complex Agencies.' *Children & Society* 29, no. 6: 524–34. <https://doi.org/10.1111/chso.12092>.
Siraj, Asifa. 2011. 'Meanings of Modesty and the Hijab amongst Muslim Women in Glasgow, Scotland.' *Gender, Place & Culture* 18, no. 6 (1 December): 716–31. <https://doi.org/10.1080/0966369X.2011.617907>.
Sjursen, Helene. 2002. 'Why Expand?: The Question of Legitimacy and Justification in the EU's Enlargement Policy.' *JCMS: Journal of Common Market Studies* 40, no. 3 (September): 491–513. <https://doi.org/10.1111/1468-5965.00366>.
Skilling, Peter. 2007. 'New Scots: The Fresh Talent Initiative and Post-Devolution Immigration Policy.' *Scottish Affairs* 61 (First Series), no. 1 (November): 101–20. <https://doi.org/10.3366/scot.2007.0054>.
Skills Development Scotland. 2017. 'Jobs and Skills in Scotland: The Evidence.' Skills Development Scotland, 2 November. <https://www.skillsdevelopmentscotland.co.uk/media/43852/jobs-and-skills-in-scotland-2017-main-report.pdf>.
Slack, Becky. 2014. 'Immigration and Diversity: Britain Must Integrate to Accumulate.' *The Guardian*, 30 September. <http://www.theguardian.com/uk-news/2014/sep/30/uk-capitalise-on-immigration-integration-diversity>.
Slaven, Jim. 2018. 'The Irish Experience in Historical Perspective.' In *No Problem Here: Understanding Racism in Scotland*, edited by Neil Davidson, Minna Liinpää, Maureen McBride, and Satnam Virdee, 54–68. Edinburgh: Luath Press.
Smith, Anthony. 1996. *Nations and Nationalism in a Global Era*. Cambridge: Polity Press.

Smith, David J. 2015. 'Minority Rights, Multiculturalism and EU Enlargement: The Case of Estonia.' *Journal on Ethnopolitics and Minority Issues in Europe* 14, no. 4: 79–113. <http://search.proquest.com/docview/178014 2383?rfr_id=info%3Axri%2Fsid%3Aprimo>.

Smith, Matthew. 2016. 'What Makes a Person Scottish, According to Scots.' YouGov, 7 September. <https://yougov.co.uk/topics/politics/articles-repo rts/2016/09/07/what-makes-person-scottish>.

Smout, Alistair. 2020. 'Majority of Scots Support Independence from UK – YouGov Poll.' *Reuters*, 12 August. <https://www.reuters.com/article/us -health-coronavirus-scotland-independe-idUSKCN2581BD>.

Sniderman, Paul M., and Sean M. Theriault, eds. 2004. *Studies in Public Opinion: Attitudes, Nonattitudes, Measurement Error, and Change*. Princeton, NJ: Princeton University Press.

Spencer, Ian R. G. 1997. *British Immigration Policy since 1939: The Making of Multi-racial Britain*. New York: Routledge.

Stanley, Ben. 2008. 'The Thin Ideology of Populism.' *Journal of Political Ideologies* 13, no. 1 (1 February): 95–110. <https://doi.org/10.1080/135 69310701822289>.

Stephan, Ute, and Lorraine M. Uhlaner. 2010. 'Performance-Based vs Socially Supportive Culture: A Cross-National Study of Descriptive Norms and Entrepreneurship.' *Journal of International Business Studies* 41, no. 8 (1 October): 1347–64. <https://doi.org/10.1057/jibs.2010.14>.

Stolle, Dietlind, Stuart Soroka, and Richard Johnston. 2008. 'When Does Diversity Erode Trust? Neighborhood Diversity, Interpersonal Trust and the Mediating Effect of Social Interactions.' *Political Studies* 56, no. 1 (1 March): 57–75. <https://doi.org/10.11 11/j.1467-9248.2007.00717.x>.

Strang, Alison, and Alastair Ager. 2010. 'Refugee Integration: Emerging Trends and Remaining Agendas.' *Journal of Refugee Studies* 23, no. 4 (1 December): 589–607. <https://doi.org/10.1093/jrs/feq046>.

Stubley, Peter. 2019. 'Boris Johnson's Most Infamous Lies and Untruths.' *The Independent*, 24 May. <https://www.independent.co.uk/news/uk/politics /boris-johnson-lies-conservative-leader-candidate-list-times-banana-bre xit-bus-a8929076.html>.

Sturgis, Patrick, Ian Brunton-Smith, Jouni Kuha, and Jonathan Jackson. 2013. 'Residents of More Ethnically Diverse Neighbourhoods Actually Reported Higher Levels of Social Cohesion.' Online resource. British Politics and Policy at LSE. Blog post from London School of Economics & Political Science, 25 November. <http://blogs.lse.ac.uk/politicsandpo licy/>.

Sturgis, Patrick, Ian Brunton-Smith, Sanna Read, and Nick Allum. 2011. 'Does Ethnic Diversity Erode Trust? Putnam's "Hunkering Down" Thesis

Reconsidered.' *British Journal of Political Science* 41, no. 1 (January): 57–82. <https://www.jstor.org/stable/41241641>.

Tatham, Michaël. 2008. 'Going Solo: Direct Regional Representation in the European Union.' *Regional & Federal Studies* 18, no. 5 (1 October): 493–515. <https://doi.org/10.1080/13597560802351523>.

The Guardian Editors. 2015. '*The Guardian* View on Immigration: It's Not More Talk We Need, It's More Honesty | Editorial.' *The Guardian*, 24 March. <http://www.theguardian.com/commentisfree/2015/mar/24/guardian-view-immigration-not-more-talk-more-honesty>.

The Newsroom. 2016. 'Hate Crimes in Scotland "Fell after Brexit Vote".' *The Scotsman*, 22 September. <https://www.scotsman.com/news/hate-crimes-in-scotland-fell-after-brexit-vote-1-4237818>.

The Smith Commission. 2014. 'The Smith Commission: Report of the Smith Commission for Further Devolution of Powers to the Scottish Parliament.' 27 November. <https://webarchive.nationalarchives.gov.uk/20151202171029/http://www.smith-commission.scot/wp-content/uploads/2014/11/The_Smith_Commission_Report-1.pdf>.

The Social Marketing Gateway. 2013. 'Mapping the Roma Community in Scotland.' 26 September. <https://www.romasupportgroup.org.uk/uploads/9/3/6/8/93687016/mappingtheromacommunityinscotlandreport-2.pdf>.

Thewliss, Alison. 2015. 'Maiden Speech.' Presented at the Skills and Growth (Opposition Day Debate), 17 June. <https://publications.parliament.uk/pa/cm201516/cmhansrd/cm150617/debtext/150617-0002.htm#15061738001609>.

Thompson, Louise. 2018. 'Understanding Third Parties at Westminster: The SNP in the 2015 Parliament.' *Politics* 38, no. 4 (November): 443–57. <https://doi.org/10.1177/0263395717740585>.

Thomson, J. M. 1995. 'Scots Law, National Identity and the European Union.' *Scottish Affairs* 10 (First Series), no. 1 (1 February): 25–34. <https://doi.org/10.3366/scot.1995.0004>.

Thomson, Richard. 2020. 'Maiden Speech.' Presented at the Economy and Jobs, 20 January. <https://hansard.parliament.uk/Commons/2020-01-20/debates/246E9FDE-1333-421A-A696-0D2A976122D7/EconomyAndJobs#contribution-0DB55429-A281-43DD-9D6A-A78E149967D3>.

Thorburn, Mike. 2018. 'Scotland Is Now – A New Way of Looking at Scotland.' 11 April. <https://www.scotland.org/features/scotland-is-now-a-new-way-of-looking-at-scotland>.

Thurman, Neil. 2017. 'Newspaper Consumption in the Mobile Age: Re-assessing Multi-platform Performance and Market Share Using "Time-Spent".' *Journalism Studies* 19, no. 10 (1 February): 1409–29. <https://doi.org/10.1080/1461670X.2017.1279028>.

Thurman, Neil, and Richard Fletcher. 2018. 'Has Digital Distribution Rejuvenated Readership?' *Journalism Studies* 20, no. 4: 542–62. <https://doi.org/10.1080/1461670X.2017.1397532>.

Tierney, Stephen. 2005. 'Reframing Sovereignty? Sub-state National Societies and Contemporary Challenges to the Nation-State.' *International & Comparative Law Quarterly* 54, no. 1 (January): 161–83. <https://doi.org/10.1093/iclq/54.1.161>.

Tindal, Scott, David McCollum, and David Bell. 2014. 'Immigration Policy and Constitutional Change: The Perspectives on Scottish Employer and Industry Representatives.' Monograph, 14 February. <https://eprints.soton.ac.uk/362122/>.

Torrance, David. 2011. *Salmond: Against The Odds*. Edinburgh: Birlinn.

Transport Scotland. 2018. 'Scottish Transport Statistics No 37 2018 Edition.' <https://www.transport.gov.scot/media/44025/scottish-transport-statistics-no-37-2018-edition.pdf>.

Travis, Alan. 2014. 'PM Is Accelerating a Race to the Bottom on Immigration.' *The Guardian*, 28 November. <http://www.theguardian.com/uk-news/2014/nov/28/cameron-immigration-debate-obama-change>.

Trevena, Paulina. 2019. 'Post Study Work Visa Options: An International Comparative Review.' Scottish Government. <https://dera.ioe.ac.uk/33953/1/post-study-work-visa-options-international-comparative-review.pdf>.

Trewby, Peter. 2017. 'Migrating Doctors.' *Clinical Medicine* 17, no. 1 (February): 4–5. <https://doi.org/10.7861/clinmedicine.17-1-4>.

UK Parliament. 2016. 'UK Government Must Take Post-Study Visa Problems Seriously – News from Parliament.' UK Parliament, 15 February. <https://www.parliament.uk/business/committees/committees-a-z/commons-select/scottish-affairs-committee/news-parliament-2015/post-study-work-schemes-report-published-15-16/>.

UK Parliament. 2020. 'NHS Staff from Overseas: Statistics.' UK Parliament, 4 June. <https://commonslibrary.parliament.uk/research-briefings/cbp-7783/>.

University of Glasgow. 2018. 'Misleading Fantasy that Scotland Has No Problem with Racism.' <https://www.gla.ac.uk/news/archiveofnews/2018/may/headline_584609_en.html>.

van der Linden, Meta, and Laura Jacobs. 2016. 'The Impact of Cultural, Economic, and Safety Issues in Flemish Television News Coverage (2003–13) of North African Immigrants on Perceptions of Intergroup Threat.' *Ethnic and Racial Studies* 40, no. 15 (8 December): 2823–41. <https://doi.org/10.1080/01419870.2016.1229492>.

van Klingeren, Marijn, Hajo G. Boomgaarden, Rens Vliegenthart, and Claes H. de Vreese. 2015. 'Real World Is Not Enough: The Media as an Additional

Source of Negative Attitudes toward Immigration, Comparing Denmark and the Netherlands.' *European Sociological Review* 31, no. 3 (1 June): 268–83. <https://doi.org/10.1093/esr/jcu089>.

Vargas-Silva, Carlos. 2013. 'Migrants in Scotland: An Overview.' Migration Observatory, 18 September. <https://migrationobservatory.ox.ac.uk/resources/briefings/migrants-in-scotland-an-overview/>.

Vargas-Silva, Carlos, and Mariña Fernández-Reino. 2019. 'Migrants and Housing in the UK: Experiences and Impacts.' Migration Observatory. <https://migrationobservatory.ox.ac.uk/resources/briefings/migrants-and-housing-in-the-uk-experiences-and-impacts/>.

Vargas-Silva, Carlos, and Cinzia Rienzo. 2017. 'Migrants in the UK: An Overview.' Research. Migration Observatory, 21 February. <http://www.migrationobservatory.ox.ac.uk/resources/briefings/migrants-in-the-uk-an-overview/>.

Vaughan, Geraldine. 2005. 'Irish Protestants in the West of Scotland (1851–1914): An "Invisible" Community?' *Études irlandaises* 30, no. 1: 177–91.

Virdee, Satnam, Christopher Kyriakides, and Tariq Modood. 2006. 'Codes of Cultural Belonging: Racialised National Identities in a Multi-ethnic Scottish Neighbourhood.' *Sociological Research Online* 11, no. 4 (1 December): 1–9. <https://doi.org/10.5153/sro.1424>.

Vliegenthart, Rens, Hajo G. Boomgaarden, and Joost Van Spanje. 2012. 'Anti-immigrant Party Support and Media Visibility: A Cross-Party, Over-Time Perspective.' *Journal of Elections, Public Opinion & Parties* 22, no. 3 (August): 315–58. <https://doi.org/10.1080/17457289.2012.693933>.

Wadsworth, Jonathan. 2013. 'Mustn't Grumble: Immigration, Health and Health Service Use in the UK and Germany.' *Fiscal Studies* 34, no. 1: 55–82. <https://doi.org/10.1111/j.1475-5890.2013.00177.x>.

Walgrave, Stefaan, and Knut de Swert. 2010. 'The Making of the (Issues of the) Vlaams Blok.' *Political Communication* 21, no. 4 (29 October): 479–500. <https://doi.org/10.1080/10584600490522743>.

Walgrave, Stefaan, Stuart Soroka, and Michiel Nuytemans. 2008. 'The Mass Media's Political Agenda-Setting Power: A Longitudinal Analysis of Media, Parliament, and Government in Belgium (1993 to 2000).' *Comparative Political Studies* 41, no. 6 (1 June): 814–36. <https://doi.org/10.1177/0010414006299098>.

Walker, Graham. 1992. 'The Orange Order in Scotland between the Wars.' *International Review of Social History* 37, no. 2: 177–206.

Walker, William. 2014. 'International Reactions to the Scottish Referendum.' *International Affairs* 90, no. 4 (1 July): 743–59. <https://doi.org/10.1111/1468-2346.12138>.

Weale, Sally. 2019. 'Seventy-Five Bogus Universities Shut Down in Past Four Years.' *The Guardian*, 8 April, sec. Education. <https://www.theguardian.com/education/2019/apr/08/seventy-five-bogus-universities-shut-down-in-past-four-years>.

Weishaar, H. B. 2008. 'Consequences of International Migration: A Qualitative Study on Stress among Polish Migrant Workers in Scotland.' *Public Health* 122, no. 11 (1 November): 1250–6. <https://doi.org/10.1016/j.puhe.2008.03.016>.

White, Roger. 2020. 'What Might a Land Border between the United Kingdom and a Separate Scotland Look Like?' *The Nation Said No Thanks!* (blog), 16 January. <https://mercinon.wordpress.com/2020/01/16/what-might-a-land-border-between-the-united-kingdom-and-a-separate-scotland-look-like/>.

Whitehead, Christine, Ann Edge, Ian Richard Gordon, Kath Scanlon, and Tony Travers. 2011. 'The Impact of Migration on Access to Housing and the Housing Market.' London: Migration Advisory Committee, LSE.

Williams, Charlotte, and Philomena de Lima. 2006. 'Devolution, Multicultural Citizenship and Race Equality: From Laissez-Faire to Nationally Responsible Policies.' *Critical Social Policy* 26, no. 3 (1 August): 498–522. <https://doi.org/10.1177/0261018306065606>.

Wintour, Patrick, and Nicholas Watt. 2015. 'Ed Miliband: I Won't Have Labour Government If It Means Deals with SNP.' *The Guardian*, 1 May, sec. Politics. <https://www.theguardian.com/politics/2015/apr/30/ed-miliband-snp-opposition-question-time-election>.

Wray, Helena. [2011] 2016. *Regulating Marriage Migration into the UK: A Stranger in the Home*. London: Routledge. <https://doi.org/10.4324/9781315604510>.

Wright, Robert. 2013. 'A Post-Independence Scottish Immigration System: How Might It Be Shaped by European Union Requirements.' *Fraser of Allander Economic Commentary* 37, no. 2 (5 November): 47–53. <https://strathprints.strath.ac.uk/45854/>.

Wright, Robert. 2017. 'Analysis: Our Future Prosperity Is Dependent on Our Ability to Attract Foreign Workers.' *The Herald*, 8 December. <https://www.heraldscotland.com/news/15709840.demographic-time-bomb-a-huge-threat-to-the-economy/>.

Wright, Robert. 2018. 'Home Office Told Thousands of Foreign Students to Leave UK in Error.' *Financial Times*, 1 May. <https://www.ft.com/content/2ae9b7d2-4d0c-11e8-8a8e-22951a2d8493>.

Wright, Robert, and Irene Mosca. 2009. 'Devolved Immigration Policy: Will It Work in Scotland?' *Fraser of Allander Economic Commentary* 33, no. 2 (November): 55–60. <https://strathprints.strath.ac.uk/46775/>.

Zimmer, Oliver. 2003. 'Boundary Mechanisms and Symbolic Resources: Towards a Process-Oriented Approach to National Identity.' *Nations and Nationalism* 9, no. 2: 173–93. <https://doi.org/10.1111/1469-8219.00081>.

Zorlu, Aslan, and Joop Hartog. 2005. 'The Effect of Immigration on Wages in Three European Countries.' *Journal of Population Economics* 18, no. 1 (1 March): 113–51. <https://doi.org/10.1007/s00148-004-0204-3>.

Zucker, Harold Gene. 1978. 'The Variable Nature of News Media Influence.' *Annals of the International Communication Association* 2, no. 1 (1 December): 225–40. <https://doi.org/10.1080/23808985.1978.11923728>.

INDEX

acculturation, 124–5
Africa/African, 22, 29
Ager, Alistair, 123–4
Alexander, Colin, 245–7
Aliens Act (1905), 20
Allan, Alasdair, 110
Angell, Frank, 59
Anglophobia, 132–3, 216, 220, 236–7
Anholt Ipsos Nation Brands Index (NBI), 243–4, 280–1
anti-Catholic *see* sectarianism
anti-English *see* Anglophobia
anti-Muslim *see* Islamophobia
anti-racism, 32, 133–5, 138n
Archbishop of Canterbury, 192
Asia/Asian, 27, 28, 30, 51, 81, 85, 86, 89n, 118, 129, 131, 138n, 152, 162, 199, 200, 209–11, 214–18
assimilation, 10, 49–50, 123–4
asylum seekers, 39, 45n, 58, 106, 108, 128, 166, 177, 198, 220, 222, 227n, 242–3, 258; *see also* refugees
Australia, 20, 22, 27, 40, 45n, 71, 152

Bardell, Hannah, 155
Belgium, 8, 17n, 50, 205n, 248n
Better Together, 5
Blackford, Ian, 150, 151, 153
Blunkett, David, 164
Bond, Ross, 74, 83, 236
Bonnar, Stephen, 154
Boswell, Christina, 178
Boswell, Philip, 155
Brain family, 145, 172n
Brexit, 4, 6–8, 40–1, 55–6, 94, 98–9, 145, 146, 147, 148–9, 165, 169, 235, 238, 241–2

Brexit referendum *see* referenda: European Union
British National Party (BNP), 3–4
British Social Attitudes Survey (BSAS), 222–5, 268–74, 278, 279
British unionism, 86–7, 89n, 127, 160, 168, 169, 171n, 241
Brown, Gordon, 34, 139, 146

Cameron, David, 4, 6, 22, 36, 38, 101, 147, 187, 206
Canada, 17n, 20, 23, 27, 40, 45n, 50, 59, 64n, 71, 113n, 119
Carlaw, Jackson, 149, 165, 172n
Catalonia, 8–12, 50, 242
Catholic/Catholicism, 25–6, 77, 86–7, 108–9, 127
Cherry, Joanna, 156
Church of Scotland (The Kirk), 25–6, 51
citizenship, 10, 18n, 20, 31, 40, 48, 58, 64n, 119, 123–4
  British, 20–1, 137n, 183, 236
  European Union, 55
  Scottish, 60, 64–5n, 78–9, 88n, 235–6, 231, 235–6
Clark, Steven, 1–2
Clarke, Amy, 245–6
Coalition Avenir Québec, 10
Common Travel Area, 5, 235, 243, 248n
Commonwealth, New, 20, 27, 28
Commonwealth, Old, 20, 23, 26, 27
Commonwealth Immigrants Act (1962), 20
community cohesion *see* social cohesion
conflict, 10, 23, 24, 47, 69, 116, 118, 122, 126, 258
  identity, 82, 87, 88n

331

conflict (cont.)
  political, 170, 173n, 174n, 184, 191–2, 202, 252
  religious, 19, 25, 86, 87, 116, 127
conflict theory, 118–19, 121
Conservative and Unionist Party, 3–5, 16, 21, 54, 142–3, 147–9, 165–6, 177, 216, 260, 261; see also Scottish Conservative and Unionist Party, 165–6, 261
Constance, Angela, 38, 57
contact theory, 117–18, 119–20, 125, 256
Convergència i Unió, 10, 242
Cooper, Yvette, 5
Corbyn, Jeremy, 146–7
cosmopolitanism, 195, 214, 228n
Cowan, Ronnie, 156

Davidson, Neil, 89n, 136, 138n, 232–3
Davidson, Ruth, 73, 148, 165
demographic decline see population: decline
devolution, 8, 17n, 32, 36, 41, 45n, 51, 56, 60, 191–2; see also immigration policy: devolved
diaspora, 22–4, 59–61, 64n, 247n
diplomacy, public, 244–7, 249n, 280–1
discrimination, 26, 44n, 82, 105–6, 127–33; see also sectarianism; Anglophobia; Islamophobia
Doogan, Dave, 154, 157

East/Eastern Europe, 21, 81, 99, 130, 200–1, 210–12,
economy, 22–4, 33, 36–7, 53–4, 93–102, 103, 104–5, 111, 113n, 120, 218–19, 248n
Edinburgh, 16, 27, 28, 97, 159, 220, 221, 277
education, 22, 34–5, 57, 107–9, 114n, 117, 125, 137n, 220, 225, 228n, 253
emigration, 19, 22–4, 42, 43n, 59–61, 65n, 9, 245–7
entrepreneurship, 27, 28, 97, 117, 121, 153–4, 254

European Economic Area (EEA), 45n, 96, 101
European Union (EU), 5–8, 17n, 54–6, 64n, 204n, 237–43, 248n, 249n
  Blue Card Network, 243
  Committee of the Regions, 239
  Council of the European Union, 239
  European Commission, 5, 100, 239–40, 249n
  European Parliament, 16n, 17n, 170–1n, 240
  Scottish membership, 241

faith schools, 108–9, 114n, 152
family immigration, 7, 17n, 21, 34, 41, 137n, 146, 154, 242–3, 258
Farage, Nigel, 4, 16n, 102, 171n, 190, 194
Fellows, Marion, 152
Ferrier, Margaret, 153
FitzPatrick, Joe, 58
free movement, 4, 5, 7, 41, 54, 55–6, 62, 94, 100–1, 113n, 142, 145, 147, 148, 149, 163, 184, 193, 211, 218, 228n, 231, 235, 239, 241, 249n, 252, 257; see also Schengen Agreement
Fresh Talent Initiative, 31, 33–9, 44n, 57, 91, 96, 98, 144, 163, 164, 174n, 246
Fresh Talent Working in Scotland Scheme, 33, 57; see also Fresh Talent Working in Scotland Scheme; post study work visa

Gardner, Mark, 85
Gethins, Stephen, 151, 154
Gibson, Patricia, 154
Glasgow, 2, 25, 27, 28, 29, 44n, 82, 86, 106, 108, 118, 121, 126, 128, 130–2, 135, 152–3, 221, 258, 277
  Govanhill, 130–2
  Pollokshields, 118
Gove, Michael, 7, 102
Green Party, 225, 260; see also Scottish Green Party
Greer, Ross, 39

332

Guardian, The, 53, 178–80, 182–4, 185–6, 186–202, 203n, 204n, 205n, 262
Gypsy *see* Roma

Habermas, Jürgen, 179
health, 6, 44n, 45n, 99, 102–4, 113n, 128, 137n
Hechter, Michael, 51, 94
Hendry, Drew, 154, 173n
Hepburn, Eve, 11, 17n, 144, 161, 169, 170, 234, 254–5
Herald, The, 178–9, 188, 191–3, 195–7, 198–202, 203n, 204n, 205n, 262
Highland Clearances, 22–3, 61–3, 155
Holyrood *see* Scottish Parliament
Hopkins, Peter, 118, 129, 136, 233–4
House of Commons *see* UK Parliament
housing, 44n, 101, 104–7, 113n, 114n, 126, 128, 253–4
  social housing, 101, 105–7, 113n, 114n
Howard, David, 128, 134, 233, 248n
Hughes, Kirsty, 6
Hussain, Asifa, 53, 129, 132, 133, 162, 216, 220, 222, 228n, 236–7, 248n, 257
Hyslop, Fiona, 92, 115

identity
  British, 77–80, 83–5, 89n, 217
  dual/hybrid, 78, 83, 86, 89n
  English, 78, 83–4, 89n, 225
  Scottish, 60, 66–87, 88n, 89n, 209–10, 213–18, 228n, 229n
identity marker, 67–74, 77, 88n, 132, 257
immigrants
  English, 74, 75, 81, 132–3, 236–7; *see also* Anglophobia
  EU, 21, 98–9, 101–2, 109, 112–13n, 187, 218
  see also Africa/African; Asia/Asian; East/Eastern Europe; India/Indian; Ireland/Irish, Pakistan/Pakistani
Immigration Acts (2014, 2016), 106–7, 114n

immigration policy, 4, 19–22, 31, 112n, 148, 170–1n, 189, 235–6, 242
  devolved, 31, 33, 40–2, 45n, 95, 99, 110, 144–5, 149, 151, 154, 158, 172n, 162, 188; *see also* Scottish Green Card; post-study work visa
  'hostile environment', 22, 35, 114n, 151, 170n
  points-based, 7, 21–2, 34, 40–1, 43n, 45n, 95, 99, 103, 144, 148, 149, 165, 191, 218, 234, 257–8
Independent, The, 178–202, 203n, 204n, 205n, 262
India/Indian, 20, 27–8, 29, 44n, 84, 112n, 128, 245–6, 249n, 250n
integration
  immigrant, 10–11, 31, 38–40, 49–50, 116–17, 123–7, 135, 137n, 138n
  European, 55, 204n, 237–42, 248n, 249n
International Graduates Scheme, 34
international students, 33–8, 45n, 57
Ireland/Irish, 5, 19, 21, 24–7, 29–30, 43n, 77, 86, 94, 95, 112n, 114n, 127, 152, 235, 243, 248n, 251
irregular/illegal immigration, 34–5, 114n, 178, 234–5
Islam, 82, 89n, 130, 209; *see also* Islamophobia; Muslims
Islamophobia, 129–30

Jardine, Christine, 153
Jock Tamson, 1–2, 152, 154
Johnson, Boris, 4, 6, 16–7, 22, 37, 42, 45n, 148
Johnson, Jo, 37

Kearns, Ade, 124–6, 135
Kerr, Callum, 156
Kerr, Stephen, 153–4
Khan, Sadiq, 84

labour
  high-skill labour, 4, 36, 92, 96–7, 140, 145, 148, 218–19, 229n, 243

labour (*cont.*)
  immigrant labour, 4, 17n, 22, 25, 27–8, 43n, 58, 91–2, 95–101, 103, 112–13n, 126, 140, 144, 187, 243
  labour shortage, 22, 96–9, 103, 114n, 146, 218, 253, 254
  low-skill labour, 4, 7, 21, 92, 96, 98, 99, 125, 138n, 144, 165, 218–19, 229n
Labour Party, 54, 55, 89n, 142, 144, 146–7, 149, 172n, 173n, 174n, 196, 198, 216, 225, 260; *see also* Scottish Labour Party
Law, Chris, 152
Liberal Democratic Party *see* Scottish Liberal Democratic Party
Linden, David, 155
Livingstone, David, 245

McAuliffe, Naomi, 40
McConnell, Jack, 33, 45n, 59, 91–2, 163, 164, 174n, 246–7
McCrone, David, 67–8, 94, 111, 142, 143, 159–60, 248n
McDonald, Stewart, 156–7
McDonald, Stuart, 145, 151, 173n
McDougall, Blair, 5
McKay, Derek, 95
Macpherson, Ben, 111
maiden speeches, 62, 151–8, 173n
Malawi, 245, 250n
Masterson, Paul, 152, 250n
May, Theresa, 7, 22, 34–5, 37, 41, 102, 115, 147–8, 170n, 191, 206
media
  frame, 178–82, 186–202; identity, 195–8; moral, 192–4; political, 189–92; utilitarian, 186–9
  tone, 182–4, 186–92
  see also newspapers
Migration Advisory Committee, 41, 99, 100, 110, 111, 113n, 116–17, 120
Miliband, Ed, 146, 149, 171n
Miller, William, 53, 129, 132, 133, 162, 216, 220, 222, 228n, 236–7, 248n, 257
minoritised groups, 28–30, 32, 44n, 72, 74, 80–7, 89n, 103, 105–7, 113n, 117, 118, 120–1, 127–32, 136, 137n, 138n, 162, 200–1, 214–18, 220, 224, 233–4, 236, 241, 253–4, 257
Monaghan, Paul, 62, 155
Mullin, Roger, 156
multicultural/multiculturalism, 19, 21, 32–3, 49–50, 56–7, 63–4, 66, 124, 134, 140, 152–3, 195–8, 214, 231, 241
Murray, Chris, 99
Muslims, 29, 81–4, 89n, 108–9, 118, 129–30, 133, 152, 177, 183, 199–200, 209–12, 214–18, 220–1, 222, 229n, 234, 236, 257

nation-building, 2, 12–13, 15–16, 42, 47, 48, 56, 58, 60, 83, 136, 141, 161, 192, 242, 246, 252
National Health Service (NHS), 102–3, 144, 206, 251
Nationalism
  civic, 8, 10–12, 46–55, 56–8, 63–4, 68–70, 74, 75–6, 77–9, 80–2, 87, 88n, 134, 156, 159–60, 161–2, 196, 202, 209, 225, 233, 241, 252, 253, 258; civic republican, 48–9; liberal civic nationalism, 48–9, 50–4, 57, 64n
  English, 89n, 136, 232
  ethnic, 47–50, 51, 52, 54, 60, 69, 76–7, 87, 88n, 156, 162, 241
  Scottish, 50–63, 64n, 65n, 132, 156, 159–60, 232, 236–7
New Scots Refugee Integration Strategy, 31, 38–40, 39, 57, 124, 135
New Zealand, 20, 22, 23, 27, 40, 45n, 59
newspapers, 175–203
Northern Ireland, 44n, 51, 52, 86, 127, 235, 251

One Scotland campaign, 31, 32–3, 39, 42, 56–7, 124
  One Scotland, Many Cultures, 31, 32–3, 124, 134, 163, 244

334

Orange Orders, 26, 86, 127, 138n
Oswald, Kirsten, 152

Pakistan/Pakistanis, 20, 27, 28, 29, 44n, 83, 84, 89n, 116, 118, 128, 129, 131, 251
Parti Québécois, 10–11
Patel, Priti, 92, 149
Penrose, Jan, 128, 134, 233, 248n
Peterson, Margaret, 62
points-based immigration policy *see* immigration policy
Poland, 27, 28, 29, 114n, 227n, 254
population
    decline, 5, 10, 30, 31, 32, 56, 61, 90–4, 104, 108, 112n, 168
    growth, 58, 90–4, 95, 104, 109, 169, 252, 254, 255
populism, 3–5, 6–7, 11, 16n, 141, 142, 232, 252
post-study work visa, 13, 31–8, 42, 57, 96–7, 98, 144–5, 154–5, 167, 172n, 231; *see also* Fresh Talent Initiative; Fresh Talent Working in Scotland Scheme
Powell, Enoch, 115, 190
Protestant/Protestantism, 25, 26, 86–7, 127, 138n, 171n
public finances, 101–2, 113n, 187
public opinion, 70–80, 81–3, 198–201, 206–27, 243–4

Quebec, 8–12, 40, 45n, 50, 64n

race, 25–6, 30, 48, 68–9, 72, 82, 88n, 134, 232–3, 255
Race Equality Plan, (2017), 132
Race Relations Acts (1965, 1976), 105, 130
racism, 30, 32–3, 56–7, 84, 87–8, 89n, 105–6, 127–33, 136, 138n, 139, 193, 232–33, 248n
    anti-racism, 32–3, 44n, 133–5, 166, 256–7
referenda
    Catalonia independence referendum (2017), 8–9

European Union referendum (2016), 3, 4, 6–8, 17n, 35–6, 153, 154, 156–7, 206, 249n, 252
Quebec independence referendum (1980, 1995), 9
Scottish independence referendum (2016), 5–6, 9, 12, 17, 45n, 84–5, 148, 179, 249n
refugees, 2, 27, 31, 38–40, 43n, 44n, 57–8, 61–3, 92, 106–7, 121–2, 124, 126, 128, 129, 134–5, 137n, 138n, 152–5, 162–8, 177, 192, 194, 255, 258
Syrian refugees, 29, 38–40, 45n, 252, 254
Right to Rent, 106–7, 151
Roma, 19, 121, 130–2, 177
Rosie, Michael, 169, 170, 254–5
Roxburgh, Angus, 53

Salmond, Alex, 5, 17n, 50, 55, 144, 161–2
Sarwar, Anas, 87
Schengen Agreement, 235, 241, 243, 248n
Schengen Area, 54, 235, 243, 248n, 257
Schengen Border Code, 235
see also free movement
Scotland Acts, 56
Scotland in Europe, 55, 238
Scotland is Now, 50, 59, 242, 249n
Scots Asians for Independence, 86, 162
Scots Law, 52
Scotsman, The, 7, 178–9, 188, 190–1, 195–7, 198–202, 203n, 204n, 205n, 262
Scottish Affairs Committee, 35, 173n
Scottish Conservative and Unionist Party, 147–9, 165–6, 172n, 261
Scottish Constitutional Convention (1989), 52, 159
Scottish Green Card, 99, 162; *see also* immigration policy: devolved
Scottish Green Party, 39, 160, 166–8, 216, 228n, 261

Scottish Labour Party, 146–7, 151, 160, 163–5, 172n, 174n
Scottish Liberal Democrat Party, 151, 160, 166, 172n, 261
Scottish National Party (SNP), 5, 6, 9, 10–12, 16n, 17n, 55–6, 85, 86, 87, 99, 113n, 133, 136, 141, 143, 144–5, 149–51, 157–8, 160, 161–3, 171n, 172n, 173n, 174n, 196, 216, 228n, 238, 240, 242, 248n, 252, 260, 261
Scottish Parliament, 5, 9, 39, 40, 42, 58, 67, 75, 91, 126, 129, 131–2, 191, 158–69, 251, 261
  architecture, 159–60
Scottish Referendum Study, 85
Scottish Refugee Council, 39, 44n, 57, 78, 126, 135, 249n, 258
Scottish Social Attitudes Survey (SSAS), 70–2, 75–9, 81, 199, 200, 201, 207–21, 224–6, 264, 270–4, 276–7, 279
Scottish Trades Union Congress, 36, 121–2
Scottish visa *see* immigration policy: devolved
sectarianism, 25–6, 86–7, 108–9, 121, 127–8
Shabi, Rachel, 139
Sheppard, Tommy, 154
skill shortage *see* labour: labour shortage
Smith Commission, 36, 191, 204n
Smith, Adam, 156
Smith, David, 241
Smith, Robert, 36
Smith, Susan, 118, 128, 136
social capital, 97, 108, 112n, 117, 118, 120, 135, 253, 255
  bonding, 118
  bridging, 118, 136
social cohesion, 14–15, 61, 108, 112n, 115–25, 130–1, 135–7, 152, 167, 198, 220, 255
Strang, Alison, 123–4
Sturgeon, Nicola, 6, 7, 9, 38, 45n, 50, 55, 73, 85, 172n, 242, 251
surveys *see* Scottish Social Attitudes Survey; British Social Attitudes Survey

Telegraph, The, 177–80, 182–202, 203n, 204n, 205n, 262
Thatcher, Margaret, 54, 55, 171n, 190
Thewliss, Alison, 152
Thomson, Richard, 155–6
threat perception
  cultural, 10, 37, 47, 53, 54, 115, 140, 195, 208–9, 213–26
  economic, 37, 140, 177, 210–12, 213–26, 227n, 228n
  identity, 51, 80–3, 199–201, 208–9, 213–26, 227n, 228n
  security, 177, 189
  social cohesion, 130–1, 198
Traveller *see* Roma

UK Parliament, 3, 8–9, 19–20, 21, 34–5, 42, 94, 141–58, 163, 164–5, 166, 167, 168, 171n, 172n, 191, 204n, 232, 260
United Kingdom Independence Party (UKIP), 3–5, 6, 16n, 17n, 102, 142, 180, 189, 191, 196, 198,
United States (US), 23, 27, 60, 119, 146, 213

Vince, John, 183
Virdee, Satnam, 89n, 136, 138n, 232–3
voting rights, 39, 58, 64, 75–6, 89n, 151, 153, 156–7, 163

Westminster *see* UK Parliament
Whitley, Elise, 124–6, 135
Wright, Robert, 95, 110

xenophobia, 4, 7, 30, 86, 88n, 127, 133, 156, 232, 255, 256, 258;
  see also racism; discrimination; Islamophobia; Anglophobia; sectarianism

Yousaf, Humza, 35

Zazai, Sabir, 57–8